LET
HEROES
SPEAK

LET
HEROES
SPEAK

ANTARCTIC EXPLORERS, 1772–1922

MICHAEL H. ROSOVE

NAVAL INSTITUTE PRESS

Annapolis, Maryland

Naval Institute Press
291 Wood Road
Annapolis, MD 21402

Library of Congress Cataloging-in-Publication Data
Rosove, Michael H., 1948–
    Let heroes speak : Antarctic explorers, 1772–1922 / Michael H. Rosove.
        p. cm.
    Includes bibliographical references (p.).
    ISBN 1-55750-967-0
    1. Explorers—Antarctica—Biography. 2. Antarctica—Discovery and exploration.
    I. Title.

G874.R67 2000
919.8904—dc21   99-056907

Printed in the United States of America on acid-free paper ♾
07 06 05 04 03 02 01 00   9 8 7 6 5 4 3 2
First printing

*To the men of that era who risked and gave their lives to discover
the unknown, and who have inspired me*

*To today's men and women who seek to preserve the Antarctic
continent for the magnificent work of nature that it is*

*And to the memory of my father and mentor, Leon Rosove, M.D.,
and to my mother, Eve Bay Rosove*

CONTENTS

PREFACE

My interest in the Antarctic dates back to 1954, when I was six years old. I had a boyhood fascination with atlases and wondered about that remote territory at the bottom of the world—illustrated in white and so very distorted (except in polar projection)—with its Ross Ice Shelf, Wilkes Land, Antarctic Peninsula, and the South Pole. For the next twenty-four years, I developed interests in books, photography, birding, nature, and backpacking into remote areas. I have always preferred the less civilized parts of the world. My interest in Antarctica, however, remained dormant. Then, one day in 1978, I was browsing in a bookstore when Eliot Porter's magnificent newly published photographic work *Antarctica* (New York: E. P. Dutton, 1978) caught my eye. Who could not be enthralled by the otherworldly beauty of the southern land and its unique wildlife? Porter's brief reference to Scott's tragic story, with which I was only vaguely familiar, made me aware that there has been a dramatic and inspiring human side to mankind's contact with the continent. That side is the subject of this book.

The Antarctic has a human history that is only 228 years old. Prior to the late eighteenth century, the most southerly regions of the globe were inaccessible, forbidding, and unexplored, being the subject only of speculation and imagination. Our ancestors simply had no means by which to get there and back alive. The Antarctic continent, temperate millions of years before the dawn of man but long since relegated to the cold, southernmost part of the globe by continental drift and climatic change, lay in secrecy.

Then things changed. James Cook tried to find a southern land in his circumnavigation at high southern latitudes in 1772–75; he only just missed sighting the continent. William Smith discovered the South Shetland Islands in 1819, an event that unleashed a flurry of sealing and Antarctic exploration. Since then, the Antarctic continent has been visited and investigated by people of many nations, with recent rules of conduct established under the Antarctic Treaty, ratified by an ad hoc consortium of twelve nations in 1961.

Since then, many more nations have acceded to the treaty. Men and, more recently, women have been drawn south to flee the humdrum of civilization and to pursue scientific investigations, high adventure, the enjoyment of wildlife and nature and—regrettably, in my opinion—commercial and political gain. People may now visit or work in the Antarctic in relative safety and comfort. Such was hardly the case in the early years of discovery and exploration. Indeed, conditions then were extremely difficult, and those times are full of tales of almost inconceivable hardships. Many, too, were the lessons of leadership—and followership.

This book begins with James Cook, who made the first broad exploration of the highest southern latitudes. His circumnavigation, proving that no previously known lands composed the Antarctic continent, ushered in what may be considered the classical age of Antarctic exploration. I have ended the book with the death of Sir Ernest Shackleton in 1922, which occurred during his *Quest* expedition. Shackleton's passing marked the end of the colorful heroic age of Antarctic exploration that had begun in the middle of the 1890s. After Shackleton, Antarctic exploration and science experienced a rapid surge in mechanization; ships became bigger and stronger, aircraft were used as the principal vehicle of exploration of the Antarctic interior, and companies of explorers grew in size. In the first 150 years of Antarctic exploration, from 1772 to 1922, Antarctica was in actuality rarely visited: the southernmost region of the globe was the object of only a hundred or so voyages, many of which were sealing expeditions, in the early 1820s, to the region of the Antarctic Peninsula. The remainder were voyages of discovery and exploration, and those are the emphasis of this book. Today more people—scientists, government personnel, tourists—visit Antarctica in a single year than visited in all the first 150 years combined, yet those who visit now are still a privileged few.

This book is based on published primary and secondary sources. I have quoted liberally from the primary sources for the purpose of conveying the quality of writing found in much of this literature. None among the Antarctic explorers were authors by profession, but a few of them had considerable writing talent: the narratives of Robert F. Scott, Ernest H. Shackleton, and Apsley Cherry-Garrard are especially familiar and are classics of the literature of exploration. The writings of other explorers may be less well known, but they, too, contain compelling tales, beautiful images of the Antarctic and its wildlife, and descriptions of the profound spiritual effects that the magnificent continent had on the explorers who first saw it.

I wish to thank my wife, Maxine, for her extensive and helpful comments, generous support, and enduring patience, particularly when I would steal away to write in the middle of the night, only to be too exhausted or preoccupied to be good company the following day. I am sincerely grateful to Delores Bryant of Tallahassee, Florida, and to Martin Hanft of Gilsum, New Hampshire, for their insightful editing, to the editorial staff of the Naval Institute Press for their expertise and professionalism in shepherding the book through the review and publication process, and to T. H. Baughman and many others who have offered suggestions and encouragement.

And now, let heroes speak.

LET
HEROES
SPEAK

1

THE SECOND VOYAGE OF CAPT. JAMES COOK IN THE *RESOLUTION* AND *ADVENTURE* (1772–1775)

We cross'd the Antarctic Circle . . . and are undoubtedly the first and only Ship that ever cross'd that line.

James Cook, journal

FEW EXPLORERS HAVE BEEN AS highly regarded as Capt. James Cook (1728–79). Originally from Yorkshire, Cook first worked in the coal and North Sea trades as a seaman; later he joined the navy. Navy life was hard in Cook's day. Discipline was severe—a man might be flogged, hanged, or shot—and deaths by drowning, scurvy, or typhus were common. Furthermore, Cook was a lower-deck man; only occasionally were such hands promoted, but Cook was one such individual. He was given charge of surveying the Newfoundland coast, a treacherous task because of unpredictable weather, icebergs, and the deceptive shoreline, but Cook produced outstanding charts and proved himself a capable leader. His reputation well established, he went on to conduct three Pacific voyages for which he is famous, explorations that remain among the most celebrated of all times.

Long before Cook, a southern continent had been postulated by the ancients, and navigators in the two centuries preceding Cook had claimed discovery of lands they thought might be part of such a continent. Cook's second voyage led him to the Antarctic regions. He was instructed by the British Admiralty to explore the southern latitudes "in as high a Latitude as you can, & prosecuting your discoveries as near to the South Pole as possible."[1]

To move forward with his plans, Cook had certain requirements for the vessels he would employ. The ships had to have shallow drafts for safety on uncharted coasts, but their holds had to be sufficiently large for a long voyage. They had to be strong enough to withstand grounding, but small enough to be laid on their sides for repairs. The North Country colliers of the coal trade best satisfied Cook's requirements, and the navy purchased two, built in Whitby, England, in 1770. Cook was in command of the *Resolution,* a 462-ton, 111-foot ship that carried 118 officers and men. Capt. Tobias Furneaux (1735–81) commanded the *Adventure,* a 336-ton, 97-foot ship that carried 83.

The parties included Johann Reinhold Forster (1728–98), a petulant but brilliant scientist, and his son George Forster (1754–94), who ensured that careful work would be done in the fields of botany, zoology, and anthropology. The experienced navigators Charles Clerke (1741–79) and Joseph Gilbert, and the astronomers William Wales (1734–98) and William Bayly (1737–1810) were on board. The scientists had bought magnetic compasses, sextants, and chronometers from the best instrument-makers and used magnetic variation charts. Their estimated positions were as exact as any of that time. Latitude was accurate to within a few miles, and longitude to within thirty miles in Antarctic latitudes. Because Cook included sauerkraut in the men's diet, carried a medicinal preparation of lemons and oranges to prevent scurvy, and paid strict attention to cleanliness, illness was infrequent. The expedition, well outfitted in every way, departed from Plymouth on 13 July 1772.

During the course of the expedition, Cook twice circumnavigated the globe at high southern latitudes. He made four southward passages, two each during the austral summers of 1772–73 and 1773–74. In the first excursion, the ships sailed from Cape Town on 22 November 1772. Approaching the ice, the men noted abundant bird life and marine mammals. Cook correctly guessed, although he was never able to prove it, that the avifauna indicated land to the south, since the birds would require places to nest. He and Furneaux continued toward the Antarctic Circle; the Irish gunner's mate aboard the *Resolution,* John Marra, in what was the first published narrative of the expedition and writing anonymously in the third person to disguise his identity, noted mankind's first entry into the southern realm of the midnight sun. "The sun now shewed himself about 12 at night, and as they advanced the stars disappeared, and the sun continued to cheer them with his light till their return again to the same latitude."[2] The line was crossed at about a quarter to noon on 17 January 1773, in 39°35' E. Cook gave his noon position as 66°36.5' S and noted, "We cross'd the Antarctic Circle . . . and are undoubtedly the first and only Ship that ever cross'd that line."[3] Later that day the vessels were stopped by ice at 67°15' S, approximately ninety miles

An immense field of ice blocked the way.
[Marra], *Journal of the Resolution's Voyage*, 1775

north of what later became known as the Prince Olav Coast. According to George Forster, "An immense field of solid ice extended beyond . . . to the south, as far as the eye could reach from the mast-head. Seeing it was impossible to advance farther that way, Captain Cook ordered the ships to put about."[4] The parties retreated to lower latitudes.

Cook and Furneaux were separated in a gale on 8 February 1773 in 49°53' S, 63°39' E. Both parties just missed discovering Heard Island (located at 53°0' S, 73°35' E), which would have antedated Peter Kemp's sighting by sixty years. With no possibility of rescue from another sailing craft in the event of calamity, Cook made his second passage south alone, reaching his farthest point on 23–24 February. Cook recounted: "We were in the latitude of 61°52' South, longitude 95°2' East . . . which was exceedingly stormy, thick and hazy, with sleet and snow. . . . Surrounded on every side with danger, it was natural for us to wish for day-light. This when it came, served only to increase our apprehensions, by exhibiting to our view, those huge mountains of ice, which in the night, we had passed without seeing. These unfavourable circumstances . . . quite discouraged me from putting into execution a resolution I had taken of crossing the Antarctic Circle once more. Accordingly . . . we stood to the North."[5] Again Cook had the misfortune of having to turn too soon: he was about 260 miles north of the Queen Mary Coast and the Shackleton Ice Shelf. During this passage the men often had excellent views of the aurora australis—"exceeding beautifull from the variety and vividness of their colours,"[6] according to Richard Pickersgill (1749–79), third lieutenant of the *Resolution.*

The two parties arrived in New Zealand in late March 1773 and made surveys and scientific observations there until early June. They explored at sea until August, then spent several weeks at Tahiti and other islands. On their return to New Zealand, the ships were separated once again in a gale on 25 October 1773. Cook arrived at the rendezvous point in Cook Strait on 3 November, but the sister ship was not to be found. Cook did not see Furneaux and the *Adventure* again until he returned to England.

After the separation, Furneaux struggled for land, short on food, water, and supplies. He arrived at New Zealand on 9 November and laid in stores. On 17 December, a boatload of ten men under John Rowe went ashore to gather wild greens at Grass Cove, now Whareunga Bay. When they did not return, a search party set out under Lt. James Burney (1750–1821) and made the gruesome discovery that their mates had been cannibalized by the Maoris.[7] Rowe's party had been taking their meal on shore and got into a quarrel with the local inhabitants, probably over the theft of food. The Europeans fired two muskets and killed two natives, whose companions then attacked and killed all ten men, immediately cooking and eating them.[8]

The *Adventure* departed for open sea on 23 December 1773. Furneaux headed toward the Cape of Good Hope and, in the vicinity of Cape Horn, stayed mostly south of 60° S. In February 1774 he passed just out of sight of the as-yet-undiscovered South Shetland Islands and the South Orkney Islands. Had the weather been clear, he would have seen Elephant Island and Clarence Island, but because haze and fog limited visibility throughout the critical ten-day period, they lay unsighted for another forty-five years.[9] The *Adventure* arrived at the Cape of Good Hope on 17 March, and in England on 14 July.

Meanwhile, Cook set out on his third southward passage on 1 December 1773, recrossing the Antarctic Circle on 20 December at longitude 147°30' W. Two days later the *Resolution* reached its highest latitude of 67°31' S, 142°54' W, where it was stopped by pack ice at the frontier to what was eventually named the Ross Sea. The men explored the edge as they proceeded eastward. George Forster described "the sight of immense number of icy masses, amongst which we drifted at the mercy of the current, every moment in danger of being dashed to pieces."[10] Having found no land, they withdrew to high forties latitudes and then made to the south again in late January 1774.

On this fourth and final southward cruise, Cook described fantastic ice islands, as tabular icebergs were commonly called at the time, "one of which . . . could not be less than two hundred feet in height, and terminated in a peak not unlike the cupola of St. Paul's church."[11] They crossed the Antarctic Circle on 26 January, sailing through what was later named the Bellingshausen Sea, at 109°31' W. Now little ice was seen. The men were weary from cold and demoralized by the monotony of salted food, but sea conditions were good; Cook pushed south unimpeded.

On 30 January he sailed in clear weather until he was stopped by ice, attaining the farthest south of the entire voyage, "being at this time in the latitude of 71°10' South, longitude 106°54' West."[12] Neither Cook nor any of his company believed that they had sighted land beyond the ice fields. Cook remarked, "I will not say it was impossible any where to get farther to the South; but the attempting it would have been a dangerous and rash enterprise. . . . It was, indeed, *my* opinion, as well as the opinion of most on board, that this ice extended quite to the pole, or perhaps joined on some land to which it had been fixed from the earliest time. . . . I, who had ambition not only to go farther than any one had been before, but as far as it was possible for man to go, was not sorry at meeting with this interruption; as it, in some measure, relieved us; at least, shortened the dangers and hardships inseparable from the navigation of the southern polar regions."[13]

Johann Reinhold Forster, in uncharacteristic understatement, wrote in his journal merely, "I believe, it is so far South, as ever any man in future times shall choose to go."[14] His son George later stated, "As it was impossible to proceed farther, we put the ship about, well satisfied with our perilous expedition, and almost persuaded that no navigator will care to come after, and much less attempt to pass beyond us."[15] Anders Sparrman (1748–1820), the elder Forster's assistant, profiting from a physical quirk of the ship's design, believed that he was farther south than any man on board. "We began to turn the ship to the northward. . . . In order to avoid the bustle and crowd on the deck, usual in such operations, I went below to my cabin to watch more quietly through the scuttle the boundless expanses of Polar ice. Thus it happened, as my companions observed, that I went a trifle farther south than any of the others in the ship, because a ship when going about, always has a little stern way before she can make way on the fresh tack when the sails fill."[16] The *Resolution* was probably less than fifty-five miles from the limit of visibility of Mount Caldwell (72°04' S, 101°46' W) on Thurston Island in perfect weather.[17] For the third time, Cook narrowly failed to discover the great southern land, stalled by the guardian ice that encircles the Antarctic continent.

Cook abandoned high southern latitudes and arrived at Easter Island on 11 March. The party then visited the Marquesas Islands, Tahiti, Huaheine, Ulietea, the Friendly Isles, and the New Hebrides, and were the first Europeans to see New Caledonia. In the middle of October 1774 they arrived once again in New Zealand. On 10 November they headed south and east across the Pacific Ocean to explore in lower latitudes than previously, holding to about 53° to 57° S. No land was sighted, and the *Resolution* arrived in Tierra del Fuego in the middle of December.

Cook then sailed to the east in search of land that had been described in 1675 by Anthony de la Roché and in 1756 by the party of the Spanish merchant ship *Leon*. Land was indeed sighted on 14 January 1775, and soon the *Resolution* was cruising the north coast of what Cook named the Isle of Georgia, now South Georgia. On 17 January, Cook accomplished the first of three landings at Possession Bay, so named because there he took possession for England. He described the dramatic South Georgian landscape in terms that have never been improved upon: "The head of the bay was terminated by perpendicular ice-cliffs of considerable height. Pieces were continually breaking off, and floating out to sea; and a great fall happened while we were in the bay, which made a noise like cannon. The inner parts of the country were not less savage and horrible. The wild rocks raised their lofty summits, till they were lost in the clouds, and the valleys lay covered with everlasting snow. Not a tree was to be seen, nor a shrub even big enough to make a toothpick. The only vegetation we met with, was a coarse strong-bladed grass growing in tufts . . . and a plant like moss, which sprung from the rocks. Seals, or sea bears, were pretty numerous. . . . Here were several flocks of penguins, the largest I ever saw . . . and . . . albatrosses."[18] Until Cook sailed southeastward along the north coast and rounded the east end, he thought that he might have discovered the southern continent, but he was forced to conclude that South Georgia was an island. He tellingly named the point of revelation Cape Disappointment. His report of abounding marine life at South Georgia fell on eager commercial ears, and within a few years the area was plundered for animal skins and oil.

Optimistic that the South Atlantic might surrender additional discoveries, Cook sailed to the southeast and on 31 January 1775 discovered Sandwich Land, now known as the South Sandwich Islands. At 59° S latitude the islands constituted the most southerly land known. Over the ensuing days, haze, fog, rain, and snow permitted only occasional observations of several islands. Cook finally quit the area on 6 February. Unable to imagine that explorers might some day follow him, he commented gloomily, "The greatest part of this southern continent (supposing there is one) must lie within the polar circle, where the sea is so pestered with ice that the land is thereby inaccessible. The risque one runs in exploring a coast, in these unknown and icy seas, is so very great, that I can be bold enough to say that no man will ever venture farther than I have done; and that the lands which may lie to the South will never be explored. Thick fogs, snow storms, intense cold, and every other thing that can render navigation dangerous, must be encountered; and these difficulties are greatly heightened, by the inexpressibly horrid aspect of the country; a country doomed by Nature never once to feel the warmth of the sun's rays, but to lie buried in everlasting snow and ice. . . . It would have been rashness in me to have risqued all that had been done during the voyage, in discovering and exploring a coast, which, when discovered and explored, would have answered no end whatever, or have been of the least use, either to navigation or geography, or indeed to any other science."[19]

His exploration now completed, Cook headed for Cape Town and then for England, arriving on 30 July. He had lost four men, considered a very good record at the time, three of them to accident, only one to illness. During the year following his return, Cook wrote the narrative of his second voyage and made preparations for his third. On that voyage Cook was murdered by natives at Kealakekua Bay, Hawaii, on 14 February 1779.

Although Cook did not sight the Antarctic continent, he proved beyond doubt that no previously known lands could be part of a southerly landmass. He showed that an ocean encircled the globe to the limit of the polar sea ice, and that a continent, if one existed, must lie within the frozen interior at latitudes higher than he was able to penetrate. The expedition's findings defined mankind's southern limit of unsupported habitation on the globe. The scientists substantiated the worth of highly accurate chronometers in determining longitude. Cook believed that his discoveries effectively closed the door to further Antarctic exploration. He did not comprehend that what he had actually done was to lay the groundwork for the future—that others just as zealous as he, and better equipped, would someday go farther.

2

The Voyage of Fabian Gottlieb von Bellingshausen in the *Vostok* and *Mirny* (1819–1821)

> Words cannot describe the delight which appeared on all our faces at the cry of "Land! Land!"
>
> Fabian G. von Bellingshausen, *The Voyage of Captain Bellingshausen to the Antarctic Seas*

IN THE WORDS OF THE GREAT turn-of-the-century Antarctic historian Hugh Robert Mill (1861–1950), the voyage of Fabian G. von Bellingshausen (1778–1852) was "one of the greatest Antarctic expeditions on record, a voyage well worthy of being placed beside that of Cook."[1] Like Cook, Bellingshausen was a man of high moral character. He was a captain of the Imperial Russian Navy and was commissioned by Tsar Alexander I—likely acting upon the advice of the Marquis of Traversey, chief administrator of the Russian Admiralty—to circumnavigate the globe as far south as possible to expand on Cook's discoveries.

Most of the expedition's preliminaries were completed under the Marquis of Traversey. Bellingshausen, with merely six weeks' notice, set forth in two ships. The 129-foot *Vostok* ("East"), carrying 117 officers and men, was under his command. Lt. Mikhail Lazarev (1788–1851), second in command of the expedition, was the commander of the 120-foot *Mirny* ("Peaceful"), which carried 72 officers and men, plus a chaplain. The ships, a frigate and sloop of war, were made of pine and had coppered hulls; only the *Mirny* was strengthened for ice. Even after mast and sail modifications, the *Mirny* was slow, and the *Vostok* was obliged to proceed with abridged sail for the entire voyage. Bellingshausen had no choice but to make the best of the vessels designated for his use. He obtained the finest British navigational instruments; in Antarctic latitudes, his determination of longitude was accurate to within four miles.

Bellingshausen had many volunteers for the voyage, despite the expected hardships and risks. The minister of the navy specified that the health of the officers and seamen was of paramount importance: scurvy was avoided through a careful selection of provisions, and great care was paid to proper warm clothing. Two German naturalists were to have joined the expedition in Copenhagen but declined at the last moment. Bellingshausen, anxious that he would not be able to carry out the scientific program, scrambled to find substitutes through an appeal in England to the president of the Royal Society and the venerable Sir Joseph Banks (1743–1820), who had accompanied Cook on his first voyage; but even Banks was unable to produce any last-minute recruits.

Bellingshausen departed Buenos Aires on 3 December 1819 and headed for South Georgia. (Dates in Bellingshausen's narrative are in accordance with the Julian calendar; dates given here are in accordance with the Gregorian calendar—that is, eleven days have been added to the Julian dates.) Over a three-day period, from 26 to 29 December, Bellingshausen charted the south coast that Cook had been forced to omit and gave Russian names to many newly charted geographical features. He then proceeded to the South Sandwich Islands, previously discovered by Cook, and on 3 and 4 January 1820 discovered three new islands at the north end of the group. He named them Leskov Island (after the lieutenant of the *Vostok*), Visokoi Island (meaning "high island" in Russian), and Zavadovski Island (after Ivan Zavadovski, the first officer of the *Vostok*). The three islands were collectively named the Traversey group. Bellingshausen landed on Zavadovski Island, actively volcanic and occupied by chinstrap penguins. Over the next several days he made detailed surveys of the islands discovered by Cook to the south, showing conclusively that they were indeed islands and not part of a larger coast, as Cook had surmised.

Bellingshausen then made south and crossed the Antarctic Circle on 26 January 1820. He was apparently unimpressed with this accomplishment, since he makes no particular mention of it in his narrative, giving only the latitude.[2] The following day the ships' southward progress was halted by impenetrable ice. What the men actually saw has been the subject of much discussion. The early historians Karl Fricker (1865–?) and Mill gave no particular emphasis to this moment in the voyage,[3] but Frank Debenham and A. G. E. Jones believed that on 27 January the men may have sighted for the first time ice contiguous with and covering the continental landmass.[4] Jones believed that Bellingshausen understood what he saw, though Debenham and others believe he may not.[5] Bellingshausen noted in his official account only that "we observed that there was a solid stretch of ice running from east through south to west . . . which was covered with ice hillocks."[6] He gave a more provocative account, however, in a letter dated 8 March 1820 to the Marquis of Traversey:[7] "Having reached latitude 69°25', and longitude 2°10' W . . . we could see icy mountains to the south."[8] Lazarev wrote, "We encountered continental ice of exceptional height and on that magnificent evening, looking from the cross-trees, it extended as far as the eye could see."[9] The ships were in the approximate position of the Fimbul Ice Shelf.

Another attempt south was initiated on 31 January 1820, but the ships were stopped by pack ice the following day at 69°25' S, 1°11' W. Nothing of importance was recorded; the ships retreated and headed east. On 3 February the ships again pushed southward, but ice stopped them once more. Bellingshausen comprehended the origin of the huge icebergs and presumed the existence of an immense landmass when he commented, "Flat ice islands . . . show clearly that pieces are broken off this continent, because they have edges and surface similar to the continent."[10] The ships continued east, remaining south of Cook's track, until mid-March, when Bellingshausen decided to head for Australia, arriving in Sydney Harbor on 29 March; there the men were treated cordially by the Australian authorities. The Russians spent the next several months in the South Pacific, returning to Sydney on 19 September, where Bellingshausen learned of William Smith's discovery of New South Shetland (see chapter 3).

In the second season of 1820–21, Bellingshausen headed south on 11 November and visited Macquarie Island, where he gave a detailed account of the British oil industry and wildlife depredation. Sailing south, he was stalled by ice on 9 December at 62°18' S in an area eventually named the Ross Sea. Bellingshausen carefully avoided large pieces of ice that might damage the ships and followed the pack edge eastward, remaining south of 60° S for a remarkable 145 degrees of longitude. He reached his most southerly point on 21 January 1821, at 69°53' S, 92°19' W. "As there was no possibility of going south because of the icefield we had encountered, we were obliged against our will to continue our course to the north."[11]

Later on the same day, the men spotted a dark outcrop in the distance and soon confirmed land. In an uncharacteristic, emotion-filled statement, Bellingshausen wrote, "The sun coming out from behind the clouds lit up the place and to our satisfaction we were able to assure ourselves that what we saw was land covered with snow. Only some rocks and cliffs, where the snow could not hold, showed up black. Words cannot describe the delight which appeared on all our faces at the cry of 'Land! Land!' Our joy was not surprising, after our long monotonous voyage, amidst unceasing dangers from ice, snow, rain, sleet and fog."[12] Bellingshausen named this land, the first seen since leaving Macquarie Island, Peter I Island. The ships made a close approach the following day but were barred by ice from landing. Lying in 69° S, 90° W, Peter I Island rose four thousand feet out of the ocean and was the most southerly land yet discovered—and the only known land within the Antarctic Circle.

The ships proceeded east, skirting the pack ice. Another yet larger land-scape came into view on 28 January; the Russian commander named it Alexander I Land (now Alexander Island). The vessels were unable to approach any closer than forty miles, but the perfectly clear weather permit-ted the men to record the land's features. As no exploration could be carried out to the south, Bellingshausen remained uncertain of the nature of this land. (It is now known to be a large island about two hundred miles in length, connected to the continent beyond by a twenty-mile-wide ice shelf.)

Once Bellingshausen had left these newly discovered and remote islands, much time elapsed before they were seen again. Seventy-one years later, in 1892, Captain Evensen in the *Hertha* sighted Alexander Island (chapter 8); eighty-nine years later, in 1910, Jean-Baptiste Charcot in the *Pourquoi-Pas?* observed Peter I Island (chapter 18). Bellingshausen proudly named these distant lands for great Russian rulers: "Monuments erected to great men are erased from the face of the earth by time the destroyer, but 'Peter I Island' and 'Alexander I Land' are indestructible monuments which will commem-orate the name of our Emperors to the remotest posterity."[13]

The men now headed the ships north and east toward the South Shetlands, arriving there 4 February 1821. The following day, Bellingshausen met with eight American and British sealing vessels and encountered Nathaniel Palmer (1799–1877), an American sealer. The event has been ro-manticized by the account of sealing master Edmund Fanning (1769–1841), the only description available in English for many years; Fanning, twelve years after the encounter, re-created Palmer's recollections. As the fog lifted, Palmer in his tiny boat found himself in the company of Bellingshausen's large ships. Bellingshausen spoke no English, but Fanning recounts the meeting: "'[We] concluded we had made a discovery, but behold, when the fog lifts, to my great surprise, here is an American vessel apparently in as fine order as if it were but yesterday she had left the United States; not only this, but her master is ready to pilot my vessels into port; we must surrender the palm to you Americans,' continued he, very flatteringly."[14] Fanning's clear implication is that Palmer discovered the coast of the Antarctic Peninsula, even though the land had already been sighted by Edward Bransfield and William Smith. Regarding the encounter, Bellingshausen simply stated, "I lay to, despatched a boat, and waited for the Captain of the American boat. . . . Soon after Mr. Palmer arrived in our boat and informed us that he had been here for four months' sealing in partnership with three American ships."[15] The Russian captain then went on to describe the sealing activities in the area as related by Palmer. Encounters regularly took place between ships plying the South Shetlands at that time: how significant this particular one was remains enshrouded in a fog as mysterious as that which often envelops the islands themselves.

After his visit to the South Shetlands, Bellingshausen passed by the South Orkneys, completed a circumnavigation of South Georgia, had a harrowing time in a gale near Shag Rocks (53°33' S, 42°2' W), reached Rio de Janeiro, and arrived home in Kronstadt on 4 August 1821. He had lost only three men during the voyage, an exceptional record. His circumnavigation included a remarkable 242 degrees of longitude south of 60° S, and 41 degrees south of the Antarctic Circle, compared to Cook's 125 and 24 degrees, respectively.[16] He closed all the gaps left by Cook, strengthening the proposition that a continuous ocean circles the globe at latitude 60° S.

His immense accomplishments went unacclaimed by his Russian contemporaries, and Bellingshausen encountered ten years of obstacles in getting his narrative and carefully prepared charts published.[17] Neither was Bellingshausen's work recognized in his own time outside of Russia: not until the turn of the century did any translation or summary of the work in English become available.[18] A full English translation was not published until 1945.[19] The Russian navy was unimpressed with prospects for the far south, and Russian envoys did not officially visit the Antarctic regions again until 1946. Even so, Russian officials have claimed that Bellingshausen was the discoverer of the Antarctic continent.

To this day, relatively little is known about the great Russian explorer's life. After the 1819–21 voyage, Bellingshausen continued to serve in the navy and rose to the rank of admiral in 1831. In 1839 he became the governor of Kronstadt, where he died in 1852.

3

Sealing and Early Scientific Voyages
(1819–1830)

The beaches were as good as paved with guineas, such was the number of
seals, and so valuable their skins.

William Smith

THE SEALERS OF THE EARLY NINETEENTH CENTURY explored the southern regions near the Antarctic Peninsula for profit, and a decade of slaughter
nearly exterminated the seal populations of the area. William Smith, who
discovered the South Shetland Islands in 1819, stated: "The beaches were as
good as paved with guineas, such was the number of seals, and so valuable
their skins." Taking the animals was easy, as they "regarded a man as no more
that they did a bird." Another sealer, Robert Fildes (1793?–1827), remarked
that "going amongst these unconcern'd creatures put me in mind of Adam
when surrounded by the beasts of the field at the time of Creation."[1]

The sealers, caught up in greed and intense rivalry, disregarded human
decency and even their own safety. Thomas W. Smith, a sailor aboard the
schooner *Hetty* of London in 1820, recorded a fierce encounter between the
men of the *Hetty* and another British vessel, the *Indian*: "The leading men of
our party . . . collared their leaders. . . . This act immediately threw the parties into confusion [and] a general and bloody engagement. . . . The seals
which had been killed were a total loss to both parties, as they were left to rot
upon the beach."[2] Accidents and shipwrecks were numerous; the beaches of
many islands in the South Shetlands are still littered with the artifacts of
sealing vessels and the seal slaughter.

By 1829, William Webster, the expedition surgeon who chronicled Henry
Foster's scientific voyage in the *Chanticleer*, observed, "The islands of South
Shetland . . . formerly abounded with seals; but such is the havoc made by
sealers among them, that they are now scarce and seldom seen. The shores of
[the interior of Deception Island] must have formed a delightful retreat for

these persecuted creatures before it was found out by man, retired and secluded as it is; but during our stay we did not see a solitary fur-seal."[3]

Eighty-five years after the seal massacres, historian Hugh Robert Mill poignantly portrayed the sadness of the atrocities: "The southern summer of 1820–21 was a dark one for the fur-seals whose ancestors had basked upon the shores of the South Shetlands for untold centuries, following their quaint semi-civilised life and pursuing their patriarchal customs of war and love undisturbed by any being capable of contending with them. . . . The killing of seals, perhaps from the total ignorance of the victims of the threatened fate, perhaps from the almost human family affection they display, perhaps from the pathos of their innocent eyes, seems nearer murder than any other form of butchery or sport, and the first assault upon such a tribe of creatures is really painful to think about."[4]

Some of the men, however, who voyaged south during the 1820s made new and important contributions to geographic discovery, even though their chief purpose was sealing. Unfortunately, many records and logs of the period, which the sealers themselves considered far less important than their booty of animal skins and oil, have been lost. No one knows whether these records might have contained important historical insights and accounts of discoveries. Amid the slaughter, some expeditions went south purely for scientific reasons. An overview of the most significant and best-known voyages of this period follows.

William Smith was an experienced and capable English merchant captain in command of the brig *Williams*. He left Buenos Aires for Valparaiso with a crew of twenty-five men in January 1819. Strong westerlies in the vicinity of Cape Horn forced him to choose a route far to the southwest, into the ice. The risk was significant, since his ship was copper sheathed but not strengthened against ice. On 19 February, at about 62°40' S, 60° W,[5] Smith recorded the following in his journal: "At 7 AM land or Ice was discovered."[6] After standing off this possible land for the brief night, he became convinced of land the following day.[7] John Miers, a mining engineer who obtained information from one of Smith's officers and from Smith's log and who subsequently wrote about the voyage, stated that Smith, who had been brought up in the Greenland whale-fishery and was experienced in distinguishing land from ice, was indeed convinced of a land sighting.[8] Smith had discovered what he first named New South Britain and, later, New South Shetland. His first sighting was probably of what is today known as Williams Point on Livingston Island.[9] The South Shetland Islands are intimately associated with the Antarctic mainland nearby and are Antarctic in the geographic sense. Thus Smith's discovery constituted the lifting of the veil from the last continent and a great moment in the history of exploration. He headed north to Valparaiso the following day, arriving on 11 March.

Smith reported his remarkable findings to Capt. William Henry Shirreff, the senior naval officer, who was skeptical of the merchant service in general and particularly of Smith, since he had taken no depth soundings to substantiate the fact that he was close to land. As Miers related, "All ridiculed the poor man for his fanciful credulity and his deceptive vision; no one, in fact, gave the least credit to his tale, all endeavouring to persuade him that what he had seen was no more than ice-islands. Mr. Smith was not, however, to be thus easily laughed out of his own observation."[10] Smith vowed to return to confirm his discovery. He left Valparaiso for Montevideo on 16 May and detoured south despite the season. He managed to reach 62°12' S, 67° W on 15 June, in the depth of autumn and with scant daylight; he found himself surrounded by ice. He retreated north without delay and, without a land sighting, happy to have escaped.

When Smith arrived in Montevideo, he learned that news of his discovery had already arrived, reflecting, no doubt, the commercial sealing potential in the area. Smith spurned American offers of large sums to charter the *Williams* or to provide information on the position of the land. Rivalry between British and American sealers was already intense, and Smith decided that he would divulge the crucial information only to his British compatriots.[11] Already the lure of large seal harvests was so great, however, that ships were heading south on little more than rumor.

Smith departed south from Montevideo in September 1819, and on 15 October he confirmed the existence of a string of islands. Three days later he made a landing on King George Island, probably at Venus Bay, taking possession for Great Britain. He described the abundant wildlife and the absence of any but the most primitive vegetation.

He returned to Valparaiso in late November and related his discoveries to the British Admiralty. The admiralty organized an expedition under the command of Edward Bransfield (1795?–1852), with Smith as pilot; it departed Valparaiso in the *Williams* on 20 December. The men made another landing on King George Island and carried out charting as far as Livingston Island. They circumnavigated Tower Island and sighted Deception Island, failing, however, to note its remarkable interior harbor.

At three o'clock in the afternoon of 30 January 1820, the mainland of the

Antarctic Peninsula, and thus the Antarctic continent, was seen for the first time. Bellingshausen's observation three days earlier of ice contiguous with the continent notwithstanding, Bransfield and Smith had recorded the first sighting of actual land. The men aboard ship were aware that they had made a major discovery, but over a century was to elapse before the Antarctic Peninsula was conclusively shown to be a part of the continent.

Proceeding northeast, the party made landings at Cape Bowles on Clarence Island and on an islet near Elephant Island. The expedition finally turned north on 18 March, arriving in Valparaiso on 14 April. Smith made another sealing voyage the following season, by which time almost fifty American and British sealers were in the area.

Among the Americans, James P. Sheffield in the *Hersilia* was under orders from sealing entrepreneur Edmund Fanning, operating out of Stonington, Connecticut, to find new sealing grounds. Sheffield was in the Falkland Islands when he learned from the British of prospects to the south, so he headed for the South Shetlands late in 1819. Sealing was good, and by late 1820, Fanning had five ships going south under the command of Benjamin Pendleton in the *Frederick*. Twenty-one-year-old Nathaniel B. Palmer in the *Hero* was sent ahead to find a safe harbor; in the course of his sail he discovered that volcanic Deception Island had a narrow chasm in its rim and that the sea filled the interior, providing a sheltered haven for ships. From near Deception Island, Pendleton and Palmer saw the continental mainland in clear weather on 17 November 1820. Palmer sailed as far south as 66° S.

In the following season, near Elephant Island, Palmer in the *James Monroe* met and befriended the twenty-six-year-old British captain George Powell (1795?–1824) of the *Dove*. The two men proceeded east together and discovered another major island group, the South Orkney Islands. These islands, which Powell claimed he had seen first,[12] were sighted on 7 December 1821.[13] Powell wrote, "At 3 am the man at the mast-head discovered land and ice, bearing E. by S.: at this time the '*James Monroe*' was about four miles a-stern of us; I shortened sail for her, and hailed her: they had not seen it till close up with us, and then Captain Palmer doubted whether it was land or ice."[14] The next day Powell landed on the largest island of the group. He took possession of it for Great Britain and named it Coronation Island, in honor of the coronation of King George IV. The two ships sailed together along the island's north coast, and on 11 December, Powell sailed through Lewthwaite Strait and Palmer through Washington Strait. In honor of Powell, the South Orkney Islands were briefly known as the Powell Group in England, France, and the United States. Palmer was not particularly interested in the newly found islands, because few seals were found there.

Another British sealer, James Weddell (1787–1834), achieved greatness in the Antarctic. He began life at sea early, joining the British Navy at the age of nine. Weddell was first mate in the merchant service at age twenty-one, rejoined the navy, and became master two years later.[15] He visited the Antarctic regions in 1820–21 and again in 1822–23. He was different from most sealers in that he had a bent for scientific observation and a strong explorer's determination. He also proved himself to be a superb leader.

In the first season, in the small 160-ton brig *Jane,* Weddell could not find the Aurora Islands east of the Falkland Islands. These islands had first been reported in 1762 and several times later confirmed, but reported positions were imprecise. To the various observers the purported islands may have been Shag Rocks, icebergs seen in poor light, or illusions. Weddell turned south and produced charts of the western portion of the South Shetland Islands, and, in the company of the small sixty-five-ton cutter *Beaufoy* under the command of Michael McLeod, sighted the South Orkney Islands only six days after their discovery by Palmer and Powell.

This voyage seems not to have been profitable,[16] but Weddell promptly launched another. The *Jane,* with twenty-two men, was under his own command, and the *Beaufoy,* with thirteen men, was captained by Matthew Brisbane (?–1833). Again, the main purpose was sealing, but Weddell had a contingency plan—if sealing was unproductive, he would search for new lands. The ships visited the Falkland Islands, the South Shetland Islands, and then the South Orkney Islands, where Weddell sought seals and spent eleven days charting the islands, unaware that Powell and Palmer had already done so the previous year. Like Palmer, Weddell and Brisbane found few seals at the South Orkney Islands, so on 4 February 1823 they agreed to probe south into what eventually was named the Weddell Sea. "I accordingly informed Mr. Brisbane of my intention of standing to the southward, and he, with a boldness which greatly enhanced the respect I bore him, expressed his willingness to push our research in that direction."[17] To improve the comfort of the crew, Weddell allotted to each man three wine-glasses of rum daily and placed a cooking stove in the men's quarters for warmth and the drying of clothes. Thus began the most interesting and significant aspect of Weddell's voyage.

Although neither ship was prepared for ice travel, Weddell and Brisbane persevered in a difficult southward penetration through the ice pack and bergs that guard the Weddell Sea like so many ramparts. The two vessels happened to have sailed in a year of unusually light ice conditions, however, and on 18 February at 72°38' S, in fine weather, there was suddenly no further ice to bar the way. In capitalized letters, Weddell wrote, "NOT A PARTICLE OF ICE OF ANY DESCRIPTION WAS TO BE SEEN."[18] (Unknown to Weddell, these conditions were produced by cold, dense air cascading down from the altitudinous continental interior northward to the sea. James Clark Ross later found the same ice-free conditions, also produced by these so-called katabatic winds, in the Ross Sea.) The *Jane* and *Beaufoy* were able to proceed south unimpeded as long as the weather and the season held.

Two days later the ships established their farthest south position, surpassing Cook's record by 185 nautical miles. Given a contrary wind and the lateness of the season, Weddell decided not to press on further. Even at this, the climactic point of his voyage, Weddell simply stated, "Our latitude at this time, 20th February, 1822 [*sic*], was 74°15', and longitude 34°16'45"; the wind blowing fresh at south, prevented, what I most desired, our making farther progress in that direction."[19] The officers and crew celebrated with a hoisting of colors, the firing of a gun, three cheers, and an extra round of rum. Weddell delivered a brief speech. To ascertain the direction of the water current, Weddell placed a note in a bottle secured with cork and tossed it over-

Brig *Jane* and cutter *Beaufoy* in the latitude of 74°15' S
Weddell, *A Voyage towards the South Pole*, 1825

board. No land had been sighted—a disappointment. Taking advantage of a fresh southerly wind, Weddell and Brisbane retreated northward, wisely resisting the lure of open water to the south so late in the season, in what is now known as an area of dangerous and fickle conditions. Even sailing under prudent guidance, the two ships were separated in a storm on the way north. Anxiety prevailed until their reunion six days later. The parties anchored temporarily in a bay of the southwest portion of South Georgia, and wintered in the Falkland Islands.

Weddell and Brisbane headed south again, early the following season, 7 October 1823, to hunt seals in the South Shetlands. They met with ice islands at 59°16' S. At 61°21' S the vessels reached extensive ice fields. The ships became enveloped in bitterly cold hurricane-force winds from the southwest. High seas swept clear the deck of the *Jane,* and the ship's rudder was frozen fast. The ships lost sight of each other, but that mattered little; one could not have helped the other. The storm moderated the next day, but many of the men had been injured in falls, all were frostbitten, and virtually none had spare clothing. Weddell wrote, "I never, during my experience at sea, have seen an equal degree of patience and firmness as was exhibited by these seamen. No dastardly request to reach a better climate was ever hinted at, but they continued in the strictest obedience and determination to make light of difficulties."[20] More hardships were to follow. The helmsman made an error, and as a result the port bow struck an ice mass so forcefully that men were thrown out of their bunks and the *Jane* was damaged. In the shifting pack ice, another collision tore down the starboard bulwarks and mainguard board; leaks were repaired with tarred canvas, lead, and planks. At last, the men abandoned prospects for a landfall and headed north for Cape Horn. They ended their voyage in England.

Weddell was unusual among sealers in that his quest for knowledge appeared at least as strong as his commercial bent. "I pity those who, when they meet with an appearance that is likely to throw some light on the state of the globe, are led through pusillanimity to forego the examination of it. But the extreme reluctance I have to excite painful feelings any where, restrains me from dealing that just censure which is due to many of my fellow seamen, who, by negligence, narrow views of pecuniary interest, or timidity, have omitted many practicable investigations. . . . If I have contributed, by my private adventure, to the advancement of hydrography, I conceive that I have only done that which every man would endeavour to accomplish, who, in the pursuit of wealth, is at the same time zealous enough in the cause of science to lose no opportunity of collecting information for the benefit of mankind."[21]

Weddell anticipated that his farthest south position might be subject to doubt, so he brought the chief officer of the *Jane* and two seamen to swear to the truth of his log before the commissioners of His Majesty's Customs in London. His claim of having penetrated so far south in the vicinity of 30° W longitude was, indeed, taken skeptically by some of his contemporaries, inasmuch as ice had forestalled all others in lower latitudes. But there was never any reason to doubt his claim. As James Clark Ross later stated, "Weddell was favoured by an unusually fine season, and we may rejoice that there was a brave and daring seaman on the spot to profit by the opportunity."[22] Weddell was honored by election to fellow of the Royal Society of Edinburgh. He never became rich from his sealing endeavors and died in abject poverty. As for Brisbane, he became the head of the British establishment at Port Lewis on East Falkland and was murdered there in 1833 by mutinous gauchos.

Several other voyages during the decade of the 1820s deserve mention. Richard Sherratt, a British sealer, visited the South Shetlands during the 1820–21 season in the *Lady Trowbridge* and was wrecked on King George Island. His surveys, made while awaiting relief, were among the first performed in those islands.

Another sealer, Robert Fildes of Liverpool, sailed in the *Cora* and arrived off Livingston Island in December 1820. While he and his party were collecting sealskins, a gale caused the ship to drag anchor. The vessel struck a rock, drifted ashore, and was wrecked. The stranded men salvaged timber from the ship for bunks, and survived on seal meat, penguin eggs, and supplies left by other vessels until their rescue. Fildes spent his time preparing a compendium of South Shetland harbors and anchorages. In the *Robert*, Fildes again visited the South Shetland Islands late in 1821. Unlucky once more, Fildes was wrecked in March 1822, but this time his party was quickly relieved.

The British sealing vessel *Lord Melville*, under the command of one Captain Clark, was wrecked during the 1820–21 season. A boatload of ten men under the command of the mate was stranded at Esther Harbor, King George Island, and they were not taken off until the following season. The ten endured the miserable winter in fairly good spirits. The involuntary nature of their stay detracts only slightly from the fact that these were the first men to winter over in the Antarctic regions.

In search of seals, the American captain John Davis took his ship *Cecilia* southward, and, on 7 February 1821, made a landing on a large body of land.

His observations were recorded in the log of another vessel, the *Huron*: "I think this Southern Land to be a Continent."[23] The site may have been what was later named Hughes Bay; if it was, his landing was the first on the Antarctic continental mainland, but the location remains in dispute.

Another American, Benjamin Morrell (1795–1839), sailed the *Wasp* in the years 1822–23. Morrell searched for and could not find the Aurora Islands, visited South Georgia and the Kerguelen Islands, and then voyaged south into the Weddell Sea. His account contains so many inconsistencies and unconfirmed claims that precisely what he accomplished is difficult, if not impossible, to assess.[24] Morrell benefited in 1823, as had Weddell, from relatively ice-free conditions in the Weddell Sea. Amusing to modern readers, Morrell boasted, while in 70°14' S latitude late in the season on 14 March, "I should then have been able, without the least doubt, to penetrate as far as the eighty-fifth degree of south latitude. . . . The way was open before me, clear and unobstructed; the temperature of the air and water mild; the weather pleasant; the wind fair."[25]

The British captain Edward Hughes, on a sealing expedition in the *Sprightly* in 1824–25, visited the South Shetland Islands and conducted a survey of Hughes Bay on the west coast of the Antarctic Peninsula.

Henry Foster, a capable British captain with a scientific background, was sent out in the *Chanticleer* by the British Admiralty to the South Atlantic in the years 1828–31. He visited the South Shetland Islands and made magnetic and pendulum observations, extending Edward Sabine's work in the South Atlantic. Foster resided at Deception Island from 9 January to 8 March 1829, where he also studied flora and fauna; his chart of the island remained the best available through the turn of the century. Later in the voyage he fell into the raging rapids of a river in Panama and was drowned, a sorry loss to his men and to British scientific inquiry.

After an absence of eight years, the Americans Benjamin Pendleton and Nathaniel Palmer returned to the Antarctic in 1829–30 in the *Seraph* and *Annawan,* reexamined Palmer's previous land discoveries in the South Shetland Islands, and hunted seals. Weather and ice frustrated them in all their endeavors, and the crew, which had signed on for a share of the profit, became impatient. The unproductive voyage was ended after five weeks in the ice. James Eights (1798–1882), the first American scientist to work in Antarctica, later published a report on the discovery of a previously unknown species of crustacean,[26] constituting the first purely scientific paper by an American concerning the Antarctic. The general failure of the expedition, however, convinced Fanning that private enterprise could no longer take the financial risk of sponsoring substantial geographical and scientific investigations—in the Antarctic or anywhere else. He thus became a prominent lobbyist for what eventually grew to be the government-sponsored United States Exploring Expedition of 1838–42 under Charles Wilkes (see chapter 6).

4

JOHN BISCOE, JOHN BALLENY, AND THE
ENDERBY VOYAGES
(1830–1850)

The cliffs of it, which bore the marks of icebergs having been broken
from off it . . . then ran away to the southward with a gradual ascent,
with a perfectly smooth surface. . . . It was then lost in the general glow
of the atmosphere.

John Biscoe, from his log

THE LONDON FIRM OF ENDERBY BROTHERS, which commenced sealing
and whaling operations in the southern oceans in 1785, was noted not only
for its enterprise but also for its keen interest in geographic exploration. In
the latter respect, the company was unusual among commercial operations
of its time, since such expeditions were financially unprofitable. Enderby
captains were carefully selected for sea experience and education. Some
already had made important contributions to geographical discovery:
Abraham Bristow had discovered the Auckland Islands in 1805; James
Lindsay and Thomas Hopper likely saw Bouvetøya (then Bouvet Island) in
1808; and George Norris landed there in 1825.

When the elder Samuel Enderby died in 1829, his sons took over the firm.
One son in particular, Charles (1797–1876), was also interested in geographi-
cal discovery and continued the tradition of the firm's support of explo-
ration. Enderby Brothers, under the sons, sponsored several voyages to the
Antarctic regions. Two of these, those of John Biscoe (1794–1843) and John
Balleny, resulted in major discoveries.

John Biscoe's expedition sailed in the brig *Tula* and the cutter *Lively* on
what became the third circumnavigation at high southern latitudes. Biscoe
never published an account of his voyage, but his journal was preserved by
the Royal Geographical Society, which published the Antarctic portions of

the narrative.[1] Biscoe left London on 14 July 1830 and departed from the Falkland Islands on 27 November. Heading east, the parties made a fruitless search for the Aurora Islands, were then separated in fog and gales for three anxious days, and at the South Sandwich group were forced north and east by ice. The parties were eventually able to make their way south again and crossed the Antarctic Circle at 2°30' E on 21 January 1831. For several weeks Biscoe proceeded eastward, south of Bellingshausen's track, without sighting land. Conditions were so arduous that Biscoe connected the two ships by a line to avoid another separation, but while unlashed on 14 February, the ships were separated for four days in a gale.

Biscoe saw Antarctic petrels and snow petrels flying toward the southwest, making him believe he was close to land.[2] On 25 February his supposition was confirmed when he glimpsed ice-covered land forming part of the continent at 66°29' S, 45°17' E. "At noon ... [an] appearance of land ... now bore from E.S.E. to W.S.W. .... The cliffs of it, which bore the marks of icebergs having been broken from off it, and which was exactly similar to their sides in every respect ... then ran away to the southward with a gradual ascent, with a perfectly smooth surface, and I could trace it in extent to at least from 30 to 40 miles from the foretop with a good telescope; it was then lost in the general glow of the atmosphere."[3] He was convinced of an actual land sighting on 28 February, at 65°57' S, 47°20' E. "4 p.m. saw several hummocks to the southward ... and at 6 p.m. clearly distinguished it to be land, and to considerable extent; to my great satisfaction what we had first seen being the black tops of mountains showing themselves through the snow."[4] The land is now known as Enderby Land.

The crews struggled to get closer, but the way was barred by ice. On the night of 2 to 3 March, the men's attention was distracted by an extraordinary aurora. Biscoe was afraid that the crew's awe of the lights would make them negligent and jeopardize the ships' safety in the dense ice. But he, too, was impressed: "Nearly the whole night, the Aurora Australis showed the most brilliant appearance, at times rolling itself over our heads in beautiful columns, then as suddenly forming itself as the unrolled fringe of a curtain, and again suddenly shooting to the form of a serpent. . . . [It] was without exception the grandest phenomenon of nature of its kind I ever witnessed."[5]

Biscoe gave the name Cape Ann to the headland at 66°25' S, 49°18' E. Just as a final approach seemed possible, a strong gale on 5 March turned into hurricane-force winds, and the ships were separated. In the storm's fury, one of the *Tula*'s boats was swept away, and the bulwarks were damaged as the brig ran out of control for 120 miles. Only because the sea ice was moving with a speed comparable to that of the ship did no serious collisions occur. The *Tula* regained Cape Ann by 16 March but could not approach, and the cutter was nowhere seen. The *Tula* was beset by ice, and the men were afflicted by cold and scurvy. On 3 April, only three crewmen were fit enough to sail. Biscoe thus abandoned his plans to winter at the desolate Kerguelen Islands and retreated instead to the warmer climate of Hobart. Two men died on the voyage northward, and several more were hospitalized upon arrival in Hobart on 10 May. The crew of the *Lively* had fared even worse. By the time the cutter reached Port Philip, Australia, only Captain Avery, a seaman, and a boy with a crushed hand were still alive.

Despite the terrible hardships, Biscoe had ships and crews ready for a fresh departure from Hobart on 10 October. He sailed south on 4 January 1832, following the bearing of seabirds in flight, hoping that they might indicate the direction of land. By early February the cutter's sails were so badly damaged that Biscoe confided in his journal his decision not to prolong the voyage, finding it "absolutely necessary to make as quick a passage as possible."[6] Nevertheless, the ships remained far south well into autumn, probably because Biscoe found the temptation to explore too great to resist.

On 15 February, at 67°15' S, 68°20' W, Biscoe discovered Adelaide Island and its associated island chain. Apparently unaware of Bellingshausen's discoveries of Peter I Island and Alexander Island farther to the south, Biscoe wrote, "This island being the farthest known land to the southward, I have honoured it with the name of H.M.G. Majesty Queen Adelaide. It has a most imposing and beautiful appearance, having one very high peak running up into the clouds. . . . About one-third of the mountains, which are about four miles in extent from north to south, have only a thin scattering of snow over their summits. Towards the base the other two-thirds are buried in a field of snow and ice of the most dazzling brightness."[7] Biscoe sent a boat ashore on one of the Pitt Islands on 19 February. Two days later, Biscoe landed on the "mainland" (later named Anvers Island), took possession for King William IV, and named the tallest mountain Mount William after his sovereign.[8]

The men sailed north to the South Shetland Islands to hunt for any elephant seals they might still find that late in the season. There Biscoe cooperated with the British sealer Captain Kellock in the schooner *Exquisite*. Afterward, Biscoe explored islands to the south. On 10 April a wind sprang up with a huge swell, and the *Tula*, having a deeper draft than the *Lively*, was grounded in the shallows at Low Island. The rudder was damaged, and both ships made for the Falklands, arriving 29 April. The *Tula* returned to England, ending its voyage on 30 January 1833. The *Lively*, having survived its arduous Antarctic voyage, was wrecked in the Falklands, with no loss of life.

Upon completing his circumnavigation, Biscoe knew that he had produced the first strong evidence of a large southern continent, although the existence of such a continent—as opposed to numerous islands—was not yet generally accepted.[9] He had circumnavigated 160 degrees south of 60° S and almost 50 degrees south of the Antarctic Circle. His work was well received, and he was awarded gold medals by the Royal Geographical Society and the Paris Geographical Society.

Following Biscoe's success, tribulations notwithstanding, the Enderbys sent the *Rose* and the *Hopefull* in 1832?–33 under the command of Henry Rea (1804?–?) to explore south between 0° and 20° E. The *Rose* was crushed in the ice north of Clarence Island, and the crew was rescued by the men of the *Hopefull*. The surviving ship was now overladen, and the expedition had to be aborted.

On 27 November 1833, Peter Kemp (?–1834), a sealer in the *Magnet*, sighted Heard Island at 52°30' S, 69°15' E (although Capt. John Heard was later given credit for the discovery, in November 1853). Kemp sailed as far as 66° S and at about 60° E longitude discovered an easterly extension of Enderby Land, later named Kemp Coast. Sadly, Kemp's chart and logbook were lost in a London cab, and no narrative of his voyage was ever published.

In the 1838–39 season, John Balleny in the 154-ton schooner *Eliza Scott*, and Capt. H. Freeman in the 54-ton cutter *Sabrina*, made notable geographical discoveries on their Antarctic sealing voyage. Balleny's journal of the voyage and the log of John McNab, the second mate, have been published.[10] The natural elements of the far south were not the only sources of hardship: even before the ship's departure, some of the crew behaved mutinously, and a young crewman was beaten for insubordination during the Antarctic portion of the voyage.

The expedition sailed south from New Zealand on 7 January 1839. After a six-day stay in Perseverance Harbor at Campbell Island, Balleny reached 69°2' S, 174° E before being halted by ice. At eleven in the morning on 9 February, the Balleny Islands were sighted for the first time, the latitude being given as 66°37' S (now considered 66°35' S, 162°50' E). By eight in the evening the men were close enough to confirm three distinct islands of considerable size and elevation, two smaller ones, and a number of islets.

On 12 February, Balleny and Freeman went ashore on Young Island. "At 6 p.m. went on shore in the cutter's boat, at the only place likely to afford a landing; but when we got close with the boat it proved only the drawback of the sea, leaving a beach of 3 or 4 feet at most. Captain Freeman jumped out and got a few stones, but was up to the middle in water. . . . But for the bare rocks where the icebergs had broken from, we should scarce have known it for land. . . . The cliffs are perpendicular, and what in all probability would have been valleys and beaches are occupied by solid blocks of ice."[11] Balleny described abundant seals, whales, penguins, and petrels.

The ships then turned westward, the first time sailing vessels in the Antarctic regions had attempted exploration against the prevailing winds. On 2 March, an important discovery was made at about 65° S, 121° E. Balleny simply stated: "Saw land to the southward, the vessel surrounded by drift-ice"; and the following day: "To the S.W. the ice was quite fast, with every appearance of land at the back of it, but, the weather coming on thick, were obliged to steer to the northward."[12] McNab recorded only slightly more: "The supposed land not more than one mile to windward."[13] The following day, he wrote: "At 8 it cleared off a little. Saw the appearance of land to the south, but there being so much ice between the vessels and it, we were glad to get out again safe. . . . At 11, still saw the appearance of land to the west, but it coming on thick, and the vessels surrounded with ice, we steered as requisite to gain the open sea."[14] What was not widely appreciated at the time but is accepted now is that Balleny's "appearance of land" was the continental mainland south of Australia at the place Jules Dumont d'Urville saw the following year and called Côte Clarie (Clarie Coast).

On 24 March, at about 52° S, 94° E, the ships were caught in a ferocious gale and high seas. The *Sabrina* burned blue lights, an indication of distress, but the schooner could not close on her. At dawn the *Sabrina* was nowhere to be seen, and indeed she was never seen again. All souls were lost. Meanwhile, Balleny and his men were still in jeopardy. An enormous wave had swept clear the deck of the *Eliza Scott* and laid the ship on its beam: the vessel arighted only after ten anxious minutes. The men headed home and arrived in London on 17 September, the accomplishments and tragedies of the expedition duly recorded.

In 1847, the Enderby firm secured from the British government permission to establish a whaling station at New Zealand's subantarctic Auckland Islands. The town of Hardwicke was established at Port Ross in 1850. At the height of Hardwicke's brief existence, a Captain Tapsell, in 1850, sailed south from Hardwicke in the *Brisk* to the Balleny Islands and then proceeded to 143° E, without sighting land.

5

THE VOYAGE OF JULES S.-C. DUMONT D'URVILLE
IN THE *ASTROLABE* AND THE *ZÉLÉE*
(1837–1840)

Jamais vin de Bordeaux ne fut appelé à jouer un rôle plus digne; jamais bouteille ne fut vidée plus à propos.

[Never was Bordeaux wine called on to play a more worthy part; never was a bottle emptied more fitly.]

Joseph Dubouzet, in Jules S-C Dumont d'Urville,
Voyage au Pole Sud

THE STUDY OF TERRESTRIAL MAGNETISM became a scientific priority in the early to mid nineteenth century, and the polar regions north and south beckoned scientists in pursuit of scientific knowledge and national pride. Three nations, France, the United States, and England, sent expeditions south at approximately the same time. At the order of King Louis-Philippe of France, Jules Sébastien-César Dumont d'Urville (1790–1842) led an expedition in two ships, *L'Astrolabe,* under his own command, and *La Zélée,* under the command of Charles Jacquinot. These men were seen by their countrymen as followers in the French exploring tradition established in the Southern Hemisphere by Paulmyer de Gonneville, Jules Marie Crozet, Marie-Joseph Marion-Dufresne, and Yves-Joseph de Kerguélen-Trémarec.

Dumont d'Urville was already distinguished for maritime exploration, in particular for his voyage in the *Astrolabe* in 1826–29 to Australia, New Zealand, and the South Pacific. He was also lauded for securing for France the ancient Greek statue *Venus de Milo* during his visit to the island of Melos in 1820, and he was a founder of the Paris Geographical Society in 1821. In spite of his acclaim, Dumont d'Urville's personal life had fallen into a shambles by the late 1830s.

His tactlessness cost him the goodwill of colleagues and, excepting his wife and son, that of his family and in-laws as well. He lost his beloved two-year-old daughter to cholera. This new expedition served to resurrect his life and purpose. Dumont d'Urville's greater interest was not the physical sciences but rather botany, entomology, and the various peoples he encountered on voyages. Nevertheless, his love for France and desire to uphold its honor compelled him to command this expedition. His ships and crews were poorly chosen for the rigors of such work, ultimately affecting the results of the expedition and the lives of the men.

In the 1837–38 season, after surveying the Strait of Magellan, Dumont d'Urville and Jacquinot headed south with orders to better Weddell's southern record. They passed between the South Orkney Islands and the Elephant and Clarence Island group and were soon stopped by ice at only 63°39' S on 22 January 1838. After a retreat to the South Orkney group, they made another southward attempt. Dumont d'Urville called the magnificent scenery "austere and grandiose beyond words."[1] When the ships were stopped and nearly trapped by the ice at 62°20' S, the men broke their vessels free with axes and saws. Dumont d'Urville openly questioned Weddell's achievement in the same area, but there was no justification for doing so, beyond his bitterness at his own lack of better success.

Dumont d'Urville and Jacquinot retreated once again to the South Orkney Islands, made a landing on Saddle Island, and then visited the South Shetland Islands, noting the tiny volcanic Bridgeman Island in active eruption. Here Dumont d'Urville charted the northern part of Graham Land in late February to early March, described Joinville Island and Terre Louis Philippe (now Louis Philippe Plateau, a portion of the Trinity Peninsula, the northernmost extension of the Antarctic Peninsula), and assigned names to some of the mountains. Even though Bransfield Strait and Orléans Strait farther to the south were relatively ice free and visibility occasionally was quite good, the parties were forced to retreat to Chile because of scurvy, a death, and discontent among the crew. Progress northward was slow, and as soon as the ships arrived in Talcahuano Bay on 6 April, many of the men deserted.

From May 1838 to October 1839, Dumont d'Urville performed extensive Pacific explorations. Then, during the voyage from Sumatra to Hobart during the months of October to December, many officers and crewmen alike became seriously ill from dysentery, and sixteen men—among them some of the most capable and liked—died from the epidemic aboard the two ships. More of their numbers were hospitalized upon arrival in Hobart. The death of one additional man, just as the ships were about to depart again for the Antarctic, had a profound effect on all. That man was Ernest Goupil (1814–40), a twenty-five-year-old artist. According to Lt. Joseph Dubouzet, another expedition member, "Everyone beheld with distress a young man so remarkably talented cut off in the flower of his age, after a long and difficult voyage, to which the passion of art and travel had led him to sacrifice everything. . . . Never . . . was his noble character so markedly shown as during his long and severe sufferings, which he bore with so much courage and resignation. . . . To the last moment his thoughts were with his family and his friends."[2]

The expedition left Hobart on 2 January 1840, in the direction of the south magnetic pole. Dumont d'Urville was interested in exploring between 120° and 160° E south of 60° S, a region not previously examined by the three circumnavigators Cook, Bellingshausen, and Biscoe. Again the ships were marked—a number of men had relapses of dysentery, and one more seaman died.

When the parties encountered tabular icebergs, Dumont d'Urville surmised correctly that land was near. An appearance of land, or, more accurately, a rise in the ice that presumably covered land, was seen from the *Astrolabe* on 19 January, but the men, unsure as they strained to gaze through the opaque scene, had to await better visibility and independent confirmation from the *Zélée* the next day. Finally, in magnificent weather, the men stared upon a landscape rising over three thousand feet. Their calculations placed them at 66°30' S, 131°21' E. The magnetic dip was 86°, and they realized that the magnetic pole lay inland. The land was a continuation of that seen by Balleny, but Dumont d'Urville did not know of Balleny's discovery. News of it had not reached Hobart by the time of his departure.

The ships advanced among gathering icebergs. Jacquinot and expedition hydrographer Clément Vincendon-Dumoulin (1811–58) described them eloquently: "Their perpendicular walls towered above our masts; they overhung our ships, whose dimensions seemed ridiculously diminutive compared with these enormous masses. The spectacle which presented itself to our gaze was at once grand and terrifying. One could imagine oneself in the narrow streets of a city of giants. At the foot of these immense masses we perceived vast caverns hollowed out by the sea, where the waves rushed in with a roar. The sun darted oblique rays on the immense walls of ice, which

Reconnaissance of the Adélie Coast, 20 January 1840
Dumont d'Urville, *Voyage au Pole Sud, Atlas Pittoresque*, 1846

resembled crystal. The effects of light and shade were truly magical and striking. From the top of these ice mountains there leaped into the sea numerous streams, caused by the apparently very active melting of the snow."[3]

No landing on the mainland was possible, owing to the sheer cliffs of ice. However, shortly after six in the afternoon on 21 January 1840, J.-A. Duroch, on watch aboard the *Astrolabe*, spotted some rocks offshore and quickly put out a boat under his own command. Not to be outdone, the men of the *Zélée* launched a boat under Dubouzet's command, and the two boats raced each other for shore. Duroch, who had the head start, reached shore first. Later reflecting on the experience, he wrote, "Over these majestic ruins there reigns a deathly stillness, an eternal silence; never before had man's voice rung out through these icy solitudes. Surrounded by this sublime spectacle, our boats, the French flag on the prow, glide in. We are quite silent and enraptured but our hearts are beating wildly and then suddenly a long shout of '*Vive le Roi!*' greets our landing."[4] The boats had landed on one of a string of islets about a third of a mile offshore, much to the displeasure of the resident penguins. The French tricolor was hoisted, possession was taken, and a

[31]

libation, brought along with great prescience, was shared. Dubouzet was inspired to exclaim, "Never was Bordeaux wine called on to play a more worthy part; never was a bottle emptied more fitly."[5]

Dumont d'Urville gave to the land the name Terre Adélie (now the Adélie Coast), after his wife, and the ships proceeded west. The twenty-fourth of January was harrowing as blinding whirlwinds of snow enveloped the parties. The ships were coated with rime, and, so close to the magnetic pole, the compasses were useless. The two vessels lost sight of each other, and the *Astrolabe*, its mainsail torn to shreds, heeled so severely that it seemed the ship must be engulfed. A tortured Dumont d'Urville wrote, "How painful were my reflections at such a moment! If we had perished that day, all the records of the expedition would have been destroyed. . . . For myself, life was nothing: condemned to constant suffering, death would be almost a deliverance; but how different was the position of the young sailors with a most honourable future before them, who several days before had been so joyous and hopeful at the sight of the land we had just discovered."[6] A change in the weather the following day was the men's salvation, but the leader's anxiety for the *Zélée* was intense until the parties found each other late that day.

On 29 January, the French ships unexpectedly encountered Charles Wilkes's brig *Porpoise* but failed to communicate because of a misunderstanding of signals. Dumont d'Urville and Jacquinot sailed on and the following day followed a 100- to 160-foot-high ice barrier for nearly ninety miles. Dumont d'Urville assumed the ice was connected to land, and he named this land Côte Clarie (Clarie Coast) after Jacquinot's wife. His work in the south now finished, he turned north on 1 February and arrived in Hobart on 17 February. There the men met with more sorrow—they learned that three more of their company, left behind, had died. Dumont d'Urville visited the Auckland Islands in March, and then returned to France.

Only two years later, having by now lost three of his four children, Dumont d'Urville perished with his wife and son in a fiery train accident near Versailles. Jacquinot and Dumoulin were left to complete publication of the expedition's work.

6

CHARLES WILKES AND THE UNITED STATES EXPLORING EXPEDITION (1838–1842)

It required all the hope I could muster to outweigh the intense feeling of responsibility that hung over me. I may compare it to that of one doomed to destruction.

Charles Wilkes, *Narrative of the United States Exploring Expedition*

THE TEMPERAMENTAL LT. CHARLES WILKES (1798–1877) was chosen by the U.S. Navy to lead an expedition for geographic and scientific discovery only after other naval officers had declined the opportunity. The U.S. Exploring Expedition was an enormous venture that set out with six ships and more than four hundred men. Only half the men lasted to the end, because of desertions, discharges for insubordination, and deaths. And one by one, most of the ships dropped out as well. Even so, the expedition was a great achievement in maritime exploration on a grand scale for such a relatively young nation. The effort gave the United States international stature in the field of geographic exploration. Wilkes, however, incurred substantial personal hardship from this expedition, first from its organization and execution and then from official attacks on his reputation, criticism of some of his results, and finally from his years-long struggle to see the scientific work published.

Seeds of discontent were sown from the outset. Wilkes was a strict and often capricious disciplinarian. He kept secret from his scientific staff the objectives of the expedition and treated them as common sailors. The navy prohibited expedition members from making public any journal, memoir, work of art, or communication upon the expedition's return, so no man had a sanctioned outlet for expressing his views. None of the ships were reinforced for work in the ice; provisions and equipment included no antiscorbutics, no ice saws, only poor clothing for cold weather, and, for the southern voyages, insufficient shiphold capacity for even one year's provisions. The oak timbers of one ship, the *Peacock*, were already in a fairly advanced state of decay. Wilkes acknowledged that the chances of their surviving an Antarctic winter, if trapped in the ice, would be slim. But for this lack of preparation he was not entirely to blame, as he had expressed his concerns beforehand to the navy. Discontent among the men was predictable. Wilkes remarked upon departure, "It required all the hope I could muster to outweigh the intense feeling of responsibility that hung over me. I may compare it to that of one doomed to destruction."[1]

The entire fleet consisted of the 780-ton flagship *Vincennes*, the 650-ton sloop *Peacock*, and the 230-ton brig *Porpoise;* two tiny pilot boats, the 110-ton *Sea Gull* and 96-ton *Flying Fish*; and the store ship *Relief*. The fleet left Norfolk, Virginia, on 18 August 1838. In preparation for the first Antarctic season, all of the ships met in Orange Harbor in Tierra del Fuego, the last time all would be together.

Wilkes in the *Porpoise* and Lt. Robert E. Johnson in the *Sea Gull* departed late in the season, on 25 February 1839, and explored the South Shetlands as instructed; their voyage was uneventful and relatively unimportant. Closed in by ice, with the miserable weather of approaching autumn and scurvy appearing in a number of the men, Wilkes and Johnson ended their southward push on 5 March. Johnson's party spent a week in Deception Island's interior harbor, where the men collected geological specimens and birds. Later the next month, as they were heading for Valparaiso, the *Sea Gull* and the *Flying Fish* were separated in a gale in the vicinity of Cape Horn. The *Flying Fish* retreated to Orange Harbor, but the *Sea Gull* and its party of fifteen men were never seen again. Wilkes had a difficult time accepting that the ship could have foundered in the hands of his trusted officers, but he resigned himself to the fact when a search revealed no traces of either the ship or its party.

Meanwhile, the *Peacock*, under Capt. William Hudson, and the *Flying Fish*, under Lt. William M. Walker, composed a separate party. The ships lost each other in a gale one day after departure and were reunited only by chance on 25 March. The unexpected meeting occurred at about 68° S, 97°58' W, as far south as the *Peacock* was to reach; the ship had been stalled by gales and ice. Titian R. Peale (1799–1855), scientist and artist aboard the *Peacock*, recorded on 22 March: "[Icebergs] and detached floes . . . seemed to say, 'thus far shalt thou come, and no further.'"[2] The men of the *Peacock* now learned that the

Flying Fish, while attempting to better Cook's farthest south of 71°10', had reached a remarkable 70°4' S on 22 March, at 100°16' E, about 5 degrees east of Cook's incursion. Walker believed that all was well until, on 24 March, he discovered his ship closely hemmed in by ice extending in all directions in an almost dead calm. "Never did fond ear strain for the sigh of love, more anxiously than those devoted men listened to each gasp of the wind, whose breath was now their life."[3] Forcing a passage through narrow leads, Walker steered his ship to the safety of open water and then had his welcome encounter with the *Peacock.* In an unreinforced, leaky ship that Walker thought "would at least make . . . an honourable coffin,"[4] the southern penetration was a courageous achievement. Both parties headed north together. The entire entourage left Valparaiso and spent the rest of the year exploring the South Pacific, Australia, and New Zealand. The *Relief* was forced to return home early because of unseaworthiness.

The second southern voyage, of far greater significance and the most important contribution to geographic exploration of the entire expedition, set out the following season from Sydney on 26 December 1839. The objective was to sail as far south as possible, then explore west. Wilkes was in the *Vincennes,* Lt. Cadwalader Ringgold in the *Porpoise,* Hudson in the *Peacock,* and Lt. R. F. Pinkney in the *Flying Fish.* A storm soon separated the ships. One of two rendezvous points was the nonexistent Emerald Island, but, astonishingly, the *Vincennes* and the *Porpoise* did reunite with the *Peacock* in the vast ocean. The leaking *Flying Fish,* with a complement of sick men, returned to New Zealand.

The three remaining ships pressed on and reached the ice fields and an ice barrier. The men were plagued by fog much of the time, but on 14 January 1840 the fog lifted and revealed sixty icebergs in the vicinity. The remarkable sight prompted inspired words from midshipman George Colvocoresses aboard the *Vincennes*: "Masses assuming the shape of a Gothic church, with arched windows and doors, and all of the rich drapery of that style, composed, apparently, of crystal, showing all the shades of opal, or of emerald green; pillars and inverted cones, pyramids and mounds of every shape, valleys and lakes, domes supported by round transparent columns of cerulian [*sic*] hue, and cities and palaces as white as the purest alabaster. The liveliest imagination could not paint to itself a scene more rich and grand, and we stood gazing at it with astonishment and admiration until it was again enveloped in the fog."[5]

Two days later, Wilkes tentatively thought he had sighted land. "On this day (16th January) appearances believed at the time to be land were visible from all the three vessels."[6] The next day, seaman Joseph Clark aboard the *Vincennes* recorded: "The loom of land was plain in the horizon"; and then the next day: "Every indication of land."[7] Wilkes was convinced, once visibility improved. On 19 January he recorded: "Land was now certainly visible . . . and my own opinion was confirmed by that of some of the oldest and most experienced seamen on board. . . . We were at this time in longitude 154°30' E., latitude 66°20' S.; the day was fine, and at times quite clear."[8] Lt. William Reynolds, aboard the *Peacock,* recorded his experiences of 19 January: "I spent more than one hour at the mast head. . . . I was alone on my airy perch . . . naught to disturb the solemn and almost awful stillness. . . . I thought there was no one but God near me and as I looked upon the mighty scene around which was neither Earth nor Sea, I was more impressed with the idea of His creative power and of the insignificance of man, than by any prospect that ever Earth afforded, or Sea assumed. . . . Once we thought we saw Land and as it happened I had been the first to discern the appearance . . . and its high and broken sides and summit confirmed our conjectures. We were sure it was a portion of the Southern Continent and were elated beyond measure."[9] Colvocoresses was also convinced,[10] and Clark commented that land "was plainly visible from the deck, stretching from the south and east as far as the eye could extend, with a towering top some two and three thousand feet on a level."[11]

The *Peacock* was taken in closer to land but on 24 January suffered severe damage in the ice and narrowly escaped annihilation. Its rudder incapacitated, the helpless ship was repeatedly slammed by the wind onto floating pieces of ice, as more and more damage was inflicted on the decaying oak. Hudson first tried sending men out by boat to anchor the ship to the ice; the maneuver failed, with near catastrophe for the men who had left the mother ship. Hudson found uncertain shelter for his wounded vessel in a bay in the ice barrier. Frantic repairs were made over several days of intermittently threatening weather. He then took the ailing ship north to Sydney and arrived with all men well. Hudson later received Wilkes's highest praise for the manner in which he had handled the treacherous position. The ship, under Hudson's command, was later wrecked without loss of life in North America, during the course of a voyage in shallows and difficult seas at the mouth of the Columbia River.

Only the *Vincennes* and the *Porpoise* now remained to continue the examination of the coast south of Australia. The ships parted to explore separately on 27 January at about 65°41' S, 142°31' E. Ringgold in the *Porpoise* had an unexpected meeting with Dumont d'Urville in the *Astrolabe*, explored as far west as 100° E, sighted the ice barrier in a number of places, and then on 24 February headed north, returning to New Zealand.

Wilkes in the *Vincennes* made additional land sightings along fifteen hundred miles of coast, often amid hardships brought on by ice and stormy weather. On 28 January the ship was in the middle of a gallery of tabular bergs when a gale nearly wrecked it. Seaman Charles Erskine related, "Suddenly many voices cried out from the to'-gallant forecastle, 'Icebergs on the weather bow!' then, 'On the lee bow, and abeam!' Destruction seemed certain. . . . Return we could not, for we had just passed large bergs to leeward. . . . Louder and more furious raged the gale. Now the lee guns were under water; the next instant the ship rose upright on an even keel. At last we entered a narrow passage between two monster icebergs that were gradually closing together. Every officer and man was at his station with bated breath and blanched face; yet true to discipline there they stood like specters. . . . One thought of the dear ones at home, a brief prayer to our God, then we nerved our hearts to meet our fate. But . . . Providence was indeed kind. . . . Our hearts grew lighter and lighter as we heard the whistling of the gale grow louder and louder over our heads, while we gradually emerged from the passage. . . . As we dashed along in clear water, we felt that we had escaped an awful death, and thanked God in our hearts for our preservation."[12] Clark wrote, frenzied, "All this day a gale and a dreadful sea . . . nothing but ice! ice!! ice!!!"[13]

The gale ended, but not Wilkes's difficulties. Two surgeons and most of the wardroom officers attested to the increasingly poor health of the crew; the vessel could be jeopardized for lack of hands to man it. Wilkes was not moved by the men's sickness. Out of his sense of duty to country and responsibility to the world he decided, overriding his surgeons' opinions, to continue exploration of the extensive coast rather than turn north. He commented that he would "not give up the cruise until the ship should be totally disabled, or it should be evident to all that it was impossible to persist any longer."[14] Indeed, the sick list swelled from fifteen to twenty men, but with a spell of favorable, sunny conditions the ship was aired, clothes were dried, and soon all the men were improving.

On 12 and 13 February, in fine weather, the party obtained splendid views of a snow-covered mountain range rising to over three thousand feet at 64°57' S, 112°16' E. The following day, a landing of sorts was made on a large iceberg about eight miles offshore; the berg contained boulders, stones, and

Landing on the iceberg
Wilkes, *Narrative of the United States Exploring Expedition*, 1845

gravel. "Many specimens were obtained, and it was amusing to see the eagerness and desire of all hands to possess themselves of a piece of the Antarctic
Continent. These pieces were in great demand during the remainder of the
cruise. In the centre of this iceberg was found a pond of most delicious
water, over which was a scum of ice about ten inches thick. We obtained
from it about five hundred gallons. We remained upon this iceberg several
hours, and the men amused themselves to their hearts' content in sliding. . . .
We found many species of zoophytes. . . . This day, notwithstanding our disappointment in being still repelled from treading on the new continent, was
spent with much gratification."[15] Finally, on 21 February, the ships headed
north. The remainder of the voyage was devoted to exploration of the
Hawaiian Islands, the U.S. Pacific Northwest, the South Pacific again, the
Philippines, Singapore, the Cape of Good Hope, and St. Helena.

Both Wilkes and Dumont d'Urville believed that they had first discovered
the mainland; neither was aware of Balleny's prior sightings. Wilkes, based
on the magnitude of the coast he explored, correctly surmised the existence
of an Antarctic continent.

Upon his return to the United States, however, Wilkes learned that his Antarctic discoveries had been discredited, his leadership criticized. James Clark Ross claimed to have sailed south of Wilkes's latitude in the same longitude. Wilkes defended his position poorly. He faced a court martial for a variety of charges, nearly all of them petty, and he was deeply angered. His sometimes arbitrary and harsh discipline of his subordinates was, no doubt, part of the motivation for the allegations against him. The insult was all the more unjust, however, because Wilkes had been forced to lead an underprovisioned expedition with an ill-adapted fleet. Despite the poor light into which he was cast, Wilkes was acquitted in his court martial. He fought for the North in the American Civil War until age forced his retirement in 1864. Wilkes unflaggingly supervised the production of the scientific reports from the 1838–42 U.S. Exploring Expedition over the course of many years and managed to maintain funding for the effort until 1872. He died five years later, in 1877.

7

The Voyage of James Clark Ross in the *Erebus* and *Terror* (1839–1843)

... for we might with equal chance of success try to sail through the Cliffs of Dover.

James C. Ross, *A Voyage of Discovery and Research*

THE 1839–43 VOYAGE OF JAMES CLARK ROSS (1800–62) was the most significant Antarctic expedition since James Cook's circumnavigation and the discovery of South Shetland by William Smith. Ross had already gained considerable stature as an explorer, but his accomplishments on this Antarctic voyage made him a hero in his own time and a legend ever since. He made geographic discoveries of enormous importance, and his scientific investigations yielded a huge amount of new and important data in several disciplines.

The British Association for the Advancement of Science, the Royal Society, and the British government all supported an Antarctic expedition for the study of the earth's magnetism in the vicinity of the south magnetic pole. Thirty-nine-year-old Capt. James Clark Ross was the first choice to lead. He had first gone to sea at age twelve with his uncle Sir John Ross. The younger Ross then served under William E. Parry on four Arctic expeditions between 1819 and 1827. Starting as midshipman on the first voyage, Ross had command of his own vessel by the fourth. He developed skills in magnetic and lunar observing, botanical collections, zoology, and taxidermy, and he discovered the Ross's gull. The fourth Parry expedition achieved a farthest north of 82°43' that stood for almost fifty years. James Ross made the significant acquaintances of Francis R. M. Crozier (1796?–1848), Edward Bird, and Robert McCormick (1800–90) on these expeditions, men who eventually served on his own expedition. In 1831, while serving as second in command under his uncle, James Ross set out over the northern ice and planted the British flag at the north magnetic pole.

In the late 1830s, he was appointed to conduct the first magnetic survey of England. During that survey the ship was pounded by a ferocious storm and nearly lost, prompting one of the officers to state, "The Captain is, without exception, the finest officer I have ever met with, the most persevering indefatigable man you can imagine. He is perfectly idolised by everyone."[1] Following this scientific voyage, Ross was elected fellow of the Linnaean Society and fellow of the Royal Society.

His experience made him a logical and fitting choice to lead an Antarctic expedition. Ross was instructed to establish a series of magnetic observatories in the Southern Hemisphere and, if possible, to reach the south magnetic pole itself. The scientific program was to include pendulum experiments to measure gravity, observations of tides, weather, atmospheric refraction, sea temperatures, and auroras, as well as the taking of ocean depth soundings and work in botany and zoology. He was given a free hand to pursue these endeavors in the way he thought best, and he was to document new geographical discoveries.

The expedition departed quietly from England on 30 September 1839. Ross was in command of the 370-ton *Erebus,* and Commander Crozier was in charge of the 340-ton *Terror.* Each had a crew of sixty-four men. The men were superbly provisioned for maximum comfort, and special attention was paid to antiscorbutics. The ships were of unequal speed, however, and the *Erebus* often had to heave to so that the other might catch up. The two vessels touched at Madeira, the Canary Islands, and the Cape Verde Islands, landed at the remote and rarely visited St. Paul's Rocks, and crossed the equator on 3 December and—to Ross's particular interest—the magnetic equator (the line of no dip) four days later. Landings were made at Trinidad Island and St. Helena. The men reached the Cape of Good Hope, departed Cape Town on 6 April, and headed east for subantarctic Marion, Crozet, and Kerguelen Islands.

The parties had great difficulty making their landing at the desolate Kerguelen Islands; unfavorable winds in early May kept them offshore for eight days. They spent two months at the head of Christmas Harbor taking magnetic observations, and the highly edible Kerguelen cabbage was an excellent addition to their diet. The ships departed on 20 July, the botanist Joseph Dalton Hooker (1817–1911) commenting, "I was sorry at leaving Christmas Harbour; by finding food for the mind one may grow attached to the most wretched spots on the globe."[2]

Heading east in gale-force winds, the ships ran ahead of their expected positions in the easterly currents. A brief spell of hurricane-force winds separated the ships and kept them under reduced sail while waves broke in sheets and flooded the decks from astern. The boatswain of the *Erebus* fell overboard, and two boatloads of men were unable to rescue him; one boat was struck hard by heavy seas, and four men washed overboard were saved only by the efforts of the men in the companion boat.

The men's hardships were over for the time being, and the *Terror* sailed up the Derwent in Tasmania on 15 August; the *Erebus* followed the next day. Ross was received with effusive hospitality by Lt. Gov. Sir John Franklin, Ross's friend and fellow Arctic explorer. Ross set up a metal-free magnetic observatory, named Rossbank, on nonmagnetic sandstone, with the assistance of two hundred convicts. He had learned of the magnetic work of Dumont d'Urville and Wilkes south of Australia; Wilkes had written Ross an amicable letter the previous April, detailing his explorations and including a track map.[3] Now Ross became angry with both the Americans and the French because he had made known his specific intentions prior to departure and felt that they had committed an impropriety. He resolved to avoid the tracks of the French and American expeditions and thus explored the south in a more easterly direction, a highly fortuitous decision.

The ships sailed down the Derwent at daylight on 12 November 1840, with Franklin aboard the *Erebus*. At the mouth of the river, Franklin went aboard the *Terror* to say good-bye. He was given three cheers.

Ross's parties arrived at Rendezvous Harbor in the Auckland Islands and found records from Dumont d'Urville and Wilkes documenting their Antarctic visits. The rock foundation there was so magnetic that it spoiled the magnetometric readings. There was no time to survey the islands, but Hooker described numerous new plant species, and Robert McCormick, the expedition's surgeon and zoologist, prepared numerous bird skins. Abraham Bristow had left pigs on the island in 1807, and although they were noted to have destroyed some of the native flora, Ross landed several types of game animals and fruiting plants, to provide for future expeditions.

The ships reached Campbell Island on 13 December. Tacking up Perseverance Harbor, the *Erebus* ran briefly aground, while the *Terror* had a more suspenseful episode: the vessel grounded at high tide. The men hurriedly pumped out water and landed stores, permitting the ship to float off before the tide fell. The scientists set up a small magnetic observatory, but the intrinsic magnetism of Campbell Island frustrated them once more. Perseverance Harbor was surveyed, botanical and zoological specimens were collected, and the ships departed for the far south on 17 December. Ross remarked, "Now that we had at length the prospect before us of entering upon those labours from which we all hoped the most remarkable and important results of our voyage might be fairly anticipated, joy and satisfaction beamed in every face; and although I could not but look forward with much anxiety of mind to the issue of our exertions, yet this was greatly diminished by the assurance that we were in possession of the best of human means to accomplish our purposes. . . . I felt that we had nothing to desire but the guidance and blessing of Almighty God."[4]

The first iceberg was sighted on 27 December. Antarctic fulmars and snow petrels, harbingers of the ice, were seen three days later, and soon the ships encountered pack ice. McCormick, like many before and after him, was overcome by the unique beauty of the snow petrel and was prompted to record, "This morning, for the first time, I saw the beautiful and elegant white petrel (*Procellaria nivea*), its black beak and feet forming a striking contrast to its pure, unsullied, snow-white plumage, rivalling in its whiteness the snow-clad berg itself; several were hovering round the ship, rising higher as they swept to windward, in their rapid and graceful evolutions."[5]

New Year's Day was spent in conviviality; Ross visited the *Terror*, extra food was provided, cold-weather clothes were distributed, and the ships crossed the Antarctic Circle. On 5 January 1841, in a dramatic departure from prior expeditions, the men worked their ships into the pack ice, dependent solely on the northwesterly wind for their progress. "The signal was made to the Terror, and we bore away before the wind."[6] Without a chance of retreat, dependent on sail alone, and with the dangers of the packed sea ice and bergs, the men courageously advanced their ships. They were entertained by the penguins, noted seals atop the floes, and described and named after Ross a new species of seal.

Four days later, on 9 January, at 69°15' S, 176°15' E, the parties made the extraordinary discovery of an open sea to the south that now bears Ross's name. McCormick, using words reminiscent of Weddell's own statement upon discovering open water in the Weddell Sea eighteen years earlier, recorded in his diary, "At noon we had a most cheering and extensive view; not a particle of ice could be seen in any direction from the masthead."[7] Of Ross's great moment, historian Hugh Robert Mill proclaimed, "It was an epoch in the history of discovery: the magic wall from before which every previous explorer had to turn back in despair, had fallen into fragments at the first determined effort to break through it. The opportunity opening before the triumphant ships was one of those that occur but once or twice in the course of the ages."[8] Roald Amundsen, who almost seventy years later was the first to arrive at the South Pole, wrote, "Few people of the present day are capable of rightly appreciating this heroic deed, this brilliant proof of human courage and energy. With two ponderous craft—regular 'tubs' according to our ideas—these men sailed right into the heart of the pack, which all previous explorers had regarded as certain death. It is not merely difficult to grasp this; it is simply impossible—to us, who with a motion of the hand can set the screw going, and wriggle out of the first difficulty we encounter. These men were heroes—heroes in the highest sense of the word."[9] Unimpeded, the ships continued south, headed in the direction of the south magnetic pole, the focus of Ross's desire.

On 11 January 1841, a magnificent new land, Victoria Land, loomed up ahead, a glorious glaciated mountain range, rising to over twelve thousand feet. The sea abounded in whales, seals, and penguins. Ross soon became aware that the land would obstruct the way to the south magnetic pole and was disappointed, but he fully appreciated the significance of his discovery and considered the potential for commercial exploitation of the marine life. Soon the parties sighted Cape Adare, named after Ross's friend, Viscount Adare, and mountains that were later found to be part of the Transantarctic Mountains. Tall peaks in what was called the Admiralty Range (now Mountains) were named Mount Minto and Mount Adam after lords commissioner of the Admiralty, including the First Lord Earl Minto and Vice-Admiral Charles Adams; Ross named what he thought at first was the tallest peak Mount Sabine for his friend and supporter, the great magnetologist Edward Sabine. On 12 January, a twenty-five-minute landing was made on one of the Possession Islands, site of an enormous, age-old penguin colony. The men cheered as they planted a flag and toasted Queen Victoria and Prince Albert. The party was prevented by ice and heavy seas from making what would have been the first landing on the nearby Antarctic mainland.

The morning of 15 January was perfectly clear. Visibility along the mountain range of Victoria Land to the south was extraordinary, prompting inspired words from many of the men. From McCormick: "The lofty, magnificent-looking coast-line appeared to a great advantage this evening. . . . The thickly grouped, angular-shaped, small peaks, or hummocks, clad in snow of the purest white, the whole resembling a vast mass of crystallization, but on such a huge and splendid scale, as nature's laboratory alone could produce."[10] Coulman Island was discovered on 17 January, and Ross named Cape Anne for his fiancée (whom he had met in 1834 and had fallen in love with at first sight),[11] the island for her father, and Cape Wadworth for her uncle's hospitable home where the two would eventually marry. On the clear and beautiful evening of 22 January, the expedition exceeded Weddell's farthest south of 74°15'. Extra grog was passed all around, with toasts to "sweethearts and wives."[12]

On 27 January, a landing was made on Franklin Island at 76°8' S, 168°12' E. Ross, Crozier, and officers made for shore on the only beach they could see. McCormick as medical officer was angrily disappointed at having been left behind on ship. The landing was rough due to a huge swell, and the men were soaked in the frigid water; Hooker was almost crushed between some rocks and the stern of the boat, nearly ending the life of the man who became one of the nineteenth century's greatest botanists. The party made note of nesting south polar skuas and snow petrels.

The "High Island," years later fittingly renamed Ross Island, was sighted on 26 January. An active volcano, Mount Erebus, as well as Mount Terror, Beaufort Island, Cape Crozier (the eastern flank of Mount Terror and easternmost extension of Ross Island), and a great ice barrier (now called the Ross Ice Shelf) were seen on 28 January. Ross described Mount Erebus "emitting flame and smoke in great profusion."[13] Of the ice barrier he wrote: "As we approached the land under all studding-sails, we perceived a low white line extending from its eastern extreme point as far as the eye could discern to the eastward. It presented an extraordinary appearance, gradually increasing in height, as we got nearer to it, and proving at length to be a perpendicular cliff of ice, between one hundred and fifty and two hundred feet above the level of the sea, perfectly flat and level at the top, and without any fissures or promontories on its even seaward face. What was beyond it we could not imagine. . . . It was, however, an obstruction of such a character as to leave no doubt upon my mind as to our future proceedings, for we might with equal chance of success try to sail through the Cliffs of Dover."[14] Ross learned from soundings that the barrier was a floating mass of ice. The men were tricked by the light into believing there were mountains beyond the barrier, and they named them the Parry Mountains. These were subsequently proven not to exist. Even an observer as conservative and careful as Ross was fooled by the Antarctic light.

One can only imagine the sensations of the men as these Antarctic scenes revealed themselves to human eyes for the first time. The ships explored the ice front for two hundred miles, and a farthest south of 78°4' was achieved on 2 February. After standing off the barrier for six days, the ships made an approach on 8 February and sailed between the pack ice on the port side and the barrier to starboard. Within a bay a quarter mile wide and one to two miles deep, the barrier descended to a height of only fifty feet, allowing the men a view of the upper surface. Ross's description was purely descriptive, whereas the Irish blacksmith of the *Erebus,* Cornelius Sullivan, could not contain his emotion: "All hands when they Came on Deck to view this the most rare and magnificent Sight that Ever the human eye witnessed Since the world was created actually Stood Motionless for Several Seconds before he Could Speak to the man next to him. Beholding with Silent Surprize the great and wonderful works of nature in this position we had an opportunity to discern the barrier in its Splendid position. Then i wishd. i was an artist or a draughtsman instead of a blacksmith and Armourer. We Set a Side all thoughts of mount Erebus and Victoria's Land to bear in mind the more Imaginative thoughts of this rare phenomena that was lost to view In Gone by Ages. When Captn. Ross Came on deck he was Equally Surprizd. to See the Beautiful Sight Though being in the north Arctic Regions one half of his life he never see any ice in Arctic Seas to be Compard. to the Barrier."[15] Of the magnificent sights, McCormick wrote, "The wondrous scene nature has unfolded here, even beyond what might have been anticipated in this land of wonderment, has had the effect of riveting me to the deck for the last twenty-four hours . . . myself most anxious to trace this mighty wall of ice continuously . . . a night never to be effaced from memory's tablet to the latest hour of existence; and well was I rewarded for the temporary sacrifice of a night's rest and sleep by the grand and sublime panorama which . . . arrested my gaze . . . as the "noon-day" night of this high latitude wore on, and scene succeeded scene in nature's unrivalled display of her great Creator's works."[16]

The approach of autumn with its gathering cold stopped the men's eastward progress. Course was reversed on 14 February, and two days later the men watched Mount Erebus erupt in fire. The deep bight on the west side of Ross Island that would figure later so significantly in the expeditions of Robert F. Scott and Ernest H. Shackleton was found and named after Archibald McMurdo, first lieutenant of the *Terror.* The men made another attempt to reach the south magnetic pole, and a maximum magnetic dip of 88°40' was obtained on 17 February. Heading north, the men reached Cape Adare four days later, but over eight miles of sea ice blocked the way and prevented a landing.

Ross hoped to find safe southern winter quarters, but such were not to be found. So on 26 February he hauled off to the north. He wrote, "But few can understand the deep feelings of regret with which I felt myself compelled to abandon the perhaps too ambitious hope I had so long cherished of being permitted to plant the flag of my country on both the magnetic poles of our globe; but the obstacles which presented themselves being of so insurmountable a character was some degree of consolation, as it left us no grounds for self-reproach, and as we bowed in humble acquiescence to the will of Him who had so defined the boundary of our researches, with grateful hearts we offered up our thanksgivings for the large measure of success which he had permitted to reward our exertions."[17] In fact, Ross carried aboard *Erebus* the same flag that he had erected at the north magnetic pole, hoping that this single piece of cloth might wave over both magnetic ends of the earth.

Heading west, Ross still clung to the hope that a passage to the south magnetic pole might be found between Victoria Land and the various lands or islands discovered by Balleny, Dumont d'Urville, and Wilkes. The ships sustained some damage in the ice in early March, and the Balleny Islands were sighted on 2–4 March. Again ice barred an approach. The men sailed south of Wilkes's reported land but saw none. Unfortunate accusations and recriminations later arose between the two leaders as a result of the apparent incongruities. Ross proceeded west until he reached the meridian of the magnetic pole and crossed it twice at different latitudes so that he could determine a line of no variation. The expedition returned to Hobart on 7 April, with everyone in excellent health and the ships in outstanding condition.

The following day, Hooker wrote a letter to his father concerning the cruise: "I can give you no idea of the glorious views we have here, they are stupendous and imposing, especially when there was any fine weather, with the sun never setting, among huge bergs, the water and sky both as blue, or rather more intensely blue than I have ever seen it in the Tropics, and all the coast one mass of beautiful peaks of snow, and when the sun gets low they reflect the most brilliant tints of gold and yellow and scarlet, and then to see the dark cloud of smoke tinged with flame rising from the Volcano in one column, one side jet black and the other reflecting the colors of the sun, turning off at a right angle by some current of wind and extending many miles to leeward; it is a sight far exceeding anything I could imagine and which is very much heightened by the idea that we have penetrated far farther than was once thought practicable, and there is a sort of awe that steals over us all in considering our own total insignificance and helplessness. Everything beyond what we see is enveloped in a mystery reserved for future voyagers to fathom."[18] Little could Hooker have known that he alone among his mates would live long enough to witness Scott and Shackleton, more than sixty years later, determine what indeed lay beyond.

With Ross's new geographical discoveries, the continent of Antarctica had finally surrendered many of its secrets. The news of Ross's scientific work aroused sensation at home and in the rest of Europe. There were no subsequent accomplishments of comparable magnitude until the turn of the century, when the regions discovered by Ross would serve as the staging area for the first penetrations to the Antarctic interior and ultimately to the South Pole.

After spending the austral autumn and winter in Australia and New Zealand, Ross and his men sailed south a second time, departing from the Bay of Islands, New Zealand, on 23 November 1841. Ross now sought to penetrate the pack ice at about 146° W, since this was as far east as he had explored the barrier the previous season. He remarked on the migrating penguins and their "wonderful instinct, far beyond the powers of untutored reason, that enables these creatures to find their way, chiefly under water, several hundred miles, to their place of usual resort."[19]

The parties entered the pack ice on 18 December, and this time it took fifty-six trying days to get through instead of four. The men were scarcely able to enjoy their sumptuous Christmas Day dinner, since most attention had to be given to warping and tacking. Soon the vessels were firmly stuck in the ice. The ships were anchored in a calm, fifty yards apart on opposite sides of a floe. The men made the best of the windless respite by enjoying games on the sea ice. Come New Year's Day, each ship's party tried to outdo the other in production of noise and revelry as the stroke of midnight approached. Following dinner, the officers and crews alike went out to the "ball" on the floe, where silliness was the rule.

On the evening of 19 January 1842, still amid the pack ice, the ships were hit hard by a driving gale that lasted twenty-eight hours. Waves broke over the tops of the tallest icebergs. The ships collided repeatedly with floating ice. Both rudders were severely damaged, and Ross was doubtful of the ships' survival, "watching with breathless anxiety the effect of each succeeding collision, and the vibrations of the tottering masts, expecting every moment to see them give way."[20] The ships at one point were so close to each other as to be on adjacent, towering waves. After the storm, Ross visited the *Terror* to review the men and survey damage. John E. Davis (1815–77), second mate of the *Terror,* recorded, "The usual smile had gone from Captain Ross's countenance and he looked anxious and careworn."[21] Only on 12 February did the ships finally clear what remained of the pack ice, and they sailed south, unimpeded, in open sea.

The ships approached the barrier and on 23 February attained a new farthest south of 78°9.5' at 161°27' E longitude. Both ships tacked in the same spot, each attaining the same latitude. The men were able to follow the barrier eastward another 10 degrees of longitude, but the closing season and a freezing sea forced them to retreat northward. They followed the pack edge with a southeasterly breeze strong enough to propel the ships through the crusting surface. The two parties anxiously dodged heavy masses of sea ice and recrossed the Antarctic Circle on 6 March. Three days later, the men thought they were free of the ice and set a course for Cape Horn and the Falkland Islands.

Then on 12 March, in foul weather, the parties found themselves unexpectedly amid many icebergs. Sails were close-reefed, and Ross planned to wait out the dark night. But the ships were uncomfortably close, and while on opposite tacks with no room to maneuver in the rough seas, they collided. The entire expedition came within a hair's breadth of perishing. Davis aboard the *Terror* described "the *Erebus* striking this ship heavily on the starboard cat-head, breaking our anchor right in two and taking the cat-head and part of the anchor away, carrying away flying jib boom and jib boom, the former of which broke in three places and snapped close off at the cap, and carried away the lower studding-sail boom. . . . After striking several times very hard she worked further aft . . . near the gangway, she then splintered the immense strengthening pieces outside which prevented our being cut down. Our yard-arms were now striking at every roll and broke all the booms and boom-irons, which came tumbling down. . . . She then (working further aft) struck us abreast the mizen-mast several times, smashed the quarter boat, broke the ice planks, and again shattered the strengthening piece outside and tore off all the iron work. We then separated, she carrying away our spanker-boom."[22] Meanwhile Ross, aboard the *Erebus*, recorded: "We instantly hove all aback . . . but the concussion . . . was such as to throw almost everyone off his feet; our bowsprit, foretopmast, and other smaller spars, were carried away . . . the ships hanging together, entangled by their rigging, and dashing against each other with fearful violence."[23]

As soon as the crippled ships cleared each other, two very broad bergs, towering 200 and 120 feet high, loomed in the men's path, with only a narrow, dark channel between them through which to escape. Ross described the *Erebus* "falling down upon the weather face of the lofty berg under our lee, against which the waves were breaking and foaming to near the summit of its perpendicular cliffs. . . . The wreck of the spars so encumbered the lower yards, that we were unable to make sail. . . . The only way left to us to extricate ourselves from this awful and appalling situation was by resorting to the hazardous expedient of a stern-board, which nothing could justify. . . . But no sooner was the order given than the daring spirit of the British seaman manifested itself—the men ran up the rigging with as much alacrity as on any ordinary occasion."[24] Of Ross's composure as he resorted to the stern-board, McCormick wrote: "Captain Ross was quite equal to the emergency, and, folding his arms across his breast, as he stood like a statue on the after-part of the quarter-deck, calmly gave the order to loose the main-sail. His whole bearing, whilst lacking nothing in firmness, yet betrayed both in the expression of his countenance and attitude, the all-but despair with which he anxiously watched the results of this last and only expedient left to us in the awful position we were placed in . . . as but for the howling of the winds, and the turmoil of the roaring waters, the falling of a pin might have been heard on the *Erebus*'s deck, so silent and awestruck stood our fine crew in groups around, awaiting the result."[25] Ross continued: "The ship gathered stern-way, plunging her stern into the sea . . . the "under tow," as it is called, or the reaction of the water from its vertical cliffs, alone preventing us from being driven to atoms against it. . . . The difficulty now was to get the ship's head turned round and pointed fairly through between the two bergs. . . . This however, we happily accomplished . . . and the next moment we were in smooth water under its lee."[26]

Meanwhile, aboard the *Terror,* Davis continued, "A dreadful shipwreck and death then appeared inevitable; there was no alternative but to run for the dark place we had seen before, which might be an opening, or be smashed on the face of the cliff. The helm was immediately put a-starboard, and with the assistance of the sails she answered it very well. We were immediately rushing past an enormous berg, the ship being perfectly covered with the foam caused by the sea breaking against it. Every moment we were expecting the ship to strike ice right ahead. 'Hard-a-port' was screamed out from forward. . . . The men flew to the ropes, although I should think at that moment that there was not one on board but thought all hope was fled. She came round, and passed through an opening between two bergs not twice the breadth of the ship, the foam and spray dashing over us on each side as we passed."[27]

The *Erebus* passing through the chain of bergs
John E. Davis, from Ross, *A Voyage of Discovery and Research*, 1847

Davis confided his feelings to his sister: "I have often been in danger, and perhaps have had more than my share of it, but never till those moments did I in reality know what fear was; and, Emily, what were my fears? I was afraid to stand before a severe though merciful and just God; I was not fit to die. What would I not have given at that time for a single day to prepare myself for such an awful change! What thoughts passed in rapid succession through my brain! The events of a life passed in review before me in a few moments, and what had I to trust to except mercy? Alas, nothing. . . . The men on the whole behaved very well throughout; only one was running about out of his senses, but two or three were crying. . . . I looked round me when the first blue light was burnt, and, to see the ghastly appearance of everyone's face, in which horror and despair were pictured, the half-naked forms of the men thrown out by the strong light, oh! it was horrible, truly horrible. That time will never be effaced from my memory."[28]

The men had a short service of thanksgiving and set about their repairs; a course was set for Cape Horn. On 2 April the popular quartermaster of the *Erebus*, James Angelly, fell overboard from the mainyard in a freshening gale; he succeeded in reaching a life buoy thrown out to him, and he perched himself upon it. But by the time the men in the ship reached the life buoy in the turbulent sea, Angelly, who had failed to lash himself to the pole, had disappeared.

On 6 April 1842, the ships anchored in Berkeley Sound, East Falkland. A magnetic observatory was set up; Hooker resumed his botanical studies; and the ships were refitted. The lieutenant governor of the Falklands consulted Ross and Crozier concerning the best location at which to establish the British settlement of forty-six people. Ross recommended Port Williams over Port Louis, and the town of Stanley was accordingly established on the southern shore of what was then called Jackson Harbour. The ships left the Falklands on 8 September for Tierra del Fuego. There the men observed the native Fuegans, whom Ross perceived as "the most abject and miserable race of human beings"[29] because of their difficult subsistence. Ross's parties arrived back in the Falklands on 13 November.

The expedition headed south for a third and last time, on 17 December 1842. Ross intended to sail along the coastline of Louis Philippe Plateau, discovered by Dumont d'Urville. If this proved impossible, he would try for a greater southing than Weddell's 74°15' in the Weddell Sea. Ross's parties sighted Joinville Island; just to the east they discovered a group of low rocks camouflaged amid the ice, which they named the Danger Islands because they posed considerable danger for an unwary captain. Ross gave the large bay to the south of Joinville Island the cumbersome name of Erebus and Terror Gulf, surmised the existence of a channel (later named Antarctic Sound) between Joinville Island and the Trinity Peninsula, and discovered Paulet, Snow Hill, and Cockburn Islands. A landing was made on Cockburn Island. McCormick was once again annoyed that as medical officer he was excluded; as geologist and ornithologist he was interested in the craterlike peak and the nesting birds. Hooker was included, however, and found nineteen botanical species, the most southerly vegetation known.

In January the ships were restrained by heavy sea ice and drifted at the whim of the current; the weather was overcast with nearly constant snowfalls. The ships were often beset, heeling in the pressure, timbers cracking. Further exploration was out of the question; the exhausted crews spent hours warping the ships out of the ice and entered open sea once more.

Ross now decided to enter the Weddell Sea. On 5 March 1843, the ships were stopped by ice at 71°30' S, 14°51' W. The men turned just in time, as a northeasterly gale threatened to force them onto the pack ice in their lee. Sea spray froze as it fell upon the rigging and decks in the darkness. Ross praised

Crozier and Bird, the first lieutenant of the *Erebus,* for their handling of the perilous situation. The season's work was disappointing compared with that of the first; but Ross succeeded in getting farther south in the Weddell Sea than any of his predecessors except Weddell, and some important geographic and scientific discoveries had been made. En route home, Ross and his parties stopped at St. Helena, Ascension, and Rio de Janeiro, and arrived in England on 5 September 1843, ending an extraordinary four-year voyage.

Many years later, at the turn of the century, the Antarctic historian Karl Fricker stated, "The voyage of James Clark Ross . . . must be regarded as one of the most brilliant and famous of all voyages of discovery that have ever been made."[30] Another historian, J. Gordon Hayes (1877–?) was prompted to say that Ross had "opened the gates. . . . He, like Captain Cook, marked the end of one stage in the history of Antarctic discovery, if not the beginning of another. He altogether overshadowed his contemporaries."[31] And Erich von Drygalski, who led the German expedition to the Antarctic in 1901–3, wrote: "In my consideration of earlier achievements, Ross's account stood preeminent. It has such a depth of content and he approaches every problem with such a fine imperturbability."[32]

The passage of time has certainly confirmed these impressions, but in its own age the expedition returned to no great fanfare. The events of the second and third seasons could not rival the excitement generated by the first, and interest had naturally declined. The general public was especially interested in voyages that encountered new tribes or that might have commercial possibilities; much of Ross's voyage concerned the uninhabited and desolate far south, and the public was largely uninterested. Also, Ross was not given to self-promotion, and the delay in publication of his generally dry narrative surely lessened his renown.

Occasional discontent among the crew was probably no greater than on comparable voyages of the day. However, the dreary winter at the Falklands—a site that Ross deliberately chose to avoid desertions and sickness before the final southern program—the extraordinary dangers, the hard work, and the long absence from normal society certainly taxed the tolerance and goodwill of many of the men, even Hooker. Ross was not adored by many who served under him—Crozier and Bird excepted—but he was respected; he never lost an opportunity to praise his men for their work or to recommend promotions.

Ross was knighted upon his return and received the Founder's Medal of the Royal Geographical Society, as well as the Gold Medal of the Royal Geographical Society of Paris. Ross and Anne Coulman had exchanged letters during the explorer's long absence, and their affections had endured. The two were married only six weeks after Ross arrived in England.[33] In 1857, however, a great misfortune was to change the rest of Ross's life: his beloved wife died from pneumonia at forty years of age. Ross rewrote his will, appointed two executors, one of whom was his loyal friend Bird, and requested that upon his death he be buried next to his wife: "Thus our dust may mingle in the grave, while our souls rejoice together in glory everlasting." Ross fell into a profound depression from which he never recovered. In 1862 he died, a recluse and alcoholic, and was buried with his Anne at Aston Abbotts.[34]

8

WHALING, SEALING, AND SCIENTIFIC VOYAGES (1841–1899)

> We are filled with an intense longing to land and make a closer acquaintance with these shores, which have but once before been seen by man. . . .
> We are in an unknown world, and we stop—for *blubber.*
>
> W. G. Burn Murdoch, *From Edinburgh to the Antarctic*

THE AMERICAN WILLIAM SMILEY was one of very few sealers who persisted in investigating the South Shetland Islands after the near extermination of the seals. He sailed in 1841–42, landed at Deception Island, and investigated islands to the south. Unfortunately, Smiley lost many of his records, leaving in doubt what he had accomplished.[1]

Lt. Thomas E. L. Moore, a junior executive officer on Ross's expedition, sailed in the *Pagoda* in 1844–45 with instructions to make magnetic observations south of 60° S between 0° and 100° E longitude, a region not investigated by Dumont d'Urville, Wilkes, or Ross. He reached a latitude of 67°50' S and, in a position east of 50° E, cautiously reported an appearance of land that was a northeasterly extension of Enderby Land.

After the 1840s, the Antarctic regions were seldom visited until the beginning of the "heroic era" in the 1890s. For some of those who did head south the motivation was science, but for most the stimulus remained marine mammals and the promise of riches. By the latter part of the nineteenth century, the Norwegians had developed superior whaling techniques that included harpoon guns mounted on ever-smaller, motorized boats. The result was the near elimination of whales in the northern seas, and attention inevitably turned southward. Like the sealers of the 1820s, some among this new generation of opportunists also made significant geographical discoveries.

In the nineteenth century, right whales provided the best material for women's corsets and other products requiring a light, flexible construction. The German Polar Navigation Company under the influence of Georg

Neumayer (1826–1909) sent Capt. Eduard Dallman (1830–96) in the *Grönland* in 1872–74 to investigate the south polar regions. He reached the South Shetland Islands and proceeded as far as 64°45' S. No right whales were seen, but the sealing was profitable. Dallman explored the Trinity Peninsula coast and has been credited with the discovery and naming of the Neumayer Channel (between Anvers Island and Wiencke and Doumer Islands, all these islands being named by later explorers), the Bismarck Strait (separating Anvers and Wiencke Islands from a group of small islands farther south), and those latter islands, which he called the Kaiser Wilhelm Archipelago (now Wilhelm Archipelago).

Great Britain, too, was active in scientific pursuits that would maintain its stake in the Antarctic. The *Challenger* voyages (1872–74) revived the science of oceanography through an extensive investigation of the world's oceans. The *Challenger* became the first steam-powered ship to cross the Antarctic Circle, reaching 66°40' S at 78°30' E longitude. There scientists brought up samples from the ocean floor that contributed to Antarctic oceanographic science. No land sightings were made, but the expedition helped revitalize interest in the Antarctic and set the stage for the future surge in exploration. Sir John Murray (1841–1914), a member of the scientific staff, spent thirteen years as editor of the expedition's voluminous reports, completing them in 1895.

The Dundee Whaling Expedition (1892–93), with its complement of four wooden ships built for work in the ice, the *Balaena, Diana, Active,* and *Polar Star,* set out for the northern part of the Weddell Sea in search of the right whales Ross had reported there. The ships' captains were Alexander Fairweather, Robert Davidson, Thomas Robertson, and James Davidson, respectively. Whaling was the principal interest, but a limited scientific program was included, and the Royal Geographical Society and Meteorological Office had expressed interest in the expedition's program. William S. Bruce, who later led the Scottish National Antarctic Expedition of 1902–4, served as naturalist; W. G. Burn Murdoch (1862–1939) was artist on the *Balaena*; and C. W. Donald, who had a strong bent toward the natural sciences, was the surgeon on the *Active.*

The *Balaena* and the *Diana* departed from Dundee on 6 September 1892; the *Active* and *Polar Star* set out two days later. Two among more than twenty stowaways escaped notice and were signed on to replace deserters. The ships sailed south independently. Murdoch, who recorded life at sea aboard the *Balaena,* called the cruise lazy and monotonous. The men entertained themselves by telling yarns of Arctic whaling experiences and singing chanteys. At the equator, the men dressed in costumes and shaved the heads of new initiates to the Southern Hemisphere in honor of King Neptune. The *Balaena* party demonstrated little respect for animal life. Two sparrow hawks wandering 130 miles off the Irish coast took respite on the ship and were shot for no apparent reason. Superstitious men made "a Jonah of the cat."[2] Farther south, albatrosses were taken because they "might" have been of value.

The *Balaena* and *Active* coincidentally arrived in the Falkland Islands on the same day, 8 December, and spent three days making final preparations for the southward voyage. The *Diana* arrived just after the other two ships had departed. Murdoch was inspired by the scene of floe ice and bergs: "You can scarcely dream of the delicate beauty of the forms, or the infinite subtlety of the harmonies in white, and silver, and green, and pale yellow and blue . . . an endless fairy picture, painted on silk, with a ghostly brush from a palette of pearl."[3] His heart was won over by the penguins: "No matter how melancholy a man may feel, if he sees one of these jolly little fellows he cheers up."[4]

The first land sightings were the Danger Islands. A few associated islets missed by Ross amid the icy confusion were now recorded for the first time. Robertson examined the south coast of Joinville Island and there discovered and named Dundee Island. He also described and navigated the strait between the two islands. Three of the four ships made their planned rendezvous in Erebus and Terror Gulf, the tiny, underpowered *Polar Star* arriving late. No whales were found, but seals were taken. Commercial exploits had priority over exploration, much to Murdoch's frustration. "We are filled with an intense longing to land and make a closer acquaintance with these shores, which have but once before been seen by man. What might we not discover . . . we could lay out the chart over leagues of undiscovered lands. . . . We are in an unknown world, and we stop—for *blubber*."[5]

The ships plied the waters east of the Antarctic Peninsula, north of 65° S, for the remainder of the season, often in the company of Capt. Carl A. Larsen (1860–1924) of the *Jason*. The Dundee ships were tantalizingly close to new geographical discoveries, but the priority was seals. The horrible lessons of the 1820s had never been learned, and the scenario of bygone years was being repeated. The crews were literally awash in blood as they harvested fourteen thousand sealskins. Even that enormous number was only just sufficient to make the voyage profitable. Murdoch lamented, "How mean and ugly we of the world of people feel in this lovely world of white beauty, making bullets sing through the cold, silent air, fouling the snow with blood and soot. . . . All the majesty and beauty of the seal has gone."[6]

Larsen's whaling expedition (1892–94), under the auspices of the whaling entrepreneur Christen Christensen and the Oceana Company of Hamburg,[7] spanned two seasons and included investigations of the Graham Land coast and the Bellingshausen and Weddell Seas. In the first season, Larsen sailed in a single ship, the *Jason*. No suitable whales were found, but seals made the voyage profitable and justified another season.[8] During the course of the voyage, Larsen discovered what were believed at the time to be the first fossils found in Antarctica, petrified wood on Seymour Island. He reached 64°40' S, 56°30' W and believed he saw land to the west, which in fact was the east side of the Antarctic Peninsula, opposite Graham Land, as it was known from the other side.

In the second season, three ships proceeded south, the *Jason, Hertha,* and *Castor,* the latter two under the commands of Captain Evensen and Capt. Morten Pedersen, respectively. Again seals were taken, and ice observations were recorded. Larsen visited Erebus and Terror Gulf, and penetrated southward in favorable ice conditions. At about 66° S, 60° W, Larsen sighted land to the west, and he assigned names to King Oscar II Land (now Oscar II Coast), Cape Framnes, and Mount Jason (now Jason Peninsula). He achieved 68°10' S, where further progress was blocked by ice; there he discovered mountain peaks to the west that he named Foyn Land. All of these sightings were of the Antarctic Peninsula. On the way north at 66° S on 9 December 1893, Larsen discovered Robertson Island, naming it for William Robertson, co-owner of the Hamburg firm that had sponsored his voyage; Larsen also charted many islets. At about 65° S, he made a brief landing at Christensen Nunatak. Larsen was frustrated by the lack of time to explore further but felt duty bound to obtain his seal booty. He headed north, deposited his sealskins in the Falklands, and headed south once more to Erebus and Terror Gulf before the season closed. Larsen's geographical work constituted the greatest gains in Antarctic exploration since Ross.

Meanwhile, Evensen sailed from the South Shetland Islands past the Biscoe Islands. He sighted Adelaide Island and on 21 November 1893 reached 69°10' S, 76°12' W; he saw Alexander Island the following day and made a closer approach than Bellingshausen had. Pedersen accompanied Evensen part of the way, at least as far as 64°23' S, 53°20' W.

Professor Carl Chun led a German scientific expedition for deep-sea studies in the *Valdivia* in the 1898–99 season. After departing from the Cape of Good Hope, Chun, at 54°26' S, 3°24' E on 25 November 1898, found Bouvetøya. The island had first been reported in 1739, but Cook had not found it; despite two additional sightings in 1808 and 1825, the position and therefore the existence of the island had remained in dispute after the voyage of Ross, who, like Cook, could not locate it. Chun's achievement was all the more notable since he found the island amid storm, thick clouds, and icebergs. From Bouvetøya the ship was steered east along the edge of the pack ice, and the party reached 64°15' S, 54°20' E on 16 December, at a point only 102 nautical miles from Enderby Land. Most soundings yielded depths greater than sixteen thousand feet, a surprise to the scientists. Such depth soundings were risky: a single reading took twelve hours, and a sudden, severe weather change could have put both equipment and men in danger. Geological specimens and marine invertebrates were brought up in dredging operations. The men closed out their season's work in visits to the Kerguelen Islands and St. Paul and Amsterdam Islands.

9

The Voyage of Henryk Johan Bull
in the *Antarctic*
(1893–1895)

The sensation of being the first men who had set foot on the real
Antarctic mainland was both strange and pleasurable.

Henryk Johan Bull, *The Cruise of the 'Antarctic'*

The landmark accomplishment of this expedition was the first confirmed
landing on the Antarctic mainland. What also distinguished it from previous voyages is that while adventure and exploration were its principal moti-
vations, passage was to be paid for by a take of marine mammals.

Henryk Johan Bull (1844–1930), a Norwegian businessman, was engaged
in the mercantile trade in Melbourne in the late 1880s when talk in scientific
circles turned on the possibility of an Australian expedition to the Antarctic.
For lack of funding, no such project went forward, but Bull became enraptured with the idea and believed that an expedition for science and exploration could pay for itself by even a modest whaling success. His work over
the next three years to get financial backing in Australia failed, so he went to
Norway and visited the venerable and wealthy eighty-four-year-old whaling
master Svend Foyn (1809–94), whom he had known for many years. After fifteen minutes of conversation, Bull had the use of a ship and funding. The
budget was extraordinarily low, about £5,000.

The vessel was a 226-ton steam whaler built in 1872. The hull and engines
were thoroughly overhauled in Tønsberg and Kristiania (now Oslo), and the
refurbished ship was renamed *Antarctic*. Capt. Leonard Kristensen was
selected to command. The division of responsibilities between Kristensen
and Bull was poorly defined, and conflict grew. Bull later had no reservation
in criticizing the captain for lack of experience in whaling and ice navigation, or for indecisiveness. At times Bull had little authority: "It was galling
in the extreme."[1]

The expedition departed Tønsberg on 20 September 1893. A landing at the Canary Islands was forbidden because the men forgot to bring papers verifying sanitation—they were assumed to be a party of lepers seeking asylum. After visiting Tristan da Cunha, they arrived at the Kerguelens, having had no success in finding right or sperm whales. So they turned to seals and in six weeks took sixteen hundred elephant seals for their skins and oil, the value of which Bull expected would pay off the entire expedition. Bull described the killing of these defenseless and trusting creatures in pathetic, sorrowful terms. "The details of seal-hunting are so particularly nauseating that I will spare my readers an exhaustive description . . . . The sportsman can find nothing attractive in the capture of the kind of seals we met with. They generally look on with quiet curiosity and interest at the preparations for their own execution."[2] Bull also pondered the rugged and desolate but inspiring landscape of the island group. The ship was nearly wrecked in a storm that, typical for the area, rose to hurricane force without warning.

The expedition arrived with fanfare in Australia on 23 February 1894, and the men spent weeks in Melbourne. Bull was in for an unpleasant surprise when his ninety-five tons of oil realized only £1,775 and the skins, which he had expected to bring over £1 apiece, were appraised to be of generally poor quality and netted him virtually nothing. While Bull remained in Australia disposing of the cargo and making final preparations for the southern voy-

Killing seals
W. G. Burn Murdoch, from Bull, *The Cruise of the 'Antarctic,'* 1896

[61]

age the following season, Kristensen departed with the ship on 12 April to prospect for whales.

The ship's party visited Tasmania and then Campbell Island, where the *Antarctic* ran aground on Terror Shoal in Perseverance Harbor, sustaining serious damage. After the staff of another ship in the area provided new anchors and coal, Kristensen resumed whaling operations, but hunting techniques remained terribly faulty. Despite the sighting of numerous right whales, the crew captured only a single whale. The party retreated to Australia, arriving in a despondent mood on 21 August. The ship was repaired and overhauled, costing the profits from sealing at the Kerguelens, and the expedition was provisioned for the upcoming season. Prominent Australians stepped forward to assist the expedition.

William S. Bruce, the Scottish naturalist who had accompanied the *Balaena,* was to have joined the *Antarctic,* but he did not reach Australia in time. Instead, Carsten E. Borchgrevink (1864–1934) of Norway, residing in Australia and possessing only a meager scientific background, applied for the position.[3] He failed to be appointed as scientist, but eager as Bull was to have companionship on board, Borchgrevink was taken on as an ordinary seaman and received highly deferential treatment. Borchgrevink figured significantly in this expedition and, later in the decade, led his own expedition to the Antarctic.

The *Antarctic* headed south from Melbourne Wharf with a warm public farewell on 26 September. In place of the largely Norwegian crew that had sailed the previous season, the crew was now a mixture of Swedes, Danes, Poles, and Englishmen. The ship stopped at Tasmania, Macquarie Island, and Campbell Island. Bull, relatively aged for a polar explorer of that era, celebrated his fiftieth birthday and shortly thereafter his silver wedding anniversary, without the benefit of his wife's presence.

The expedition headed south to challenge the pack ice. Given the magnitude of the undertaking and potential dangers that lay ahead, Bull forced himself to get along with Kristensen. The discovery at 58° S of "Svend Foyn Island" was celebrated with a round of brandy, but the discovery was soon retracted as the island resolved itself into an immense iceberg. On 7 November, at 59°20' S, the propeller malfunctioned, forcing a retreat to Port Chalmers, New Zealand, for repairs. The problem stemmed from damage sustained at Campbell Island. The engineer had reported the concern to Kristensen at the time, but the captain chose to ignore the matter. Bull was now incensed but mostly kept his own counsel: he contemplated what might have happened if steam power had been lost in, or south of, the pack ice. Now, at the very least, the season's proceedings would have to be delayed.

The dispirited crew brought the ship into dry dock on 27 November and spent three days completing repairs. Two crewmen deserted and seven more resigned. Bull requested that the New Zealand authorities not telegraph Foyn about the issue until the ship was beyond recall, for fear that his sponsor would halt the expedition for incompetence. His fears were justified— that was exactly Foyn's reaction,[4] but it was then too late. Foyn died shortly thereafter, and the men of the expedition learned of their benefactor's death only upon their return to civilization.

The party headed south on 30 November, increased its number to twenty-six by taking on four recruits at Stewart Island, made excellent progress in fair weather, and, thus newly inspired, entered the ice. The men were awed by the beauty of the surroundings, particularly in the long light when the sun was low on the horizon. With hopes high for a good take of seals and whales, they risked an extended stay in the ice by taking a westerly course toward the Balleny Islands. But whaling proved to be poor there, in large part due to persistently faulty hunting methods. The take of seals was small, the first engineer broke a leg and lost a finger in an accident, and the ship was encircled in pack ice. The year's close found the men once more gloomy. Kristensen wanted to abandon any further attempt to penetrate into the Ross Sea, and to do more hunting in the pack before retreating northward. Bull persuaded him to persist so that they could accomplish an essential aim of the expedition—namely, to assess the numbers of right whales south of the pack, where Ross had reported them in abundance.

Heading south, the men finally left all the ice behind on 13 January 1895 and became the first party since Ross's, fifty-three years earlier, to enter the Ross Sea. Cape Adare was sighted on 17 January, but an immediate landing was prevented by ice. They landed instead on 19 January on the Possession Islands, where Borchgrevink found lichens, proving that the fringes of Antarctica were not too hostile for vegetation. Bull tried to land the next day at Cape Hallett, site of an enormous Adélie penguin colony, but was once again frustrated by ice. The most southerly point reached was near the southern extremity of Coulman Island at 74°0' S. The ship was turned north, as there seemed no certain commercial value in going on. Not a single right whale had been seen.

Bull was greatly inspired by the landscape of Victoria Land: "It is impossible for me to render even a moderately fair description of the other-worldly beauty and perfect uniqueness of the landscape. The pinnacled mountains towering range beyond range in majestic grandeur under a coverlet of matchless white; the glittering and sparkling gold and silver of the sunshine, broken or reflected through the crystals of ice and snow; the sky of clearest blue and deepest gold when the sun is at its lowest; but perhaps more than all, the utter desolation, the awesome, unearthly silence pervading the whole landscape—all this combines to form a scene which is worth many a sacrifice to behold for once, although living alone in such surroundings would undoubtedly end in speedy madness."[5]

Now the crowning event of the expedition, and one of the most significant and interesting historical events in mankind's history on the southern continent, was to unfold. At one in the morning on 24 January 1895, a boatload of seven men cast off from the *Antarctic* toward the mainland. About an hour thereafter, a landing was made on what later became known as Ridley Beach at Cape Adare, the first confirmed landing on the Antarctic mainland. Who actually stepped ashore first is a matter of dispute; Borchgrevink, Kristensen, and a New Zealand recruit named Alexander H. F. von Tunzelman all made the claim.

The landing on South Victoria Land at Cape Adare
Kristensen, *Antarctic's Reise til Sydishavet*, 1895

Borchgrevink took credit thus: "We landed at Cape Adare that night, being the first human creatures to put foot on the mainland. A peculiar feeling of fascination crept over each of us, even to the most prosaic natures in our boat, as we gradually drew near to the beach of this unknown land. Some few cakes of ice were floating about, and looking over the side of the boat, I even discovered a jelly-fish, apparently of the common light blue, transparent kind. I do not know whether it was to catch the jelly-fish, or from a strong desire to be the first man to put foot on this *terra incognita*, but as soon as the order was given to stop pulling the oars, I jumped over the side of the boat. I thus killed two birds with one stone, being the first man on shore, and relieving the boat of my weight, thus enabling her to approach land near enough to let the captain [Kristensen] jump ashore dry-shod."[6]

Kristensen recorded the event quite the opposite: "When we were so close to the promontory straight across from Cape Adare that I could see with the naked eye the movement of the penguins there, I lowered a boat manned by six men and rowed together with steerman Mr. Bull to land on the promontory, where we hauled the boat in. It was very easy to land there, as the sea was quite calm, and there was hardly more than a slight undertow. During the rowing I sat forward at the bow, and when the boat approached the shore, I slid down onto the beach with the words, 'Now I am the first to set his foot on South Victoria Land.' Immediately thereafter Carsten Borchgrevink, whom I had commanded into the boat to row, hopped over the gunwale at the stern of the boat, waded ashore and shouted, 'And I am number two.'"[7]

Tunzelman maintained for the rest of his life that he was the first, that he had jumped out of the boat to steady it for Bull, Kristensen, Borchgrevink, and the others.[8] Bull neither claimed to be first nor indicated in his account who actually was. He simply stated, "The sensation of being the first men who had set foot on the real Antarctic mainland was both strange and pleasurable, although Mr. Foyn would no doubt have preferred to exchange this pleasing sensation on our part for a Right whale even of small dimensions."[9]

Bull described the Adélie penguin colony there at Cape Adare, admiring the little birds for their courage in eking out such a difficult existence. "Myriads . . . fairly covered the flat promontory . . . [and] further lined all accessible projections of the rocks to an altitude of 800 or 900 feet. . . . Our presence was not much appreciated. . . . Our seaboots were bravely attacked. . . . The mortality in the colony must be frightful, judging by the number of skeletons and dead birds lying about in all directions. A raptorial (skua) gull was present . . . busily occupied with its mission in life—viz., prevention of over-population in the colony. . . . The patience and endurance of the penguins are beyond praise."[10] The men erected a pole with a box, on which were painted the Norwegian colors, the date, and the name of the ship. After a two-hour visit ashore, the men returned to their vessel.

The *Antarctic* then skirted the Balleny Islands and arrived in Melbourne on 12 March. The expedition's achievements were well received in Australia, and the party disbanded there. The expedition was a financial failure, but it was a success for its first continental landfall, its stimulus to further exploration, and its occasional contributions to geography, geology, and biology.

For a time, Bull and Borchgrevink continued a cordial relationship and attempted to obtain funding for another Antarctic expedition. But the two had a falling out when Borchgrevink went to England and Norway and usurped credit for the expedition's successes in a presentation before the Sixth International Geographical Congress in London and a spate of journal articles.

Following Bull's expedition, a period of exploration lasting until the death of Ernest H. Shackleton in 1922 included some of the most exciting years of Antarctic history-making. The men who voyaged there were driven by nationalistic pride and penchants for scientific discovery, adventure, and fame. Some of the men sailed south again and again: their overwhelming drive, as it had been for Bull, was the ineluctable lure of the ice and the magical spell the Antarctic continent casts over its visitors. Bull concluded his narrative: "I do not know whether it will ever be my lot to revisit Antarctica, but the years spent in realizing my dream of an Antarctic expedition will ever remain among the most pleasant, certainly the most interesting, part of my life, disappointments and tribulations notwithstanding."[11]

10

ADRIEN V. J. DE GERLACHE AND THE
VOYAGE OF THE *BELGICA*
(1897–1899)

Ce jour-là, un fragment du disque du soleil nous apparut encore, grâce à
la réfraction; puis commença une nuit de seize cents heures.

[That day, a fragment of the sun's disk appeared to us once more, thanks
to refraction; then began a night of sixteen hundred hours.]

Adrien de Gerlache, *Quinze mois dans l'Antarctique*

"THE SIXTH INTERNATIONAL GEOGRAPHICAL CONGRESS, assembled in
London, in the year 1895, with reference to the exploration of the Antarctic
Regions, expresses the opinion that this is the greatest piece of geographical
exploration still to be undertaken; and in view of the additions to knowledge, in almost every branch of science, which would result from such a scientific exploration, the Congress recommends that the various scientific
societies throughout the world should urge, in whatever way seems to them
most effective, that this work should be undertaken before the close of this
century." Upon being presented to representatives at the meeting, the resolution was carried unanimously.[1]

Adrien Victor Joseph de Gerlache (1866–1934), a lieutenant in the Royal
Belgian Navy, had for years harbored a burning desire to explore the Antarctic
regions. He presented his first prospectus to the Royal Geographical Society of
Brussels in 1894, the year before the Sixth International Geographical Congress
convened. Gerlache journeyed to Norway and Greenland to learn about travel
and survival in the polar regions. He had great difficulty at first raising funds,
but he wrote for the press and popularized the value of a scientific expedition
to the Antarctic. The Brussels Geographical Society obtained financial backing
for him by subscription, and with help from the government $60,000 was
raised, just sufficient for the expedition's essentials.

The officers and scientists came from several countries. Georges Lecointe, a Belgian navigating officer and astronomer, was second in command. The Norwegian Roald Amundsen (first to arrive at the South Pole, in 1911) volunteered and was taken on as first mate. In his later years, Amundsen stated that he had gone to obtain the necessary experience to qualify for a skipper's license. He aspired to command his own polar expedition one day, and to avoid the potential conflict of shared leadership with a ship's captain, he resolved to qualify himself for both posts.[2] The American Frederick A. Cook (1865–1940) (later of North Pole fame and controversy) joined in Rio de Janeiro as a last-minute replacement for the original surgeon, who had backed out. Scientists included Lt. Émile Danco (1868–1898) (Belgian; magnetics), Émile Racovitza (1868–1947) (Rumanian; naturalist), and Henryk Arctowski (1871–1958) (Polish; geology, oceanography, meteorology). In addition, the party included two Belgian engineers, a Russian assistant meteorologist, and nine sailors (four Belgians and five Norwegians). It was a polyglot group that set sail, nineteen in all, but enough shared languages ensured that communications were mostly satisfactory. The officers and seamen lived apart on board, but fellowship was good and the ship's comforts were inviting.

The ship, a 250-ton Norwegian steam sealer renamed *Belgica,* had been built in the late 1880s. The vessel was 110 feet long and 26 feet wide; it was equipped with a 150-horsepower engine and had a maximum speed of seven knots under steam. The *Belgica* was iron sheathed, with a strengthened rudder and a propeller that could be replaced easily if damaged. The bow would rise over the sea ice and crush it under its weight. The party had equipment and supplies for thorough scientific investigations, cameras for what would become the first extensive photographic record of Antarctic land- and seascapes, and an extensive library in multiple languages.

After a visit from King Leopold, the party departed Antwerp on 24 August 1897, stopping at Madeira, Rio de Janeiro, Montevideo, Punta Arenas, and finally at Staten Island, the group's last port of call before heading south into the Antarctic on 13 January 1898. Gerlache's plan was to visit the South Shetland Islands, to explore Graham Land and possibly its east coast to the limit of navigability, and then to head toward Alexander Island and finally Victoria Land, making soundings and dredgings along the way. But they had spent an inordinate amount of time exploring Fuegan channels and studying the native peoples, and their departure south was a late one by any standards; the season was well advanced. Gerlache thus abbreviated his plans.

The scientists performed the first soundings of the Drake Passage: the sharp drop-off of the ocean shelf south of Staten Island led them, unaware of the Scotia Arc, to believe that the Antarctic Peninsula was disconnected from South America. One week after departing Staten Island, the South Shetland Islands were sighted.

In a gale, Carl Wiencke, a young sailor, was freeing the scuppers from coal washed in by the waves when he fell overboard. Amundsen and Cook on the bridge "heard an unearthly cry"[3] and went aft to find Wiencke struggling in the mountainous sea. Wiencke was thrown a log attached to a line, which he grasped; he was drawn in, and Lecointe, "with a bravery impossible to appreciate,"[4] volunteered to be lowered to haul him in. Lecointe himself was inundated by the backwash and almost drowned. Wiencke was towed to the side of the ship, but in the ice-cold, turbulent sea, he let go his grasp and went down. He had made many friends on board, and his loss was taken hard. Wiencke Island is his memorial.

As the men sailed on, they were impressed by the region's distinctive character: leaden skies, glassy black water, snow-clad mountains, ice cliffs and stark granite, and the bustling dissonance of gulls, cormorants, penguins, and seals. Entering Hughes Bay, the party discovered Belgica Strait (later renamed Gerlache Strait); they made twenty landings on various islands and described many miles of new coastline. Gerlache named the peninsular coast after Danco; the land was fronted by an ice wall fifty to one hundred feet high and had a mountainous spine rising two to four thousand feet or more. The men gave the name Palmer Archipelago to a group of four large islands forming the western boundary of the Gerlache Strait that, in addition to Wiencke Island, they named Liège, Brabant, and Anvers after places in Belgium. All of the officers had a turn ascribing names to newly discovered geographical features. Scientific studies and collections went forward to a greater extent than ever before.

To reconnoiter the area better, Gerlache, Danco, Arctowski, Amundsen, and Cook made a seven-day trip up and inland at d'Ursel Point on Brabant Island, the first sledge journey in Antarctica. Heavy hauling, crevasses, poor visibility, and wind all made for an arduous trip. But when the men reached an altitude of fifteen hundred feet and had gorgeous views, they felt their efforts justified. To the northeast they could see the strait through which they had come, and to the southwest they could see its extension toward new lands and its debouchement into the sea. They viewed the mainland to the east, and the eastern shores of Liège and Brabant Islands. Meanwhile,

Lecointe had taken the ship south, discovered several islands and a penguin colony, and reached the southernmost extremity of the strait.

On a particularly glorious and clear day, the men eagerly made charts, sketched and photographed landscapes, and recorded the magnificent, otherworldly light effects. Cook wrote: "The night . . . fixes my attention and makes sleep impossible. There is a glitter in the sea, a sparkle on the ice, and stillness in the atmosphere . . . a solitude and restfulness about the whole scene which can only be felt; it cannot be described. . . . The face of the mysterious land is clothed by the successive sheets of snows of the sleeping years of countless silent centuries. . . . [The] hues, with their indescribable gradations, are spread over the whites and blacks of the waters, and the snow and the rocks of the land. It all seems like an artist's dream."[5]

After three weeks in the strait, Gerlache proceeded south into the Bellingshausen Sea. The ship cruised amid sea ice and bergs, and wildlife was abundant. The party skirted Adelaide Island and Alexander Island, then ice forced the ship in a westerly direction, away from land. Gerlache continued despite the lateness of the season and against the sentiments of others on board. He took advantage of open leads whenever they appeared, close pack occasionally squeezing the ship, and managed to penetrate about ninety miles to the south. The closing season issued a firm warning on 20 February when ice held the ship immovable despite full steam, but wildlife suggested to Gerlache that land lay to the south. The leader hoped for a major discovery, and he was not turning back.

Cook was only one of many who were ambivalent about the wisdom of pushing on, even in such an ice-worthy ship: "We are hoping to continue our voyage of exploration as long as possible, and when the darkness and cold become too great we expect to steal away and winter in more congenial latitudes. . . . Shall we succeed, or will the ice seize us with a final and relentless embrace?"[6] Cook also believed that Gerlache deliberately intended to winter in the ice despite the attendant dangers. On 23 February, Cook wrote: "The fact is forced more and more upon us that we are fixed for the winter. . . . Gerlache has all along manifested an inclination for wintering in the pack, but every officer has been so much opposed to this that the Commandant did not openly betray his disposition."[7] Gerlache acknowledged the general dissent, but he obtained Lecointe's support in a brief meeting that ended with a handshake, and he pressed on.[8] Amundsen was deeply concerned, commenting, "They [Gerlache and Lecointe] could not have made a greater mistake. I saw and understood fully the great danger they exposed the whole expedition to, but I was not asked for my opinion, and discipline required me to keep silent."[9]

Days passed, progress was nearly nil, and the sunlight and relative warmth of summer were vanishing. After more foreboding entanglements with the ice, the ship was at about 71°30' S latitude when the sea froze over on 3 March. The ship was locked in, and the party became only the second to winter over in the Antarctic. The first had been Captain Clark's party in 1821 on King George Island; Gerlache's party was the first to winter south of the Antarctic Circle. Cook commented, "All blame the director for entering the main body of the pack at the season's end. After airing opinions, though adverse and bitter to the men in charge, everybody feels better. . . . Even the most disheartened among us now begins to see new charms in the curious chance which may make us the first of all human beings to pass through the long antarctic night."[10] On 16 March, Cook and Arctowski saw from the crow's nest many open water lanes, but now that Gerlache was agreeable to an escape from the ice, a way through was not practicable. It was too late.

The drift of the *Belgica* in the frozen sea was to last thirteen months; the ship was carried by wind and current from about 85° to 103° W longitude,

Obtaining snow for drinking water
Gerlache, *Quinze mois dans l'Antarctique,* 1902

and between about 70° and 71°30' S. The ship's movement tended east during the winter, and west at other times. As autumn advanced, the numbers of birds and seals diminished, and some days there were no signs of wildlife at all. The departing sun left in its wake ever-deepening and long nights but resplendent noontime effects toward the north. The men busied themselves observing weather and atmospheric phenomena, the bergs, the development of ice-flowers on newly formed sea ice, and the effects of the tide and wind on the pack. For entertainment, some took short trips by ski. The group celebrated King Leopold's birthday, the birthdays of each man on board, and all legal holidays of each country represented—and the men discussed at length their ideals of feminine beauty. But the ship was not as accommodating for a winter in the ice as it initially appeared to be: it was underprovisioned, cold, damp, and dark. The food was dull and nutritionally poor, and the men, to their detriment, did not eat fresh penguin, cormorant, or seal. Amundsen observed: "The commander . . . developed an aversion to the flesh of [seals and penguins] that amounted almost to a mania. He was not content only to refuse to eat it himself, but he forbade any of the ship's company to indulge in it."[11] Depression beset the party. Even as early as 21 March, Cook wrote, "We are imprisoned in an endless sea of ice. . . . We have told all the tales, real and imaginative, to which we are equal. Time weighs heavily upon us as the darkness slowly advances."[12]

On 19 May 1898, the men became the first human witnesses to the onset of an Antarctic winter night. Gerlache commented: "That day, a fragment of the sun's disk appeared to us once more, thanks to refraction; then began a night of sixteen hundred hours."[13] Cook described "the weird outline of the dying face of the setting sun . . . heatless, rayless, and sad";[14] they would not see it again for sixty-three days. The farthest south of their drift, 71°36', was reached on 31 May. Danco weakened over a number of weeks and died in early June. Cook thought the difficult conditions had exacerbated his chronic valvular heart disease. He was buried at sea through a crack in the sea ice, in the presence of his despondent companions. The mood on ship deteriorated. Even the cat was affected; once spirited and friendly, the cat turned to growling, became withdrawn, and eventually died. The darkness that had descended over their world now descended over their spirits. Somehow the men continued scientific work in a variety of fields, but many among the company had physical complaints. One became insane, others mentally unstable. Cook noted irregular heart action in a number of the men. He attributed the problems to depression, darkness, and poor nutrition. Midwinter Day passed with a few touches of orange on the northern noontime horizon.

The gradual reappearance of midday light in the north was cheering, and each of the would-be sun worshippers took up a favored post on ship from which to witness the sun's reappearance on 22 July. Cook described the event: "These positions were taken at about eleven o'clock. The northern sky at this time was nearly clear and clothed with the usual haze. A bright lemon glow was just changing into an even glimmer of rose. At about half-past eleven a few stratus clouds spread over the rose, and under these there was a play in colours, too complex for my powers of description. The clouds were at first violet, but they quickly caught the train of colours which was spread over the sky beyond. There were spaces of gold, orange, blue, green, and a hundred harmonious blends, with an occasional strip like a band of polished silver to set the colours in bold relief. Precisely at twelve o'clock a fiery cloud separated, disclosing a bit of the upper rim of the sun. . . . For several minutes my companions did not speak. Indeed, we could not at that time have found words with which to express the buoyant feeling of relief."[15]

Men nevertheless continued to turn ill, and temperatures outside reached their lowest some weeks later. Gerlache and Lecointe wrote their wills. Cook and Amundsen took moral command; Cook kept up the company's humor, made sure of proper clothing and dry bedding, made every sick man spend time each day in front of the coal or wood fire, and forced them to eat fresh meat. These treatments helped, and soon all were craving penguin. On 31 July, Lecointe was healthy enough again to join Amundsen and Cook in a sledging trip to escape the claustrophobic confines of the ship.

With the coming of spring, the health of the party returned. But the *Belgica* was still trapped in a two-mile floe with no certain exit, even though open water was only half a mile away. By January, the possibility of another year in the ice loomed. After explosives failed to break the floe, Cook suggested digging two trenches to open water, one from the ship's bow and the other from the stern, with the hope that this would speed up the melting. Through extraordinary effort this was accomplished, and the men applied saws and axes to open the channel. After several weeks, on 14 February 1899, the *Belgica* emerged safely from its prison. Pack ice remained tight, however, and the ship was restrained for another month before being freed at last from its icy confines.

The party reached Punta Arenas on 28 March and finally arrived in Antwerp on 5 November, to a grand reception that Gerlache said he would never forget. Gerlache received honors from King Leopold and gold medals from the Royal Academy of Belgium, the Royal Belgian Geographical Society, the Royal Geographical Society of Brussels, and the municipalities of Brussels and Anvers. He became Grand Laureate of the Geographical Society of France in 1925.

Amundsen had climbed a rung in his quest toward achieving captain's qualifications; during the years until his South Pole expedition of 1910–12, he explored the Arctic and, in the *Gjøa* in 1905, became the first to conquer the previously elusive Northwest Passage. In 1907, Arctowski attempted unsuccessfully to launch a second Belgian Antarctic expedition for scientific investigation of the relatively unknown region between 105° and 150° W.[16] Cook's future was marred by scandal, both in geographical exploration and in business. He laid claim to being the first to reach the North Pole, but his latitudes and character fell into serious question. Later he spent time in jail for illegal business activities, but his contribution to the *Belgica* has never been in question. It accorded him his just measure of indisputable greatness.

11

CARSTEN E. BORCHGREVINK AND THE VOYAGE OF THE *SOUTHERN CROSS* (1898–1900)

> We slowly moved towards the low beach whereon man had never ventured to live before, and where we were to live or perish.
>
> Carsten E. Borchgrevink, *First on the Antarctic Continent*

AFTER THE BULL EXPEDITION, Carsten Egebert Borchgrevink, member of that expedition and one of the seven men who had accomplished the milestone event of landing at Cape Adare, was convinced that spending a winter there was feasible. He planned to return as leader of his own expedition specifically to achieve that goal.[1] Borchgrevink was zealous and enterprising, qualities that undoubtedly contributed to his success in obtaining the requisite financial backing and in outfitting his expedition, but he was lacking in certain qualities of leadership. He was not easy to get along with, he did not take advice well, and he alienated his scientific staff by failing to comprehend a rigorous approach to scientific observation and interpretation.[2] In spite of these flaws, he achieved a great deal as an Antarctic explorer.

Borchgrevink was a man driven by ambition and ideals. "Man's philosophy has . . . reached the glittering gates of the Poles where eternity rules in stern silence, awaiting the hour when time is ripe through the sacrifice of mortals, for man to be allowed to follow his philosophy and to enter the Polar crystal palaces, and to satisfy his thirst for certainty."[3] He secured substantial backing from the successful London publisher Sir George Newnes (1851–1910), for which he was harshly and enviously criticized by the Royal Geographical Society, which was planning a large-scale scientific Antarctic expedition of its own.

Borchgrevink sailed in an old Norwegian whaler that was renamed *Southern Cross*. The ship weighed 276 tons; it was 146 feet in length and 31 feet abeam and was equipped with a steam engine that allowed closer approaches to Antarctic shores than were possible under sail alone. The ship had been designed and built by Colin Archer, who also designed the *Fram,* which carried Fridtjof Nansen to his farthest north and which later served as Roald Amundsen's ship to the Antarctic. The *Southern Cross* was under the command of the Norwegian captain Bernhard Jensen (1853–?), who had been second mate under Leonard Kristensen during the voyage of the *Antarctic.* Although the *Southern Cross* sailed under the British flag, Borchgrevink himself was an Anglo-Norwegian who lived in Australia, and only three expedition members were actually British.

The expedition departed Kristiania on 30 July 1898. The multinational flavor of the expedition was evident at the departure ceremonies in the hoisting of the Union Jack, toasts to both Queen Victoria of England and King Oscar of Norway, and the presence of both the British consul-general and prominent Norwegians. In addition, two expedition members were Finns. The ship arrived in London, where Newnes held a luncheon attended by various notables including the prominent Antarctic historian Hugh Robert Mill. Toasts were again made to both crowns, and the ship departed on 22 August with a complement of thirty-one men and ninety dogs. The party put in stops at Madeira, Santa Cruz, and St. Vincent, and arrived in Hobart on 28 November for a two-week layover.

Heading south from Hobart, the *Southern Cross* arrived at the edge of the Ross Sea pack ice on the last day of 1898. Forty-three days, an extraordinarily long time, were spent getting through. Despite the season—the height of summer—a gale produced so much ice pressure that on one occasion the ship was lifted four feet. The party's position, far west in the Ross Sea ice belt, was to blame. In good weather, the men spent time hunting seals and letting the dogs run loose on the floes. The British members of the expedition attempted to keep pace on skis with their Norwegian companions.

As the party approached the Balleny Islands, Louis Bernacchi (1876–1942), the twenty-four-year-old expedition scientist from Australia whose account of the expedition contains many beautiful literary depictions of the Antarctic, commented: "Sunset and sunrise mingled. . . . The sumptuous colouring of the sky beggars description; the water was a mass of quivering and shifting colour. . . . The lofty peaks of perennial snow in the distance were lit up with a tender rose pink . . . the fantastic dream of some imaginative painter."[4]

The *Southern Cross* arrived at Cape Adare and dropped anchor on 17 February 1899. A scout party of three, including Borchgrevink and Bernacchi, went ashore in a small boat. Bernacchi congratulated Borchgrevink, who related: "It was a moment which, I believe, will always remain in the memory of my staff and self as we slowly moved towards the low beach whereon man had never ventured to live before, and where we were to live or perish, under conditions which were as an unopened book to ourselves and to the world."[5]

The lead party found conditions good, so over the next ten days equipment, stores, and hut-building materials were landed for the ten men who would remain to spend the winter. Borchgrevink named the site Camp Ridley after his mother. Seventy-five dogs were landed, the first time dogs had been employed in the Antarctic. Bernacchi and Hugh Blackwall Evans (1874–1975) seized a fleeting opportunity to climb the thousand-foot summit of Cape Adare, the first men to stand on a summit of Victoria Land. During the landing operations, the entire expedition was nearly lost in a severe, four-day blizzard. When the vessel lost its anchor, only the power of the engines and the indefatigable efforts of the stokers kept the ship from running ashore. Meanwhile, a marooned shore party of seven men was lucky to have had a tent: they survived by bringing all of the dogs in to lie on top of them for warmth.

The *Southern Cross* returned north on the evening of 1 March 1899. The men on shore watched the ship and their comrades depart across the bay in perfect weather, the pack ice shining silver in the moonlight. When they thought about how two thousand miles of ocean would separate them from

"The 'Southern Cross' was about to leave us at our pioneer settlement."
Borchgrevink, *First on the Antarctic Continent*, 1901

the nearest humans, they realized that they would be the most isolated party on earth.

Among the men, Borchgrevink was thirty-six and the oldest. Seven of the party served in scientific and miscellaneous capacities, including Bernacchi (magnetics, astronomy, photography); two Englishmen, Lt. William Colbeck (1871–1930) (magnetics) and Evans (assistant in zoology); and four Norwegians, Nicolai Hanson (1870–99) (zoology), Herluf Klövstad (1868–1900) (physician), Anton Fougner (1870–1932), and Kolbein Ellefsen, who also was cook. Two Finns, Ole Must (1877–1934) and Persen Savio (1877–1905) were the youngest, both age twenty-two, and the smallest, but very strong and loyal; they tended the dogs. Borchgrevink wrote high praise of Must and Savio: "More faithful and devoted companions than them I do not think any commander could wish for."[6] The Finns knew little English at the outset of the expedition but were conversant by the end of the long winter night.

The men quickly adapted to the bleak and austere surroundings, the windswept, gravelly, and irregular terrain, the stark, mountainous backdrop, and the few remaining Adélie penguins. A hut, merely fifteen feet square, was erected on a foundation dug two feet deep in the gravel. The roof was anchored by cables and insulated with sealskins. This insulation was a blessing against cold, but the heat inside the hut was a curse when the stove was burning. A shed for equipment and provisions was erected only a few yards away, and the space between was used for storage. The seals, penguins, and other birds were largely gone by the end of March, and the men and dogs were totally alone—without the wildlife that contributes so much to the character of the Antarctic coast.

The wintering party settled into routine activities that included specimen collections, meteorological and magnetic observations, coastal surveys, and photography. Unfortunately, exploration from Cape Adare was extremely limited by the surrounding land features. The sun disappeared on 15 May, Bernacchi commenting, "It is scarcely possible to adequately comprehend how much we are indebted to the sun even for the principle of our own existence. It is the direct and indirect agent of all the vital transformations which occur on our planet. . . . We watched the departing sun as it slowly skimmed along the horizon like a tired traveller after a long weary march."[7]

Despite Borchgrevink's prediction that a winter at Cape Adare could be accomplished with relative ease, there was much adversity. A storm packing ninety-mile-per-hour winds blew the dog kennels out to sea and lifted a boat into the air, smashing it two hundred yards away. East-southeasterly autumn gales destroyed the wind vane and anemometer. On a sledge journey to the southern end of nearby Robertson Bay, Borchgrevink, Bernacchi, Fougner, and Savio were almost swamped when a gale blew out the trusted sea ice and replaced it with sheets of frozen spray and huge seas; the men's only route back to camp was around the frightfully perilous coast by means of ropes and uncertain footholds. At Camp Ridley, Evans was lost for three hours in a furious blizzard after taking a meteorological observation, unable to see his way back to the hut. A fire resulting from a candle left burning in a bunk scorched a wall of the hut; after that, Borchgrevink assembled survival provisions and tents in case another accident forced them out. On another occasion, Bernacchi, Hanson, and Ellefsen were asleep in the hut and narrowly escaped death from coal fumes. Savio had a horrific fall sixty feet into a crevasse, alone and untethered, and was jammed in head downward—had he fallen two feet farther to one side he would have been lost. He could hear one of his companions above, but his own frantic cries for help were unheard. Adopting an inner calm and remembering he had a pocket knife, he cut toe holds into one wall of the crevasse while leaning his back against the other. He emerged atop the ice, where Borchgrevink found him exhausted and unable to speak.

During the deepest part of the winter, very little work was done except for scientific measurements taken at the hut and occasional sledge journeys in the immediate vicinity. The men found themselves often getting up as late as eleven in the morning, lazing away the time apathetically, and gaining weight from the lack of activity. Borchgrevink noted: "We were getting sick of one another's company; we knew each line in each other's faces. Each one knew what the other one had to say. Our whole repertoire was exhausted, but knowing the fact, all kept cheerful."[8] They read, played whist and chess, and found reason for occasional celebration. When it was cold enough, the men could "eat" their whisky. The cold also froze the chemicals used to develop photographs.

An astonishing event occurred on 30 June. One of the dogs had been blown out to sea on a floe on 23 April, and it now showed up, quite well nourished and spirited. How it had survived was a mystery, but it proved the survival capacity of dogs introduced to the region. Some of the dogs occasionally turned murderously on each other; a few were killed and eaten by their canine comrades.

Hanson grew ill during the winter and deteriorated rapidly in early October. On 14 October, when Hanson knew he was about to die, he asked to see each expedition member to say good-bye and shake hands. When asked where he would like to be buried, he designated the spot next to a large boulder at the summit of Cape Adare; the men promised to grant this last wish. By a strange and wonderful coincidence, the first Adélie penguin arrived back at Cape Adare only thirty minutes before Hanson died, and the bird was brought to him. Hanson, always the eager zoologist, took great delight in this creature in his last moments. Klövstad's official doctor's report stated that Hanson had died from "occlusion of the intestines,"[9] but Hanson's numbness in the legs, edema, rapid heart rate, and difficulty in breathing[10] all point to beriberi (now known to be caused by dietary thiamine deficiency) and resulting heart failure.

Atop Cape Adare at Hanson's chosen grave site, the party excavated the frozen ground with dynamite. Hanson had been a cheerful and unselfish companion to all; because the men were eager to honor Hanson's last request, the difficult work was not too great for them. The burial service was read, and the Finns sang a sad melody. Of the site, Bernacchi lamented, "There amidst profound silence and peace, there is nothing to disturb that eternal sleep except the flight of sea-birds."[11]

Soon tens of thousands of penguins were about, initiating nesting rites, and the men took the opportunity to supply the hut's larder with penguin meat and eggs. November and December brought particularly fine weather that allowed the scientists to gather data in earnest and study the penguins and other nesting pelagic birds. Not fully appreciative of the skua's important role in the Antarctic ecosystem, the men killed a number of the birds for their predatory and aggressive behavior. While examining lichens on an islet at the head of Robertson Bay, Klövstad discovered live insects, a species of springtail,[12] and the party discovered eight new species of fishes.[13] Bernacchi considered many of the magnetic readings unreliable due to local background disturbances and the limitations of the instruments, but he was able to conclude that since Ross's time the position of the south magnetic pole had shifted significantly to the northwest.[14]

In January the weather turned gloomy, and worry filled the camp as the month rolled on with no sign of the ship, expected since late December. Early on the morning of 28 January 1900, while all the men except Ellefsen, the cook, were asleep, the *Southern Cross* returned to Camp Ridley. Ellefsen had just gone outside the hut to get a bag of coal when he spied a creature approaching. Was it a large penguin? Ellefsen quickly recognized Jensen, who entered the hut, dropped the mail sack, and called out, "Post!" arousing all the sleepers. Borchgrevink related: "It was a great moment as we again shook hands."[15] The shore party's isolation was over. The men were handed letters from home, received news of the ship, and learned of the Boer War. On 2 February, the men paid a last visit to Hanson's grave and erected a cross. Then they all boarded ship and left their winter home for destinations south, as long as the season held out.

The following day, a cold, windy, snowy landing was made on a rough beach on the western side of the largest of the Possession Islands. They found the Bull expedition's pole with tobacco box attached, containing a note, and the men added a note of their own, signed by each. The ship approached Coulman Island and on the morning of 4 February was cruising along the western shore. The coast was mostly inaccessible because of steep cliffs and walls of ice, but a spot for a possible landing was sighted. Borchgrevink, Colbeck, Bernacchi, and two sailors set out in a boat and leapt ashore at the base of a cliff, the first landing ever made on Coulman Island. When they returned to the ship, they headed south and landed at the foot of Mount Melbourne to make magnetic observations.

On 8 February, a party of seven including Borchgrevink, Jensen, Colbeck, Bernacchi, Evans, and two sailors landed at Franklin Island on a large pebbly beach on the west side. There they gathered specimens of rock and primitive vegetation and took magnetic readings. They found the Adélies there had not progressed as far in their nesting cycle as their counterparts at Cape Adare, owing to their more southerly latitude.

The party then headed for Ross Island and the great ice barrier. Mount Erebus and Mount Terror came into view on 10 February. A small headland between Cape Bird and Cape Crozier on Ross Island was named Cape Tennyson for the English poet, and Borchgrevink decided on a landing there, since the weather was fair. He took with him Colbeck, Jensen, and two sailors; a small Union Jack and a letter were to be left ashore. Borchgrevink and Jensen had not yet returned to ship when a loud roar signaled the calving of an iceberg immediately to the west. A cloud of water and ice crystals obscured visibility, and a fifteen- to twenty-foot tidal wave rushed toward the beach. The two men instinctively sought the highest ground, and as they clung to the perpendicular rock they were swamped over their heads. Several reverberating waves washed them up to the chest, but they remained clinging to their holds, surviving their ice-cold bath.

As the ship cruised eastward along the great ice barrier (Ross Ice Shelf), the men noted it had receded thirty miles since Ross's visit. On 11 February, the ship passed Ross's farthest south of 78°9.5'. The event was celebrated that night: the saloon was decorated with flags, and there was plenty of revelry, with toasts and a speech by Borchgrevink. On 16 February, at 164°10' W, the wall of ice was seen to open up into a bay several miles across. (This site has been called Borchgrevink's Inlet, Balloon Bight by Scott, and the Bay of Whales by Shackleton.) The barrier receded to only a few feet above the sea in the eastern portion. Here, at 78°34' S, the ship was moored to the sea ice and a remarkable first "landing" on the barrier was made. Borchgrevink led a party south over the gentle plain. The leader recorded the event simply and without fanfare: "Here I effected a landing with sledges, dogs, instruments and provisions, and while I left the sledge in charge of Captain Jensen with the rest of the Expedition, I myself, accompanied by Lieut. Colbeck and Savio, proceeded southwards, reaching 78°50', the farthest south ever reached by man."[16]

Borchgrevink commenced his northward passage on 19 February. Five days later the party visited Franklin Island again, but weather and the lateness of the season forced them to hurry on. They anchored in Port Ross in the Auckland Islands to hunt ducks and goats, take on fresh water, and clear the boiler pipes. At Stewart Island, Borchgrevink wired Newnes: "Object of Expedition carried out. South Magnetic Pole located. Farthest south with sledge record 78°50'. Zoologist Hanson dead. All well on board. — Borchgrevink."[17] The expedition ended upon arrival in Hobart on 6 April, where Borchgrevink was greeted by his wife and cheered by enthusiastic citizens.

Borchgrevink's accomplishments were considerable. His party had been the first to winter over on the Antarctic mainland, in a well-constructed hut. He was the first to employ dogs in the Antarctic. His men carried out careful scientific observations, discovered new species of lichens and fish, and found the first live insects in the region. The men made several first landings, including one upon the Ross Ice Shelf during which a new farthest south was established. Their ascent onto the barrier was a particularly significant link in the sequence of historical events culminating in man's arrival at the South Pole.

Despite their achievements, Borchgrevink and his men did not receive timely recognition. Vagueness over the expedition's nationality, discredit by the Royal Geographical Society, the attention given to preparation for Scott's *Discovery* expedition, and Borchgrevink's lack of charisma all contributed. Eventually, however, in 1930 the Royal Geographical Society bestowed on Borchgrevink the Patron's Medal, and the historical significance of his important expedition is now well appreciated.

12

ROBERT F. SCOTT AND THE
VOYAGE OF THE *DISCOVERY*
(1901–1904)

Nothing but this terrible limitless expanse of snow. . . . And we, little
human insects, have started to crawl over this awful desert.
                                   Robert F. Scott, *The Voyage of the Discovery*

THE BRITISH NATIONAL ANTARCTIC EXPEDITION OF 1901–4, perhaps
better known as Scott's *Discovery* expedition, was the fruition of eight years'
dogged determination by Sir Clements R. Markham (1830–1916), president
of the Royal Geographical Society. The project was backed by the Royal
Society and its Antarctic Committee; it had parliamentary funding, private
donations, plus the encouragement of Sir Joseph Hooker, other prominent
scientists, and naval officers. The enormous sum of £92,000 was raised to
fund what was intended to be a large-scale scientific enterprise. The government gave £45,000, and £25,000 alone came from a private contributor,
Llewellyn Longstaff, a wealthy London businessman who supported the
expedition for the sake of scientific advancement.[1]

The significance of this voyage's accomplishments cannot be overesti-
mated. Well organized, the program was a logical and thorough extension of
Ross's geographic discoveries and research in all relevant branches of science.
Considering that Scott and most of the officers had no polar experience, their
achievements were enormous, but inexperience also led to mishaps and to one
death in the far south. The expedition in one way or another influenced all
succeeding British Antarctic expeditions of the heroic era.

Robert Falcon Scott (1868–1912) was born in Devonshire to a family of
naval tradition, which he carried on by entering early into a naval career. In
1887, at the age of eighteen, he met Markham and left a lasting favorable
impression. Scott was a first lieutenant on leave in London in 1899 when he
applied to Markham for command of the expedition: a year later he was

awarded it. Scott was an excellent choice, but he was not infallible. Years later, Louis Bernacchi, who had sailed with Borchgrevink and later became physicist on the *Discovery* expedition, summed up Scott well when he said, "Captain Scott, with his striking personality and charm of manner, his courage, his enthusiasm for science, had the ability to inspire loyalty and devotion. He had understanding and knowledge and never failed to stand up for what he considered right: an ideal leader for such an expedition— although he had his weaknesses too, for he was very human."[2]

The *Discovery*, constructed in Dundee for £51,000, was the first vessel designed and built in Britain specifically for scientific exploration. The vessel (485 tons, 172 feet long, 34 feet broad) was made of solid English oak and other fine hardwoods. The hull was strengthened with girders, struts, and beams. The *Discovery* was slow under sail in a light wind, however, so extra coal had to be provisioned for steam power. The ship also had a tendency to roll, and the source of an annoying leak could not be found.

Several committees moved plans along. Scott, steeped in naval tradition, emphasized a naval crew. George Murray (1858–1911) directed the civilian scientific staff and edited the expedition manual. The officers were all highly capable men whose names are immortalized in Scott's narrative and in the Antarctic geographic features named after them in the McMurdo area. They included Albert B. Armitage (1864–1943) (navigator); Reginald Koettlitz (1861–1916) (senior physician, botany); Thomas V. Hodgson (1864–?) (biology); Charles W. R. Royds (1876–1930) (first lieutenant, meteorology); Michael Barne (1877–1961) (second lieutenant); Edward A. Wilson (1872–1912) (second doctor, vertebrate zoology, artist), who became one of the most beloved figures of the heroic era; Reginald Skelton (1872–1952) (chief engineer, photographer); Hartley T. Ferrar (1879–1932) (geology); Bernacchi (physics); and Ernest H. Shackleton (1874–1922) (third officer), who later led three Antarctic expeditions of his own and achieved immortality in Antarctic legend. Another significant member was Ernest E. M. Joyce (1875–1940), selected by Scott from among four hundred applicants seeking a position advertised at the last moment. Joyce impressed Shackleton, who included him on his 1907–9 and 1914–17 expeditions. Two petty officers, Edgar Evans (1876–1912) and William Lashly (1867–1940), emerged as the strongest men of the lower deck; Scott included both in his 1910–13 expedition. Tom Crean (1877–1938), a seaman who joined the expedition at Port Chalmers, served as a sledger. Scott seldom mentioned him but took him again in 1910–13; Shackleton took him in 1914–17. Crean performed deeds of heroic proportion on each expedition. Armitage and Koettlitz had had Arctic polar experience, but only Bernacchi had been in the Antarctic. All the others, including Scott, were novices.

Markham chose the Ross Sea sector as their destination. The chances of attaining a high southerly latitude appeared greatest there, with the possibility of sledge journeys over the Ross Ice Shelf. The scientists could check if magnetic readings had changed since Ross's time. The barrier face could be explored to define its eastern extremity. The mountains fringing the western edge of McMurdo Sound could be investigated, and a wintering over seemed feasible.

The *Discovery* departed Cowes Harbour on 6 August 1901 after a royal visit. Proceeding east from the Cape of Good Hope in difficult seas, the ship displayed its propensity to roll, often to more than 40 degrees, the buoyant stern rising in the following sea. Once the ship broached to and flooded: "Chaos reigned below and discomfort everywhere."[3] Scott made a southward diversion to the sea ice to obtain magnetic readings and then anchored briefly in Fisherman's Cove at Macquarie Island to observe and collect penguins. The men foolishly steered the ship close to windward of the Auckland Islands, barely weathering the cliffs in a freshening gale. At one point the ship heeled to 55 degrees.

The party hurried on to Lyttleton, New Zealand, where the men received a very warm reception. Armitage learned that his wife had given birth to a daughter, the only child of any of the officers. The party spent three weeks refitting, restocking, and taking on enough coal (330 tons, in all) to last two years before heading south heavily laden on 21 December. They sailed away from a throng of thousands, two men-of-war, five dressed steamers, bands, whistles, and the fluttering of handkerchiefs. Despite the gaiety, Scott revealed misgivings embarking on the stormiest ocean in the world in a heavily laden ship. Two days later, the death of seaman Charles Bonner, who had been drinking whiskey atop the mainmast before his fall, sobered the party, which was en route to its scheduled coaling stop at Port Chalmers. There they left the body, and Scott, in a cheerier mood, put the matter behind him.

On 3 January 1902, the ship entered the first streams of pack ice, where Scott was delighted by the wildlife. The men celebrated their penetration into the open water of the Ross Sea with champagne. They anchored in Robertson Bay, landing at Cape Adare on 9 January. The Borchgrevink hut was intact, as was Hanson's gravesite, and Bernacchi reminisced. Wilson's impressions were hardly subtle: "The Adélie Penguin. Such a sight! There were literally millions of them. They covered the plain . . . they covered the slopes. . . . The place was the colour of anchovy paste from the excreta. . . . It simply stunk like hell, and the noise was deafening. There were a series of stinking foul stagnant pools. . . . The rest of the plain was literally covered with guano. And bang in the centre of this horrid place was the camp with its two wooden huts, and a midden heap of refuse all round and a mountain of provision boxes, dead birds, seals, dogs, sledging gear, ski, snow shoes, flags, poles and heaven only knows what else."[4]

The men departed the following day in a difficult current, amid grinding pack and grounded bergs—fine initiation into the hazards of Antarctic navigation. Scott and Armitage were apprehensive of the peril, while most of the party slept below, "happily unconscious."[5] Members of the party made a landing on Coulman Island near Cape Wadworth under the "fearful and wonderful"[6] cliffs, where the men erected a staff with a cylindrical tin container containing a record of the voyage. They observed the Victoria Land coast south of Cape Washington in fine weather, then sailed into McMurdo Sound to seek winter quarters. But the ship was shut out by ice, so Scott turned east.

On 22 January, a landing was achieved at Cape Crozier for the first time, sixteen men straining at oars in heavy surf. They erected a tin cylinder in the Adélie rookery, took magnetic readings, and ascended 1,350 feet to view the barrier surface to the south before returning to ship. Proceeding east along the barrier face, they disproved the existence of Ross's Parry Mountains. They were south of Ross's positions along most of the barrier front, indicating that the barrier had receded during the intervening sixty years.

By 29 January, Scott was east of Ross's most eastward position. The following day, the barrier was seen to rise hundreds of feet, with crevasses suggesting land beneath, and soundings were shallower. Later, land was unmistakably seen poking through the ice at about two thousand feet, representing the eastern limit of the five-hundred-mile-long barrier front. The land (now Edward VII Peninsula) was named after that monarch. Shackleton was on watch and first sighted the land. He wrote in his diary: "It is a unique sort of feeling to look on lands that have never been seen by human eye before."[7] The discovery constituted one of the expedition's greatest geographic achievements.

The party found Borchgrevink's Inlet and anchored where the ice met the sea. On 3 February, Armitage, Bernacchi, and four others took a sledge up a valley to the south. The twenty-hour journey was grueling: transport was by manhauling, the men lacked a stove to heat their food, and all six tried to sleep in a three-man tent. When Bernacchi could stand the squeeze no longer, he slept outside.

The next day, Scott became Antarctica's first aeronaut as he ascended eight hundred feet in a hydrogen balloon secured by a rope. He obtained fine views of the barrier and noted long undulations two to three miles between crests that ran parallel to the edge. He could pick out the sledge party about seven to eight miles from the ship. The cautious Wilson was highly critical of the ballooning enterprise. "The Captain, knowing nothing whatever about the business, insisted on going up first and through no fault of his own came down safely. . . . Then Shackleton went up. . . . I refused. . . . I think it is perfect madness to allow novices to risk their lives in this silly way, merely for the sake of a novel sensation. . . . Happily, after lunch, the balloon was found to have leaked. . . . Had anyone used the valve in the morning, when the balloon was up, it would not have closed properly and nothing could have prevented the whole show from dropping to earth like a stone! . . . If some of these experts don't come to grief over it out here, it will only be because God has pity on the foolish."[8] Bernacchi didn't think the activity yielded enough new information to justify the endeavor. But Skelton was more enthusiastic and appreciated ballooning's logical extension into the future: "For when we once more reach civilization, we may find flying machines en route for the Poles."[9] The project had been the idea of the venerable Sir Joseph Hooker, botanist on Ross's expedition.[10]

Scott decided to hurry on west. He knew the season would soon be closing—the sea was already starting to freeze at times—and he did not wish to winter where little exploration could be done. In addition, his supply of coal was limited. The *Discovery* rounded Cape Bird on what Scott fittingly renamed Ross Island and sailed as far south into McMurdo Sound as ice conditions could ever permit, to Winter Quarters Bay at Hut Point. There Scott discovered White Island, Black Island, and Brown Island (now Peninsula) to the south, around which the barrier ice flowed. The men erected a hut as a shore station for supplies and scientific work, no small chore with the supports placed almost four feet into the frozen ground. They called the hut Gregory Lodge after its Australian designer, but it is now known as the Discovery hut. The ship was anchored, and the men settled in, the *Discovery* serving as principal quarters.

From the outset, the enterprise was marked by the mishaps of inexperience, but also by the men's dogged determination. Very soon after arrival, C. Reginald Ford, the ship's steward, fractured a leg skiing, Hodgson was almost swept out on a floe, Royds fell into the frigid water alongside ship and saved himself by climbing a rope ladder at the stern, and Scott was laid up after pulling a hamstring skiing. Skelton and Barne were almost lost in a dense blizzard just yards from the ship. Shackleton, Wilson, and Ferrar made a three-day sledge journey seventeen miles south to White Island, where they scaled its twenty-seven-hundred-foot peak and made the momentous observation of an extended line of mountains to the south. They also discovered the hazard of concealed crevasses too near the projecting land.

A far worse fate awaited the group attempting a sixty-mile journey in early March to Cape Crozier across the barrier on the south side of Ross Island. Because of his injury, Scott deferred leadership to Royds, and he later acknowledged that the group was ill prepared. Four officers and eight seamen set out on 5 March with two sledges and eight dogs. The sea was still open past the east slope of The Gap, a low-elevation passage between Crater Hill and Observation Hill used to traverse Hut Point Peninsula, so they reached the barrier surface to the east by a detour requiring an eight-hundred-foot ascent. Four days later, the party was on the soft snow of Windless Bight. Only three pairs of skis were on hand, so Royds decided to go on with Koettlitz and Skelton; he sent the other nine back to the ship under Barne's direction. A blizzard struck, and the nine inexperienced men, inadequately clothed, their stoves out of order, needlessly fearful that the tents would not hold, and believing the ship only a mile away, made the fateful error of abandoning their shelter to run for the *Discovery*, leaving the sledges behind.

The party got onto a steep slope near Castle Rock in poor visibility. Suddenly Clarence Hare went missing, and then Edgar Evans slipped and was out of sight. Barne went after them, lost his footing, and slipped down the slick ice, landing next to Evans on a soft patch of snow. Hare could not be found. Arthur Quartley became impatient and decided to slide down; he, too, lost control but slipped down safely next to the other two. Evans, Barne, and Quartley soon realized that they had only just been saved from going over a precipice by the forgiving snow; a dog already had been lost to that very fate. A brief lapse in the wind permitted them enough visibility to reach a safer position.

The five men who had remained higher up—Frank Wild (1873–1939), F. C. Weller, William Heald, Frank Plumley, and George Vince—went on alone.

Wild had the forethought to put a few nails in his boots and was able to steady himself and help the others, but in the gloom they all suddenly realized they had descended to a precipice above the sea. The danger of their predicament became all too evident. Vince, in fur footwear because he had been unable to don his frozen leather boots, could not maintain his footing and shot down and over the precipice into the sea in front of his horrified companions. The only salvation for the rest was a terrifying ascent using jack knives to cut footholds in ice hard as glass. Every step was life threatening until they reached safety.

Wild's party arrived at the ship on 11 March, and search parties were sent out. Vince was never seen again; all of the remaining men eventually reached safety, although frostbitten and exhausted. Barne's fingers on one hand were so severely injured by the cold that a week passed before any circulation returned to the fingertips. Hare returned miraculously unharmed on 13 March, having unwittingly slept thirty-six hours in the snow. Royds's party returned 19 March, having discovered the route to Cape Crozier over the windswept east slope of Mount Terror, but the men had been unable to go the whole distance because of inadequate equipment and clothing. One night they shivered and huddled as the temperature dropped to minus 42 degrees Fahrenheit.

Once the sea froze over, Scott led an autumn sledge journey south consisting of twelve men plus dogs, but the party did not get far. The dogs pulled poorly, the men were overworked, temperatures were below minus 40 degrees Fahrenheit, and there were few hours of light. At least this time there were no serious mishaps, although the entire undertaking was perhaps too optimistic. Life in the tents was miserable. Wilson related: "Our furs . . . are frozen stiff. . . . One can do literally nothing but lie as one falls in the tent. One cannot turn . . . without upsetting both your companions. . . . Your only chance of keeping warm is to lie still. . . . Rime coating the inside of the tent . . . drops on your face and melts there and runs where it chooses as you can't possibly get a hand up or wipe it. . . . Reinskin hairs tickle your nose . . . and you can't do anything for it, except move your head which brings the ring of ice on the balaclava . . . into close contact with warmer skin, so that it melts and runs down your neck."[11] Armitage, with prior polar experience, noted: "The short trip was not quite useless, as it had shown those who were totally inexperienced in sledging work something of the realities of it."[12]

As the season closed, Scott noted the southward movements of emperor penguins and deduced that they must winter in the far south after all other

Manhauling the sledge
Edward A. Wilson, from *The South Polar Times*, 1907

birds had migrated north. He was also fascinated by peculiar ice formations on the newly frozen sea: "This is a season of flowers, and behold! they have sprung up about us as by magic: very beautiful ice-flowers, waxen white in the shadow, but radiant with prismatic colours where the sunrays light on their delicate petals."[13] The sun was seen for the last time on 20 April: "A highly refracted elliptical ball of red, giving little light and no appreciable heat. For a few minutes it bathed the top of Observation Hill in soft pink light, then vanished beneath a blood-red horizon."[14]

The polar night officially began three days later, and the men of the *Discovery* now became the most southerly party ever to winter over in the Antarctic. Winter passed fairly easily. Scientific studies were pursued in earnest. Seals were hunted for food, although Scott could not bring himself to do the killing and delegated the responsibility: "It seemed a terrible desecration to come to this quiet spot only to murder its innocent inhabitants and stain the white snow with blood."[15]

Scott formulated his plan for the southern journey in the spring and selected Wilson to accompany him; he was undecided on a two- versus three-man party when he opened the subject with Wilson on 12 June. Wilson favored three because survival was more likely if one became incapacitated. Scott and Wilson independently selected Shackleton as the third.[16] Wilson and Shackleton had often taken long walks together during the autumn; Scott and Wilson both appreciated Shackleton's strengths. In retrospect, Scott should have chosen differently.

For entertainment, the wintering party had games and extensive reading material, including a library of polar literature. A number of the men kept diaries. A "Discovery Debating Club" was formed: they debated women's rights, each man (married or not) having twelve minutes to spew as much hilarious nonsense as possible. They staged talent shows, comedy routines, and a play. The men produced an expedition magazine, *The South Polar Times*. Shackleton was editor; officers and men contributed poetry, prose, acrostics, and caricatures, often anonymously, most in a light, amusing vein; Wilson worked indefatigably as principal illustrator. Only the best submissions were included, since it was Scott's intention to have the issues published on their return to England.[17] Five issues were produced during the first winter, each in a single copy. Armitage remarked, "A most fortunate thing it was, too, that we were able to see the humorous side of our existence in those regions; otherwise our life in the secluded South would have been a most melancholy affair."[18] The rejects of the first issue were printed separately on the ship's press as *The Blizzard*, and each expedition member received a copy; but the lagging quality of the contents did not justify a second issue.

While officers and men shared many activities, Scott adhered to strict naval routine: the officers and men messed apart, though Scott ordered they have the same food. "Without subverting discipline, it silences complaint."[19] For a bit of solitude, many of the officers enjoyed lone walks away from the ship. The sun returned on 22 August. "For long our blinking eyes remained fixed on that golden ball and on the fiery track of its reflection; we seemed to bathe in that brilliant flood of light, and from its flashing rays to drink in new life, new strength, and new hope."[20] With the advancing daylight, Koettlitz grew mustard and cress with seeds in Antarctic soil under the wardroom skylight.

By the end of August, preparations for spring sledging were in full swing. The men gave attention to every detail of sledging equipment, clothing, food, and transport. Scott knew that dogs were valuable in polar transport, but he had had little experience with them and was too sentimental to make serious beasts of burden of them; he was disdainful of their role. "In my mind no journey ever made with dogs can approach the height of that fine conception which is realised when a party of men go forth to face hardships, dangers, and difficulties with their own unaided efforts. . . . Surely in this case the conquest is more nobly and splendidly won."[21] This hidebound view was to limit his success in the coming season, and to cost him his life on his next expedition in 1912. But to Scott, sledging as he conceived of it was so virtuous that he could not compromise his philosophy. "Sledging draws men into a closer companionship than can any other mode of life. In its light the fraud must be quickly exposed, but in its light also the true man stands out in all his natural strength. Sledging therefore is a sure test of a man's character, and daily calls for the highest qualities of which he is possessed."[22]

Scott awaited the southern journey with anxious anticipation. The initial southward run was a short depot and reconnaissance journey. Meanwhile, other spring reconnaissance journeys were made to the west, southwest, and north, and all the men suffered the severe cold of early spring sledging. Armitage was away two weeks, reconnoitering a way up through the western mountains; three of his party returned with scurvy. Scott was merely two days out when he was caught in a cold blizzard—temperatures were below minus 30 degrees Fahrenheit—with the tent skirt improperly secured. Whirling drift permeated everything while the miserable party waited out the storm.

Scott's party made a second start and cached six weeks' provisions out on the barrier, but on the way they got into fractured ice north of Minna Bluff, a prominent land projection running east-west just south of White and Black Islands, named for Clement Markham's wife. One of the warrant officers, and then an entire sledge, had to be hauled out of crevasses. Scurvy afflicted some of the men. Scott and his contemporaries were aware that fresh food prevented the disease, but they mistakenly believed that a toxin in their prepared foods, rather than a dietary deficiency, was the cause. Seal meat was a preventative and not unappealing, but the cook knew only how to fry it; many of the men became bored of seal and avoided it altogether.

Royds headed a party of six to Cape Crozier in early October to leave a message in advance of the relief ship's arrival. In the process, on 12 October Skelton made the momentous discovery there of the first known emperor penguin breeding colony. The chicks were well developed, confirming the scientists' suspicions that the breeding cycle began in the depth of winter. Scott said of the event, "We gathered no small satisfaction from being the

Emperors' rookery under the broken ice cliff at Cape Crozier
Scott, *The Voyage of the Discovery,* 1905

first to throw light on the habits of a creature that so far surpasses in hardi-hood all others of the feathered tribe."[23] Royds departed again for Cape Crozier on 2 November, only to find that the emperor chicks were already gone. One egg, abandoned and frozen, was found, however, the first ever seen; the coveted prize was taken back to the ship for study.

The southern journey, with its optimistic but wholly unrealistic plan for the South Pole, began on 30 October 1902. A supporting party of twelve headed by Barne departed first to an enthusiastic send-off and display of banners. Scott, Wilson, and Shackleton, who would all achieve independent fame and eventually die in the Antarctic, left with nineteen dogs and sledges three days later to resounding cheers. The trio caught up with their support-ing party the next day at White Island. On 13 November, Scott remarked, "Sights to-day showed us to be nearly up to the seventy-ninth parallel, and therefore farther south than anyone has been. The announcement of the fact caused great jubilation, and I am extremely glad that there are no fewer than fifteen of us to enjoy this privilege."[24] At that point, half the supporting party turned north, and the remaining men pushed on south. Two days later, the

The Southern Party (left to right): Shackleton, Scott, and Wilson
Scott, *The Voyage of the Discovery*, 1905

last of the supporting party turned, and Scott, Wilson, and Shackleton went on alone.

Scott was euphoric, and he now seemed more enthusiastic about dog transport; but he was also becoming more realistic about what he could accomplish with them. "Each footstep will be a fresh conquest of the great unknown. Confident in ourselves, confident in our equipment, and confident in our dog team, we can but feel elated with the prospect that is before us. The day's work has cast a shadow on our highest aspirations, however."[25] Warm temperatures, soft snow, overloaded sledges, and poor pulling forced them to move their loads in two smaller portions, thus tripling the distance traveled to move a given distance south. The dogs became listless, and Scott condemned them for the party's poor progress; the dogs' poor fish diet and the heavy loads were to blame. The party traveled at night to avoid overheating the animals, and sometimes the men made selfless sacrifice by carrying sick ones on the sledge. But it did little to help.

Soon Scott was writing of their own hardships—sunburn, blistered lips, snow blindness—and their increasingly voracious appetites. To divide their food fairly, Shackleton invented "shut-eye": portions were divided as equally as possible and assigned by one whose back was turned.[26] Surfaces and poor work from the dogs hampered progress, but on 25 November the party crossed the eightieth parallel. Scott spiritedly remarked that "the most imaginative cartographer has not dared to cross this limit. . . . It has always been our ambition to get inside that white space, and now we are there the space can no longer be a blank; this compensates for a lot of trouble."[27]

By 3 December they had views of the magnificent range of mountains running in a southeasterly direction that formed the western boundary of the Ross Ice Shelf. But the marches were increasingly dreary. One of the dogs broke into the men's seal meat and gorged a week's supply. Wilson had arthritis. The enthusiasm disappeared from Scott's writings. Each day Scott's narrative became more and more forlorn, whether food, dogs, surfaces, or weather were to blame. The men were haunted by fantasies of foods they could not have. A few of the dogs died and became food for the other dogs. Scott lamented, "I think we could all have wept."[28]

Furthermore, according to biographer George Seaver, relations between Scott and Shackleton unraveled from "temperamental incompatibility. . . . Vexation turned to irritability and thence to anger openly expressed, till Wilson saw that plain speaking was necessary if they were to proceed at all. He took his leader aside at the end of a march and said, as only he could do, exactly what he thought, expecting an explosion. Scott heard him out in ominous silence, then to the other's surprised relief, said simply: 'Thank you, Bill.' From that night 'everything seemed to improve.'"[29] This was a key moment: one more episode for the two men who were forging an intimacy out of mutual understanding that would forever bind them.

Finally, on 16 December, the men got an emotional lift when they could give up the relay work. Confidence and exhilaration returned to Scott's record. However, on 24 December, Wilson noted discoloration of both Scott's and Shackleton's gums: scurvy. He confided the information to Scott, but Shackleton remained unaware. The signs were not severe enough to make Scott turn back; the magnificent mountains and mysterious south were too much of a lure. Christmas Day was gloriously fine and was celebrated with a special supplemented menu at each meal, and for Scott, two pipes of tobacco after dinner. But hardships returned quickly; the next day Wilson was so severely snow blind that he had to ski and haul blindfolded.

On 30 December, Scott and Wilson left Shackleton behind at their mid-day camp in thick weather and skied a mile or so to the south. Scott decided this was the place to turn; it was the point of their most southerly advance. "Observations give it as between 82.16 S. and 82.17 S."[30] The following day the men headed west across the barrier toward shore to try for a landing at the foot of the mountains, but ice, heaped up under pressure, and crevasses blocked the way. Here they assigned some of the expedition's most memorable names to geographic features: a summit (now Longstaff Peaks) beyond the eighty-third parallel was named Mount Longstaff for the expedition's generous benefactor; another particularly inspiring and magnificent twin peak ten miles to the west was named Mount Markham after the expedition's founder. Other features received the names Cape Wilson and Shackleton Inlet. Scott declined to ascribe his name to any feature. (But during the same month, on 25 December, the relief party aboard the *Morning* discovered an island group in the Ross Sea on their way south. The men initially named the largest, a mere quarter-mile long, Markham Island;[31] later the name was changed to Scott Island.[32])

Scott's narrative of the early days of January are a lamentable, pitiful tale of the dogs' rapid weakening and being put down one by one until all were gone. "I personally have taken no part in the slaughter; it is a moral cowardice of which I am heartily ashamed."[33] The men could not bring themselves to eat their canine companions, even though the fresh meat was an antiscorbutic. Realizing they must make their next food depot without delay, the men pushed on with a sail on the sledge. Since Wilson's first observations of Shackleton's discolored gums, Scott had become alarmed over Shackleton's fatigue, breathlessness, and bloody cough. Ice surfaces turned bad again, and progress was poor despite the lightening load. By 13 January, almost out of food, the men could not find their food depot. Despondent, they camped midday and cut their lunch rations. At midnight, with visibility improved, Scott went out of the tent with the telescope. "I sprang up and shouted, 'Boys, there's the depot.' We are not a demonstrative party, but I think we excused ourselves for the wild cheer."[34] The cache contained three weeks' provisions for the next 130 miles, a supply they were confident would be ample. But Shackleton was worse, and Wilson considered his friend's life in danger; Scott and Wilson had early signs of scurvy as well.

The party reached the depot on 28 January 1903, where they found abundant food and gastronomic delicacies, as well as letters and notes. "Supper did not last twenty minutes, but the amount we put away in that time would have excited the envy of any gourmand."[35] Both Scott and Wilson paid for their overindulgence with severe cramps. Upon Wilson's advice, the party hurried for the ship because Wilson believed that Shackleton's chances for survival would be better there despite the plenitude of provisions. During the morning of 31 January, Shackleton was carried briefly on the sledge.[36] On 3 February, the men approached Observation Hill and were met by two "penguins" who turned out to be Skelton and Bernacchi. Scott, Wilson, and Shackleton now got news of the rest of the party—as well as of the outer world, as the relief ship *Morning* had arrived. A shave, a hot bath, clean clothing, and a feast welcomed them at the ship. So ended a historically momentous ninety-three-day journey of 960 miles, the deepest penetration ever into the Antarctic interior. The toll on the men had been substantial. Wilson remained mostly bedridden for ten days. And Scott, who considered himself to have been least affected, had swollen legs and painful gums; his physical and mental lassitude persisted for weeks.

Exploration to the west under Armitage had resumed on 29 November 1902. Armitage, Skelton, and ten men including Edgar Evans and Frank Wild left with a support party under Koettlitz, with Ferrar and seven men. Uncertain of the way up through the mountains, and hauling loads of about 225 pounds per man, they made slow progress. However, by 7 December they were five thousand feet up overlooking the Ferrar Glacier, and on 4 January 1903 they made their last camp at 8,985 feet, having achieved the plateau 134 miles from the ship. They knew they were the first to set foot on the interior of Victoria Land, but they did not realize that their ascent constituted man's first arrival on the same plateau that bears the South Pole. All arrived back at the ship on 19 January in good health, having been inspired by spectacular mountain scenery, glaciers, moraines, running streams, and meltwater ponds along the way. Armitage later recalled, "All on board were eager to hear about our experiences, and all wished, when they had heard what we had to tell, that they, too, had been able to see the wonderful valleys of ice up which we had travelled to the summit of a land at once so forbidding and so fascinating, and warmly congratulated us on being the first human beings to storm and carry the heights of South Victoria Land."[37]

All available officers and men readied the ship for departure. Scott, against Bernacchi's advice and telling him in no uncertain terms to stick to his own specialty,[38] had made the mistake of setting the whaleboats beside the ship on the sea ice; the weight of the winter snows had forced the floes down until seawater had engulfed and frozen the boats into an ice encasement fourteen feet thick. The men now had an extraordinary labor of chiseling and sawing the boats out.

The relief ship *Morning* had arrived. The concept of sending a relief ship had originated with Markham and the Royal Geographical Society as early as 1897;[39] funding was secured via a subscription list headed by the king. About £22,600 had been raised from a variety of sources, including, once again, Longstaff, to refit, staff, and supply the small and slow wooden Norwegian whaler. The vessel sailed with twenty-nine officers and men under Capt. William Colbeck, who had had prior Antarctic experience with Borchgrevink. Edward R. G. R. Evans (1881–1957) was second officer; later he was second in command on Scott's 1910–13 expedition. Gerald S. Doorly, already Evans's best friend,[40] who later wrote the narrative of the relief voyages, was third officer. Scott had said he would attempt to leave messages for the *Morning* at Cape Adare, Possession Islands, Coulman Island, Wood Bay, Franklin Island, and especially at Cape Crozier.

The *Morning* had an extremely difficult, at times harrowing, passage south. But on a beautiful Christmas afternoon, "Evans, who was on watch, added greater interest to the day by sighting an island, of which no record could be found in books, journals, or charts. With great pride, therefore, we claimed the discovery."[41] A landing was made on Scott Island, the largest of the outcrops. Colbeck next picked up Scott's message at Cape Adare, but Scott had been unable to land at the Possession Islands or Franklin Island, and Colbeck could not land at Coulman Island and Wood Bay. Thus Colbeck made a difficult landing at Cape Crozier on 18 January to pick up the crucial, determining information—the whereabouts of the *Discovery*. He sailed directly toward McMurdo Sound, but the ship was briefly stalled in the ice between Cape Bird and Beaufort Island. Scotty Paton, a sailor, took the opportunity to leave ship and jump floes a distance of one mile to "land" on Beaufort Island, the first man to do so. His accomplishment was received with a reprimand. In McMurdo Sound, ten miles of ice separated the ships. Some of the *Discovery*'s men immediately set out across ice and slush for the relief ship, and excitement prevailed as they saw new faces from home and received mail. Armitage commented, "Amongst my correspondence I found photographs of my wife and of the little one whom I had never seen; and it suddenly dawned upon me, as it had never done before, that I was a father."[42]

By the middle of February concerns mounted, as the ships were still seven miles apart. Autumn was gathering, and the relief ship would not be strong enough to charge through a solidifying sea. Explosives were of no avail. The men transferred stores in earnest, realizing that the *Discovery* would have to spend another year. At least a variety of excellent foods, fresh clothing, repair materials, and paraffin oil would ensure their comfort.

Scott decided to reduce his party by eight in order to eliminate "one or two undesirables;"[43] eight volunteered to go, including those Scott wished to expunge. "Of course, all the officers wish to remain; but here, with much reluctance, I have had to pick out the name of one who, in my opinion, is not fitted to do so. It has been a great blow to poor Shackleton."[44] Wilson concurred, recording in his diary, "Poor old Shackleton has been sent home as the result of his break down . . . upset him a great deal. . . . It is certainly wiser for him to go home though."[45] However, according to Armitage, Scott sent Shackleton off "in spite of my strong protest."[46] Scott apparently had manipulated Koettlitz, the senior surgeon, to agree with him in writing,[47] even though Koettlitz, according to Armitage, actually told Scott that Shackleton "was not such an ill man as he, Scott, was."[48]

As the *Morning* sailed northward, Evans "watched till Scott's men vanished out of sight, when poor Shackleton, whose heart was greater than his strength, broke down altogether and wept."[49] Shackleton was replaced by a twenty-year-old naval sublieutenant and surveyor, George Mulock. Scott was outwardly relieved and expressed great satisfaction at the harmony he now felt prevailed among his party. Scott, who depended on his naval rank for authority, was probably intimidated by Shackleton's strong persona and popularity.

By late February, the *Discovery* party was teased by a northerly swell that promised to break the ice, but three and a half miles of it remained. Scott abandoned all remaining hope of a release, and the men committed themselves to laying in stores of fresh meat for the winter. They had been brought twenty sheep, and to these they added 144 seals and 551 skuas. To their regret, penguins were no longer about.

The men were now considerably more experienced than they had been during their first autumn and winter, and the seasons proceeded without mishap. They enjoyed their hockey matches in autumn, and, to vary the teams, played officers versus men, divided teams by age, or by married and engaged (or suspected engaged) versus single. A record minus 67.7 degrees Fahrenheit was recorded on 16 May. The midwinter dinner celebration on 22 June consisted of delicacies including turtle soup, tinned halibut, roast beef with artichokes, deviled wing of skua, and champagne. The men watched the puppies born the previous season growing up. Mulock collated a large body of disjointed survey data into coherent charts, to Scott's immense satisfaction. Sledges and equipment were overhauled, and scientific observations went forward. Three issues of *The South Polar Times* were produced, with Bernacchi as editor. (The entire output of eight issues from the two winters was eventually published in two volumes by Scott's London publisher, Smith, Elder, in 1907.) For several days at the end of July, the weather was calm, and Scott remarked, "We have been able to enjoy delightful walks in the light noontide. The northern horizon at this hour is dressed in gorgeous red and gold, and the lands about are pink and rosy with brightness of returning day. I am not sure that a polar night is not worth the living through for the mere joy of seeing the day come back."[50] The sun returned on 21 August.

All was made ready for the preliminary sledging journeys. Scott headed west up the Ferrar Glacier and left a depot at two thousand feet. Barne and Mulock prepared to explore the coast to the south, closer to land than previously, and left a depot southeast of White Island. Royds and Wilson would make periodic visits to Cape Crozier to study the emperor penguins. And Royds and Bernacchi would head southeast over the barrier surface to search for possible land. These brief excursions ran into an extraordinary cold snap. Barne's and Mulock's thermometer broke at minus 67.7 degrees Fahrenheit. Joyce was severely frostbitten, and his foot, frozen to the ankle, was warmed by passing it from the chest of one companion to another.

The Cape Crozier party found a thousand adult emperor penguins and well-developed chicks. The men were astonished to realize that the eggs must have been hatched in the dead of winter. They harvested a number of abandoned eggs for study. Jacob Cross mothered two chicks tenderly and brought them back to ship, housing them in Wilson's cabin. The chicks delighted the party and ate voraciously, but they did not survive their human environs.

The next set of journeys began in early October. Barne and Mulock, with a supporting party, traveled south around Minna Bluff to Barne Inlet. Away for ten weeks, Mulock prepared excellent surveys, charting some two hundred mountain peaks. Royds and his party headed southeast across the barrier, and, finding no land, had a monotonous time. Skelton made photographic studies, and Ferrar performed surveys. Wilson headed out to Cape Crozier and arrived in time to observe both the egress of the emperors and the arrival of the Adélies; the group also studied Windless Bight and collected geologic specimens from the slopes of Mount Terror. Armitage and Wilson later led a party that explored the Koettlitz Glacier.

The journey of greatest interest was the one into the mountains to the west, headed by Scott himself. Armitage had hoped to lead this journey and extend his work of the previous year but found himself excluded. In his autobiography many years later, Armitage said that Scott brushed him aside;[51] the relationship between the two men was indeed strained at times. Armitage had been Markham's first choice as navigator and second in command, but Armitage sensed a potential for conflict with the leader at their first meeting. He consented to join the expedition against his instinct but insisted that his appointment be independent of Scott's control, to which both Markham and Scott agreed.[52] But Scott gave his second in command the opportunity to leave on the *Morning*, ostensibly for the sake of his wife and child. Armitage declined the offer and later mistrusted Scott's motive. Historian Roland Huntford believed Scott was jealous and wished to limit Armitage's achievements.[53]

Scott departed on 12 October with twelve men, four sledges, and over twenty-four hundred pounds of equipment and provisions. Within three days the parties were ascending the Ferrar Glacier, and after three days more, they had achieved an altitude of six thousand feet. However, the silver sledge runners had been damaged by the hard ice, forcing an exasperating return. Scott intended to make haste, and, taking a calculated risk, he left the one good sledge and everything but half a week's provisions to make the eighty-seven-mile return. At record pace, the parties were back at the ship on 21 October. Repairs were made; two parties of nine men left the ship five days later.

The sledge runners continued to give trouble, but Scott was determined to go on. A Weddell seal carcass at five thousand feet greatly mystified the men. Why would the animal have expended such effort to gain so great an altitude with no hope of finding any sustenance? Scott described the scenery in exalted terms.

On a long expanse of hard, blue ice, the parties were caught in a driving, cold wind; they bivouacked on a tiny snow patch, the only spot yielding to their shovels. There they were stranded seven days in the unceasing gale and driving snow, with only one book for entertainment; they suffered from boredom and icy sleeping bags. Finally, Scott resolved to leave despite the weather, but quick frostbites forced a retreat back into the tents. They were away at last on 11 November but had lost their invaluable navigation book, *Hints for*

Travellers, prepared by the Royal Geographical Society. Without it, the men lacked critical information about the declination of sun and stars and logarithmic tables for performing their latitude and longitude calculations. But Scott could not bear another return to the ship; he decided to go on, even though they could not know exactly where they were, or how to get back.

Three days later the party was on the verge of the plateau at eighty-nine hundred feet. Some of the men were weakening, but out of personal pride none would confess to it. Scott divided the remaining six men into two parties and proceeded with Edgar Evans and William Lashly. Scott was enormously impressed with his companions: "I remember the splendid qualities and physique of the two men who remained with me by such a severe process of selection. Evans was a man of Herculean strength, very long in the arm and with splendidly developed muscles. . . . Lashly, in appearance, was the most deceptive man I have ever seen. He . . . a teetotaller and non-smoker all his life . . . was never in anything but the hardest condition."[54] Scott was impressed with their bulk, 178 and 190 pounds, respectively, compared with his own 160. "My companions are undefeatable."[55] And so Scott, in actuality no less strong than his companions, went on in the company of his two men from the lower deck. The experiences they were to have on this journey, one of the greatest polar sledging journeys on record, bonded them and brought the three together again on Scott's next (and last) expedition.

The plateau was an unforgiving place of rarefied, cold winds, sastrugi, barren solitude, and monotony. On 30 November, the men made their last outward march after having covered two hundred miles of changeless conditions. "Here, then, to-night we have reached the end of our tether, and all we have done is to show the immensity of this vast plain . . . a scene so wildly and awfully desolate . . . it is not what we see that inspires awe, but . . . what lies beyond our view . . . hundreds and even thousands of miles which can offer no change . . . nothing but this terrible limitless expanse of snow. It has been so for countless years, and it will be so for countless more. And we, little human insects, have started to crawl over this awful desert, and are now bent on crawling back again."[56] Scott, who admitted to depression and gloomy thoughts in these environs, was grateful for the cheering company of his companions.

Scott's narrative of the return is largely a soliloquy of inner thoughts, alternating moments of euphoria and depression, of sleeplessness, food fantasies, and descriptions of weather and poor surfaces. By 9 December, the men had cut their oil use and increased their sledging hours in anxiety and uncertainty over landmarks as they approached the threshold of the glacier. A week later, they were still uncertain as to their whereabouts. Short on provisions, they held a "council of war"[57] and decided that they had to proceed downward despite poor visibility. The men were all in crampons and tethered to the sledge when Lashly slipped on the hard ice. In an instant all were in a wild fall down a three-hundred-foot slope, providentially ending up not only unhurt but also at the head of the glacier, with a clear direction ahead.

The most harrowing moment of the journey occurred later the same day, during the descent of the glacier. Scott and Evans both suddenly fell through the lid of a concealed crevasse; the sledge jumped to the opposite side, one side of its frame cracking in the sudden jerk, and Lashly dug himself in above, just missing going through himself. As Lashly held the trace with one hand, he withdrew the ski from the sledge to anchor it, while the two men below dangled twelve feet down, freezing in the chill air with scarcely a ledge for support. The stability of the sledge was too tenuous for Lashly to be able to help the men below, so they were on their own to ascend their traces with freezing hands, encumbered by bulky clothing and crampons. Scott climbed out first. "Thank God!" Lashly uttered. Evans climbed out next, and for the first time his demeanor was shaken. "Well, I'm blowed." Scott later told of this event with great drama,[58] but Lashly confided the episode to his diary stoically in stride: "Captain and Evans disappeared down a crevasse. . . . I at once secured the sledge with a pair of ski, and held on to the other end while the Captain climbed up out. . . . We then pulled Evans up and once more proceeded on our way."[59]

The weather and the descent were favorable; they picked up their depot and were back at the ship on 25 December, completing a journey of fifty-nine days and 725 miles on the last outing alone. Scott was somewhat daunted by the effort but very proud of it. "We may claim, therefore, to have accomplished a creditable journey under the hardest conditions on record, but for my part I devoutly hope that wherever my future wanderings may trend, they will never again lead me to the summit of Victoria Land."[60] (But they did, to the same interior plateau, eight years later.)

Only four men were at the ship when Scott returned. The rest were ten miles north on the sea ice at the Dellbridge Islands, laboring around the clock to create a channel. Regarding the work and the tent life there, Wilson remarked, "We all thrived on it! There never was a healthier crowd of ruffians than the 30 unwashed, unshaven, sleepless, swearing, grumbling, laughing, joking reprobates that lived in that smoky Saw Camp."[61] But their efforts failed, and the men soon abandoned the work. In anticipation of another winter, stores of seals and penguins were laid in. On 4 January 1904, Wilson discovered the nearby Adélie penguin rookery and skuary at Cape Royds.

The British government underwrote the relief effort and ordered two ships south, the *Morning* and *Terra Nova*, under the respective commands of Colbeck and Capt. Harry MacKay. Authorities back home were not as optimistic as Scott about the prospects for the *Discovery* and, much to Scott's dismay, gave peremptory orders to evacuate the entire party and abandon the ship if need be. Armitage wrote, "I am confident that there was not a single man on board who, if given the choice of staying another two years in the *Discovery* ice-bound, or of deserting her to return safe home, would not have chosen the former course."[62] That was a strong commitment to the enterprise from a new father who had never seen his child.

On 28 January, an ocean swell reached the *Discovery*. The ship began to jostle, but eight miles of tight pack ice separated the vessel from open water. Explosives failed again. But on 14 February, a strong southeast wind, a mighty gesture of nature that dwarfed human efforts, quickly broke up the ice, and the relief ships were suddenly in Winter Quarters Bay. Doorly recalled: "The three ships, secured to each other in the winter harbour, created a thrilling sensation, and our hearts thumped with pardonable pride."[63] Two days later, the *Discovery* was free at last. Coal was transferred from the *Terra Nova*, and a cross was erected for Vince atop Hut Point, to "stand for centuries" in remembrance of "the silent caretaker of the land."[64]

A southerly gale sprang up; Colbeck and MacKay hurried to depart. A fast north-running current off Hut Point was a formidable obstacle to the *Discovery*'s escape. Scott gambled, and the ship was spun around, grounding at the base of the peninsula, masts shivering in the wind. The men waited helplessly. Each descent onto the shoal sent sickening thuds through the ship, stressing its foundation. Scott lamented: "How many times I wandered from the dismal scene on deck to the equally dismal one below. . . . I tasted something very near akin to despair."[65] Late on 17 February the current reversed, the wind slackened, and the ship lifted off the shoal. The *Discovery* was free, having sustained damage only to the false keel. Coaling and watering operations were completed near Erebus Glacier Tongue, which projects into McMurdo Sound at the north end of Hut Point Peninsula, and the ships headed north.

Freeing of the *Discovery* and junction of the fleet at midnight, 14 February 1904
Scott, *The Voyage of the Discovery,* 1905

The *Discovery* now had enough coal for further exploration; the other ships headed directly north. All would rendezvous in Ross Harbor in the Auckland Islands and proceed together to New Zealand. The *Discovery* party performed more surveys of the Victoria coast, then harbored in Robertson Bay to ship a spare rudder to replace a badly damaged one while some of the men went ashore at Cape Adare. Then they proceeded west to better Ross's record, sighted the Balleny Islands, did not find Wilkes's land, and reached 154°7' E before reluctantly turning north on 5 March because of a shortage of coal. The northward journey was miserable in gales and high seas; the ship rolled and pitched, decks leaking.

The ships docked in Lyttleton on 1 April to a warm welcome, and the men stayed in New Zealand for two months. Magnetic surveys were made in the Pacific as far as 56° to 60° S. They stopped briefly at Punta Arenas and Port Stanley. The expedition, a triumphant endeavor, officially ended on its return to Spithead on 10 September 1904. Scott was promoted to captain the same day. He was made a Commander of the Victorian Order and an officer of the French Legion of Honor; he received gold medals from the geographical societies of several nations. He embarked on an enormously successful lecture tour, even if he was self-admittedly shy at times. His account of the expedition, *The Voyage of the 'Discovery,'* was hailed as one of the finest narratives of exploration ever written, and it went far to promote Scott's fame.

13

ERICH D. VON DRYGALSKI AND THE GERMAN NATIONAL ANTARCTIC EXPEDITION (1901–1903)

Als wir nach Jahresfrist an demselben Ort wohl sagen mussten, dass wir fannten, was die Natur dort bot.

[After a year spent in the same place, we could say we knew what Nature offered there.]

Erich von Drygalski, *Zum Kontinent des Eisigen Südens*

IN RESPONSE TO THE Sixth International Geographical Congress, a German South Polar Commission and science advisory panel were formed to plan a voyage to the Antarctic regions for scientific and geographic discovery. To send a German expedition to the Antarctic had long been the focus of Georg von Neumayer (1826–1909), director of the German Marine Observatory. Erich Dagobert von Drygalski (1865–1949), professor of geography and geophysics at the University of Berlin, had prior polar experience in Greenland and proved that he could carry out serious scientific studies. Thus he was appointed leader of what became known as the German National Antarctic Expedition. The entire effort was funded by the government.

The expedition ship *Gauss* was named after the great mathematician and exponent of terrestrial magnetism Karl Friedrich Gauss (1777–1855) and built especially for the voyage by the Nautical Branch of the Reich Admiralty at a cost of 500,000 marks (about £25,000). The ship was strong and capacious, a barquentine 152 feet long and 37 feet wide with an auxiliary 325-horsepower engine. Each officer and scientist had his own cabin. The vessel was designed with two dining and social areas, one for the officers and scientists and another for the crew. Finished with fine woods including German oak, Oregon pine, teak, and greenheart, with steel reinforcements to the bow and the stern, the ship was the object of fond praise.

Later, however, as a number of design faults became glaringly obvious, the vessel was found to be far from ideal. The *Gauss* was slow, rarely achieving the seven knots expected. The interior of the ship was too dark, and the vessel was prone to disagreeable motion in rough seas. The galley and engine room were too hot in the tropics; engine room temperatures approached 150 degrees Fahrenheit, melting the pitch in the planking seams. A bad water leak kept the noisy pumps busy, consuming coal; the source of the trouble, the rudder well, was only discovered later, when caulking provided relief at last.

The Reich Interior Ministry and Drygalski collaboratively organized the expedition. Drygalski's relationship with the ship's captain was carefully delineated: the captain was in charge of the ship and personnel, while Drygalski held all other authority as leader. The captain was to keep the leader informed about the state of the ship; the captain could disobey the leader only if he sensed a threat to life or ship. The party was to examine the Antarctic sector between 60° and 90° E, since that was close to the south magnetic pole and no study of ocean currents had been made there. An ancillary station would be built in the nearby Kerguelen Islands: it would be to the Germans what New Zealand and Australia were to the British. However, the Kerguelens were essentially uninhabited, and even at the height of summer the islands were often enshrouded in fog and battered by squalls of rain and sleet.

Drygalski was a scientist, not a glory seeker—how high a latitude he might achieve was of little importance to him. He respected the rights of the British to further investigate the Ross Sea area, and he believed that the Antarctic seas south of the Kerguelens held as many oceanographic secrets waiting to be discovered as did the Weddell Sea. The leader and the other four scientists were highly capable men, and Drygalski later gave high praise to his colleagues. Ernst Vanhöffen (1858–1918), zoologist and botanist, had been with Drygalski in Greenland and aboard the *Valdivia* with Carl Chun: "To know that the entire biological aspect of the expedition would be in his hands was already a relief for me. . . . He was always a rock."[1] Hans Gazert (1870–?) was medical officer, bacteriologist, and meteorologist: "A man of quiet and self-contained nature, rejecting all dissimulation and superficiality, calmly competent, he never failed when called upon to provide comradeship and support. His loyalty to his family, his profession and his duties won him absolute trust."[2] Emil Philippi (1871–1910) was a well-rounded scientist who served as chemist, geologist, and photographer: "His academic career and his travels . . . had given him an intellectual stimulus."[3] Friedrich Bidlingmaier (1875–1914), the youngest of the scientists, was meteorologist and magnetologist: "Bidlingmaier became not only equal to the task he had undertaken: he became master of it. Geomagnetic observations have probably never been made at sea with such totality and precision as he achieved, in spite of the storms and mountainous seas. . . . He never failed us even when his own favourite schemes had to be subordinated to the more general good."[4]

The ship's officers were Capt. Hans Ruser (1863–?), who had been aboard the *Valdivia*, Albert Stehr (chief engineer), Wilhelm Lerche (first officer), Richard Vahsel (1868–1912) (one of two second officers, who later became the controversial captain on Wilhelm Filchner's Antarctic expedition), and Ludwig Ott (second officer). Twenty-two men composed the crew.

The *Gauss* departed Kiel on 11 August 1901 after inspection by the German king and Chancellor Graf von Bülow. The men stopped at the Cape Verde Islands, made a noteworthy 24,000-foot sounding in the Romanche Deep, and crossed the equator, where those—including Drygalski—passing for the first time submitted to a ceremonial tub dunking. In Cape Town, six men were "paid off," five for trouble-making; each was easily replaced. Two Swedes had stowed away, and both proved useful. In all, the crew included three Swedes and two Norwegians.

The party arrived at the Crozet Islands on 25 December. Six men made a first landing on the south coast of Possession Island, a feat neither James Clark Ross nor members of the *Challenger* expedition had been able to carry off. The men were ashore only a few hours as the ship beat back and forth along the coast, waiting anxiously in fog and rain squalls. The area was a paradise of seals, penguins, bird life, and previously unknown plant species.

The men reached the Kerguelens on the last day of the year. A German contingent had already set up the scientific and supply station at Observation Bay. The station was under the direction of the robust and energetic Joseph Enzensperger (1873–1903), a mountaineer and meteorologist with an enthusiastic interest in several branches of science. He had collected dogs, stores, and equipment in Sydney. The *Gauss* party was cheerfully escorted ashore at the station, where they spent a month, setting out again on 31 January 1902. Enzensperger later died of what was thought to be beriberi. Drygalski remarked, "All honour then to his memory, who found death on a lonely island in the service of science!"[5]

The party anchored in Corinthian Bay at Heard Island, long enough for Drygalski and four scientists to go ashore. Drygalski then headed his party south into the pack ice. The ship proceeded slowly through narrow leads among bergs; the scene was sometimes clear, at other times obscured, and sometimes it was a strange world of optical illusions.

On 19 February, a depth sounding showed only 792 feet. Two days later the party viewed to the south a magnificent, ice-covered land rising to a thousand feet, which they named Kaiser Wilhelm II Land (now Wilhelm II Coast). Now the ship was held fast in the sea ice. The crew unsuccessfully tried explosives to loosen the ship; the *Gauss* was locked where it was, forty-six miles from the coast.

The men set up huts on the ice for weather, magnetic, and astronomical observations, drilled holes in the ice for dredging, and gathered rocks and debris from nearby bergs. They were busy, healthy, happy, and awed by the magnificent sunsets and earth shadows. The dogs were chained to keep them from wreaking havoc among the Adélie penguins waddling by. Sledging had to wait until the men were confident in the stability of the floes and the ship's position.

A reconnaissance party of Philippi, Vahsel, and a crewman headed south on 18 March with two sledges, eighteen dogs, and ten days' supplies. The party returned, all well, eight days later, reporting a thousand-foot mountain at 66°40' S latitude. Gaussberg, as they named the spot, was volcanic and inhabited by lichens, mosses, and seabirds.

For further reconnaissance, a hydrogen balloon was lofted on 29 March, Drygalski himself making the first ascent. The day's heat expanded the gas, and the release valves were stiff; Drygalski could have been carried away had the cable broken. He ascended to sixteen hundred feet and saw that Gaussberg was the only ice-free land: ice covered all the terrain rising beyond. Drygalski could see the open pack to the north, the arrangement of ice, and how an escape with the ship could eventually be made. Ruser and Philippi went up in a second and final ascent. Night fell, the gas was let out, and the balloon was packed up, never to be used again. The results of these ascents would determine their future plans.

Two more autumn sledging trips to Gaussberg were made, to erect an igloo and a meteorological hut, and to depot supplies. The last trip was led by Drygalski, who obtained a remarkable view from the summit. "To the south we gazed into infinity. There were no bounds. . . . The mountain was in effect surrounded by a stream of ice . . . unbroken, in all probability, as far as the Pole and beyond. The mountain is but a tiny spot in this desert, and yet how important for us, how fundamental to all the expedition's experi-

Gaussberg
Drygalski, *Zum Kontinent des Eisigen Südens,* 1904

ence! Here we really had rock beneath our feet . . . a point of association between the South Polar Continent and the other regions of the earth, our life and its familiar images."[6]

At Gaussberg, samples of lava, quartz, sandstone, granite, and sulfur were collected. Flocks of snow petrels sheltered in rock crevices and niches. The birds were tame, oblivious to man or dog; food for the dogs was short, so they were put on half rations and caught petrels. On the return, the dogs howled in hunger and discovered by scent alone the drift-covered remains of a seal killed by the first party. The men could not determine their latitude for lack of sun but by luck picked up tracks. The ship had been half buried by snow and drift in a storm.

During the winter, the men busied themselves with science, a few brief sledge journeys to nearby bergs, and an overhaul of the ship's machinery. Nineteen lectures were well received, the topics including emergency medical care in the polar regions, facts about the ship itself, and various branches of science. For entertainment, the men put on a midwinter celebration, four formed a glee club, and they had card games and a library. Drygalski preferred reading history and politics, to remind him of the rest of humanity. Puppies were born: fifty dogs became sixty-seven. Many of the men, despite their occupations, became depressed in the cold and scant daylight, although they fared as well as other wintering parties of the era.

Drygalski began to contemplate how to escape from the ice, and he read with particular interest the circumstances of the *Belgica.* The *Gauss* had to deal with thicker ice still, sixteen to nineteen feet with drifts of up to forty feet. During the *Belgica* expedition dark objects had absorbed enough heat to melt ice, so in June Drygalski began to have all ashes and garbage saved for such a purpose. The order was initially greeted with jibes, but it was later appreciated.

In the middle of September, Drygalski led a four-week journey of eight men, four sledges, and twenty-eight dogs. Early spring weather made the efforts very trying. He divided the group into two parties: one proceeded toward Gaussberg to study the inland ice; the other headed southwest to examine a ridge of compressed blue ice twenty-five miles away. Atop a high, old moraine above Cape Lewald on the western end of Gaussberg, the men built a cairn containing the expedition's history sealed in a bottle, with a German flag alongside. Drygalski made no attempt to travel south of Gaussberg, as there was no clear scientific value in doing so. To reach 72° to 73° S would have been the limit of possibility, and Drygalski could justify neither the time nor the resources.

Spring returned. Seals, emperor and Adélie penguins, skuas, and seabirds became abundant again. Philippi and three men departed on 26 October on a ten-day excursion to extend Drygalski's observations of the nearby blue ice; two more trips were made through early December. The compacted pressure ridges were afloat and sheltered the ship from moving ice, explaining why the ship had at no time experienced any pressure. Emperors and chicks came by in groups, and the men concluded correctly that the birds must breed on the ice, since they had no land access.

Soot from the ship engine's exhaust had been settling nearby and causing the ice to decay. Drygalski now determined to put his ash-and-garbage plan into action and chose the line along which the material was to be strewn. The ship was readied for escape to freedom a mere third of a mile away. Explosives and ice saws had little effect, but the strewn debris, with the help of ocean currents, opened up cracks. Soon pools of water became interconnected, and some of the men entertained themselves paddling about in kayaks. Optimism rose, but on 21 January 1903, a gale carrying heavy drifts covered and closed the pools and cracks as if they had never been. The group resigned itself to a second winter.

Then on 28 January there was unexpected ice movement, and the scene was suddenly shifting bergs and ice floes. The *Gauss* began to drift. All equipment was brought on board. Drygalski had a premonition and dream of emancipation on the night of 7 February, and the next day a strong swell came up. "We suddenly felt two shocks, one upon the other. The first left me holding my cup to my lips, listening attentively, and when the second came it was like a revelation. With a cry of: 'There she goes!' I hurled myself on deck, and with a repetition of the cry the mess emptied and the entire crew assembled as one, as if by order all dressed just as they were. . . . A gully had already opened up."[7] As winds threatened to close the ice about the ship once more, the vessel was maneuvered out.

By 16 March the ship had cleared the ice. Drygalski and Ruser cruised the edge seeking another site at which to spend the next winter, but by early April no safe position was found. With the season far advanced, Drygalski decided at last to forgo another winter in the ice. No longer able to support all the dogs, the men undertook the horrible job of killing some. The dog keeper, Björvik, was so upset that he would not permit Gazert, who arranged the killing, to treat him for an illness.

Soon the party sighted the Kerguelen Islands. The ship arrived at St. Paul and New Amsterdam, where the men saw lush green vegetation for the first time in over a year. Drygalski, eager for the news from which they had been cut off for a year and a half, hailed a Norwegian barque, the first vessel they saw. The scientists hastily wrote up a compendium of reports to send home from Cape Town.

On 9 June, the ship put in at Simonstown, an hour by rail from Cape Town, where the party was warmly received. Drygalski hoped the German government would grant him another year in the south, perhaps on a sub-antarctic island, and he had the support of his officers and scientists. But Drygalski did not get the approval he sought, because, he believed, the expedition's reports were not seriously reviewed. Perhaps his lack of major geographical discoveries or sensational adventures cost him backing. He received word on 2 July to return to Germany. The scientists conducted oceanographic studies to the west, then the party headed home via St. Helena, Ascension Island, and the Azores, arriving in Kiel on 24 November. The *Gauss* was sold to Canada to pay off the expedition's debts.[8]

The scientists' achievements won high praise. Twenty volumes of reports were generated from 1905 to 1931, fourteen of them concerning zoology, botany, and bacteriology and describing 1,440 species endemic to the Antarctic. The expedition provided the strongest evidence to date for the existence of the Antarctic Convergence, the interface of Antarctic and temperate waters and the boundary between polar and temperate ocean life. Explorations along the Antarctic coast had authenticated six hundred miles of new continental coastline at the latitude of the Antarctic Circle. Penguin vocalizations were recorded for the first time.

The expedition's accomplishments were overshadowed in the public eye, however, by contemporary voyages achieving higher southern latitudes. Drygalski felt forced to defend himself. "After a year spent in the same place, we could say we knew what Nature offered there. . . . The lack of . . . perils and adventures has been frequently regretted, although we said nothing about them in order to concentrate on positive experiences, such as how to overcome events rather than fall victim to them. Every polar expedition has, beside all the fine things, a list of privations, of conflict with the powerful compulsion of a superior Nature. These are not to be dismissed in arrogant fashion, but neither are they to be paraded in the front line. Finally, the most frequently voiced complaint was about our failure to reach a record high latitude, an accusation which was itself a complete failure to recognize that the *Gauss* was working alone in a totally new region, and had therefore found and made public totally new discoveries. This appeared to be different from what was happening elsewhere, but it was no less of an achievement. . . . We are pleased with what we did."[9]

14

Otto Nordenskjöld and the Swedish Antarctic Expedition (1901–1904)

Vetenskapens bjudande kraf, att ingen del af jorden skulle få förblifva oberörd af undersökningar, var det som förde vår lilla detta den yttersta söderns land.

[The demand of science, that no part of the globe shall remain untouched by the hand of investigation, was the force that drew our little band to the land of the farthest south.]

Otto Nordenskjöld, *Antarctic*

Nils Otto Gustaf Nordenskjöld (1869–1928), geologist and lecturer at the University of Uppsala, led this remarkable Swedish expedition that became a complex tale of courage and survival. Nordenskjöld had planned to explore new areas about the Antarctic Peninsula on both the west and east sides, to penetrate as far south as possible, and to leave a wintering party of six men at a suitable, snow-free site from which further exploration and scientific studies could be carried out. The party would be picked up when the ship returned the following season. The nonwintering men would conduct scientific studies in the Falkland Islands, South Georgia, and Tierra del Fuego during the autumn and winter. Little could any of them have imagined the drama that was to unfold.

Nordenskjöld was thirty-six years old when the adventure began. Capt. Carl A. Larsen was forty-one and already experienced in the region of the Antarctic Peninsula. Some of the other twenty-seven men were Johann Gunnar Andersson (1874–1960) (who would head the ship's party after Nordenskjöld was landed in the south), Samuel A. Duse (1873–1933) (lieutenant in the Norwegian artillery, cartography), K. A. Andersson and Axel

Ohlin (zoology), Carl Skottsberg (1880–1963) (botany), Gösta Bodman (hydrography, meteorology, and magnetics), Eric Ekelöf (bacteriology, medical officer), and the American Frank Wilbert Stokes (1858–1955) (artist).

Dependent on private contributors, the expedition had considerably less funding than the government-supported British and German expeditions. The *Antarctic*, Bull's old ship, departed Göteborg on 16 October 1901, to the well wishes of an enthusiastic crowd. During a brief stop at Falmouth, England, coal was loaded, and Nordenskjöld traveled to London. There he was entertained by Sir Clements Markham at a Royal Geographical Society luncheon and received personal greetings from William S. Bruce. Bruce was preparing for his Scottish National Antarctic Expedition, which would be operating within several hundred miles of the Swedish expedition; the two leaders agreed that one would attempt to rescue the other in case of distress. The *Antarctic* left England, put in a brief stop at St. Vincent, and sailed directly on to Buenos Aires.

The director of the Argentine Observatory on Staten Island, in a communication to Nordenskjöld the previous year, had requested that an Argentine naval officer accompany the expedition. Nordenskjöld agreed, hoping that would induce South American nations to become more involved in Antarctic polar research. Now, in Buenos Aires, Nordenskjöld learned that the Argentineans wanted their man to be a member of the wintering party. The Swedish leader kept his hesitation to himself until he met the man, José M. Sobral (1880–1961), a naval sublieutenant selected by the Minister of the Navy. Nordenskjöld developed an immediate, strong liking for Sobral and willingly included him. In return the Argentineans promised Nordenskjöld full support, amply demonstrated later in the course of the expedition. Sobral served as assistant to the Swedish scientific staff, and he eventually wrote an account of the expedition for his countrymen.[1]

The expedition called at Staten Island and arrived in the Falkland Islands on 30 December. They received the governor's hospitality. Dogs that had died in the heat of the tropics were replaced, and sheep were taken on board for food. After a three-day stay, the *Antarctic* headed south. King George Island in the South Shetland Islands was sighted on 10 January 1902. Nordenskjöld was moved to comment, "The overpowering feelings cannot be described which were awakened in me when this long-wished-for land thus suddenly rose before my view. . . . A loneliness and a wildness reigned here such as could, perhaps, be found nowhere else on earth."[2] At Nelson Island, Nordenskjöld and five officers rowed ashore to a beach covered with

Weddell seals, penguins, and birds. The men hiked inland, staying a few hours to make rock and plant collections.

The party sailed toward the Trinity Peninsula and entered the Orléans Strait between the mainland and Trinity Island, an area that Nordenskjöld had determined to examine. The Orléans Strait was known to be between the Trinity Peninsula to the north and Graham Land to the south, but at the time it was unknown if the strait was a bay or channel. They proceeded south: "We were now sailing a sea across which none had hitherto voyaged.... We pressed onward, seized by that almost feverish eagerness which can only be felt by an explorer who stands upon the threshold of the great unknown."[3] They pressed on for two days, hoping to determine the relationship of Orléans Strait to the Gerlache Strait further south still, and made two more landings, but the answer had to wait until the following season when the *Antarctic* visited the area again. At that time, Larsen found that the Orléans and Gerlache Straits were confluent, and the Trinity Peninsula and Danco Land were connected. Nordenskjöld later considered these the most significant geographical discoveries of the expedition.

The *Antarctic* now sailed northeast along the coast of the Trinity Peninsula, turned southwest, and was the first ship to navigate the channel between the Trinity Peninsula and north-lying Joinville Island to the east side of the Antarctic Peninsula. Nordenskjöld named the strait Antarctic Sound after his ship. The party discovered another sound that divided what they named D'Urville Island from Joinville Island; the ship navigated that channel the following season. Nordenskjöld noted a broad, snow-free shore in a bay on the coast of the Trinity Peninsula that led into a beautiful glacial valley; he immediately recognized its potential as a depot or wintering site. He didn't stop, but Hope Bay later figured prominently in the story of the expedition.

To the east of the Antarctic Peninsula, a landing was made on Paulet Island. There the men spent a long day noting the island's volcanic character, observing the enormous Adélie penguin colony, and dredging the coastal waters for marine plants and animals. (The men could have had no idea that Paulet Island would save the lives of twenty of their party the following year.) They proceeded south across Erebus and Terror Gulf, encountering enormous icebergs, and left a depot on the northern coast of Seymour Island. Further southward progress was stopped at 66°15' S by a perpendicular barrier 130 feet high extending as far as the eye could see: Oscar II Coast loomed in the distance. Following the ice edge eastward into the Weddell Sea but making no significant progress south, the men turned the ship at 63°30' S, 45°7' W to conserve coal and to set up winter quarters before the season ended. Sidney Herbert Bay (now Herbert Sound), with its magnificent glaciers and red-brown hills, was the last area explored by ship that season.

For a wintering site, Seymour Island was attractive for its many landing places and deep, ice-free valleys; but nearby Snow Hill Island (often referred to simply as Snow Hill) had a broad, low shore, excellent building sites, and more fossils (including ammonites, the first found in the Antarctic), which made it the better choice. The surrounding hills and walls of ice appeared to provide safety from the weather, a protection that later proved deceptive. Nordenskjöld had already selected Bodman to be his second in command; Sobral, Ole Jonassen, Ekelöf, and Gustav Åkerlund (the youngest) composed the remainder of the wintering party. All expedition members but one were willing to stay; Stokes backed out because the wintering site was too far north for the auroral displays he had hoped to portray in his artwork.

To bring supplies and coal ashore, two whale boats were bridged with planks to make a "raft," which was towed back and forth by rowboat during a three-day operation. Two boats were left for the wintering party's use. The men first erected a magnetic observatory to provide shelter while they built the main hut. Construction proceeded rapidly; the living quarters measured twenty-one by thirteen and a half feet. After the men said their good-byes, the *Antarctic* had a very rough passage in a terrifying storm in the Bransfield Strait en route to the Falklands. Larsen and company spent the autumn and winter charting and conducting scientific studies in South Georgia and Tierra del Fuego.

Nordenskjöld contemplated his surroundings after the ship departed: "I stood there amid the grandeur of the scenery, while the sun sank slowly behind the haughty, ice-covered crown of Mount Haddington [on nearby James Ross Island], and gilded the ice-field far away on the eastern horizon. No sound was to be heard around me; one could not be more alone, more isolated. This desert spot is to be, for a long time forward, home, everything, for me, for my companions! Here we shall stand face to face with Nature in its mightiest majesty, and combatting with it, shall strive to make it reveal to us its many secrets. Shall we succeed? At the moment I felt a strong faith in the future, everything lay bright and promising before me, I felt full of gratitude at being at last able to begin our real work."[4]

Nordenskjöld, Sobral, and Jonassen made a short reconnaissance journey south with dogs in March 1902 to establish a depot. They were forced to

The Snow Hill wintering party (left to right, top then bottom):
Jonassen, Ekelöf, Åkerlund, Bodman, Nordenskjöld, Sobral
Nordenskjöld, *Antarctic,* 1904

steer their boat in a winding course through the sea ice, which in places was piled so high under pressure that they had to disembark and climb to reconnoiter. All the while, the tide jostled the ice in a groaning, crackling roar. The men camped on a solid ice foot attached to shore half a mile from Cape Hamilton (now Hamilton Point) on James Ross Island. They noted how variable the barometer could be and how storms could appear suddenly. One storm fractured the trusted ice on which they camped, and water flooded the tent. To their credit, the men established that Admiralty Bay was properly Admiralty Sound, and Snow Hill an island. Nordenskjöld, Ekelöf, and Jonassen made a short sledge journey at the end of April to Seymour Island to check a signal post and look for fossils. They forgot a lamp, realized the three-man sleeping bag was not their style, and lost all their butter to an unrestrained dog.

Soon Snow Hill was racked by autumn storms lasting days at a time. The living quarters were secured by wires, but the wooden magnetic hut was dashed to splinters. Several dogs died in the storms, raising the men's anxieties for the coming season's sledgework. A special house was therefore built to shelter the animals. A June storm packing high winds tossed one of the boats more than seventy feet; it landed upside down, its oars, thwarts, and planks smashed and scattered, the zinc sheeting torn away.

The men busied themselves with the study of meteorology, bacteriology, biology, and tides. Their free time was taken up in reading, amicable conversation, and as many celebrations as they could invent. Burning coal and blubber kept the hut cozy, but there was still a temperature gradient of 20 degrees between head height and floor; as a result, the men gave their feet special attention. Eventually, everything in the hut took on a grayish cast from the soot of burning fuel. When warm weather thawed the ice on the walls and roof, the hut interior became a sopping mess. Food rations were unlimited: no one imagined having to reserve anything for a second winter.

During interludes between the storms, the men enjoyed taking walks to break the monotony. They were far enough north to have several hours of usable though wan daylight even in June. Nordenskjöld turned philosophical during the calms. "The long row of icebergs, glimmering in the last rays of the sun, resembled white castles in an enchanted city. . . . When the dark came on . . . I went out alone a little way on the ice until the camp became invisible, until nothing met the eye but the dark outline of that precipitous coast, the far-stretching ramparts of snow and towering blocks of ice. Not a breath of air was in motion, not a sound could be heard. . . . The mind grasped how infinitely small was the rôle played by a chance visit of a few men and their attendants to this desert world of ice."[5]

In July, Nordenskjöld, Sobral, Jonassen, and Åkerlund made a short journey at minus 30 degrees Fahrenheit to Admiralty Sound to test clothing and equipment for a longer winter expedition, and for charting, photography, and rock collecting. In a sudden, brief storm their tent poles collapsed. Undaunted, Nordenskjöld immediately planned a longer journey: the ship was due back in November, and time was running out. He had only a few serviceable dogs, but he was eager to investigate the coast of the Antarctic Peninsula to the south. Departing 30 August on a preliminary depot journey, Nordenskjöld, Sobral, and Jonassen were barely away from Snow Hill when two of the three dogs broke free in a storm and scampered back to the hut. The men aborted the journey and planned another start for late September. In the meantime the men refurbished the sledges, reconstructed the tent, prepared new canvas sacks, organized the scientific equipment, and weighed and sorted food rations.

Embarking on what would be the most significant sledging journey of the expedition, the same trio set out for Oscar II Coast with two sledges and five dogs. Their clothing was made of reindeer, guanaco, and canvas. Food was pemmican, meat biscuits, bacon, lentils and peas, meat-chocolate, bread, butter, sugar, and coffee. By 8 October the men had covered the first eighty-four miles and reached Robertson Island, noting its volcanic nature. They climbed the island and viewed a cluster of nunataks to the west. They proved that the Trinity Peninsula and Oscar II Coast were connected. A low ice terrace or barrier attached to the peninsula intercepted Robertson Island, its edge swinging north-northwest and south-southwest; traveling over the ice sheet, the three men negotiated its inconstant and sometimes chaotic surfaces. Soon the southern extension of Oscar II Coast loomed ahead. A landing, the first on the peninsula's east side, was made on 18 October. There, at about 65°57' S, 62°17' W, Nordenskjöld's party camped at the base of a mountain, and the leader honored Carsten Borchgrevink by naming this nunatak after him. A nearby narrow, ice-filled sound running westward was named Richthofen Valley (now Pass).

The men now began their return to the hut but had to wait for the weather to clear. During that wait, a storm split the tent, Jonassen injured his arm, and the dogs ate all the pemmican; the party hastened their return. The men followed the land more closely and made for Cape Desire, which they renamed Cape Disappointment when uneven ice and crevasses blocked them. Poor visibility and snow blindness hampered them further. Supplies were running low, and a storm confined the men to the tent for two days. Nordenskjöld lamented, "It is like a prison . . . to lie thus uninterruptedly in the same sleeping-bag with another becomes almost a torture. One feels almost like a fever patient, lying there without occupation, staring at the roof and making the spots in the cloth assume strange forms and . . . dreaming of the past and the future and, above all, of action. . . . I dream of an ordered and thorough investigation of the unknown and most interesting region which is the field of our operations. . . . It is not easy to reconcile oneself to lying here uselessly and listen to the howling of the storm, and to know nothing but that our provisions are coming to an end and that our poor dogs are becoming weaker."[6] By 31 October the three men were on the sea ice again. They picked up their depot and made a thirty-eight-and-a-half-mile final run on their last day out, arriving at the hut with the dawn at half past one on 4 November. Unkempt and exhausted, each having lost about fifteen pounds despite full rations, the three men felt compensated for their struggle by their considerable accomplishments on the thirty-three-day, four-hundred-mile journey.

The men made several brief journeys to fill time before the ship's return. The most notable was the four-day sledging trip that Bodman, Ekelöf, and Jonassen made to Cockburn and Seymour Islands to check the sign post, collect penguin eggs and cormorant meat, and gather fossils. The party's contribution of fossilized ammonites, plants, ferns, and firs added considerably to the scope of the collections made nine years earlier by Larsen.

The ship, however, did not appear. On 9 January 1903, Jonassen climbed a nearby hill and all around saw only closely packed ice. Relief seemed impossible, and stores for another winter were inadequate. Fuel use was cut. Four hundred penguins, thirty seals, and skuas were taken for food and fuel. Nordenskjöld wrote: "It would be difficult to imagine a more disgusting task. . . . It was only bitter need which could compel us to this horrible slaughter; nothing else could have prevailed upon me to take part in it. It may seem difficult in other countries to be obliged to kill animals in numbers, but it becomes still more repulsive here, where the creatures have not yet learned to fear man."[7]

A storm on 18 February froze the sea, eliminating any chance of rescue that season, and the men settled down to their fate of a second winter. Their meteorological observations compensated, in part, for the confinement, as they documented substantial differences between the two winters. For example, on one occasion it rained heavily all day, and on another, a large drop in barometric pressure brought a hurricane-force storm. The men relied on work, short sledging journeys, and various amusements to maintain harmony and sanity. "Although the scenery which surrounded us was of uncommon interest . . . with what delight should we not have greeted one little blade of grass? . . . Red, green and yellow—that is, the colours which more than all others, have a stimulating influence upon the senses—were almost entirely wanting. . . . One saw only white, blue, brown, and those almost preternaturally fine, pale, pure tints which are so characteristic of winter in Polar lands. . . . They attract the beholder with wondrous power, although they seem to radiate a something which resembles the chill of death."[8]

To escape the monotony of the camp, on 29 September Nordenskjöld and Jonassen left on a journey with dogs and thirty days' provisions. Eighteen miles out, at Lockyer Island, not only did they realize that half their bread had been left behind but, in addition, a storm blew the tent away from over their heads and a loosened pole ripped the tent cloth. The two were obliged to return to the hut for repairs and made a fresh start on 4 October.

They now discovered the Prince Gustav Channel, approaching it from the south. Nordenskjöld described the magnificent scenery and lay of the land, including the extension of Oscar II Coast to the northwest and the cliffs of James Ross Island to the east. By 12 October, they had traveled the entire west coast of James Ross Island and turned east to continue along the north coast of Vega Island, to check for a possible crossing to Paulet Island.

Approaching a prominent headland, Nordenskjöld and Jonassen saw in the distance little black specks they at first thought were penguins. But Nordenskjöld had a premonition, and to their astonishment, the specks soon resolved themselves in the field glass to be men. The parties approached each other, and Nordenskjöld and Jonassen had an extraordinary but humorous encounter with J. G. Andersson, Duse, and Toralf Grunden, who were black with soot and unrecognizable. In honor of the reunion, the spot was named Cape Well-met. Nordenskjöld and Jonassen now realized that something must have gone terribly wrong with the *Antarctic,* but they would know the full story only much later.

Before the ill-fated ship had headed south from the Falkland Islands on 5 November 1902, letters were sent to the secretary of the Swedish Anthropological and Geographical Society and to the Swedish-Norwegian consul general in Buenos Aires, requesting relief if the ship did not return as expected. The ship's party visited the South Shetland Islands and carried out the charting and scientific studies in the Gerlache and Orléans Straits previously mentioned. On 5 December, Larsen decided it was time to retrieve the Snow Hill party.

He had expected a mere two- or three-day trip, but contrary to the previous season, Antarctic Sound was now blocked with ice, barring passage to Snow Hill. Five men went ashore and ascended Mount Bransfield to reconnoiter and saw only a solid ice sheet to the east in Erebus and Terror Gulf. Larsen tried valiantly but unsuccessfully for several days to get through, directing his crew personally from the crow's nest. A new plan was adopted. On 29 December 1902, J. G. Andersson, Duse, and Grunden, a Norwegian sailor, were put ashore at Hope Bay to bring the Snow Hill party there, so all could be picked up by the ship. Larsen realized that this might be impossible, so he would sail north around Joinville Island to try picking up the Snow Hill party from the other side. The Hope Bay party quickly established a depot and headed for Snow Hill.

The men sledged to the east side of the peninsula, traversed the difficult, frozen sea to Vega Island, and then, to their intense disappointment, found open water preventing any further approach to Snow Hill. They returned to Hope Bay, arriving 13 January 1903, to await the ship. Andersson spent the time collecting stone slabs containing fossilized ferns and pines, remnants of the peninsula's ancient, verdant past. One month later the three men still had not been rescued and were increasingly uncertain whether they would be. So they built a winter shelter, a small hut of stones, planks, and a sledge, with a tarpaulin as a roof. A freezing mixture of snow and seawater served as plaster. For extra weather protection, the men set up a tent as sleeping quarters inside the hut, with penguin skins as flooring.

Still the ship did not arrive. The men secured about seven hundred penguins for their food cache and settled in for a difficult winter, burning blubber for heat. Fuel ran short, and they reduced meals to two per day. Dependent mostly on penguin and seal meat, their limited bread and twice-weekly porridge rations were cherished luxuries. The men increased their food variety each Sunday. They celebrated the first Sunday of each month, their three birthdays (which all occurred during their confinement), and several other special occasions with a "dram" apiece of Holland gin. Gratefully, temperatures inside the tent remained fairly constant at only a few degrees below freezing. The men grew accustomed to it and only seldom suffered the wet results of a thaw, but the floor and sleeping bags were soaked in a heavy August rainfall.

Grunden kept up spirits with his chanteys. Thanking the cook after each meal was an important courtesy. Despite the congeniality, the winter was exceedingly arduous. Andersson wrote: "Chat, jokes, and tales were rare oases in a desert of intellectual nothingness." But the men achieved "the knowledge of the strong power that warm and honest friendship has, to proudly subdue the dark might of isolation and of extreme distress."[9]

Spring arrived. The men knew that if the *Antarctic* and all hands had been lost, no one would know where they were, so the three struck out for Snow Hill on 29 September. They arrived at Vega Island across the frozen sea, and in the course of their travel proved that Vega Island was separate from James Ross Island by showing that Herbert Sound was connected to Prince Gustav Channel. Spring weather had been harsh; Duse's toes were badly frostbitten. On 12 October, the men had their unexpected and memorable reunion with Nordenskjöld and Jonassen at Cape Well-met. Nordenskjöld was in "stupefied amazement" that it had been possible for the Hope Bay party to survive. "The one feeling that for a long time overpowered all the others . . . was that of undivided sympathy for these men who had suffered so much for our sakes."[10] The entire group of five proceeded to Snow Hill together, where a celebration and banquet were held. Nordenskjöld was eager to continue exploring nearby islands until relief arrived, and several short expeditions were launched.

The eighth of November 1903 proved to be a most significant day at Snow Hill, one of miraculous coincidences. Seven men were at the hut—Bodman and Åkerlund were away—yet four figures were now seen approaching from the direction of Seymour Island. After some suspenseful anticipation, the extra men proved to be two Argentinean naval officers, Commo. Julian Irizar and Lt. J. Jalour of the *Uruguay*. They had come to relieve the overdue party. The Snow Hill party now believed that their comrades on the *Antarctic* were likely dead, but they managed to give the Argentinean officers a banquet in the shabby hut.

Then, at about half past ten the same evening, the dogs began to bark as six people approached the hut. Astonishingly, the men were Larsen and five companions from the *Antarctic*. Nordenskjöld exclaimed, "No pen can describe the boundless joy of this first moment. . . . I learned at once that our dear old ship was no more in existence, but for the instant I could feel nothing but joy when I saw amongst us these men, on whom I had only a few minutes before been thinking with feelings of the greatest despondency. . . . A young and able seaman of their number had died. . . . All the others had preserved both life and health. . . . We conducted the newcomers in triumph to the building."[11] The entire group departed Snow Hill in a rough trek over the sea ice to the *Uruguay,* where they were cheered on board. The Swedish scientists picked up their collections from depots at Seymour Island, and Irizar proceeded to Paulet Island to pick up the Swedes' castaway mates, arriving there on 11 November.

And so the men of the *Antarctic* told their saga. Larsen, with great difficulty, had brought the ship around Joinville Island after dropping off the Hope Bay party, but the vessel, unable to withstand the pressure of the closing pack ice, began to leak. At first the pump had been able to compensate, its constant whirring an unpleasant reminder of their danger. But by 12 February, the crippled ship was not responding to the helm. A third of the keel was gone, planks were lost, and leaks were irreparable. Paulet Island was the closest landfall, twenty-five miles away across the sea ice.

The *Antarctic* was abandoned. Skottsberg related: "Everything is ready. All of us are gathered in the gun-room—for the last time! Proudly has she lived, proudly shall she die. . . . Thanks for what has been! We go up on deck . . . a last look at the low room where so many plans have been discussed, so many scientific questions debated, so many amusing stories related, so much happy laughter heard. Good-bye to it for ever!"[12] The twenty men watched solemnly as the ship, with all their scientific collections, disappeared beneath the icy ocean surface.

Paulet Island was a land of bleak prospects. The men realized that no one would know they were there. They would have to survive a winter and then venture out in spring for help. The men garnered their courage and resolve. They made their way, struggling from floe to floe, at times carving a path with their axes, with their equipment, over a ton of food, 240 liters of petroleum, the whale boats, and the cat. The drift of the ice was usually—and very providentially—in their favor.

They arrived at Paulet Island on 28 February. "Who can describe the feelings with which we heard the boats touch the shore? What joy, what happiness there was. . . . Does not this success bear encouragement enough with it to make us fall to work with renewed vigour, and to make us determined, in spite of every difficulty, to persevere to the very end?"[13] As the season drew to a close, the stranded men secured eleven hundred of the last remaining penguins plus occasional seals for food and fuel. These creatures represented their only chance for survival.

For their hut, the men chose a site with natural weather protection up the sloping beach. They fashioned the building of flat basaltic stones from the

The stone hut on Paulet Island
Nordenskjöld, *Antarctic*, 1904

volcanic surroundings and old nonodorous penguin guano. "Paulet Island architecture,"[14] they called it proudly. The hut measured thirty-four by twenty-two feet. Two small windows allowed in some light. A man had to stoop to enter and could barely stand erect at the highest point. Two stone beds seven feet long and twenty feet wide accommodated ten men each. The common areas were the kitchen and a four-foot-wide corridor between the beds. Their diet was penguin with occasional seal and fish. Their water, unpleasant tasting and yellow-green, came from a crater lake below the penguin colony. Their clothing was adequate, except for the foot gear, which frequently left them with cold feet. Walking on the beach and the sea ice in good weather was the only outdoor entertainment. "One grows stupid lying in the bags all day."[15]

Food and rescue dominated their conversations. Boredom was constant. The men had only a few books, and interest over taking the morning temperature readings and anticipating the morning coffee or tea took up only a small amount of their time. The temperature in the hut usually stood a few degrees above freezing. The interior stank horribly of burning blubber and the putrefying penguin skins that some men used to soften their beds of stone. Ole Wennersgaard weakened and died of a heart condition on 7 June. All the men could do was to give him temporary burial in his bag in a snowdrift until he could be properly interred after the spring thaw. The solstice was an emotional turning point: the men's spirits rose as the sun became stronger, their dreams of emancipation coming closer to realization.

The ice broke up in October, and on the last day of that month Larsen and five crewmen set out from Paulet Island for Hope Bay in a whaleboat. They reached their destination on 4 November, five weeks after the Hope Bay party had left; they found a sketch map to Snow Hill left by Andersson. Antarctic Sound was open, so three days later Larsen's party launched a boat journey, using the tarpaulin from the Hope Bay hut for shelter inside the boat and a tent pole for a mast. About twelve to fifteen miles short of Snow Hill the men were stopped by ice and so covered the remaining distance in a seven-hour march. Larsen recorded the jubilant reunion: "Everybody came hurrying out of the house. The reader can easily picture our mutual gladness, but we were quite astounded . . . that an Argentine vessel lay off the island. . . . Overpowered with joy . . . we thought how glad our comrades on Paulet Island would be. . . . I met with the heartiest reception imaginable on the part of Captain Irizar and all his officers. . . . It was really affecting to be thus greeted by the representatives of a foreign nation."[16]

Meanwhile, the remaining fourteen men at Paulet Island, unsure of rescue, short on food, and finding themselves amid tens of thousands of penguins in breeding season, secured six thousand eggs for their larder. And then, on 11 November, eleven days after Larsen set out for relief, an uncommon sound penetrated the night. Skottsberg recounted what happened next: "I must have been dreaming. — The sound is repeated — it must be so — it can be nothing else — *the boat is here!* I am out of the bag. I thump at the sleepers beside me: 'Can't you hear it is the boat — *the boat* — THE BOAT! HURRAH!' Arms wave wildly in the air; the shouts are so deafening that the penguins awake and join in the cries; the cat, quite out of her wits, runs round and round the walls of the room; everybody tries to be the first out of doors, and in a minute we are all out on the hillside, half-dressed and grisly to behold. Hurrah!"[17] And later, sailing away, Skottsberg reflected sadly, even yearningly, "I see Paulet Island disappear behind the dazzling inland-ice— disappear maybe for ever. Has it not been my home?"[18]

The relief ship visited Hope Bay, and Nordenskjöld and J. G. Andersson went ashore in threatening weather to pick up the fossil and geological collections that Andersson had made; in their hurry, they had to leave some valuable specimens behind.[19] "The ruined hut ... appeared little more than an ordinary stone-heap, but ... it bore witness for the future of what human beings had done in this place. Round about swarmed the members of the large colony of penguins, glad, no doubt, at once more being undisputed rulers of their ice-covered world."[20] Nordenskjöld, in gratitude to the Argentineans, named two nearby islands after Irizar and the relief ship.

In Buenos Aires, the party transferred to the German steamer *Tijuca* for the final leg home to Stockholm, with stops in Madeira, Boulogne, Hamburg, and Copenhagen along the way. The men were greeted with cheers, flowers, and a choir in Malmö, their first stop in Sweden. Thus ended an expedition remarkable not only for its geographical and scientific contributions but also for the courage, ingenuity, and perseverance of its men.

15

WILLIAM S. BRUCE AND THE
SCOTTISH NATIONAL ANTARCTIC EXPEDITION
(1902–1904)

While "Science" was the talisman of the Expedition, "Scotland" was emblazoned on its flag.
>   William S. Bruce, *The Voyage of the "Scotia"*

WITH HIS SLIGHT STOOP and loose-fitting clothing, William Speirs Bruce
(1867–1921) appeared too delicate for any demanding occupation, let alone
the leadership of an Antarctic expedition. Modest and shy, with an intense
dislike of publicity and contempt for commercialism, he was not the kind of
person one would imagine could raise funds for a serious project. Indeed, he
was able to enlist but few large donors for his Antarctic expedition; were it
not for the Coats brothers, James and Andrew, who contributed £30,400 of
the £36,405 budget, the expedition would have been nothing more than an
idea Bruce had incubated for seven years.

When the expedition finally returned to Scotland, Bruce, again overly
modest and more intent on devoting his personal and financial resources to
seeing the scientific reports come to publication, refused to write a popular
narrative of the expedition. He believed that his expedition, lacking pole-
seeking sensationalism, would arouse little public interest or sentiment. The
story of the expedition was finally written by three of the scientists. It might
seem impossible that such an individual could have been assertive and
charismatic enough to become the leader of a major expedition, but in truth
Bruce was eminently qualified; his reclusive nature belied his determination
and endurance. His adherence to moral principles and his kindliness of
manner engendered respect and affection from the men who served under
him, even if he was most comfortable only when alone on his night watch.

Bruce was born in London of Scots ancestors and spent his childhood in
London. He was an oceanographer by profession, having developed an early

interest in natural history that ultimately prevailed over the study of medicine, which he undertook briefly at the encouragement of his father. Bruce had been a member of the Dundee expedition to the Antarctic in 1892–93 and the Jackson–Harmsworth expedition to Franz Josef Land in 1896–97; he visited Spitzbergen in 1898 in the significant company of Andrew Coats. On these adventures he obtained experience in numerous branches of science.

Bruce made efforts to return to the Antarctic as soon as he came back from the Dundee expedition: he enlisted on Bull's expedition but failed to arrive in Melbourne in time to join the ship.[1] He turned his attention to organizing an Antarctic expedition of his own but struggled unsuccessfully for support in London and Edinburgh. Bruce was not lacking determination, however, and his proposal for a Scottish National Antarctic Expedition was publicly announced by Sir John Murray, of *Challenger* renown and president of the Royal Scottish Geographical Society, at its meeting in Edinburgh on 22 March 1900.[2]

The concept of a Scottish expedition at a time when Belgium, England, Sweden, and Germany had all committed themselves to Antarctic exploration was supported widely in Scotland, and the Royal Society of Edinburgh, the Royal Scottish Geographical Society, and the Perthshire Society of Natural Science all approved. Andrew Coats was first to step forward, with a contribution of £5,000; James Coats, who ultimately contributed a total of £23,400, made an initial donation of £6,000, and the expedition was soon well under way. Sir Clements Markham, president of England's Royal Geographical Society, architect of Scott's expedition, and self-appointed dean of Antarctic affairs, was critical of Bruce, just as he had been of Borchgrevink. Markham felt that he deserved to be consulted and was currently engaged in the planning of Scott's expedition. Despite the friction Markham engendered, Scott and Bruce were quite cordial with each other. Bruce decided to confine his soliciting to Scotland, which made his expedition a truly Scottish affair, but the restriction significantly limited his potential contributions.

Bruce chose the Weddell Sea as the objective of his hydrographic investigations because little exploration had been performed there. He planned to study wildlife in the South Orkney Islands, with the islands serving as the launching point into the Weddell Sea. No land was known within the southern recesses of the Weddell Sea—that is, from the Antarctic Peninsula to Enderby Land. Only Weddell, Morrell, and Ross had penetrated beyond 70° S latitude there. Perhaps the highest possible latitude anywhere in the Southern Hemisphere was attainable by ship in the Weddell Sea, although

Bruce was well aware of the severe difficulties of ice navigation in that area.

After consulting with Fridtjof Nansen, and with Colin Archer, builder of the *Fram,* which had carried Nansen to his farthest north, Bruce purchased the 238-ton, 140-foot Norwegian barque *Hekla* for £2,620. The ship was transported to Troon, where it was overhauled at the Ailsa Shipbuilding Company. Masts, bowsprit, hull, and rotten wood needed replacement. Repairs were initially estimated to run £5,000 but in the end cost much more: by then it was too late to give up. The famous naval architect G. L. Watson gave his and his firm's services to the expedition free of charge. Frustrations abounded, and, according to R. N. Rudmose Brown (1879–1957), the expedition botanist who later became Bruce's biographer, "The best thing to do with the Hekla, in Mr. Watson's opinion, was 'to fill her with stones and take her to Ailsa Craig and sink her.'"[3] The repair work was completed in August 1902, and the ship was renamed *Scotia.* The vessel was capable of eight knots but was most coal efficient at three-quarters that speed. It had massive wooden reinforcements; excellent lighting, ventilation, laboratories, and equipment; and a 36,000-foot dredging cable attached to a powerful steam winch. The *Scotia* proved highly sea- and ice-worthy and was, after all the hardships of its restoration, one of the finest ships to ply Antarctic waters at the turn of the century.

Sir John Murray hosted a farewell dinner for the members of the expedition. Fully aware of the difficulties the small, isolated group would encounter in a remote and hostile locale, Murray told them, "You are to do battle with the fiercest forces of nature in the most forbidding region that our planet affords. I hope you will emerge victoriously. While engaged in that struggle you will be cabined and confined to a company of yourselves. That is equally terrible."[4] Bruce selected Thomas Robertson to the post of ship's captain. Robertson had twenty years of Arctic experience and had been captain of the *Active* in the Dundee expedition to the Antarctic. Although authority was divided between the two men, they worked together in remarkable harmony.

In all, the party consisted of Bruce, seven staff members, the ship's officers, and a crew of twenty-five men. The staff included Bruce himself (hydrography, zoology), Brown (botany), R. C. Mossman (1870–?) (meteorology, magnetics), J. H. Harvey Pirie (1878–?) (geology, bacteriology, medical officer), D. W. Wilton (zoology), Alistair Ross (taxidermy), and William Cuthbertson (artist). Unencumbered by committees, each scientist was entrusted to gather equipment and supplies for his respective branch of scientific investigation. In a rare, passionate moment, Bruce wrote about the venture that was about to unfold: "While 'Science' was the talisman of the Expedition, 'Scotland' was emblazoned on its flag; and it may be that, in endeavouring to serve humanity by adding another link to the golden chain of science, we have also shown that the nationality of Scotland is a power that must be reckoned with."[5]

The men sailed from the Clyde on 2 November 1902, making stops in Dublin, Madeira, and the Cape Verde Islands, then proceeding south off the South American coast. They spent three weeks in the Falklands doing scientific work and restowing the ship and then departed for the South Orkney Islands. They encountered the pack at the relatively northerly latitude of 61° S after an especially cold winter by Falkland standards. Beautiful but menacing bergs appeared out of the mist to welcome them into Antarctic waters.

The South Orkney Islands were sighted on 4 February, and a landing, the first since Dumont d'Urville, was made on Saddle Island, where they found chinstrap penguins and nesting seabirds. The party departed later that same day for a deep run into the Weddell Sea—perhaps too optimistically, for the pack ice was formidable, and the ship did not cross the Antarctic Circle until 18 February. Now in open water, the men were cheerful again. "Our hopes of a rapid run south are now strong: [we] are beginning to experience that excitement which is inevitably associated with the advent of unexplored lands and seas."[6] Two days later, however, they were halted in close pack and had no choice but to head east. The next day they received an emotional lift in passing 70° S, but after a week's battle they had achieved no more than 70°25'. Bruce decided it was time to head north to set up winter quarters at the South Orkney Islands. The ship fought its way in a closing season of increasing cold and lengthening nights.

The party arrived in the South Orkney Islands on 21 March and spent four days searching for a safe harbor amid gloom and poor visibility, high winds, and the repeated threat of offshore rocks and bergs. At last a good anchorage was found on the south side of Laurie Island, a spot they named Scotia Bay. "Needless to say, the prospect of a quiet night after such a trying week as we had experienced was much appreciated, and there were few on board who did not sleep the sleep of the just."[7] All were satisfied with the site, spectacularly scenic with bold headlands and precipitous peaks. The tallest point on Laurie Island was only about fifteen hundred feet, but the island's striking contours made up for its relative lack of elevation. The ship was anchored at a narrow isthmus, and travel by foot only a few hundred feet over "The Beach" brought the explorers to Uruguay Cove on the north side of the island.

Laurie Island, thirteen miles east to west with a highly irregular coastline and numerous deep bays, is the second largest of the South Orkney group, Coronation Island being larger and higher. One of the officers thought the islands would make a good penal colony; in winter the convicts would be kept busy "shovelling snow off the glaciers."[8] Another expedition member more seriously commented, "There is, I feel sure, no region in the world more grand in its scenery than the Antarctic, and no place more transcendent in its beauty. It is a vast wonderland laid out on a giant scale, in which littleness has no place; but its very vastness, no less than its beauty, while it quickens the traveller's daily wonder and deepens his reverence, forces him to feel that it is a world he can never conquer, a world in which the forces of nature are too tremendous to overcome, and must resignedly be bowed before in the hope that they will suffer him to come and pass again unscathed."[9]

Three days after the party's arrival in Scotia Bay, the sea froze over. The ship was prepared for winter: sails were put away, the highest yards were taken down to cut wind resistance, fires were left to go out, and snow was banked against the ship's sides for insulation. A large stone house was erected ashore, fourteen feet square and six to eight feet high; its flooring was ship's hatches, the walls were lined with canvas, and the roof was made of sail, yard, oil, and grease. The house was supplied with a stove, two mattresses, and four hammocks; the men deemed it quite comfortable. Bruce intended the hut to house some of his party next spring and summer when the *Scotia* would leave for the Falklands. The house was to become the basis of a larger perpetual observation station staffed by the Argentine government in future seasons. The building was named Omond House after R. T. Omond, an Edinburgh architect who had provided Bruce with the building plans. A prefabricated, wooden magnetic hut was also set up. The station was subject to sudden freakish weather changes; for example, on 31 May the temperature rose to 46.8 degrees Fahrenheit, and it rained.

Having settled in for the season, the staff began the enormous tasks to which they had committed themselves. Their surveys of Laurie Island were the most accurate ever performed. Hauls from the sea bottom yielded fine collections of marine organisms. Lichens and mosses were collected, and fossils were discovered. During leisure times, the men diverted to philosophy and speculation on world events; they cared for a few dogs, read and played games, listened to the phonograph, sang songs and chanteys, and celebrated special occasions. Winter evenings made for fond recollections later. "These days ... were very happy ... days of peaceful uneventfulness to think of amid the turmoil of life in crowded cities. . . . Isolation among the fastnesses of nature does not bring loneliness: that can perhaps be only felt in its full extreme among the busy haunts of men."[10]

In early autumn, penguins were still seen regularly during their northward migrations. They were taken for food, but Bruce forbade killing near the ship so they would come in without fear. The men thought so much of penguin as food as to suggest naively the establishment of rookeries on Scotland's barren west coast islets. Penguin breast, browned and fried with onion, or mixed in a soup or curry, were the favorites. Two Adélies made a meal for fifteen hungry men.

Allan G. Ramsay, the chief engineer, had left Scotland with a heart condition and was already ill by the time the ship arrived in the Falklands. But he kept his own counsel for fear the expedition would suffer without him. He gradually worsened and died on 6 August. Bruce wrote in his log: "He never said much, but always did his duty. This morning he opened up his heart to me more than he ever did before: 'I came here with the intention of doing my best, and making a name out of this job.' Then he . . . lamented having been ill, from the point of view of not getting through all the work he should. I held his head for several hours, as he wanted me to—for which he was most grateful. . . . He prayed and hoped to die. He said to me, 'I've not been very good, but I haven't had a bad life.'"[11] One of the staff wrote: "He gave his life for others, and gave it uncomplainingly. What greater praise can be given to any man? There are those, I know, who envy him his last resting-place beneath the shadow of the ice-capped hill that is named after him where throughout the ages the sea-birds wheel in their restless flight, and the waves crash on the shore save when frost holds them in its mighty grip, and there is stillness deep as death."[12]

The absence of animal life in winter contributed to a melancholy relieved only by the arrival of the first seals in late August, and then the penguins and seabirds in early October. "The spring, with its rapidly lengthening daylight and return of myriad birds and seals, brings with it tenfold more joy to those men who are privileged to experience it than any spring in temperate regions ever could."[13] The men raided the penguins' nests of thousands of eggs, many to be stored to feed the party occupying Omond House next winter. The raid made little dent in the bird population, numbering in the tens of thousands.

During late winter and spring, virtually all of Laurie Island was surveyed by sledge parties. The first excursion was a short trip to Delta Island (now Acuña

Island) in Scotia Bay commencing 8 July. The next was a trip commencing 13 August westward to Wilton Bay across the five-hundred-foot ridge separating it from Scotia Bay; the men became "walking icicles"[14] in driving sleet. On 21 September, another party left for Whitson Cape, five miles to the east, and with the aid of dogs extended their work to Cape Dundas, the easternmost point of the island. The final approach was exceedingly difficult. "If this is Science," said Willie, "she's a hard mistress; give me Art."[15] The men saw no sign of the grass reported by Weddell at Cape Dundas; all they found were green lichens, and they assumed Weddell's report to have been a mistake. The men continued their work around the island along the north shore. The sedimentary nature of the rock caused them to conclude correctly that the South Orkney Islands were part of a larger land mass, "leaving these tiny islands as the sole remains of a lost continent. . . . The probability is that the same ridge which we see bending eastwards in Southern Patagonia and Tierra del Fuego once continued still farther south-east, and the rocks of the South Orkneys, which are folded along a north-west and south-east axis, lay on one flank of this sub-Andean chain."[16]

On 2 November, a party of six led by Bruce left with two boats from Uruguay Cove to explore the north coast of Laurie Island. Part of Bruce's party returned to Scotia Bay, and the ship, once freed on 27 November, picked up the remaining men. Names were given to many of the island's features including the bays, capes, peninsulas, and offshore islets. But with characteristic modesty, Bruce did not permit his name to be given to any feature.

Bruce left a party at Omond House and headed toward the Falkland Islands. The ship's scientists dredged the Burdwood Bank, about which little was known. Upon arrival in the Falklands, Bruce learned of Nordenskjöld's plight and rescue by the Argentineans. He only just missed having to put into plan a rescue attempt he himself had promised Nordenskjöld. The *Scotia* was dry-docked in Buenos Aires for repairs, and Bruce learned that James Coats would pick up the expenses of the next season's work. Three Argentineans now joined the ship: L. H. Valette, H. Acuña, and E. Szmula. These men would be left at Omond House along with two of the ship's company for meteorological studies the next winter. The ship made an easy return to Laurie Island.

Meanwhile, six men, Mossman, Pirie, Cuthbertson, Ross, William Martin (one of the crew), and Bill Smith (the cook), had been left behind at Omond House. Bill Smith was the most colorful among the crew, a redoubtable individual whose stories of personal adventure accounted for one hundred fifty years of life—he was a "shameless liar."[17] Yarns and arguments were legion.

The scientists produced some of the finest early studies of penguins and Antarctic seabirds. The cape petrel is a widely distributed species, known to breed on South Georgia and the Kerguelen Islands. But the bird had never before been studied at the nest. Pirie made the first discovery of the nests and eggs. "He received a jet of evil-smelling fluid in his face, but the prize was worth the discomfort."[18] The pollen of a conifer was found, blown on the wind from South America, proving that biological materials could be transported to the Antarctic from more temperate regions across considerable distances.

In the warmth of December, the seaward wall of Omond House began to collapse, and the men realized that the foundation had not been set on solid rock. The wall had to be rebuilt. February was spent putting the house in proper repair in case the ship never came, and a rationing plan was formulated. But the ship did arrive and departed again on 22 February after leaving Mossman, Smith, and the three Argentineans to spend the winter; this group would be relieved the following season in an operation sponsored by the Argentine government. On the *Scotia*, Bruce completed his comprehensive survey of Laurie Island by fixing the positions of outlying rocks to the north.

Now began the most interesting portion of Bruce's expedition with respect to geographical discovery. Bruce and Robertson boldly headed the *Scotia* southeast into the Weddell Sea for a last chance to discover new land. They were favored with better ice conditions than they had been the previous year and by 1 March were south of their previous season's best, in open water. The following day, in 72°18' S, 17°59' W, soundings were shallower, and the captain went up to the crow's nest and reported land. The ship was brought to within two miles of an ice barrier similar to the one discovered by Ross; an iceblink was seen beyond. By 6 March, the men had followed the barrier southwest for 150 miles amid innumerable bergs. "The surface of this great Inland Ice . . . seemed to rise up very gradually in undulating slopes, and faded away in height and distance into the sky. . . . This made it certain that we were really off a new Antarctic land, which has been named 'Coats' Land' in honour of Mr James Coats, jun., and Major Andrew Coats, the two chief subscribers to the Expedition. Whether this land is a large island or a part of the Antarctic continent remains for future explorers to finally decide, but the latter hypothesis seems the more probable one."[19] Dredgings brought up rocks typical of an ancient continent. On a point of ornithological interest, the men, to their astonishment, spotted Arctic terns that happened to be at the southernmost boundary of their remarkably latitudinous migratory circuit.[20]

On 7 March, a northeast blizzard began, and the *Scotia* was trapped in ice and slush "like a fly in treacle."[21] The vessel creaked and groaned as it was lifted four feet by the ice pressure. Imprisoned, the ship drifted to 74°1' S, 22°0' W. On 9 March, the men anxiously waited in good weather for an opportunity to escape. But no open water was in sight, the temperature was 0 degrees Fahrenheit, and the sea was freezing: Bruce assumed they would have to winter where they were. The party was blissfully unaware of the severe danger from vortical ice movements in the Weddell Sea; the men's greater anxiety was the effect their absence would have on those at home who would not know their whereabouts or circumstances. Naively, no one seemed doubtful of the ship's eventual release.

On 12 March, a southwest air was accompanied by a rise in temperature to 17 degrees Fahrenheit, and the floes began to jostle. Two days later the men were able to move the ship. The engines worked hard against old floes up to thirty feet thick and a contrary northeasterly breeze. The last of the ice was left behind on 5 April. "Monotonous, dreary, and uncomfortable days there had been, but where do these not exist? In the future we knew there would often come a longing to be back again, however much we might rail against the present. The ice had cast its indescribable mysterious glamour over our souls."[22]

The men now headed home to Scotland. En route the ship visited subantarctic Gough Island, then Cape Town, St. Helena, Ascension, and the Cape Verde Islands before arriving in Ireland on 15 July. In Kingstown Harbor they patiently awaited the preset date of arrival six days later in the Clyde, where a triumphant return celebration had been organized by James Ferrier, the expedition secretary. The men of the *Scotia* were escorted into anchorage where cheering crowds, Murray, and James Coats with his yachts were all waiting. There the expedition formally ended, and its members dispersed.

The party of five that had stayed behind at Laurie Island spent its time monitoring the weather, taking magnetic readings, geologizing, and adding to their natural history collections. The autumn and winter seasons proceeded uneventfully except for an early April storm. On the third day of that month, seventy-mile-per-hour winds came straight onto the beach, and in the morning the winds coincided with an especially high tide. The rising sea destroyed their breakwater and reached Omond House, spewing freezing spray, bringing in ice blocks, and sweeping stores over the ridge. At that the men lost hope for Omond House. They collected bedding, clothing, other necessities, and documents, and then vacated. Tents were taken to the highest point on The Beach but could not be pitched because of the high winds. Soaked to the skin in the 15-degree-Fahrenheit air, the men waited in the

Omond House damaged by the storm
Brown, Mossman, and Pirie, *The Voyage of the "Scotia,"* 1906

magnetic hut, expecting to see the southern face of Omond House demolished. The danger passed within a few hours; a survey of the damage revealed the flooring was flooded, the porch was undermined, the covered passage to the storeroom was ruined, the south corner was gone (the buttress holding only by frozen spray), and stores were strewn about. The men set about their repairs and buttressed the house with barrels, boxes, and sacks of rubble.

Except for this unforgettable event, life was dull and the men suffered from social deprivation. They were relieved on 31 December by the Argentine ship *Uruguay,* the same vessel that had rescued Nordenskjöld. A fresh party of Argentine meteorologists was left behind with supplies and materials; the new arrivals were broken in to the rigors of Antarctic life by having to sledge twenty-five tons of coal and supplies over The Beach from Uruguay Cove. The *Uruguay* departed for the South Shetland Islands and Gerlache Strait, went as far as Wiencke Island, examined the Deception Island basin, and then headed north for Buenos Aires, arriving 8 February.

Bruce was awarded the gold medal of the Royal Scottish Geographical Society for his work. The Scotia Sea, Scotia Arc, and Scotia Ridge were geographical names given in honor of the expedition. Bruce established the Scottish Oceanographical Laboratory in Edinburgh, which published the scientific reports, paid for in part by the sale of the *Scotia* for £5,000. The vessel met a pitiable end by burning in Bristol Channel in 1916. Bruce died in Edinburgh after a long illness in 1921.

16

Jean-Baptiste Charcot and the French Antarctic Expedition in the *Français* (1903–1905)

D'où vient donc l'étrange attirance de ces régions polaires? . . . J'éprouvais
plus vivement, dans cette désolation et cette mort. Mais je sens aujour-
d'hui que ces régions nous frappent, en quelque sorte, d'une religieuse
empreinte. . . . L'homme que a pu pénétrer dans ce lieu sent son âme que
s'élève.

[From where, therefore, comes that peculiar lure of these polar regions? . . .
Amid this desolation and death, I have experienced a more vivid pleasure
of my own life. I feel that these regions make a kind of religious impression on one. . . . The man who penetrates his way into these regions feels
his soul uplifted.]

Jean-Baptiste Charcot, Le *"Français" au Pole Sud*

Dr. Jean-Baptiste Étienne Auguste Charcot (1867–1936) was the son
of the famous neuropsychologist Jean-Martin Charcot (1825–93), whose
name is still attached to diagnostic signs in the field of medicine. The famous
doctor, Charcot père, fathered an unusual son. By the age of four, the
younger Charcot was conversant in French, English, and German. He
revealed his love of navigation and adventure early: as a child, he wrote the
words "Pourquoi-pas?" ("Why not?") on a soapbox and launched himself
out on the miniature pool at Neuilly-sur-Seine. His "vessel" went down, and
he got thoroughly wet; it was, nevertheless, his first "voyage." He pursued his
medical training to satisfy his father, but the young Charcot was drawn to
the open spaces and found society superficial.

Upon his father's death in 1893, the twenty-six-year-old Charcot inherited
a fortune, about 400,000 francs (£17,000).[1] He abandoned medicine and
turned to a life of science and adventure at sea. Soon he had traveled to high

northern Scandinavian latitudes, published a respected navigation handbook, and led a scientific cruise to Iceland. He welcomed adverse conditions as a test of his mettle and was happiest in the natural world. Yet he also possessed the highest personal standards and refinements: he was the consummate gentleman and inspired respect and loyalty from colleagues. His fluency in English brought him acceptance and respect in British scientific and naval circles. He hoped that his wife, the granddaughter of the great French writer Victor Hugo, would understand and support his restless passions, but such was not possible; tension between them grew. Charcot was aware of his marital difficulties, but his wanderlust was unmitigated.

Charcot was inspired by the contemporary surge of interest in the polar regions, and he took it upon himself to uphold the pride of France in high-latitude exploration. So he invested his fortune in a voyage to the Arctic. Père Gautier of St. Malo was engaged to build a schooner, and Charcot obtained advice on its design from Adrien de Gerlache. Charcot named the ship *Le Français*. For economy, the vessel was relatively small, 104 feet and 250 tons. The small 125-horsepower engine was of poor quality and was the vessel's nemesis, but the ship itself was superior, reinforced at the waterline by transverse beams, bronze, and iron, to specifications exceeding by threefold the insurance standards of the day.

At the earliest press notices of an expedition, Paul Pléneau, director of a steamship engine company, volunteered his services, and Pléneau and Charcot struck up an immediate, warm friendship. In April 1903, news of Nordenskjöld's absence arrived in France, leading Charcot to change his plans. He decided to go south to search for the Swedish explorer and investigate the Antarctic regions, where he realized that discovery and fame might come more easily than in the north. He wrote Pléneau, asking him to come. Pléneau knew that to go would jeopardize his employment and excellent economic future, but he also understood that a chance to visit the Antarctic was a rare opportunity, and by now he was devoted to Charcot. Pléneau sent a bold telegram, remarkable, indeed noble, for its absolute commitment: "Where you like. When you like. For as long as you like!"[2]

The French Antarctic Expedition thus came into being, and Charcot obtained the support of President Émile Loubet and the Académie des Sciences. The Paris newspaper *Le Matin* opened a subscription, and numerous, mostly small, contributions came in; combined with Charcot's own funds, the expedition's financial requirements were just met. Two naval officers received normal pay; the rest of the staff and crew were volunteers. Not all the scientific instruments were the finest available; the men had to do their best with limited resources. The entire budget was only 450,000 francs (about £20,000), very lean compared with the German, British, and Scottish expeditions.

The *Français* set sail from Le Havre on 15 August 1903 to an enthusiastic sendoff by the crowds. The ship's company included Charcot (leader, medical officer, bacteriology); Pléneau (commissary, photographer); two naval officers, Lt. A. Matha (1873–?) (astronomy, hydrography, gravitation) and Sub-Lt. J. Rey (meteorology, magnetology, atmospheric electricity); two scientists, J. Bonnier and a certain Perez; Gerlache; P. Dayné (alpine guide); Robert Paumelle (Charcot's loyal steward); and eleven crewmen. One of the crew, a man known by the family name of Maignan, was killed in a freak accident moments after departure, even before the crowd had dispersed. The ship pitched in an uneven sea, and the tow rope pulled loose its cleat, which struck the sailor, killing him. The ship about-faced, and Charcot, grief-stricken, brought the body himself to Maignan's widow in her Breton village, whereupon she exclaimed, "Monsieur Charcot, Monsieur Charcot, he would have done anything for you!"[3] Two weeks later the party set sail a second time, and Charcot would hear no good luck wishes.

Charcot loved being at sea again and took enormous pride in his ship. However, he soon faced the near disintegration of his expedition. Charcot, in his official account, made no reference to this crisis; the events were recorded in 1937, a year after Charcot's death, by Marthe Oulié, Charcot's goddaughter and biographer.[4] It so happened that Gerlache, who had recently become engaged to be married, became inconsolable over the separation from his fiancée. He, along with Bonnier and Perez, for reasons unknown, elected to leave the expedition at Madeira. Charcot became despondent, doubting whether he could succeed in the Antarctic ice fields and in his scientific program without the help of Gerlache and the other two men; he feared that his entire party would splinter. He consulted Matha, Rey, and Pléneau, who declared their intention to adhere to the program. Charcot then assembled the entire crew and explained the circumstances. All expressed their intention to carry on. Charcot, relieved, took each man's hand in heartfelt thanks and appreciation.

Charcot's confidence was now restored, and the *Français* arrived in Buenos Aires on 16 November; the Argentineans saw to all repairs and entertained the party. Charcot waited for two replacement scientists to arrive from France, J. Turquet (zoology, botany) and Ernest Gourdon (geology, glaciology). Gourdon proved to be a particularly charming individual. Now Charcot received word that Nordenskjöld's expedition had been relieved, so he dropped his rescue plan. Nordenskjöld presented Charcot with five Greenland dogs in thanks.

Charcot decided to explore the west coast of the Antarctic Peninsula as far as Adelaide Island and Alexander Island while carrying out a multidisciplinary scientific research program to build upon Gerlache's discoveries. The last port of call was Ushuaia, Argentina, and the expedition departed for the Antarctic on 24 January 1904. Charcot addressed the crew and, in full candor, acknowledged the limits of his own authority and impressed the men with the responsibility each carried: "I want you all to realise that it's up to you now to play the game; I shall have no way of punishing you if you don't. I cannot put you in irons, you know that we have none on board, and anyway the crew is too small for that; I cannot deprive you of your ration of wine, you need it for your health; I cannot cut down your wages, for you wouldn't mind. So I appeal to your consciences, and rely on you doing your duty, partly out of affection for me, and more particularly because of the mission entrusted to us. You must never forget that the honour of your country is in your hands."[5]

The party entered the world of sea ice and bergs. Charcot navigated from the crow's nest as they passed Smith, Low, Hoseason, and Anvers Islands. Boiler and engine trouble forced the party to delay for repairs, without being able to anchor. They proceeded to Wiencke Island, where, on 19 February, they discovered Port Lockroy, a natural harbor in a glorious setting. The site was rich in wildlife, and Charcot, who had an aversion to hunting, ordered no molestation of the penguins and seals. The ship's party next sailed into the beautiful but formidable Lemaire Channel separating Booth Island from the Graham Land coast. By 26 February, the *Français* had reached the Biscoe Islands, but thick ice and more engine trouble forced a retreat. The men established winter quarters in a large bay, Port Charcot (named by Charcot for his father) on the north shore of Booth Island in the Wilhelm Archipelago. The ship was moored, and the men erected a hut as autumn set in.

The autumn and winter did not pass serenely. Matha was ill with a heart condition. The party was buffeted repeatedly by severe storms. Four of the crew got lost in fog and were found in a state of fairly severe exposure. When the wardroom stove malfunctioned, the ship's interior was distressingly cold.

The men slept on the ship and used the hut ashore for scientific observations, storage, and emergency shelter. For entertainment, they had the previous year's papers, chess, a large library, various celebrations, and the pleasure of strolls ashore. They were kept company by seals, some of whom snored noisily alongside the ship. A day trip southwest to nearby Hovgaard Island, an Antarctic winter picnic of sorts, was made in early June to break the gloom of confinement. A few men got wet breaking through thin ice, and ice axes were needed to cut meat and butter; but the occasion was still gleeful, helped no doubt by the rum brought along. Another trip to Hovgaard Island was made in September to establish a depot. With the coming of spring, the men added penguin and cormorant eggs to their diet.

Charcot, Pléneau, Gourdon, and two crewmen left on 24 November in their whaleboat with a collapsible sledge and twenty days' provisions on an exploratory expedition to the Graham Land coast. They spent the first night at Petermann Island, about a mile southwest of Hovgaard Island, and all together ten miles distant. The sea ice was neither compacted and solid enough for foot travel, nor open enough for boat travel, so, suffering from cold and snow blindness, they shifted their positions inside the boat or pulled the boat to win their meager advances. Five days after setting out, the men arrived at Cape Tuxen on the Graham Land coast, the first confirmed landing on the west coast of the Antarctic Peninsula. They climbed the twenty-nine-hundred-foot summit to reconnoiter, returned to the whaler, and headed south, where they sighted the Biscoe Islands to the south. They arrived exhausted at the *Français* after a journey of eleven days. Meanwhile, Matha had organized the ship, a favorable wind blew out the ice, and the *Français* left its winter quarters on 25 December.

Sailing southwest, the ship fringed the Biscoe Islands and passed by Adelaide Island. On 8 January 1905, in the height of summer, a fearsome three-day storm left in its wake clearing skies and a spectacular scene. Charcot recorded: "Never had a calm scene after a storm been more absolute, grand, and austere, and yet more radiant."[6] But the expansive ice producing this wonderful setting was blocking their way south, and they were unable to advance on any front. The party was forced to turn northward on 13 January, having obtained mere glimpses of distant mountains and Alexander Island.

Two days later the most dreadful event of the expedition occurred: near Adelaide Island the ship struck a rock. Charcot wrote: "We felt a terrible shock, the masts vibrated and swayed to the point they would come down, and the ship reared up almost to the vertical with a sinister cracking noise. . . . This surge we felt two or three times. I sprang to the telegraph and signaled 'full reverse,' but . . . the ship on its own had fallen back afloat with a muted groan. . . . The men who were sleeping below now came up to the deck half clothed. There was a moment of stupefaction and intense emotion, but no panic, and I saw all eyes turning to me. Was I afraid? I couldn't tell, but maybe so, after all, for I asked it of myself. Very calmly and collected in any case, I put my cap aright and buttoned my coat to give the proper appearance."[7]

The ship was leaking severely. The season's research was over. The men simply had to get out alive. The water pumps were hand-operated forty-five minutes per hour around the clock as the party headed for Port Lockroy. The same day, the men got sunny views of the peninsular coast, which was named Terre Loubet (Loubet Coast) after the French president.

The men arrived at Port Lockroy on 30 January after enduring adverse weather and rough seas in the crippled ship. They had spent ten days making temporary repairs, and they were worn out. The demands on Charcot had been great; he hadn't changed his clothes in a month. Meanwhile, the *Uruguay,* which had just relieved Mossman's party at Laurie Island, had gone as far as Wiencke Island, where Charcot had said he would leave information—but the *Uruguay* found nothing. With that report, Charcot's sister back in France began to organize a search-and-relief effort.

The *Français* arrived at Puerto Madryn, Argentina, at the height of the summer season, when the men should have been relishing their opportunities in the south. Pléneau rode forty-five miles by horseback to Chubut to wire home. Charcot was hit by three personal disasters—his wife, feeling deserted, wanted a divorce; one brother-in-law had died; and his sister Jeanne was divorced. Charcot's party arrived in Buenos Aires on 15 March. Only in dry-dock could the extent of the damage be properly appreciated: the bronze reinforcement on the stem had been destroyed, twenty-two feet of false keel had been lost, and planks were loose. In short, the *Français* had come close to shipwreck. The ship was repaired and sold to the Argentine government, which used it as a supply vessel to the Laurie Island meteorological station.

The party received an enthusiastic homecoming. Subsequently, Charcot became especially close to his sister Jeanne, and the two lived together. He asked her to make sure he never married again, but he met a woman named Meg Cléry who adored him and understood his love for science and the sea; the two were married early in 1907.

In all, Charcot had charted more than six hundred miles of new coastlines and islands, and he provided France a new position and precedent in Antarctic affairs. He described new features at Wiencke Island and the Loubet Coast, and fixed the names of his countrymen and important figures from former Antarctic expeditions to islands, capes, peaks, bays, and channels. Eighteen volumes of scientific reports were eventually published at government expense. Even though the work was diminished by the accident to the ship, the expedition had been a sound success. The French explorer became a national hero.

Like other polar explorers of the period, Charcot knew that he was destined to return to the Antarctic: "From where, therefore, comes that peculiar lure of these polar regions that is so powerful and tenacious that after having left one forgets all moral and physical fatigue and thinks only of going back? From where comes the otherworldly charm of these provinces, however desolate and terrifying? Is it the pleasure of the unknown, the intoxicating delight of the struggle and effort of attainment and survival, the pride of attempting and actually doing what others do not, the delight of being far from pettiness and meanness? A little of all this, but also something else. I have felt for a long time that, amidst this desolation and death, I have experienced a more vivid pleasure of my own life. I feel that these regions make a kind of religious impression on one. . . . Here is the sanctuary of sanctuaries, where Nature reveals herself in all her formidable power. . . . The man who penetrates his way into these regions feels his soul uplifted."[8]

17

ERNEST H. SHACKLETON AND THE
BRITISH ANTARCTIC EXPEDITION
(1907–1909)

We have shot our bolt, and the tale is latitude 88°23' South.
Ernest H. Shackleton, *The Heart of the Antarctic*

ERNEST HENRY SHACKLETON (1874–1922) returned south after Scott's *Discovery* expedition to lead one of the most successful expeditions ever to the Antarctic regions. After establishing a base at Cape Royds on Ross Island, Shackleton achieved a new farthest south of 88°23' and in the process discovered the Beardmore Glacier and established a route that would ultimately lead to the pole. In addition, members of his expedition were the first to stand at the south magnetic pole and climb Mount Erebus. Important new discoveries were made in the mountains to the west. Stories of personal heroism and fortitude abounded. Despite the hardships and risks, all of the men came back alive. The party also produced *Aurora Australis,* the first book published in Antarctica.

Shackleton was from Yorkshire, of Anglo-Irish origin. He found school boring but enjoyed the solitude of reading. He was hardy and favored adventure, and was well-matched to the rigorous requirements of sailing ships. He got his first taste for southern latitudes on a voyage around Cape Horn. At age twenty-four he was certified as sailing master and three years later was selected to be third mate on the *Discovery* expedition. That expedition was a perfect outlet for his burgeoning ambition, and he proved himself capable and probably too popular for Scott, who sent him home on account of ill health. Shackleton was part poet/philosopher, part romantic, and part renegade; he was fond of quoting the poet Robert Browning, and his charisma, optimism, and determination were unassailable. He was unsuccessful in business and ill-adapted to city life, but at sea and in the wild places of the world he was the consummate leader, inspiring confidence and loyalty in men who served him again and again.

After being dismissed by Scott, Shackleton remained drawn south by the "lure of little voices."[1] He designed his private expedition with the South Pole as his principal objective, but he also included enough scientific investigations to make a contribution to knowledge and to justify his requests for funds. Although he had great difficulty in raising money, he brought in £44,000 from private contributors at home and from the governments of New Zealand and Australia. He received no support from the Royal Geographical Society.

Shackleton selected as his ship the aging, forty-one-year-old *Nimrod*. The vessel was small and not his first choice, but he could not afford better. As it was, he spent a considerable portion of his financial resources refitting the vessel. Shackleton asked Capt. William Colbeck to command the ship. Colbeck, who had commanded the *Antarctic* during Borchgrevink's expedition (1898–1900) and the *Morning* on its two relief expeditions (1902–3 and 1903–4), was the most experienced Antarctic sailor alive in Great Britain. He was, naturally, Shackleton's first choice, but Colbeck was not interested. He suggested a man Shackleton already knew, Capt. Rupert A. England (1878–1942), who had been Colbeck's first mate on the *Morning*. Shackleton procured England's services. This was to be England's first command.

On 1 January 1908, the expedition departed New Zealand. The party consisted of thirty-nine men, ten ponies, nine dogs, and an Arrol-Johnston motorcar, the first motorized vehicle brought to the Antarctic. The ship was fully loaded with 250 tons of stores and coal. To save fuel, the *Nimrod* was towed more than fifteen hundred miles to the pack ice south of the Antarctic Circle by the *Koonya* under the command of Capt. Frederick P. Evans (1874–1959). Within a day of departure, the weather turned ferociously bad and remained so for two weeks. Winds increased to gale and hurricane force, waves swelled to forty-two feet, and the *Nimrod* and the *Koonya* lost sight of each other across the crests of waves. The *Nimrod* pitched and rolled perilously up to 50 degrees from vertical. Breaking seas destroyed part of the starboard bulwarks, tore the port washport from its hinges, and shifted the stores on deck. Many of the men were seasick, and their clothes and sleeping quarters were wet. When the ship began to accumulate water at three feet per hour, two men at a time worked two-hour shifts around the clock at the hand pump. Preparation and serving of meals was seemingly impossible, but no hot meals were forfeited although the galley was constantly flooded. The men could get about the deck only by the use of life lines. One horse fell in the constant wild motion and, unable to right itself, had to be killed.

The *Koonya* headed back to New Zealand on 15 January. The *Nimrod* quickly passed through the pack ice, entering the open Ross Sea the next day. The party arrived at the Ross Ice Shelf on 23 January and soon found the barrier inlet described by Borchgrevink. Shackleton had originally intended to set up his base there, but now he realized that topographical features had changed over the six years since the *Discovery* expedition, a result of the calving of ice off the barrier front; Shackleton named the new inlet the Bay of Whales. Fearful that no base would be safe on the shelf ice, Shackleton decided to establish his settlement only on solid ground. Seeking a suitable site, he sailed east toward Edward VII Peninsula but was stopped by ice at 162°14' W; on 25 January he abandoned any further attempt in that direction. The ship was turned westward, and Shackleton arrived in McMurdo Sound on 29 January with no choice but to disregard the commitment he had made Scott not to locate a base in the McMurdo area. At closest approach, twenty miles of sea ice separated the ship from Hut Point.

Thus Cape Royds, site of a large Adélie penguin rookery, was selected for the expedition's base of operations. On the last day of January, Aeneas Mackintosh (1881–1916), who was to have been a member of the wintering party, lost his right eye to an errant, swinging boat hook. On 3 February, the landing of hut materials, stores, and equipment began in earnest. The hut, made of fir and prefabricated in sections, stood thirty-three by nineteen feet and eight feet to the eaves, and was set on wooden piles driven into the frozen ground. It was made resistant to the cold by a four-inch cork insulation layer, double windows, and a series of two doors with an entry porch between. Guy ropes fixed to the roof's apex would stabilize the hut in strong winds. The winds, in fact, were not long in coming. A frigid gale lasting four days coated the ship thickly with ice and buried boxes brought to shore in up to six feet of frozen sea spray. The boxes had to be dug and chiseled out. The *Nimrod* left a shore party of fifteen men on 22 February, but not before considerable tension had arisen between Shackleton and England.[2]

England was anxious in his first command in the difficult ice conditions; Shackleton considered him overly cautious. Shackleton was the expedition leader and England's employer, but England had the prerogative over the ship's operations. The two were often at odds as they explored the barrier front between the Bay of Whales and Edward VII Peninsula, again during the unloading at Cape Royds (when England stood off and thereby delayed the delivery ashore of equipment and supplies), and still again when England wanted to retain extra coal as ballast for the voyage back to New Zealand. So Shackleton sent England north with a letter dismissing him, sealing it to preserve efficiency and harmony until the return voyage was over.

Shackleton wanted to make a southward thrust to establish food and supply depots for the following year, but the sea had to be frozen from Cape Royds south to Hut Point; it was still open water. Thus a first ascent of Mount Erebus was planned instead. Shackleton appointed an advance party of the fifty-year-old geology professor T. W. Edgeworth David (1858–1934), Douglas Mawson (1882–1958), and Alistair F. Mackay (1877–1914), and a supporting party of Jameson Adams (1880–1962), the surgeon Eric Marshall (1879–1963), and Philip Brocklehurst (1887–1975), the youngest. Shackleton's first biographer, Hugh Robert Mill, suggested that Shackleton decided not to participate so that he could get winter quarters in order.[3] Adams was to be in charge, and if the supporting party returned, David was to take over. The supporting party was not as thoroughly provisioned as the advance party but was given the option to proceed to the summit. From the moment of the plan's inception, the hut was abuzz with preparations. The parties set out the following day, 5 March, with a sledge and 560 pounds of stores.

Despite cold, sastrugi, and increasing altitude, the men made rapid progress and camped the first night at 2,750 feet and the second at 5,630 feet. Because of the increasing steepness, they left a depot consisting of the sledge, tent poles, and some of the provisions, and proceeded on foot carrying about forty pounds apiece. Although some of the men did not have adequate footwear for climbing the difficult ice terrain, the third night's camp was made at 8,750 feet. That night a ferocious blizzard struck. Brocklehurst nearly lost his life when he was blown down a ravine. The storm kept the men confined to their snow-drifted sleeping bags, and they were unable even to prepare drinking water until the morning of the fifth day, when the blizzard abated. To continue on, the men cut steps in the ice slope. Camp for the fifth night was made at 11,400 feet, just below the rim of the old crater. In camp, Brocklehurst was found to have serious frostbite on most of his toes, so after being treated he was left behind as the remaining five men went off to explore. (Brocklehurst later required amputation of a great toe.) Fumaroles in the form of ice mounds, sulfurous ice, lavas, pumice, and feldspar crystals defined the scene. Mackay fell through the deceptive ice crust into a fumarole conduit, saving himself only with his ice ax. The party returned to camp for the sixth night.

The following day the men reached the summit, which they estimated to be 13,350 feet high (it is now known to be 12,445 feet) and peered down 900 feet into the half-mile-wide active cone. Out of the crater came hissing and booming noises; steam rose to a thousand feet above their heads, and the smell of sulfur wafted through the air. The men made atmospheric observations, collected geologic specimens, took photographs, and then hastily descended, breaking camp and hurrying down the mountainside in glissades. With a descent of over seven thousand feet, they reached their sledge depot, which had been disrupted by the blizzard. There they made their seventh night's camp.

After only a few scant hours of sleep, the men rose at three in the morning to continue downward. They used ropes on the sledge runners as brakes but were repeatedly troubled by irregular surfaces and the variability of the men's foot gear. The party reached the site of the first night's camp by half-past seven in the morning. Because of the threat of another blizzard, and equipment damage, the men left the sledge and most of the equipment about six miles out and made a dash for the hut. They arrived bedraggled at eleven in the morning; their success was promptly toasted by their elated comrades with champagne and a hearty feast.

The shore party settled down to a winter routine, including studies of weather, auroras, ice, rocks, and marine life, caring for the animals, and hut maintenance. Some of the men gave descriptive and amusing names to their hut cubicles: Adams and Marshall dwelled in "No. 1 Park Lane," a neat and orderly address; George Marston (1882–1940) and Bernard C. Day (1884–?) occupied "The Gables," for the appearance of the shelves; Ernest E. M. Joyce and Frank Wild lived in the "Rogues' Retreat," with the faces of two tough-looking beer drinkers looking down from a portrait on a wall; and David and Mawson occupied "The Pawn Shop," with a multitude of miscellaneous articles strewn on the bunks, walls, and shelves. Midwinter Day and birthdays were opportunities for celebrating. Acetylene lamps kept the hut well illuminated. The men evolved some unusual traditions, including a late eleven o'clock tea for those still awake, and a retelling by the night watchman at breakfast of interesting phrases uttered by those who talked in their sleep.

Joyce, Wild, Day, and Marston, with Shackleton as editor, produced *Aurora Australis,* the first book published in Antarctica. Shackleton had edited the first of two volumes of *The South Polar Times* on Scott's *Discovery* expedition; each of the eight individual issues constituting the two volumes was prepared only in a single copy in the Antarctic, and later a collation was reproduced for the general public in a small, limited edition. Shackleton was resolved to produce a similar work on his own expedition but took the labor a step further. Rather than produce only one copy to bring back to civilization for the production of facsimiles, the entire effort including the writing, printing, illustrating, and binding was to be done on site in Antarctica. Thus was conceived and produced *Aurora Australis*—beautifully made under extremely adverse conditions by novices to the printing and binding trades.

Joyce and Wild set by hand the type for each page; after the work was checked for errors and the requisite number of pages run off, the type was distributed. The type rack was kept warm with a lamp, and the plate was heated with a candle to maintain the consistency of the ink. Marston produced the illustrations from aluminum plates. Most of the printing was done during the quieter hours, when the vibration, noise, and dust in the hut interior were minimal. Producing the illustrations was especially difficult; James Murray (1865–1914) commented: "I've frequently seen Marston do everything right— clean, ink, and press—but for some obscure reason the prints did not come right. And I've seen him during a whole night pull off half a dozen wrong ones for one good print, and he did not use so much language over it as might have been expected."[4] Day made the bindings from polished, beveled venesta case boards, leather from the horse harnesses, and silk cord. The finished work was a bound anthology of ten writings that represented the experiences and reflections of nine men (six writing under pseudonyms), plus Marston's illustrations. Fewer than one hundred copies of the book were produced.[5]

Despite the intense cold and dim twilight of mid-August, Shackleton made a preliminary ten-day southward journey in the company of David and Bertram Armytage (1869–1910) across the frozen sea of McMurdo Sound. From near Hut Point they viewed the barrier stretched out to the south. Shackleton eagerly wrote: "The fascination of the unknown was strong upon me, and I longed to be away towards the south on the journey that I hoped would lay bare the mysteries of the place of the pole."[6] Shackleton resolved to use the *Discovery* hut as a supply depot for the southern journey, and he quickly realized that the irregular barrier surface would make use of the motorcar impracticable. The men began the movement of provisions to Hut Point in earnest on 1 September. On 22 September, Shackleton, Adams, Marshall, Wild, Marston, and Joyce headed for a point one hundred miles south of Hut Point into cold that dipped as low as minus 59 degrees Fahrenheit, hauling 170 pounds per man to make a maize depot for the four remaining ponies.

Shackleton selected his polar party: Adams, Marshall, Wild, and himself. The ponies would haul as far as possible, each with about 600 to 660 pounds, after which progress would be made by man-hauling alone. Dogs and skis were not part of the program. A support party consisting of Joyce, Marston, Raymond E. Priestley (1886–1974), Armytage, and Brocklehurst would accompany the polar party for the first ten days. Shackleton planned for thirty-four ounces of food per man daily, comprising biscuit, pemmican, sugar, cheese, chocolate, emergency ration, cocoa, plasmon, oats, tea, salt, and pepper. Spirits were high on 29 October as the departing men set out, cheered by those remaining behind.

The initial barrier phase south lasted until 3 December. The men had generally fine weather except for two brief blizzards. Progress was excellent, the men took turns cooking, and they enjoyed their limited supply of tobacco and reading materials. They noted the curious appearance of two sets of Adélie penguin tracks fifty miles from the nearest water. On 26 November, the men broke out a four-ounce bottle of Curaçao and celebrated the passage of latitude 82°16.5' S, a new farthest south. The small party of four marveled at the new surroundings never before seen by man as Marshall prepared charts of the new discoveries. Shackleton wrote: "Mountain after mountain came into view, grimly majestic. We were but tiny black specks crawling slowly . . . across the white plain."[7]

The outbound trip across the barrier would prove to be the easiest portion of the journey, even though it was in fact challenging. Adams had to have a painful tooth extracted under the most primitive of conditions; for a period of time, Wild was not fit; men and horses alike had attacks of snow blindness. Surfaces were often difficult for sledges and ponies, and the pony named Chinaman along with the provisions it carried were nearly lost in a crevasse near White Island. The horses were finicky with their food and uneven of temperament, and they destroyed their tethers.

The animals gradually weakened and were shot according to plan, Chinaman on 21 November, Grisi on 28 November, and Quan (Shackleton's favorite, over which he lamented) on 1 December. The horses were flensed; some of the meat was cached for the return journey, and some was carried, either to be cooked at mealtime or eaten raw on the march. The men were relying on the antiscorbutic benefit of the fresh meat. Food was rationed after 15 November, and Shackleton wrote for the first time about hunger and food fantasies on 1 December.

Now the men had to make an ascent through the mountains. The party headed in the direction of the coast and on 4 December made a 2,750-foot ascent up Mount Hope to reconnoiter, making the first landing in the far south. Their hope was not in vain. "From the top of this ridge there burst upon our view an open road to the south, for there stretched before us a great glacier running almost south and north between two huge mountain ranges."[8] Shackleton named the hundred-mile-long glacier after William Beardmore, a supporter of the expedition.

The ascent of the Beardmore Glacier was of almost incomprehensible difficulty. The men encountered chaotic surfaces and fell repeatedly but fortunately sustained only minor injuries. Crevasses of enormous dimension and unfathomable depth were encountered, concealed by deceptive snowlids. The men were hauling a total weight of about one thousand pounds; transport required relays and rope brakes on the sledge runners to prevent sliding, and the work became increasingly exhausting with the altitude.

Disaster struck early on 7 December. Wild was leading Socks when he felt the lead rope snatched from his hand and the surface under his feet give way with a rush of wind. Socks's weight had broken through a crevasse lid and snapped the swingle-tree of the sledge, and the pony was lost. Wild miraculously escaped the same fate by grasping the sledge and scrambling out of his precarious position. Socks was to have been sacrificed that night for food; each man's daily food allotment was now reduced to twenty ounces.

Not all was hardship, however. The sun warmed the rocks alongside the glacier and melted ice, saving time and fuel. Coal was found in the hills. Everyone was safe, and the party was blessed with excellent weather. Marshall and Adams, while reconnoitering a route on 5 December in 83°40' S, reported a skua, a welcome and appreciated sign of life.

By 15 December, the party had ascended over five thousand feet up the glacier, and Shackleton mentioned for the first time cold breezes from the southwest. Four days later, the men were at almost 7,900 feet altitude in 85°5' S; two days after that they developed frostbite on fingers and ears as they faced into the frigid headwinds falling off the plateau that lay in front of them. By the day before Christmas, the crevasses were past and surfaces improved. One of the two sledges and every nonessential item, including clothing not actually being worn, was cached to lighten the total load to a little over 150 pounds per man. On Christmas Day the group enjoyed a feast of a special hoosh (a sledger's stew) made of pemmican (a meat-based, high-fat food), pony meat, emergency ration, and biscuit, then plum pudding in cocoa water with a drop of brandy, cocoa, cigars, and a spoonful each of creme de menthe. The men felt fit, but body temperatures were subnormal.

At an altitude over ten thousand feet, the men noticed the ice terrain finally flattening out—they were on the polar plateau. And with that achievement they were increasingly affected by altitude headaches, exhaustion, and hypothermia. On 31 December, at 86°54' S, they had only three weeks' food and two weeks' biscuit to make the five hundred miles to the pole and back to their last depot. On New Year's Day 1909, they claimed another first—87°54', the highest latitude, north or south, ever achieved by man. But the next day, with food supplies short and the men's physical reserves depleted, Shackleton had to admit his waning chances of achieving 90° S. "We can now definitely locate the South Pole on the highest plateau in the world, and our geological work and meteorology will be of the greatest use to science; but all this is not the Pole."[9]

By 4 January all were very weak—three men failed to register a body temperature of 94 degrees Fahrenheit. The end of the outbound journey was nearing; they could spin out neither their rations nor their luck much further. So they left a depot, departed with seventy pounds each, and trusted that their footprints would remain visible to guide their way back. With air temperatures below zero Fahrenheit, often below minus fifteen, and having endured gale-force winds in their faces with no spare clothing, the men made their last outward camp two days later. Disappointed, Shackleton wrote: "I would fail to explain my feelings if I tried to write them down."[10] On 7 January, the men were assaulted by a blizzard with temperatures of minus 40 degrees Fahrenheit. Eighty-mile-per-hour wind gusts at last confined them to the tent.

On 9 January, the men made their last southward dash—eighteen miles without the sledge. "We have shot our bolt, and the tale is latitude 88°23' South, longitude 162° East."[11] They remained at that spot only a few minutes, long enough to hoist flags, take possession for the king, take photographs, and eat a scanty meal. A scan to the south with their telescope revealed only the seemingly endless plain. They returned to their depot and made a few more miles to the north to camp, having covered forty-one miles that historic day. "Whatever regrets may be, we have done our best."[12]

With the wind at their backs and a sail on the sledge, the men made large daily distances north and were on the Beardmore Glacier in less than a week. But they suffered the loss of their sledge meter that counted the miles between depots, they were on short rations, and they were back into the areas of crevasses and slippery blue ice. Almost at the bottom of the Beardmore, the party found itself in a precarious position with only two days' food and one day's biscuit, and over forty miles over terrible terrain to the next depot.

Shackleton described the ordeal: "January 26 and 27. Two days written up as one, and they have been the hardest and most trying we have ever spent in our lives, and will ever stand in our memories. To-night (the 27th) we have had our first solid food since the morning of the 26th. We came to the end of all our provisions except a little cocoa and tea, and from 7 A.M. on the 26th till 2 P.M. on the 27th we did sixteen miles over the worst surfaces and most dangerous crevasses we have ever encountered, only stopping for tea or cocoa till they were finished, and marching twenty hours at a stretch, through snow 10 to 18 in. thick as a rule, with sometimes 2 1/2 ft of it. We fell into hidden crevasses time after time, and were saved by each other and by our harness. In fact, only an all-merciful Providence has guided our steps to to-night's safety at our depot. I cannot describe adequately the mental and physical strain of the last forty-eight hours."[13]

After the rigors of the glacier, the four weary men were happy to be on the barrier again; they dug out the deeply buried depot that would provide the security of six days' food for the next fifty miles. But a warm 30-degree-Fahrenheit snow wet everything, and a freezing wind and blizzard followed. All were affected by dysentery. Wild was especially weakened, and, on the last day of January, in an extraordinary gesture, Shackleton gave to Wild his own breakfast biscuit. Wild wrote in his diary: "I do not suppose that anyone else in the world can thoroughly realise how much generosity and sympathy was shown by this; I DO by GOD I shall never forget it. Thousands of pounds would not have bought that one biscuit."[14] Later, in the middle of February, sharing a tent, exhausted and starving, Shackleton asked Wild if he would accompany him again some day for another try on the South Pole, and Wild answered yes.[15]

Surfaces were difficult again, and travel on the featureless barrier was monotonous. The men reached Grisi depot on 2 February but two days later were stalled by dysentery. With all thoughts on food, they reached Chinaman depot on 13 February and had his "splendid" liver. While digging out the depot, the men recovered Chinaman's spilled blood, frozen in the snow, and, too hungry to pass it up, boiled it for "beef-tea."[16] Shackleton was treated on his birthday, 15 February, to a cigarette made of pipe tobacco and coarse paper. His response? "It was delicious."[17] By late February the party encountered spells of cold to minus 35 degrees but made good distance with the help of tail winds and sledge sail. As they approached the well-stocked Bluff depot, they were in a state of advanced starvation. All enthusiasm for the magnificent scenery that had captivated them on their southward journey was gone. Instead the men fantasized newly invented gastronomic delicacies and days of gorging and sleeping. On 21 February, Shackleton could comment only: "Our food lies ahead, and death stalks us from behind."[18]

While the southern party was away, Joyce, Mackintosh, Day, and Marston had departed from Cape Royds on 15 January with two sledges and eight dogs to haul eight hundred pounds of provisions to provide for the last hundred miles of the polar party's return. Joyce's party laid out the Bluff depot on 25 January; Shackleton was due on 1 February. The depot party retreated to Hut Point, then set out again, arriving at the depot once more on 8 February. They set out extra marker flags, headed south to search, returned to the Bluff depot on 16 February, and then headed back to Cape Royds.

On 23 February, Shackleton's party saw the Bluff depot looming up in the distance, and the men finished their few remaining biscuits. All food was gone when they arrived. Shackleton wrote: "After months of want and hunger, we suddenly found ourselves able to have meals fit for the gods, and with appetites that the gods might have envied."[19]

Despite the feast Marshall's health failed, and he was left under Adams's charge on 27 February while Shackleton and Wild dashed for Hut Point. Shackleton had left instructions that if he were not there by 1 March, he could be given up for dead. Thus the ship could depart for the season, and the four men would be stranded. Shackleton was already thinking of a whaleboat journey back to New Zealand.[20] Meanwhile, aboard ship, Mackintosh had a feeling that Shackleton had arrived at Hut Point, so he went aloft in the crow's nest and saw Shackleton's heliograph signal. Shackleton and Wild were aboard the Nimrod precisely on 1 March. Shackleton, Mackay, Mawson, and the New Zealander Thomas McGillan (1885–?) then went out to retrieve Marshall and Adams and reached them the following day. A monumental journey of 1,669.5 miles in 124 days was ended.

While the polar party was away, the Nimrod, under the command of Evans, who had done a remarkable job commanding the Koonya, returned in early January 1909 but was stopped short of Cape Royds by the frozen sea of McMurdo Sound. Because the party knew that the men at Cape Royds would be eager for news of the ship and the mail, the one-eyed Mackintosh and McGillan set out over the sea ice with the mail and a sledge on 3 January. But the floes broke up rapidly, and they dashed for shore, jumping open

The Southern Party on board the *Nimrod* (left to right):
Wild, Shackleton, Marshall, and Adams
Shackleton, *The Heart of the Antarctic,* 1909

water lanes, cutting their hands and getting soaked in freezing water. They
arrived three-quarters of a mile south of the penguin rookery at Cape Bird
and spent several days there, McGillan snow-blind, with no sign of the ship.
They pitched a tent, left the mail, and decided to march overland to Cape
Royds with forty pounds apiece and only three meals. They expected a brief
trip. They had no idea what lay ahead.

What ensued was a nightmare. The ice was slippery, and they had no
spikes. Due to inexperience and no foreknowledge of the terrain, the two
men proceeded unroped: McGillan fell thirty feet down a crevasse and was
luckily saved, but the stove and almost all the food and equipment were lost.
Considerably wiser now, they used a strap to link themselves together. They
ascended higher and higher to avoid the numerous chasms in their way, but
to little avail; Mackintosh described a "hot-bed" of crevasses.[21] The men had
no choice but to glissade down a three-thousand-foot slope. They tried to
use their knives as brakes, but these were torn from their grasps. They dug in
their heels and careened downward, skirting yawning crevasses, until they
reached bottom.

They could now see the Cape Royds hut, but a blizzard sprang up and obliterated the way. Mackintosh and McGillan groped about in the thick weather for eighteen hours until they happened to run into Day on the evening of 12 January, forty hours after the start of their journey. (Mackintosh recovered quickly and became a member of the Bluff depot party that departed three days later.) Meanwhile the *Nimrod* had arrived at Cape Royds on 5 January, and all feared the two men had perished. The ship went back north to find them, the tent was spotted, a boat was sent ashore, and the mail bag was picked up along with a note from Mackintosh stating that he and McGillan had set out overland for Cape Royds. The *Nimrod* arrived back at Cape Royds on 16 January to the happy news the men were safe.

The Western party was composed of Priestley, Armytage, and Brocklehurst. They ascended the Ferrar Glacier and performed survey and geological work in the dry valleys and neighboring areas to the west across McMurdo Sound. Back at Butter Point they awaited the ship and camped on what they thought was reliable sea ice; the men awoke at seven in the morning on 24 January to find two miles of open water separating them from shore. They rationed their remaining four days' food and spent the day anxiously awaiting a change in drift of their floe, since there was little hope the ship could help. Late in the evening they were indeed drifting toward the shore, and they promptly struck camp just after midnight. A six-foot edge of the floe touched the fast ice; the men rushed across in an instant. Moments later, the floe moved north again, never to return. The men were picked by the *Nimrod* the following day.

The Northern party was composed of David, who led, Mawson, and Mackay. David was a professor of geology at the University of Sydney. Beloved by his students and highly respected by his colleagues, he was possessed of a kindly and courteous manner. The goals of the party were to reach the south magnetic pole and to perform land surveys. Shackleton had carefully reviewed the provisions and how the men would be retrieved under a variety of adverse circumstances. The three-man party departed across the frozen sea ice on 25 September 1908 with the motorcar, but the wheels stuck in the sastrugi and irregular surfaces, and all of the men were injured trying to deal with the car's idiosyncrasies. They succeeded in getting away only fifteen miles, left three depots, and returned to winter quarters for a fresh start on 5 October.

By that date the snowy surface was so soft that the men decided to forgo the motor car when little more than two miles out. The men reached Butter

Point on 13 October, cached stores, and landed at Cape Bernacchi four days later, taking possession of Victoria Land for Great Britain. David became snow-blind the next day and appointed Mawson to choose the route. Mawson was so effective at route-finding that David left him in charge of that responsibility. The men traveled over the sea ice near the coast. Appalling surfaces forced them to relay and shorten their rations. Their progress was merely four miles a day. They fashioned a blubber stove out of a biscuit tin, making wicks from used food bags and a frying pan from a paraffin tin. They killed seals and emperor penguins for food, ate the meat and liver, rendered the oil, and made blood pancakes and gravy. The men regretted their three-man sleeping bag: kicking and snoring often kept them awake. They watched the sea ice break up and knew they would never be able to cross McMurdo Sound to Cape Royds after their inland journey—their rescue would hinge on the ship.

On 30 November the party reached the Drygalski Glacier (now Drygalski Ice Tongue), the point from which the inland journey would commence. The three laid in their final stores of seal and penguin meat, fixed a depot with personal letters, and set off over hazardous and irregular surfaces with a total load of 670 pounds. Mawson went down a particularly bad crevasse, swinging free eight feet below the surface while his rope cut deeply into the overhanging lid. After hoisting himself as high as he could go, he broke himself through from the underside to safety. On 20 December, they were still at sea level, with almost five hundred miles to cover before the 1 February scheduled return of the ship. They chose what they called Backstairs Passage to the south of Mount Larsen, with a 20 to 30 percent grade. They continued their collections, took occasional magnetic latitude readings with the Lloyd-Creak dip circle, made progress by relaying, and by New Year's Eve 1909 had ascended to 4,500 feet, where they were visited by a skua.

The men encountered surface undulations up to forty feet deep that increased their work of travel considerably. As they ascended, they encountered cold headwinds and blizzards from the plateau and were affected by snow blindness and frostbite. Their cracked lips were glued together overnight by congealed blood. By 11 January 1909, the party had reached an altitude of over seven thousand feet, and the ice terrain was flattening out. Mawson observed that the position of the south magnetic pole, known to be variable, had not shifted according to previous predictions. Still, they had about fifty miles to reach it. On 15 January the dip circle showed 89°45', but daily swings in the readings meant that the position of a 90° dip could only

The Northern Party at the estimated south magnetic pole
(left to right): Mackay, David, and Mawson
Shackleton, *The Heart of the Antarctic,* 1909

be approximated. Thus they made their best assumption and the next day left a depot of the sledge and all gear except the tent, sleeping bag, stove, cooker, some equipment, and food. They set out in a run for the estimated pole, leaving equipment every two miles as route markers.

The three men arrived at 72°25' S, 155°16' E under a blue sky with cumulus clouds, light breezes, and a temperature of 0 degrees Fahrenheit. They hoisted a flag, took possession, gave three cheers for the King, and took a photograph. David wrote: "It was an intense satisfaction and relief to all of us to feel that at last, after so many days of toil, hardship, and danger, we had been able to carry out our leader's instructions. . . . We were too utterly weary to be capable of any great amount of exultation. I am sure the feeling that was uppermost in all of us was one of devout and heartfelt thankfulness to the kind Providence which had so far guided our footsteps in safety to that goal. With a fervent "Thank God" we all did a right-about turn, and as quick a march as tired limbs would allow back in the direction of our little green tent in the wilderness of snow."[22]

The men were 260 miles from the Drygalski depot, where they would be picked up. That meant sixteen miles a day, not accounting for weather delays. They returned to full rations but were short on tea leaves, so they reclaimed used tea bags discarded on the outward journey and debated how best to brew them. The tea assumed a strong flavor of muslin. "Nevertheless," David remarked, "this drink was nectar."[23] The men lost their outward tracks, but Mawson, leading by hunch, miraculously picked them up. On 28 January, David, hoping for a day of larger meals, hinted to Mackay, who was cook, that it was his birthday—extra food appeared at lunch and dinner.

During the steepest descent the men had trouble controlling the sledge, lost their sledgemeter, encountered crevasses, and groped in occasional thick weather. Mawson crashed through an ice-covered lake and was soaked in the icy water up to his thighs. Even so, progress was excellent, and on 2 February they were only a few miles from the Drygalski depot. Eager not to miss the ship, they cached equipment and geological specimens and headed for the looming depot flag. But they were stopped by a barranca, a deep ravine six hundred feet wide and forty feet deep; the floor was covered with snow, and the sea ice was dotted with seals and penguins. Exhausted, David turned leadership over to Mawson. The three men descended into the barranca, found they could not ascend the far side, and had to return. They successfully negotiated a different route across a snow bridge and arrived at the depot the next day. They took up four-hour watches and wondered whether the overdue ship would ever arrive. Their talk was of a blatantly hazardous southward trek along the coast.

A booming report suddenly rang out. The men dashed out of the tent to see the *Nimrod* only a quarter-mile away. They could hear cheers from the ship. Their journey of 122 days and 1,260 miles (with 740 miles of relay work) was ended. The ice made one final mocking gesture, however; Mawson suddenly disappeared twenty feet down a crevasse and was seen perched on a ledge just above the icy seawater. A tricky rescue effort was launched by the ship's first officer, John K. Davis (1884–1967). The chasm was bridged with lumber, Davis was lowered in, and the two men were then hauled up, Mawson first. (Mawson later selected Davis as his ship's captain on his 1911–14 expedition.) On board ship, the men were photographed and given tea and letters from home. They had their first bath in four months, ridding themselves of layers of seal oil and soot. A feast and snug bunks followed.

The ship arrived at Cape Royds and preparations were made for final departure. A year's stores for fifteen men were left for any future expedition that might benefit. Shackleton's party at Hut Point was picked up, and with all aboard the *Nimrod* departed 4 March under steam and sail. As the men passed Cape Royds, they cheered their home of the previous year and recalled fond memories. Owing to a thickening, freezing sea and the lateness of the season, the geological specimens and equipment cached by the Northern party were abandoned. Shackleton planned to proceed west between the Balleny Islands and the mainland after passing Cape Adare, so as to link up the mainland to the Adélie Coast. No one had yet succeeded in doing this, owing to heavy pack ice that regularly obstructed travel in the area. The *Nimrod* did not fully succeed but reached 166°14' E, the farthest ever achieved. The ship was turned northward for New Zealand. The company landed on Stewart Island on 22 March, Shackleton sent cables the following day, and the party was welcomed to Lyttleton by cheering crowds on 25 March 1909.

Shackleton had left the door open for someone else to capture the prize of first at the South Pole. Despite his great success in achieving a high latitude, Shackleton had in his own mind failed. Roald Amundsen, who conquered the South Pole only three years later and held Shackleton in the highest regard, believed Shackleton would have succeeded had he set up base in the Bay of Whales, over seventy miles closer to the pole than Cape Royds. Once Shackleton had selected McMurdo Sound, the condition of the ice thwarted his goal. Had open water permitted him to reach Hut Point, he would have started closer to the pole and would have had the remainder of the first season to cache supplies southward. As circumstances lay for him, however, he had to accept his disadvantage. On the barrier, he had inferior transport: the British did not accept dogs as the superior means of conveyance. Whether the loss of Socks prevented success is unclear: the extra food might have encouraged Shackleton to go all the way to the pole, but the men were not fit; they would not have arrived at Hut Point until at least late March, when weather on the barrier would have been severe. If the men survived at all, the ship would have departed, and they would have had no assistance for the sick among them. They would have had to choose between wintering over or making a desperate journey home in perilous autumn seas in an open whaleboat.

18

JEAN-BAPTISTE CHARCOT AND THE SECOND FRENCH ANTARCTIC EXPEDITION IN THE *POURQUOI-PAS?* (1908–1910)

Mes yeux se portent sur la devise de la dunette que . . . nous a tous poussés et soutenus dans cette aventure, et là haut se détachant sur le ciel, battant au vent, le pavillon de notre bateau me répond *Pourquoi-Pas?*

[My eyes turn to the motto on the poop-deck which . . . has spurred on and supported us all through this expedition. . . . Standing out against the sky and flapping in the wind, our ship's ensign answers me, *Pourquoi-Pas?* (Why not?).]

Jean-Baptiste Charcot, Le *"Pourquoi-Pas?" dans l'Antarctique*

CHARCOT BEGAN PREPARING for a second Antarctic expedition to expand on the work of his first almost as soon as he returned to France in 1905. The principal purpose of the new endeavor was to extend exploration of Graham Land as far south as possible, and to determine if it and Alexander Island were part of the continent. Studies in hydrography, oceanography, bacteriology, meteorology, and atmospheric phenomena were to be included. Charcot's prospectus to the Académie des Sciences was well received, and the press was encouraging.

Even so, and despite his outstanding reputation, Charcot had trouble raising funds, as did most independent explorers of that period. But Charcot had earned the goodwill of the French people and his government when he had returned from his first expedition, and now he was awarded with 600,000 francs from the government's Ministry of Public Institutions. The final budget of 800,000 francs (about £34,000) was still modest. Charcot received additional gifts from private manufacturers and the governments of Monaco, Brazil, Chile, and Argentina. At that time in France, an expedition leader was usually able to procure a qualified but unpaid scientific staff, easing the leader's financial burdens. The Ministry of Marine supplied naval officers, coal, instruments, maps, and other materials.

Charcot once again engaged Père Gautier, builder of the *Français*, to produce a schooner to exacting standards. The new ship was named *Pourquoi-Pas?* Its construction alone consumed half of Charcot's budget. The vessel was a three-masted barque, 135 feet long and 30 feet abeam, strong and reinforced, armored at the bow with thick iron. Charcot wanted the *Pourquoi-Pas?* to be stronger and faster than the *Français*, to take advantage of the relatively brief periods of excellent visibility in the region of the Antarctic Peninsula. The interior design ensured the greatest possible comforts: a generator produced electric light, heating of the living areas was improved, and an advanced heat-efficient system for melting ice was installed. Three excellent laboratories and capacious holds were constructed. Shipbuilding was completed in eight months. Launched with a bottle of Mumm champagne, the *Pourquoi-Pas?* was the object of great admiration in sophisticated circles.

On 15 August 1908, a large crowd gathered to wish the departing voyagers well. Paul Doumer, who had persuaded the Ministry of Public Institutions to support the expedition, became president of the expedition's organization committee, and Charcot designated him father of the expedition. Doumer gave the official farewell. (Years later, Doumer became president of France.) The ship sailed away to the strains of the Marseillaise.

The ship's company comprised eight officers and scientists and a crew of twenty-two men, two of whom were over fifty, aged by Antarctic standards of the day. The staff consisted of Charcot (leader, bacteriology), H. Bongrain (second in command, astronomy, hydrography, seismology, gravity), Jules Rouch (1884–1973) (sublieutenant, meteorology, oceanography, atmospheric electricity), R. Godfroy (tides, atmospheric chemistry), Ernest Gourdon (geology, glaciology), J. Liouville (physician, zoology), L. Gain (zoology, botany), and A. Senouque (magnetics). Some men doubled as scientists and officers. Like Shackleton, Charcot engendered a loyal following—Gourdon and eight of the crew had been on the *Français*. The men's outfit included excellent cold-weather clothing, yellow-tinted goggles (no one developed snow blindness), and three motor cars. (Charcot was persuaded to take them along after joining Scott at the motor trials at Lautaret, but the cars were never used, ice surfaces being unsuitable.) Included in the cargo was the finest assortment of wines ever taken to high latitudes.

The staff of the *Pourquoi-Pas?* prior to departure (left to right): Gourdon,
Bongrain, Rouch, Liouville, Charcot, Gain, Senouque, Godfroy
Charcot, *Le "Pourquoi-Pas?" dans l'Antarctique,* 1910

Stops were made at Cherbourg, Guernsey, Madeira, St. Vincent, Rio de
Janeiro, Buenos Aires (where the ship was dry-docked for repairs and where
the Argentine government gave Charcot unlimited credit to satisfy the expedition's needs), and finally Punta Arenas, the last port of call before the voyage across the Drake Passage to the Antarctic. Charcot's beloved wife, mother
of the expedition, accompanied the ship that far. As Charcot made final
preparations for departure, he commented, "This expected and inevitable
separation was, nevertheless, a wrench. . . . Certain people may have smiled
over the presence of a woman on board during the first part of the journey
and even have found in it an excuse for belittling the grave and serious side
of our work. But others—happily the majority—only saw in it a touching
proof of love, courage, and interest in the object which I had in view; it is the
opinion of these latter for which I care."[1]
    The ship sailed from Punta Arenas on 16 December 1908 to the shouting
of a contingency of Frenchmen and Chileans ashore: "Vive la France!"
Charcot first visited the Norwegian and Chilean whalers at Deception
Island, where he was pleased to find them using his charts of Graham Land.
Charcot was ambivalent about the whaling operations: on the one hand he

hated the stench and pervasiveness of blubber and oil and was pleased when the whalers had difficulty catching their booty. "I was not sorry each time one of these magnificent, peaceful and amiable brutes managed to escape, and that it was with joy that I saw fading farther away the little black patch on the calm blue sea, with the jet of noisily spouting vapour above it."[2] However, his love of country and interest in the financial well-being of his countrymen were strong enough to override his distaste: he hoped some of his own countrymen would profit from the industry. It was not as if the great mammals were scarce—whales were so plentiful that one company at Admiralty Bay on King George Island was allowing carcasses to go to waste.

In fine weather and a favorable northeast breeze, the French sailed south from Deception Island on 25 December. In the Gerlache Strait, Charcot, Godfroy, Gourdon, and two others in a motorized boat attempted to reach Booth Island, where the *Français* had spent nine months, but, two miles short of their goal, adverse ice conditions, a freshening wind, engine trouble, and contrary currents all conspired to force them to Port Lockroy on Wiencke Island. The *Pourquoi-Pas?* later arrived there, however, with the entire party aboard, and Charcot reminisced with Gourdon and the crewmen who had been with him before, and lamented that his prior companions Matha and Pléneau could not be present. The scene and the sounds of penguins and cormorants were pleasingly familiar.

New Year's Day 1909 was spent in good cheer. "Amid the great solitude, full of the howling of the wind and the sound of the crashing floe, I pray to God on this morning of the first day of the year to give me strength and ability to rise to the height of the task . . . with the sole object of being of some use to my country."[3] That day Charcot, Godfroy, and Liouville boarded a boat to make a southern reconnaissance to Hovgaard and Petermann Islands and were drenched by rain. That same day, the entire party moved on to Petermann Island, and there discovered a sheltered cove they named Port Circumcision for the anniversary of that event in the life of Jesus.

What proved to be the most hazardous excursion of the expedition commenced 4 January. Charcot, Gourdon, and Godfroy set out on a reconnaissance to Cape Tuxen and the nearby Berthelot Islands in a motorboat in good weather, without extra provisions. Five hours later they had eaten almost all their food; they had expected to be back on ship in three hours. But ice drifted in and choked off their return, and snow and sleet were driven in a biting wind; then the motor malfunctioned. In vain the men tried to cut their way with a spade and boat hooks. The spade, their only one, slipped from Godfroy's numbed hands, and he watched, horrified, as it disappeared into the water. The ice was so thick that the spade was useless anyway, but the men were inconsolable. Soaked, freezing, and hungry, they waited on the Berthelots, Charcot lying awake anxiously preoccupied by the weight of his responsibility. After three strained days the weather finally broke, ice conditions improved, and the ship was able to approach. The men were rescued.

They had barely changed into warm clothing when, in the middle of a good meal and while the men were recounting their story, the ship grounded violently off Cape Tuxen in a falling tide. Pieces of the false keel floated about the ship as the stern deck was flooded. Rocks were apparently Charcot's nemesis. The men worked despairingly all day, shifting weight aft. Charcot lamented, "The Expedition would be at an end when barely commenced. All my efforts in organizing it, fitting it out, and bringing it here would be fruitless, and the page which I dreamt of adding to the history of French explorations would never see the light. . . . It is not only my honour which is at stake, it is my country's."[4] A rising tide released the ship, grinding and crackling. The pumps compensated for a leak, and the vessel seemed in good enough condition to continue the season's work: Charcot was unaware that his ship had been badly damaged.

The party sailed south from Petermann Island on 12 January to begin what was the most interesting part of the season's work. The *Pourquoi-Pas?* cruised between Rabot and Nansen Islands into a previously unknown bay that was named after the early-nineteenth-century American explorer Benjamin Pendleton. Charcot was not so nationalistic that he could not honor the work of a non-Frenchman. Further south the party extended Biscoe's previous charting of the vicinity of Adelaide Island, gave names to islands to the south and east, and described the mountains, nunataks, ice cliffs, huge crevassed glaciers, and conditions of the sea ice and bergs. Their investigations were hampered by the enormous number of icebergs—there were thousands of them—but the party was blessed with several days of excellent weather. Charcot, wary of vagaries in visual perception in the Antarctic regions, determined that Biscoe had made significant mistakes in estimating the dimensions of Adelaide Island. Nevertheless, in his typically gentlemanly fashion, Charcot went out of his way to praise Biscoe's work: "Nothing is so productive of error as the eyesight in polar regions. The least change in the weather alters one's estimates in truly fantastic manner. . . . I feel infinitely more pleasure in verifying the correctness of one of my predecessors . . . [than in] proving the incorrectness of his assertions."[5] He named the large bay in which they were operating after Matha (it is now called Matha Strait), his comrade on his earlier expedition.

On 16 January the *Pourquoi-Pas?* reached the *Français*'s southernmost point, where it had grounded. The men now passed the limits of Biscoe and Evensen. After a day spent skirting the floes extending south from Adelaide Island, the Frenchmen saw new lands above the glacial ice. Charcot wrote: "I confess to feeling genuine emotion over these lands, on which we are the first to set eyes."[6] Charcot discovered and named Marguerite Bay south of Adelaide Island after his wife; Jenny Island was named after Bongrain's wife. A party landed on Jenny Island and obtained magnificent views from a height of fifteen hundred feet between two of three jagged peaks. From that altitude Charcot was able to see the extension of the Loubet Coast, which he named Fallières Land (now Fallières Coast) after the contemporary French president.

As they proceeded south by ship, Alexander Island and the Fallières Coast loomed above increasingly dense pack ice. Progress eastward was exceedingly slow, but the men were rewarded with rare views of Alexander Island from a direction different than previous explorers had had. Finally, arrested by impenetrable ice floes, the party retreated to Marguerite Bay. The men hoped to winter there, because the bay seemed to be a safe haven, but they had to abandon it when ice forced them out. The party's long stretch of fair weather was now broken; coal consumption was concerning Charcot, since no winter quarters had yet been selected. But the weather turned fair again, and Charcot decided to make another attempt on Alexander Island, this time from the southwest. The ship fought its way to within two miles of the ice cliff; the mountains rose out of the ice only about fifteen miles away. This was the closest approach any expedition had ever achieved. The area was so remote that even at the height of summer marine mammals and birds were at best sparse.

The party retreated to Jenny Island, where Bongrain, Gain, and a crewman set off on a three-day excursion to determine if Adelaide Island was indeed an island or connected to the mainland. Their results, combined with observations from the ship in Matha Strait, confirmed that it was an island, in a position very close to the mainland. Even though Charcot achieved more than he had hoped for, still he regretted withdrawing with the advancing season. He had expected to winter in Matha Strait, but ice prevented it; the men reluctantly retreated to Petermann Island.

Winter quarters were established at Port Circumcision in early February. The island was just over a mile long, separated by an isthmus into two portions; the party wintered on the southern part. Excursions along the coast to various islands and a journey to the Graham Land interior would be possible, thus the wintering site was practical. But it was not secure: barriers of steel wire were stretched across the 275-foot mouth of the harbor to stop ice blocks from moving in; ten hawsers and two anchor chains running from the ship to shore were employed to fix the ship's position. Four huts were erected, and scientific studies were carried on throughout the winter. Seals for food and oil were few in number, so several hundred penguins were killed instead, grieving Charcot because he found the birds appealing and innocent. The penguins in the Adélie colony were amusing objects for scientific study. Charcot strictly forbade any unnecessary molestation. So completely had the fur seals been slaughtered in past years that not one was encountered.

The weather of late summer was occasionally too warm. A heat spell of 46 degrees Fahrenheit in late February brought about a thaw, with avalanches and torrential streams all over the island. In late March a temperature rise to 41 degrees was accompanied by rain. Charcot mused, "I always find that one of the greatest comforts of this part of the world is precisely the absence of rain and confidence with which one can go out without one's umbrella!"[7] By early April temperatures dropped, and many of the men enthusiastically took up tobogganing on the nearby slopes. Until 13 April, the living areas of the ship were left unheated to preserve coal. As a result, the wardroom was damp and only just above freezing; many of the men suffered from chilblains, cold-induced red, painful, itching patches on the feet and hands. Once the living areas were heated, those discomforts vanished. With still enough light in April, Gain and Gourdon grew hyacinths, onions, and watercress in Antarctic soil under the wardroom skylight.

Autumn was trying, as a northeasterly storm raged for four consecutive weeks; the sun was not seen from 27 April until 23 May. Finally the storm was over: "Joy beyond measure, it is absolutely calm!"[8] Some of the men made a reconnaissance journey across the channel to the glacier leading to the interior of Graham Land. Birthdays, holidays, and special occasions were celebrated. A number of the men enjoyed constructing ships in glass bottles; E. Cholet, who was first mate on both this and the *Français* expeditions, was particularly expert at this art and was given the oddest-shaped bottles as a challenge. He produced masterpieces every time. After-dinner classes were given in mathematics, grammar, geography, navigation, English, first aid, and wound care. An Antarctic Sporting Club was formed, and gold and silver medals were cut out of food boxes and awarded to the victors. Dominoes and chess were popular, but there were no card games because Charcot disliked them. The ship had a library of fifteen hundred volumes, and old magazines were issued daily. Rouch read aloud installments from his serial romance, *The Typist's Lover*.

In the middle of June, an immense drop in barometric pressure was accompanied by a ferocious storm from the northeast. The *Pourquoi-Pas?* strained at its chains and hawsers, and the ship jammed against a rock. Ice blocks swept into the harbor on heavy currents, one striking the ship's stern, tearing away two-thirds of the rudder and breaking two braces. The carpenter and blacksmith unshipped the rudder and repaired it only with great difficulty. Charcot, who regretted not having removed the rudder beforehand, was anxious for the future of the expedition. "I re-read my diary on *Le Français*, written during a period quite as agonizing as this. I light on a passage where I assert that, if ever I return to France, I will embark no more on such adventures. A few weeks after my return, I was thinking of nothing but the organization of a new Expedition, and three years later, I started off again! Is this my reward for my persistent efforts?"[9]

As midwinter passed, a number of men showed signs of depression, pallor, edema, and irregular heart rhythm—the same afflictions that had plagued the men of the *Belgica*. Charcot became quite ill and considered himself to have a serious heart condition. The sick men took a regimen of fresh meat, exercise, and antiscorbutics. By late August Charcot's health seemed to be improving, but soon afterward he suffered a setback that prevented him from leading an expedition into the Graham Land interior, a keen disappointment. "I do not wish to confess it yet, but evidently I cannot lead the excursion. I cannot walk, I crawl, and at the end of a few hours I should be obliged to have myself carried by the others."[10] Charcot remained the principal organizer, but Gourdon led the party of six that left on 18 September 1909 with two heavily provisioned sledges.

While the party was away, Charcot recorded an especially endearing interaction with a family of Weddell seals near the ship. "The men . . . hunt for seals. . . . [We] find a female Weddell's Seal, which has just given birth. . . . Nothing could have been more touching in the midst of this gloomy scenery, so little suggestive of life, than the little seal, disconcertingly human, charming . . . beside its mother with her massive and clumsy form . . . playing about and rubbing itself against its mother, with its quaint little round face and fine large eyes full of astonishment and roguery. . . . The father appeared through a hole in the ice and started to intone . . . a curious, if not particularly melodious, little song. . . . Then I drew close and took the little one in my arms. It was delighted, showing no fear, but acting just like a baby, and when I put the soft little body back on the ice again it came crawling up to me, rubbing up against my legs and asking for fresh caresses. Must I confess that the memory of a little being which I left at home in France came to me so sharply that there was a catch in my throat? . . . There was no need for me to order that these animals' lives be spared. . . . The men who accompanied me, nearly all of them fathers of a family, had felt the same emotions as myself."[11]

Sixteen days after the departure of Gourdon and his men, Charcot, Godfroy, and four others took a boat to the glacier to meet Gourdon's returning party. Gourdon had found no route to the inland ice of Graham Land, but despite wind, fog, falling snow, and bad surfaces, his party had made worthwhile observations of glaciers, topography, and weather. Gourdon had turned back sixteen miles from ship at about three thousand feet elevation in a majestic cul-de-sac that was named the Amphitheatre of the Avalanches. The men's final view was a spectacular scene of chaotic ice and six mock suns adorned by sparkling, refractive halos in an atmosphere laden with ice crystals.

Spring was soon under way as blue-eyed cormorants and Adélie penguins, some of which had been banded, returned to their homes. The men carried out surveys and collected geological specimens. Charcot found that even a brief trip to Booth Island was still almost too much for his stamina; several men became newly ill and were placed on the prescribed regimen. The ship's engine was started successfully after having lain idle for many months, and on 25 November the men departed their winter home.

The remaining eighty-ton coal supply was inadequate for another season's work in the south, so the party first made a difficult ice passage northward to Deception Island to obtain coal from the Norwegians. Unlike the turf battles waged by the sealers of the early 1820s, the Norwegian and Chilean whaling companies at Deception Island worked harmoniously together and shared limited resources, such as fresh water. Charcot was treated with special kindness; M. Andreson of the *Gobernador Bories* generously gave him the one hundred tons of coal he needed in simple exchange for Charcot's promise to repay the debt from his own supply in Punta Arenas. The men entertained each other on their respective ships. A package of mail was waiting for the men of the *Pourquoi-Pas?*, but letters to Charcot and several others were accidentally omitted from the delivery, a gloomy disappointment. Charcot learned of the North Pole exploits of Frederick A. Cook and Robert Peary, and of Shackleton's accomplishments.

The *Pourquoi-Pas?* was now leaking more than usual. Andreson offered to have the hull examined by an experienced Norwegian diver, who made a number of ominous discoveries. The vessel had sustained a long gash on the port side, fragments of the false keel had been lost, the entire stem below the water line was torn away, and a large piece of the keel was splintered. Both the diver and Andreson adamantly advised Charcot not to proceed, since even ice-free navigation was risky; even a modest ice shock might sink the ship. Charcot, in a stance unusually reckless for him, refused the advice, and, maintaining that the honor of France was at stake, resolved to carry on despite Andreson's appeal to common sense. Charcot kept the facts mostly to himself. "I think it right to tell at least a portion of the truth to my colleagues on the staff, but it seems to me useless to alarm the crew."[12] While awaiting a break in the weather at Deception Island, the party engaged itself in geology work, dredgings, and surveys; a fresh series of soundings rectified earlier charting inaccuracies. These studies would give the men something to show for the second season in the event of a mishap with the ship. The party left Deception Island on 23 December 1909.

Charcot planned first to visit Hope Bay at the northern tip of the Trinity Peninsula to recover the fossil collections left behind by J. Gunnar Andersson of Nordenskjöld's expedition, and then to seek anchorages in the vicinity of Joinville Island that might be useful to the whalers. Ice prevented both objectives, but Gourdon, Godfroy, and two others in a dinghy made the first documented landing on volcanic Bridgeman Island. The ship retreated to King George Island and made soundings, dredgings, and geologic collections in Admiralty Bay. Heading south, they were in the latitude of Alexander Island on 11 January 1910.

South of Alexander Island, at about 70° S, 77° W, Charcot achieved an ecstatic moment when he made his most important land discovery. "At last, at noon, the weather completely clears up, and I examine the horizon anxiously. . . . I will speak of it to no one before acquiring absolute and indisputable certainty. I restart the engine and to every one's great astonishment, contrary to previous orders, I steer for the east. I overhear even a few small criticisms. . . . They only make me smile. I hurry over lunch in order not to excite anyone's attention, and I climb up into the crow's-nest again with my field glasses. All doubts are gone. Those are not icebergs which lift their pointed summits to the sky; it is a land, a new land, a land to be seen clearly with the naked eye, a land which belongs to us! It is necessary to have lived through these months of waiting and anxiety, of fear of failure, of desire to do something, of eagerness to take back to one's country something important, to understand all that is conveyed by these two words, which I repeat to myself under my breath, a *New Land!*"[13] Upon Charcot's return to France, the discovery was corroborated by the authority Edwin Swift Balch, who suggested it be called Charcot Land (now Charcot Island).[14] Charcot agreed to this, but only if the name referred to his famous father.

Unable to approach on account of ice, Charcot now turned the ship west along the pack ice and achieved a higher southern latitude than either Bellingshausen or Gerlache. "The mighty sea and the monstrous icebergs are playing their giant's games . . . caressing or fighting. . . . We are merely tolerated, although a kind of intimacy may be created between us and our magnificent hosts."[15] Peter I Island was sighted on 14 January but from too great a distance to add to Bellingshausen's observations. Nonetheless, Charcot's party was the first to sight the island since the great Russian navigator discovered it in 1821.

Later that day a storm came up from the southeast, bringing fog, snow, and extreme danger. Great blocks of ice appeared in succession out of the gloom, and survival was a matter of quick maneuvering. Like others before him, Charcot believed that the bergs, shallow soundings, and birdlife were evidence of an unknown land not far away, and thus he persisted. "Happily the ship is behaving admirably, though it is evident that we cannot congratulate ourselves on being in a safe haven."[16] The party continued westward along the ice edge at latitude 69° to 70°30' S, entering bays in the ice where practicable. Finally, with the health of some of the men a growing concern and the supply of coal dwindling, Charcot decided to turn his ship north on 22 January in 124° W.

The party arrived at Tuesday Bay in the Strait of Magellan on 1 February; the ship was intact and all men were well. Ten days later they docked in Punta Arenas, where they were welcomed warmly and received telegrams of congratulations from all over the world. After dry-docking the ship in Montevideo for extensive repairs, and stopping in the Azores, where the ship was scrubbed and painted, the party arrived in Rouen on 5 June to a stupendous reception. Charcot reflected, "I ask myself if it was worth all the sorrow which accompanied our absence. . . . But my eyes turn to the motto on the poop-deck which . . . has spurred on and supported us all through this expedition. . . . Standing out against the sky and flapping in the wind, our ship's ensign answers me, *Pourquoi-Pas?* (Why not?)."[17]

Charcot and the French nation he represented had much to be proud of. In all, the French explorer and his party charted 1,250 miles of coastline and amassed an enormous quantity of scientific data that were published over the course of the following decade. They had filled in the missing pieces along the west coast of the Antarctic Peninsula and thus strengthened the importance of their predecessors' individual discoveries. Their observations of sea ice and harbors were of enormous value to navigators who followed.

Charcot's work fulfilled the ideals of scientific inquiry: accuracy of observation and impartiality of interpretation. The British had high regard for the French explorer, and the Royal Geographical Society awarded him the Patron's Gold Medal for his work. He also received the gold medals of geographical societies in Paris, Brussels, Antwerp, St. Petersburg, and New York. Charcot thereafter enjoyed a highly distinguished career in science, geography, and administration. He never lost his love for the sea, and he continued to make voyages, although not to the Antarctic regions. On 16 September 1936, Charcot went down with the *Pourquoi-Pas?* in a storm off the coast of Iceland.

19

ROALD AMUNDSEN AND THE NORWEGIAN ANTARCTIC EXPEDITION (1910–1912)

Maalet var naadd, reisen avsluttet. . . . Saa planter vi dig, du kjaere flag, paa Sydpolen.

[The goal was reached, the journey ended. . . . Thus we plant thee, beloved flag, at the South Pole.]

Roald Amundsen, *Sydpolen*

"THEN THERE IS THE QUALITY OF big leadership which is shown by daring to take a big chance. Amundsen took a very big one indeed when he turned from the route to the Pole explored and ascertained by Scott and Shackleton and determined to find a second pass over the mountains from the Barrier to the plateau. As it happened, he succeeded, and established his route as the best way to the Pole until a better is discovered. But he might easily have failed and perished in the attempt; and the combination of reasoning and daring that nerved him to make it can hardly be overrated."[1]

This complimentary postscript came from a member of the opposing camp, from Apsley Cherry-Garrard, chronicler of the Scott expedition that became engaged with Roald Amundsen (1872–1928) in a race for the South Pole. Indeed, the success Amundsen brought to his endeavor was the result of years of polar experience, his appreciation of the importance of detailed preparation and efficient transport, and the selection of his four companions for experience, hardiness, and loyalty. There was an additional spur: Amundsen knew that if he failed, he would probably incur personal ruin in fortune and reputation. Therefore, once he resolved to head south, his determination to arrive first at the South Pole became a single-minded effort, and every quantum of energy was directed toward that goal. Despite the apparent ease with which he succeeded, getting to the pole and back was by no means a simple matter.

Amundsen
Amundsen, *Sydpolen*, 1912

Amundsen's reputation as a polar explorer was already well established before he and his company left Norway. He had been in the Antarctic as the third-ranking officer on Gerlache's expedition, and he had discovered the Northwest Passage (1903–6), which had eluded many great explorers before him. His greatest dream since childhood was to be the first to conquer the North Pole, but when the Americans Robert Peary and Frederick Cook each independently laid claim to it in 1909, Amundsen, already well advanced in his own plans for a major Arctic expedition, realized he would achieve no glory in another North Pole effort. Furthermore, he would not likely recoup his expenses.

Thus he secretly determined to make a detour and take the South Pole before heading north from Cape Horn to carry out his Arctic plans. He made these plans without the knowledge of his grantors, his mentor the great Norwegian polar explorer Fridtjof Nansen (1861–1931), or, until the last moment, most of his expedition mates. Only his brother Leon, who was his business advisor, and subsequently his officers were made aware. Nansen later wrote: "This was an unheard of thing. . . . To make such an immense and entirely new addition to his plans without asking leave! Some thought it grand; more thought it doubtful; but there were many who cried out that it was inadmissible, disloyal—nay, there were some who wanted to have him stopped. But nothing of this reached him. He had steered his course as he himself had set it, without looking back."[2]

Amundsen formulated his plan at home in Bundefjord near Kristiania (now Oslo) in September 1909. Unlike Scott, he had no intention of making his southern venture a scientific expedition. By choosing a new route to the South Pole, however, he realized he could make a contribution to geographic knowledge, although the pole itself had, in all probability, been located by Shackleton on a vast polar plateau. Amundsen planned to take with him men of diverse talents who would make a perfectly complementary whole. He planned to leave Norway in the *Fram* in August 1910, and, following a last stop at Madeira, after which he would be out of reach or recall, travel directly to the Bay of Whales, described by Shackleton, arriving by the middle of January 1911. By taking up a position there, roughly sixty miles further south than McMurdo Sound, where his rival Scott would be stationed, he would be giving himself a distinct advantage in a race. With no land nearby, crevasses, too, were expected to be less of a problem than Scott would face. However, the barrier ice was afloat and could calve. For that reason Shackleton had forsaken the Bay of Whales. But based on the constancy of certain ice features since Ross's time, Amundsen believed that ice in the inner part of the bay was over the solid ground of islands, and he thought Shackleton would have made it to the pole had he started from this location. So Amundsen decided that was where he would land a shore party with two years' equipment and provisions and erect a hut. Abundant seals ensured an unlimited food supply for men and dogs, and the fresh meat would guard the men against scurvy. The ship would then depart and perform oceanographic studies in the South Atlantic. The shore party was to cache supplies as far as 80° S in the remainder of the first season. After a winter of final preparations, the men of the shore party would leave early in spring for the pole, despite the risk of extreme cold: "If we had set out to capture this record, we must at any cost get there first."[3] He planned to be back from the pole on 25 January 1912, and he was, to the very day.

Nansen lent Amundsen the *Fram,* the same vessel created for polar work that had carried Nansen to his farthest north (1893–96). The ship was an eight-hundred-ton, three-masted schooner with an auxiliary two-hundred-horsepower oil engine; it was capable of six knots. The *Fram* was constructed of fine hardwoods, with iron reinforcements and sheathing, and round-bottomed so that it would be lifted up rather than squeezed by a freezing sea. Lt. Thorvald Nilsen later recalled that when the party was caught in hurricane-force winds and a high sea, "enormous seas came surging high to windward, and we, who were standing on the bridge, turned our backs to receive them. . . . But the sea never came. A few yards from the ship it looked over the bulwarks and got ready to hurl itself upon her. But at the last moment the *Fram* gave a wriggle of her body and was instantly at the top of the wave, which slipped under the vessel. Can anyone be surprised if one gets fond of such a ship?"[4]

Because Amundsen was greatly influenced by his belief in the superior value of dog transport, he traveled to Copenhagen to arrange for the purchase of the finest Greenland dogs. He later wrote: "We had heard that Scott, relying on his own experience, and that of Shackleton, had come to the conclusion that Manchurian ponies were superior to dogs on the Barrier. . . . I do not suppose I was the only one who was startled on first hearing this."[5] Dogs could more easily cross snow bridges, travel up glaciers, and be gotten out of crevasses. Also, a dog could eat another dog, the stronger feeding on the weaker.

Amundsen left nothing to chance. The hut, built by Amundsen's own carpenter, Jørgen Stubberud, who became an expedition member, was erected at Bundefjord, then dismantled for the journey south. The structure was a modest twenty-six by thirteen feet, the length made up of a nineteen-and-a-half-foot combined dining, sitting, and sleeping area plus a six-and-a-half-foot kitchen. The building was twelve feet tall, had an attic for storage, cellulose and air insulation, two windows, and ventilation pipes. It was secured by bolts and steel wires.

For the sledging journeys, Amundsen obtained clothing of the finest quality, including reindeer skins and sleeping bags, woolens and Burberry windproofs, as well as lighter clothing. He gave special attention to footwear and its adaptability to ski bindings or crampons, because he well knew that frostbite in even a single individual could create enormous risk to an entire party. Sledging rations were of the highest quality but were simple and practical—pemmican, biscuit, milk powder, and chocolate. The tents were spacious and simple; the walls and floor were a single piece with a sack opening, and each tent required only a single pole. The men took ten twelve-foot sledges with steel-shod runners and spares, but these were heavy and over the winter were modified. The party's eight-foot hickory skis were ideal for passing over concealed crevasses in the Antarctic, but they were longer than necessary for Arctic travel, arousing some speculation among the men.

On 2 June 1910, the day before their first departure from Kristiania, the men received a memorable visit from King Haakon and Queen Maud. The party arrived in Bundefjord to load the hut, the meaning of which perplexed some of the men. They could not fathom the purpose of such a large, solidly constructed house in the Arctic, where a modest framework to provide weather protection while making observations was sufficient.[6] The men enjoyed a private supper in Amundsen's garden, then boated out to the ship and departed just after midnight in the twilight of 7 June. After a test run of the *Fram* in the seas about the British Isles and a motor overhaul in Bergen, final stores, a large amount of coal, and ninety-seven dogs were loaded in Kristiania. Many of the men began to wonder why the dogs and extra coal were taken on there, since the animals and coal could have been taken on later, after rounding Cape Horn.[7] Amundsen had already let Nilsen in on the ruse; now he told his lieutenants, Kristian Prestrud and Frederick Gjertsen, to win their confidence; Amundsen obtained their agreement to proceed south and swore them to secrecy.

Their final departure was on 9 August. The ship carried twenty men. Helmer J. Hanssen (1870–1956) and Adolf Lindström had been with Amundsen before, on the Northwest Passage. Hjalmar Johansen (1867–1913) had been with Nansen at his celebrated farthest north. Nansen, who felt duty-bound to Johansen, persuaded Amundsen to take him, but Amundsen had had reservations about the man, in whom he suspected both a character flaw, as revealed by his alcoholism and poverty, and a potential rival, due to Johansen's experience and seniority.[8]

As Amundsen got to know his men, he believed they would gladly accept his scheme; he planned to tell them in Madeira. Amundsen allowed a month to get there, and the secret was kept. On 6 September, the ship arrived; Amundsen's brother was already there. Fresh water for four months and final supplies were taken on. As the ship was about to depart, Amundsen called the entire party to the deck. It was his moment of reckoning. Hanssen recalled what happened:

> The fourth day in Madeira we were all of us ready to leave that night, when a message came from Amundsen, asking all of us to come on deck as he had something important to say to us.

When we came on deck, he had a large map of the southern hemisphere hung up, and we began to wonder if we were in for a geography lesson. Then he told us that when he had collected half of the money he needed, Peary and Cook had returned saying that they had already reached the North Pole. The job Amundsen had set himself was to be the first at the pole. Now Cook and Peary had done it, this was impossible, and it didn't matter very much when he got there. He had to round Cape Horn anyway, and he thought that being so far south, he might as well go for the South Pole on his way to the North Pole.

He said he had deceived us and also the Norwegian nation. But that could not be helped. He suggested we should all be released from our contracts when we got to San Francisco, and be given free passages home. Anyone on board who didn't want to go to the South Pole was at liberty to leave the ship right away and go back to Norway with Amundsen's brother. Now he wanted to ask us all if we were ready to go with him to the South Pole. He went round asking us one by one, and everybody said yes. "It is really more than I expected," Amundsen said, when he had asked us all. "Now you can go below and write home that we are going to the South Pole first, and from there to the North Pole. My brother will take your letters home with him."

In the evening Leon Amundsen was rowed ashore, and we weighed the anchor, and stood southwards during the night.[9]

Amundsen later wrote of the event: "I briefly explained the extended plan. . . . Now and again I had to glance at their faces. At first, as might be expected, they showed the most unmistakable signs of surprise; but this expression swiftly changed, and before I had finished they were all bright with smiles. I was now sure of the answer I should get when I finally asked each man. . . . It is difficult to express the joy I felt at seeing how promptly my comrades placed themselves at my service on this momentous occasion. . . . There was so much life and good spirits on board that evening that one would have thought the work was successfully accomplished instead of being hardly begun."[10]

Amundsen directed Leon to telegram Scott from Kristiania, as a courtesy, to inform him of his plan. Amundsen must have known the distress the message would produce in his rival. The long cruise south began. For leisure, the ship's library of three thousand volumes provided virtually unlimited reading. Caring for the dogs furnished the men amusement during four months and more at sea, and they got to know their canine companions well. Amundsen commented, "We human beings are apt to cherish the conviction that we have a monopoly of what is called a living soul. . . . Look at a dog's eyes, study them attentively. How often do we see something 'human' in their expression[?] . . . A dog is something more than a mere machine."[11] The dogs held sudden and deafening "howling concerts"[12] that ended as abruptly as they began. The men never understood their significance. The arrival of puppies cheered everyone.

The first iceberg was sighted on 1 January 1911; the ship crossed the Antarctic Circle the following day and entered the pack ice and the realm of twenty-four-hour daylight. The party passed rapidly through the ice belt and sighted the barrier on 11 January. The ship headed east and entered the Bay of Whales three days later, reaching its farthest south of 78° 41'. Now Amundsen had only to choose a site for the hut and get his men and 116 dogs ashore. The party found a suitable place a little over two miles from ship.

The men were divided into shore and ship parties. Working eighteen hours a day in a spirited air of enthusiasm, they completed construction of the hut within two weeks. The men unloaded nine hundred cases, secured a large supply of fresh seal meat, and abandoned their temporary tent dwellings in favor of their new home, Framheim. Amundsen recorded: "It is with gladness and pride that I look back upon those days. With gladness, because no discord was ever heard in the course of this fairly severe labour; with pride, because I was at the head of such a body of men. For men they were, in the true sense of the word. Everyone knew his duty, and did it."[13]

On 4 February, Scott's Eastern Party aboard the *Terra Nova* entered the Bay of Whales and found Amundsen's party. Lt. Harry Pennell, Lt. Victor Campbell, and surgeon G. Murray Levick were escorted to Framheim. Amundsen, Nielsen, and one other Norwegian lunched on the *Terra Nova*, which departed later the same day. For the British, it was unmistakable that they had just encountered a group of highly competent and affable professionals who posed a major threat to Scott's aspiration to be number one at the pole.[14]

On 10 February, a reconnaissance and preliminary depot party of four men with three sledges and eighteen dogs left Framheim and in just three miles were on top of the level surface of the Ross Ice Shelf, which appeared to extend endlessly to the south. A runner on skis went in front to give the dogs of the lead sledge a point to head toward, while the sledge driver directed the runner by compass. The driver of the rear sledge would watch for dropped articles. They proceeded carefully, for righting a capsized sledge with heavy loads was hard work. They reached 80° S, a journey of ninety-six miles, in four days and marked the route with flags on bamboo poles. At 80° S they erected a twelve-foot-high depot. (By comparison, Scott set his south-ernmost depot, far to the west of Amundsen, at 79°29' S on 17 February.) With light sledges the Norsemen rode home at phenomenal speed, jubilantly optimistic for their future prospects. They arrived back at Framheim late the following day, having traveled sixty-two miles in one day. Meanwhile, the *Fram* had departed for Buenos Aires.

The principal depot journey began on 22 February with eight men (all but Lindström, the cook, who always remained at the hut as superinten-dent), four tents, seven sledges, and forty-two dogs. The weather had be-come colder and foggier, and the men missed some markers on the way out. This experience showed Amundsen that he would have to mark his way and depots even more carefully. In five days they reached the 80° depot, where they devised a new way to mark the depot's position, with ten numbered markers to each side in the east-west direction spaced nine hundred meters apart (thus 11.2 miles from end to end). Four days later they reached 81° S and created a depot of 1,234 pounds of dog pemmican, similarly marked. Temperatures were minus 40 degrees Fahrenheit, affecting both men and dogs; Olav Bjaaland (1872–1961), H. Sverre Hassel (1876–1928), and Jørgen Stubberud returned to Framheim with Amundsen's weakest dog.

Five men and the remaining dogs headed south. Surfaces changed, and some of the dogs fell into deep, narrow crevasses, hanging by their harnesses. At 82° S on 8 March, the dogs were exhausted and indifferent to the whip. Amundsen realized he had reached his limit, though he had wished, too optimistically, to reach 83° S. The men depoted 1,370 pounds, mainly dog pemmican, and again set up markers. Amundsen later reflected, "I loved my dogs, and the feeling was undoubtedly mutual. But the circumstances we were now in were not normal—or was it, perhaps, myself who was not nor-mal? I have often thought since that such was really the case. The daily hard work and the object I would not give up had made me brutal, for brutal I was when I forced those five skeletons to haul that excessive load."[15] Amundsen left his sledge, since his dogs were too weak to pull it even empty. The other three teams were better off, but the men could not enjoy the luxury of riding on the sledges. The dogs, despite full rations, were pitiful, huddling and shiv-ering during their rests. On 22 March, all were back at Framheim.

A third, last depot journey to 80° S was made in the waning light of late March and early April, to leave another twenty-five hundred pounds of seal meat. The men's outbound course was again too far to the west, and they got into crevasses and unpleasant trouble. In all, eight dogs were lost on these journeys, seven from exposure and exhaustion, one from infection. But the season's depot work had been remarkable: six thousand pounds of food and provisions had been placed out on the barrier in three depots as far as 82° S, 2 degrees farther than originally planned.

The men's chief winter work was perfecting the entire outfit for the southern journey. The hut roof had already been extended to form a covered passage all around for stores, and the men could obtain ice without going outside. Tunnels were now constructed to extend the living quarters and workrooms, and new chambers were given such names as the Clothing Store and the Crystal Palace. Lindström painted the hut ceiling white for improved lighting. The dogs were well protected in tents sunk six feet below the ice surface. Bjaaland reduced the weight of the sledges from 163 to 53 pounds apiece, an enormous improvement. A conjoined tent for five men was devised for improved comfort. Clothing and footwear were modified. Checklists of stores were prepared for each sledge. Amundsen reflected, "The success of such an expedition . . . [is in] the way in which every difficulty is foreseen, and precautions taken for meeting or avoiding it. Victory awaits him who has everything in order. . . . Defeat is certain for him who has neglected to take the necessary precautions."[16]

The lowest temperature recorded was minus 74.2 degrees Fahrenheit on 13 August. The sun returned on 24 August, sledges were packed and readied in extremely low temperatures, and the men prepared themselves to leave as soon as the weather warmed. Out of fear that Scott might arrive first at the pole, Amundsen was prepared to risk departing too early. "It is not at all pleasant to hang about waiting like this; I always have the idea that I am the only one who is left behind, while all the others are out on the road. And I could guess that I was not the only one of us who felt this."[17] Conversations often diverted to speculating on Scott's departure date and position. (Scott did not depart until 1 November 1911.)

On 8 September, still only late winter, the temperature was temptingly warm at minus 7 degrees, and Amundsen decided the time to depart had come. The dogs were in wild excitement, twelve to a sledge, and the party of eight men was quickly off for the south. The warm lull did not last. Three days later the air was calm, clear, and minus 67.9 degrees. Next day the temperature remained in the minus sixties with an "undeniably bitter" head wind, and the dogs "were a pitiful sight. They lay rolled up as tightly as possible, with their noses under their tails, and from time to time one could see a shiver run through their bodies; indeed, some of them were constantly shivering. We had to lift them up and put them into their harness. . . . It would not pay to go on."[18]

Amundsen decided that they would turn for home after leaving all supplies at the 80° depot. On 14 September, the cold unremitting, they reached the depot. The men rode home on nearly empty sledges, occasionally running to get warm. The air temperature was so low that the aquavit and gin froze solid. Hanssen and Stubberud had severely frostbitten feet. Several dogs who could not keep up were let loose; two of them simply lay down and died. Forty miles from Framheim, Amundsen impulsively decided to do the remaining distance without a stop. The party splintered into components, the result of the differing speeds of the dog teams, and arrival times at Framheim extended over eight and a half hours, reaching past midnight. Johansen and Prestrud arrived last, out of food and fuel, Prestrud tottering and severely frostbitten.

Amundsen now divided the eight men into two groups. Prestrud, Stubberud, and Johansen were to explore Edward VII Peninsula; the remaining five—Amundsen, Bjaaland, Oscar Wisting (1871–1936), Hassel, and Hanssen—would constitute the polar party. Amundsen gave only logistical reasons for his decision, simply stating in his official account: "Circumstances had arisen which made me consider it necessary to divide the party into two."[19] In later years, Hanssen would also leave out of his own book the actual reasons for the split. His account is, in fact, blatantly disingenuous: he stated that Amundsen suddenly wished to include exploration of Edward VII Peninsula in his plans; when, after the expedition, the public thought Amundsen might not have wanted to share credit of the South Pole with Johansen, Hanssen said that Amundsen arrived at the plan only after an open discussion and general consent, and that Amundsen was at a disadvantage without Johansen in the polar party.[20] But biographer Roland Huntford, drawing on unpublished diaries, elucidated a strongly adversarial relationship between Amundsen and Johansen that had been developing for some time.[21] When Johansen and Prestrud returned to the hut, Johansen exploded in a mutinous verbal attack on Amundsen for abandoning his men in a panicked return; he blasted Amundsen's leadership. Most of the men likely shared some of Johansen's views but kept their own counsel for the general good, all except Prestrud.

Amundsen, in order to regain control, immediately divided the party to isolate Johansen. The advantages were obvious: Amundsen was now rid of his antagonist, and the value of the depots, which now had to provide for only five men instead of eight, would be considerably increased. In the event that the polar party did not return, the first exploration of Edward VII Peninsula would ensure one substantial achievement. Fortunately, Johansen had quarreled with Amundsen at the hut before conflict could have arisen out on the polar trail, but the unity of the party was now irrevocably destroyed. (Prestrud's party made three journeys from the hut from early November to January. They examined Edward VII Peninsula and explored the eastern arm and southwest corner of the Bay of Whales.)

The southern party set out again on 19 October 1911. Amundsen recalled: "I don't believe Lindström ever came out of doors to see us start. 'Such an everyday affair: what's the use of making a fuss about it?'"[22] According to Prestrud, whose relationship with Amundsen must have been strained, "The departure took place without much ceremony, and with the smallest possible expenditure of words."[23] The five men were off with four sledges and fifty-two dogs. Requiring minimal provisions to get to 80 ° S, they were so light that they sat on the sledges as the dogs pulled them jauntily along, only an occasional crack of the whip piercing the air. The party was soon up on the barrier with smoother surfaces, but again, as during the last depot journey of the previous season, the men accidentally steered west of their intended course and had some nearly calamitous crevasse trouble. The 80° depot was nevertheless made in four marches; the men rested and fed the dogs well on seal meat.

The journey south across the barrier was rapid and without incident, except that one slow dog had to be sacrificed, and Hanssen had a near disaster in a crevasse. Beginning in 80°23' S, the men built snow beacons as route markers across the barrier, 150 in all, each six feet tall and made of about sixty snow blocks. Each beacon contained a paper giving the position, direction, and distance to the next beacon northward. "It may appear that my prudence was exaggerated, but it always seemed to me that one could not be too careful on this endless, uniform surface."[24] As the men proceeded south, the crevasses dissipated, and the days warmed. The party arrived at 82° S, the last outpost of the previous season's depot journey. Amundsen here felt a distinct relief: he felt the battle half won. "Now the unknown lay before us; now our work begins in earnest."[25] Four dogs were sacrificed as food for the remaining dogs on the return. The animals were so strong that they could have covered thirty miles per day, but the party had ample food for slower travel, and by keeping the daily distances to seventeen miles, the men were able to conserve the dogs' strength and still be pulled on their skis the entire way across the barrier.

At 82°20' S, the men caught their first glimpse of a distant mountain range that they named the Queen Maud Mountains. In two days they were at 83° S; they planned to sacrifice most of their dogs at the threshold of the polar plateau and return with only twelve. Thus provisions for five men and twelve dogs for four days were now cached in a depot. Three of the best dogs unfortunately got loose and headed north, so the men redistributed the remaining ones. Soon the mountains and their spectacular, lofty peaks loomed higher and higher, and Amundsen christened two of them, rising respectively over 13,350 and 12,350 feet, Mount Fridtjof Nansen and Mount Don Pedro Christophersen (after his great benefactor). He named a distant ridge overlooking the barrier Mount Betty after his housekeeper, Betty Andersson.

The party arrived at 84° S, where similar provisions were left. The mountains were now seen to be contiguous with the mountains of Victoria Land to the west and to extend onward to the east. The barrier surface was no longer flat but was increasingly undulated. On 15 November, the men left a depot in 85° S. Expecting a great deal of ice disturbance, they were pleasantly surprised when all they encountered was a gentle ascent into the mountains. Before long they had risen a thousand feet, where they stopped and took stock of all provisions and equipment. The men left everything possible, while taking into account contingencies for unknown surfaces, unpredictable weather, and uncertainty over how the dogs would perform. Now, at the base of Mount Betty, the party had solid earth and rock under its feet for the first time since leaving Madeira.

The men, lightly clad in the warm sun, headed briskly in a southwesterly direction through the mountains, building beacons along the way. They camped beneath spectacular towering summits. At the first camp, Wisting and Hanssen went off together to reconnoiter a way up, and Bjaaland, who was the finest skier of the group, went off alone in another direction to do the same. Both found passable routes, but Amundsen heard the sounds of Bjaaland's steep, icy descent to camp; he knew he was no match for him on skis. During his sleep he "dreamed of mountains and precipices all night, and woke up with Bjaaland whizzing down from the sky."[26] He opted for Wisting's and Hanssen's route.

Even theirs proved no easy one. Ascents were steep, and chaotic ice forced a reverse; hard climbing required doubling up the dog teams. The men found themselves at 4,550 feet altitude on a plateau; a large glacier, which they named the Axel Heiberg, ran before them. It was their boulevard to the polar plateau. After camping at 5,650 feet, the men's next excursion led to a hard, steep ice slope ending in an apparently bottomless chasm. They negotiated it by putting skins on their skis for traction, but the prospect for sledges and dogs seemed doubtful; they returned to camp. The men reconnoitered another route over a ridge and at once realized success. Few hazards lay before them under the summit of Mount Don Pedro Christophersen. "Up here all was strangely peaceful. . . . We could now see to the end of this mighty glacier. . . . The last of the ascent was before us. . . . What we saw in the distance between these two mountains was the great plateau itself."[27]

The only question was where to make the last ascent. From where they stood at about eight thousand feet, surveying the surroundings, Amundsen, Bjaaland, and Hanssen found a route between Mount Fridtjof Nansen and Mount Ole Engelstad (now Mount Engelstad).[28] They happily realized that they could return to camp over two thousand feet below, and, weather permitting, make the entire ascent with sledges and dogs the following day. They arrived back at the tent, hungry and exhausted, to give the news to Wisting and Hassel: "The plateau to-morrow."[29] The Primus stove was set going with the promise of a hearty meal, the tent was warm, the red cloth absorbing the sun's rays. "The thought of fresh dog cutlets that awaited us when we got to the top made our mouths water. In course of time we had so habituated ourselves to the idea of the approaching slaughter that this event did not appear to us so horrible as it would otherwise have done."[30] The following day, they made their ascent. The group camped on 21 November at 10,920 feet in 85°36' S, having made an astounding climb of 5,720 feet over nineteen miles of ice terrain in one day. "For this . . . I must give the highest praise both to the dogs and their drivers; it was a brilliant performance."[31]

Then came the sacrifice of the dogs. Amundsen wrote: "My work . . . that night was getting the Primus started, and pumping it up to high-pressure. I was hoping thereby to produce enough noise to deaden the shots that I knew would soon be heard—twenty-four of our brave companions and faithful helpers were marked out for death. It was hard—but it had to be so. We had agreed to shrink from nothing in order to reach our goal. . . . There went the first shot—I am not a nervous man, but I must admit that I gave a start. Shot now followed upon shot—they had an uncanny sound over the great plain. A trusty servant lost his life each time. It was long before the first man reported that he had finished; they were all to open their dogs, and take out the entrails to prevent the meat being contaminated. The entrails were for the most part devoured warm on the spot by the victims' comrades, so voracious were they all. . . . The holiday humour that ought to have prevailed in the tent that evening—our first on the plateau—did not make its appearance; there was depression and sadness in the air—we had grown so fond of our dogs. The place was named the 'Butcher's Shop.'"[32]

Men and dogs spent four days resting and feasting while waiting out blizzard conditions. The rest was good for the animals, who became corpulent and content. But the men were eager to get away, and Amundsen's companions took the lead in opting to go on despite the blizzard. Amundsen later wrote: "I had already seen proofs on several occasions of the kind of men my comrades were, but their conduct that day was such that I shall never forget it, to whatever age I may live. . . . It was blowing and snowing so that when we came out in the morning we could not see the sledges. . . . When I think of my four friends of the southern journey, it is the memory of that morning that comes first to my mind. All the qualities that I most admire in a man were clearly shown at that juncture: courage and dauntlessness, without boasting or big words."[33] They proceeded with three sledges and their eighteen dogs, Hassel and Amundsen trading turns in front. The men left their crampons behind, hoping they would encounter no more hard, steep ice. Anxiety prevailed as they traveled for two days over unknown, uneven "ground" with scarcely a break in the fog. Visibility improved just long enough for them to discover the isolated Helland Hansen's Mountains (now Helland-Hansen Shoulder) on their right. Despite the conditions, they made excellent distances. Another depot was erected in 86°23' to lighten the loads.

"There was something uncanny about this perfectly blind advance among crevasses and chasms on all sides."[34] The men worked themselves into a terribly fissured area and were forced to camp on a secure spot and wait for clearing weather to find a way out. In a fog the next day, Amundsen and Hanssen set out to reconnoiter. The glacier surface was so especially chaotic and hazardous that they named it the Devil's Glacier. The weather finally cleared on 29 November, and the men got unobstructed views of the glacier, their line of travel, and the nearby mountains, including the magnificent and lofty Nilsen Plateau and a group of four peaks that Amundsen named after his companions. Skis repeatedly saved the men from disappearing into concealed crevasses. When a gale blew away all the fine snow and exposed a hard, irregular surface, they regretted having left the crampons behind. But soon the crevasses and detours became fewer, and renewed vigor filled the party of men and dogs.

In the upper part of the glacier on a surface swept free of loose snow, the party encountered an unusual district of icy haycocks. The men made camp next to one of these objects and drove their stakes into the semi-hard ice. Hassel applied his ax to a haycock and found the structure was hollow; he heard pieces of ice fall down and away into nothingness. Amundsen and his men were remarkably sanguine about it. "It appeared, then, that two feet from our door we had a most convenient way down into the cellar. Hassel looked as if he enjoyed the situation. 'Black as a sack,' he smiled; 'couldn't see any bottom.' Hanssen was beaming; no doubt he would have liked the tent a little nearer."[35]

Another day of vile surfaces followed, but the march of over fifteen miles, similar to others on rough days, was up to expectations, and the men were quite pleased. Amundsen described the evening meal: how, in the pleasant interior of the warm tent, they would "demolish" the pemmican soup, "caress" their biscuits before eating them, and how the water was "a far greater pleasure and satisfaction than the finest wine."[36] Reindeer skins were cached at 86°47' S, since the men now anticipated no need for them, except for the hoods in event of a severe headwind. They believed they had reached the end of their troubles on the glacier when suddenly before them ran a wide valley stripped of snow, gleaming in the sun, the polished surface rent with seemingly bottomless crevasses. This valley they named the Devil's Ballroom. They proceeded on to His Majesty's Ballroom, with a benign-appearing surface, but with a hollow ring beneath. Dogs, sledges, and men went through the crust repeatedly as they passed over it. This proved to be the last of the glacier, and on 4 December, at 87° S, they were on the polar plateau proper. The mountains in the northeast gradually vanished behind them.

Confident and strong, the men proceeded the following day in blindingly thick snowfall, amid difficult sastrugi, by letting the dogs, instead of a human forerunner, lead. Hanssen steered the dogs by compass, and they covered twenty-five miles. The following day was similar, and the sastrugi gradually leveled out. That evening in camp the men had the satisfaction of both having passed the 88° mark and noting that the boiling point of water was falling no further: they were confidently on the plateau with no more climbing to do. The dogs had worked hard and were extremely hungry; their daily food allotment now was not sufficient, and they would eat almost anything left unsecured, including ski bindings, clothes, and boots. Thus the men buried the sledges every night.

Each day was as gray as the last. Although travel was perfectly direct and without detours, the men had had no sun to sight to confirm their latitude since the 86°47' S depot. Amundsen began to worry that they would have to claim the South Pole on dead reckoning by compass alone; he knew that their claim would be controversial if they could not get a sun sighting. The sun finally did appear—"We looked at each other in sheer incredulity: the result was as astonishing as the most consummate conjuring trick—88°16' S., precisely to a minute the same as our reckoning, 88° 16' S. If we were forced to go to the Pole on dead reckoning, then surely the most exacting would admit our right to do so."[37]

Later that day, the men passed Shackleton's farthest south. Amundsen as forerunner was alone, some way ahead of the others in a reverie of thought, far away from his immediate surroundings. He was awakened by a shout, and he stopped and turned around. "I find it impossible to express the feelings that possessed me at this moment. All the sledges had stopped, and from the foremost of them the Norwegian flag was flying. It shook itself out, waved and flapped so that the silk rustled; it looked wonderfully well in the pure, clear air and the shining white surroundings. 88°23' was past; we were farther south than any human being had been. No other moment of the whole trip affected me like this. The tears forced their way to my eyes; by no effort of will could I keep them back. It was the flag yonder that conquered me and my will. Luckily I was some way in advance of the others, so that I had time to pull myself together and master my feelings before reaching my comrades. We all shook hands, with mutual congratulations; we had won our way far by holding together, and we would go farther yet—to the end. We did not pass that spot without according our highest tribute of admiration to the man, who—together with his gallant companions—had planted his country's flag so infinitely nearer to the goal than any of his precursors."[38]

The men camped two miles farther on, left their last depot, and marked it well. The party continued over the smooth plain, and the anxiety of being forestalled by Scott came up in conversation—needlessly, as it turned out. Hanssen commented, "I thought the first one to set foot on the South Pole should be Amundsen himself, so when, according to my calculations, we had only 5 nautical miles to go, I stopped my dog-team. . . . Then I called out to Amundsen to come on and run ahead. 'Why should I?' he asked. 'I cannot make the dogs run without someone running ahead,' I said. And then, when the 5 miles had been run, I called out to him."[39]

Amundsen recorded the events thus on the afternoon of 14 December

1911, at three in the afternoon, with only the vast white plain all around: "A simultaneous 'Halt!' rang out from the drivers . . . our Pole by reckoning. The goal was reached, the journey ended. . . . After we had halted we collected and congratulated each other. We had good grounds for mutual respect in what had been achieved, and I think that was just the feeling that was expressed in the firm and powerful grasps of the fist that were exchanged. After this we proceeded to the greatest and most solemn act of the whole journey—the planting of our flag. Pride and affection shone in the five pairs of eyes that gazed upon the flag, as it unfurled itself with a sharp crack, and waved over the Pole. I had determined that the act of planting it—the historic event— should be equally divided among us all. It was not for one man to do this; it was for *all* who had staked their lives in the struggle, and held together through thick and thin. This was the only way in which I could show my gratitude to my comrades in this desolate spot. I could see that they under- stood and accepted it in the spirit in which it was offered. Five weather- beaten, frost-bitten fists they were that grasped the pole, raised the waving flag in the air, and planted it as the first at the geographical South Pole. 'Thus we plant thee, beloved flag, at the South Pole, and give to the plain on which it lies the name of King Haakon VII's Plateau.' That moment will certainly be remembered by all of us who stood there."[40]

By sun sightings, the men realized that the South Pole was actually about four miles away; the area was encircled and crossed during the next two days. Positions were fixed by reckoning and occasional appearances of the sun. On 16 December, the men arrived at a point as close to the true position as they could estimate after a full day of sun measurements, and there they erected a tent called Polheim. (After the expedition's return, calculations performed by mathematician Anton Alexander showed that Bjaaland and Hanssen probably passed a point a little over a quarter of a mile from the actual posi- tion of the pole, which had been circumscribed.[41] That Amundsen's party achieved mankind's first arrival at the South Pole was fully accepted by Scott and has never been contested.)

On 17 December, all measurements were complete. That evening at din- ner, Bjaaland made a fine spontaneous oration and then presented Amund- sen with a case of cigars, which were shared all around. Amundsen re- marked, "A cigar at the Pole! What do you say to that? . . . I have taken good care of the case, and shall preserve it as one of the many happy signs of my comrades' devotion."[42] A small, extra tent was erected, topped by a little Norwegian flag, and underneath it was attached a pennant on which "Fram"

Oscar Wisting and his team arrive at the South Pole
Amundsen, *Sydpolen*, 1912

was written. Amundsen left a letter for Scott, a letter for King Haakon VII (which he asked Scott to carry home as proof that the Norwegians had been there, in case tragedy befell them on the return), miscellaneous equipment and clothing no longer needed, and wishes for a safe return.

The men got into their old tracks and turned northward for Framheim. Bjaaland was lead runner all the way back. "Many were the times we turned to send a last look to Polheim. The vaporous, white air set in again, and it was not long before the last of Polheim, our little flag, disappeared from view."[43] By switching to "night" travel the men avoided the sun in their faces, and they had the warmth of the midday sun on the tent while sleeping. Their beacons led them on, Bjaaland out in front on skis, the dogs close behind pulling the sledges. Wisting's sledge was aided by a sail to pick up the southerly winds. By inadvertently diverging off the outbound route, the party managed to avoid the Devil's Ballroom entirely and almost all of the Devil's Glacier. But the men missed the Devil's Glacier depot and had just decided to go on without it when Hanssen glanced back and spotted it. He and Bjaaland went back fifteen miles to retrieve it. As the party descended, the mountains often appeared very different than before; the men had been deceived that the air was clear when, in actuality, it was not.

In their final descent from the mountains, the men were so fit that they became discontent with the long rests between each day's fifteen miles. As a result, they decided to do fifteen to seventeen miles and rest only six hours, abandoning the twenty-four-hour day entirely. They were back on the barrier on 6 January. At Mount Betty, their last landfall before the barrier, they built a cairn and left an account of the expedition in the event that calamity prevented their return. (The cairn and note were found by Laurence Gould's party eighteen years later, during Richard Byrd's first Antarctic expedition.) Dog pemmican was in such excess that the animals were put on double rations, and the men ate seal meat daily. Now the height of summer, the temperatures were quite mild, well above zero. At 84°26' S, the men were visited by two skuas. "Can anyone who reads these lines form an idea of the effect this had upon us? It is hardly likely. They brought us a message from the living world into this realm of death . . . messengers from another world; they sat still a while . . . then rose aloft and flew on."[44]

On the barrier, the men followed their beacons and had so much food that they could afford to miss a depot. They passed the last beacon in 80°23' S. "Glad as we were to leave it behind, I cannot deny that it was with a certain feeling of melancholy that we saw it vanish. We had grown so fond of our beacons, and whenever we met them we greeted them as old friends. Many and great were the services these silent watchers did us on our long and lonely way."[45]

The men arrived fit and well at Framheim at four in the afternoon, 25 January 1912, having been away ninety-nine days on a journey of 1,860 miles. Their arrival aroused the other four men from their sleep. "Have you been there?" "Yes, of course."[46] Hanssen recalled that "Amundsen was the first to go in. He said: 'Good morning, my dear Lindström, have you got some coffee for us?' Lindström sat up and rubbed his eyes. 'Oh, is it you?' he said. . . . After 99 days of cocoa that coffee was delicious. There would have been a funeral in Framheim if we had been offered cocoa."[47]

The *Fram* had arrived 8 January with a complement of eleven men. The entire contingent of men and thirty-nine dogs departed Framheim on 30 January. The ship arrived in Tasmania in early March, and Amundsen sent off a concise dispatch to Norway summarizing his results.[48] Nansen commented on it: "It speaks of what is achieved, not of their hardships. Every word a manly one. That is the mark of the right man, quiet and strong."[49]

Amundsen conducted an enormously successful lecture tour in the United States, but the ice lured him, and he spent virtually the rest of his life in Arctic exploration. In his most notable achievement, he and Lincoln Ellsworth in May 1926 accomplished the first traverse of the north polar sea, in the dirigible *Norge,* piloted by the Italian designer of the craft, Umberto Nobile. In light of the controversy over the North Pole claims of Cook and Peary, Amundsen and Ellsworth may actually have been the first men to visit the North Pole, if only from the air. Amundsen and Nobile had a public falling out after the *Norge* because Amundsen thought Nobile usurped too much credit. After the *Norge,* the latest of Amundsen's many polar accomplishments, the great Norwegian polar pioneer retired from exploration. He reemerged, however, in June 1928, to attempt an air rescue of the distressed Nobile north of Spitsbergen; by doing so he desired reconciliation. During the effort, Amundsen disappeared and was never heard from again—Nobile was eventually rescued. Fitting it seems that although the celebrated Norwegian explorer's greatest exploit was his conquest of the South Pole, he died where his heart had always lived: in the far north.

Before moving on to the drama of Scott's last expedition, a contemporary of Amundsen's deserves mention, the leader of the Japanese Antarctic expedition, Nobu Shirase (1861–1946). In the Bay of Whales, the Japanese encountered the Norwegians as they were returning in the *Fram* to pick up Amundsen's party, but language differences made communication virtually impossible. Shirase's expedition account has been published to date only in Japanese,[50] so little is known about his achievement outside his native land. What is known is that Japan's excursion into the Antarctic was born out of an increasing national consciousness.

Shirase departed his country in the *Kainan Maru* on 1 December 1910 but got a late start out of Wellington on 11 February 1911. He planned to sail into McMurdo Sound and land a ten-man shore party. The following spring, with the aid of ten ponies in the manner of Shackleton, the men would attempt to reach the South Pole. But the party reached only Coulman Island

and, discouraged by bad weather, returned empty-handed to Sydney, where they met with ridicule. Only the supportive intervention of Edgeworth David, geologist on Shackleton's expedition, dissipated the censure.

The following year, Shirase reduced his aspirations to an exploration of the eastern portion of the barrier and of Edward VII Peninsula. In these endeavors, the Japanese had a measure of success. At the Bay of Whales, five men were put ashore, and while the ship's party moved on to Edward VII Peninsula, three of the shore party under Shirase sledged to 80°5' S, 156°27' W. At a height of about one thousand feet, the men flew the Japanese flag, saluted their emperor, and correctly surmised that land must lay beneath, though none was visible. Meanwhile, a shore party at Edward VII Peninsula reached the Alexandra Mountains to the north before returning to ship and picking up Shirase's party. The entire group returned triumphantly to Yokohama on 20 June 1912.[51]

20

SCOTT'S LAST EXPEDITION
(1910–1913)

"I do not regret this journey. . . . We took risks, we knew we took them: things have come out against us, and therefore we have no cause for complaint."

Robert F. Scott, "Message to the Public," *Scott's Last Expedition*

ROBERT FALCON SCOTT WILL ALWAYS BE the great, legendary, tragic hero of the Antarctic. Scott was a man of strong ambition; his writings were high-minded, full of ardor and adventure, and they were emotionally stirring. But Scott's ambition ultimately exceeded his reason and capability. On or about 29 March 1912, he became Antarctica's greatest martyr, leaving to posterity letters and a diary containing last thoughts as moving to the spirit as perhaps any ever written. Apsley Cherry-Garrard (1886–1959) stated that the expedition "achieved a first-rate tragedy."[1] Certainly that is so; the Scott story rivals the greatest of the Shakespearean tragedies.

In September 1909, Scott announced his plans for another expedition and received wide endorsement. He was able to raise only £10,000 in the first six months, however, so he and Lt. Edward R. G. R. "Teddy" Evans, his second in command, traveled throughout England to drum up financial backing. The government eventually provided £20,000, and, with private contributions including £1,000 apiece from Cherry-Garrard and Lawrence E. G. Oates (1880–1912), who became expedition members, the project came into being, although its budget was still tight given the extensive program planned. Eight thousand individuals volunteered to serve. As in the *Discovery* expedition, most of the executive officers and crew selected were navy men. Scott and Wilson organized the scientific program; Lieutenant Evans was in charge of the ship, its officers, and crew.

On his limited budget, Scott settled for the *Terra Nova*, purchased for £12,500. The ship was an old Dundee whaler built in 1884; it was one of the two vessels that had gone off to relieve the *Discovery* in 1903–4. The *Terra Nova* weighed 400 tons and was 187 feet long and 31 feet abeam; its engine produced only 140 horsepower and consumed coal inefficiently. The ship needed an extensive refit and redesign, which failed to conceal signs of wear, and the vessel was far too small for the expedition's needs. In the tropical heat, the unventilated boiler room was nearly intolerable. In high seas, the ship rolled up to 50 degrees. Cherry-Garrard was hardly kind in his assessment of the ship: "Picked up second-hand in the wooden-ship market, and faked up for the transport of ponies, dogs, motors, and all the impedimenta of a polar expedition, to say nothing of the men who have to try and do scientific work inside them, one feels disposed to clamour for a Polar Factory Act making it a crime to ship men for the ice in vessels more fit to ply between London Bridge and Ramsgate."[2]

The day before the 10 June 1910 departure, three hundred fellows of the Royal Geographical Society honored Scott and his men in London at a farewell luncheon. The party made stops at Cardiff, Madeira, South Trinidad, Cape Town, Melbourne, Lyttleton, and Port Chalmers; only at Lyttleton was the entire complement of men, animals, and supplies assembled. Scott had stayed behind in England to complete arrangements, including cinema and publishing contracts, and joined ship from South Africa to Melbourne, where he had more expedition business to attend to ("begging," as Teddy Evans called it) before joining the rest of the company in Lyttleton.

All told, the shore parties consisted of thirty-three officers, scientists, and men. Besides Scott and Teddy Evans was first officer Lt. Victor L. A. Campbell, who maintained routine on ship. Henry R. Bowers (1883–1912) (known as "Birdie" because of his profile) was in charge of stores. Lawrence E. G. "Titus" Oates, also known as "Soldier," was an army captain and in charge of the ponies. G. Murray Levick and Edward L. "Atch" Atkinson were the surgeons. Edward A. "Uncle Bill" Wilson was vertebrate zoologist, artist, and "unfailing friend-in-need of all on board."[3] The rest of the staff included Raymond E. Priestley (geology) and Bernard C. Day (motor engineer), who had both been south with Shackleton; T. Griffith Taylor and Frank Debenham (1883–1965) (geology); George C. Simpson (meteorology); Edward W. Nelson (biology); Charles S. "Silas" Wright (physics); Herbert G. "Ponco" Ponting (1870–1935) (photographer); Cecil H. Meares (in charge of the dogs); Apsley Cherry-Garrard ("Cherry") (assistant zoologist); and the Norwegian Tryggve Gran (ski expert). Among the men were Petty Officers William Lashly and Edgar "Taff" Evans, who were former *Discovery* men; another petty officer who figured significantly was Tom Crean. The ship's party had thirty-two officers and men.

What awaited Scott in Melbourne upon his arrival on 12 October was a shocking surprise: a few cryptic words from Roald Amundsen advising that he was going south—a race for the South Pole was on. Scott was enraged, for he felt that the British had precedence in the region. Teddy Evans made his position of pole over science clear, but Scott virtually denied that a threat to polar priority existed, not fully comprehending what an emotional blow arriving second would be to him.

Scott received an effusive welcome in New Zealand, where the men spent four weeks. The ship was dry-docked at Lyttleton for repairs and reprovisioned. The expedition departed to cheering crowds, musical bands, and marine escorts. The ship's deck was a menagerie of chained dogs, pet rabbits, coal sacks, and fuel drums; ponies were stabled in the forecastle. A final stop was made at Port Chalmers, and on 29 November, the overladen ship made its last departure from civilization. Scott, Wilson, and Teddy Evans each had last good-byes with their wives, who had come from England to see them off. For the first two couples, these visits would be their last.

A brief but strong gale in the first days of December came close to ending the expedition. Huge seas washed over the lee rail, tearing away the bulwarks. Cases of gasoline and coal bags broke loose; ten precious tons of coal and sixty-five gallons of gasoline were jettisoned. The animals were miserable—the ship rolled so badly that one dog was drowned on deck and others almost hanged by their chains. Two of the nineteen ponies died, while the rest waited out the storm with "sad, patient eyes."[4] The pumps choked, and rising water in the engine room put out the engine fires. All the men worked around the clock in shifts, according to Evans, "some waist-deep on the floor of the engine room . . . some men clinging to the iron ladder way and passing full buckets up long after their muscles had ceased to work naturally, their grit and spirit keeping them going." Evans, with Bowers holding an electric light, was underwater in the bilge, scooping up oily coal balls blocking the pumps. "I sent up twenty bucketfuls of this filthy stuff, which meant frequently going head under the unspeakably dirty water. . . . It was days before some of us could get our hair clean."[5] Before long the engine fires were rekindled.

The first iceberg was sighted on 7 December at 61°22' S, and two days later the men were in the Ross Sea pack ice, enraptured by the light effects and the wildlife. Scott wrote in his diary: "Stayed on deck till midnight. . . . The northern sky was gloriously rosy and reflected in the calm sea between the ice, which varied from burnished copper to salmon pink; bergs and pack to the north had a pale greenish hue with deep purple shadows, the sky shaded to saffron and pale green. We gazed long at these beautiful effects." Ponting, who was a world-traveled photographer, wrote about the icebergs: "In all my travels in more than thirty lands I had seen nothing so simply magnificent." And Cherry-Garrard commented, "No one of us whose privilege it was to be there will forget our first sight of the penguins.... We saw the little Adélie penguins hurrying to meet us. Great Scott, they seemed to say, what's this, and soon we could hear the cry which we shall never forget. 'Aark, aark,' they said ... full of wonder and curiosity."[6]

For twenty-one exasperating days, the *Terra Nova* was held up in the pack ice. The ice-worthy ship charged the floes valiantly but made little heading. With visibility poor, Scott never saw the island the men of the *Discovery* relief expedition had named after him. Christmas Day was celebrated in the wardroom with sledge flags, a new tablecloth, and a "mortal gorge."[7] By the time the pack was left behind, the 342-ton supply of coal had dwindled to 281 tons, threatening to curtail work planned at the Edward VII Peninsula.

Ice in McMurdo Sound blocked an approach to Hut Point, so Scott had to settle for a cape fifteen miles north of Hut Point, south of Cape Royds. The cape was named after Teddy Evans, and a beach suitable for winter quarters was chosen. Cape Evans was less interesting than Hut Point or Cape Royds. Skuas, penguins, and seals were infrequent. The scene was stark—lava, ice, and boulders, a hill, two small lakes, and a beach broadening to a little over half a mile. Mount Erebus towered in the east. To the west, the Dellbridge Islands were in the foreground, and their backdrop was the mountains thirty miles across the sound. The nearby islands tended to hold the sea ice in, and the winds were mostly southerly. Such was the lay of their homestead.

The ship was anchored at the edge of the ice, one and a half miles from the beach. Lt. Harry Pennell took command of the ship while Campbell supervised the landing operations. Motor sledges, thirty dogs, fifteen ponies, hut-building materials, scientific equipment, food, fuel, coal, even a pianola and gramophone were landed at a phenomenal speed—within six days. Teddy Evans was in charge of hut construction; most of the work was done by Francis Davies, the ship's carpenter, Robert Forde, Patrick Keohane, George Abbott, and Ponting. The wooden hut, measuring fifty by twenty-five feet, and nine feet to the eaves, was double-layered with seaweed insulation and had an enclosed porch entrance. During construction, all of the officers and men including Scott lived in tents. Nearby, Simpson and Wright laid the foundation for the magnetic hut. Perishable food delicacies were stored in an ice cave. Bowers kept track of the whereabouts and contents of every case. Evans remarked, "Every one happy and keen, working as incessantly as ants."[8]

The landing was not without incident. Scott admitted he was imprudent regarding the decaying ice conditions between ship and shore. One of the three motor sledges sank through the sea ice, a loss perceived as calamitous. (Later, however, when the motors gave no end of trouble, some wished the other two motors had sunk as well.) Ponting and two dogs were atop an ice floe two and a half feet thick when a group of orcas struck the floe from beneath in what was believed to be a premeditated attack. The Adélie penguins were also affected by the landing operations. Trusting and unfearful, they sometimes ventured too near the dogs—"a spring, a squawk, a horrid red patch on the snow."[9]

During the disembarkation, Scott revealed his bias toward men and ponies for transport, a position he never abandoned despite the difficult time Shackleton had had with ponies and his own experience later on: "I was astonished at the strength of the beasts [ponies]. . . . I rather fear they [the motors] will never draw the loads we expect of them. . . . The dogs are getting better . . . but they don't inspire confidence. . . . The men parties have done splendidly."[10] By the time the men had moved to the comfort of the hut on 17 January 1911, the depot journey southward lay just ahead. Scott was positively euphoric.

The men checked on the condition of the Hut Point and Cape Royds huts and were depressed to find the *Discovery* hut at Hut Point choked from drift; Atkinson and Crean cleared it out. Priestley found Shackleton's hut at Cape Royds to be exactly as it was left, lunch still on the table, perfectly preserved as it had been when the party left quickly in the lull of a blizzard on 2 March 1909. The horses' hoof marks were still discernible on the ice.

The depot sledge journey under Scott commenced on 24 January with thirteen men, eight ponies, and twenty-six dogs. They established Safety Camp two miles beyond the barrier edge, headed southeast to a point safely beyond the crevasses of White Island (about thirty miles from Hut Point), established Corner Camp there, and then turned due south.

The disadvantages of pony transport were immediately evident. Being herbivorous, the ponies could not live off the land, or off each other if circumstances required it; all their feed had to be transported. Beyond Safety Camp, the ponies were seriously slowed in the soft snow. With the differing paces of ponies and dogs, starts had to be staggered; the horses limited the distances the party could cover. Scott had to switch to "night" travel because the days were too warm for the ponies on the march, and the nights were too cold for them to be idle. Warm blizzards weakened them rapidly. Two weeks into the depot journey, on 8 February, Scott begrudgingly admitted that dogs could handle blizzards easily by comparison. A pony had to be covered with blankets and shielded behind a snow wall, constructed at the expense of extra human labor. A dog could simply curl up in the snow and let the drift provide cover.

A depot was laid down at Minna Bluff; from there Scott sent back the three weakest ponies with three men. The remaining entourage went on with two dog teams and five ponies. Cold spells warned of approaching autumn. Over the objection of Oates, who thought it better to proceed farther south and sacrifice the weakest animals, Scott called a halt to progress on 17 February at 79°29' S. One Ton Depot was established there, 130 miles from Hut Point.

Eager to complete the return as quickly as possible, Scott cut Corner Camp too close to White Island and got into the crevasses. Suddenly most of a dog team disappeared from sight; only the lead dog, Osman, and two rear dogs could be seen, grasping desperately at the edge of a crevasse. All the dogs in between were suspended and tangled in space, snapping and growling fearfully. After securing the sledge, the men hauled the dogs out in pairs. The episode was another hard experience.

While the Depot Party was away, the first Western Party, consisting of Taylor, Debenham, Wright, and Taff Evans, was taken by ship across McMurdo Sound on 27 January and deposited with sledges, tools, scientific instruments, photographic equipment, personal gear, food, and fuel. They explored the region between the dry valleys and the Koettlitz Glacier.

Pennell sailed off in the *Terra Nova* and followed the barrier face eastward to land the Eastern Party of Campbell, Priestley, Levick, petty officers Abbott and Frank Browning, and seaman Harry Dickason at the Edward VII Peninsula. Heavy pack and steep cliffs prevented their carrying out the plan, however, so Pennell reversed the ship's course to head west. On 3 February, as the vessel rounded the eastern headland of the Bay of Whales, they spotted, to their astonishment, the *Fram*, Amundsen's ship.

Campbell, Levick, and Priestley set out on ski, met some of Amundsen's men, and were informed of the Norwegians' intentions on the South Pole in the following season. Priestley summed up his and his companions' feelings: "Well! we have left the Norwegians and our thoughts are full, too full, of them at present. The impression they have left with me is that of a set of men of distinctive personality, hard, and evidently inured to hardship, good goers and pleasant and good-humoured. All these qualities combine to make them very dangerous rivals, but even did one want not to, one cannot help liking them individually in spite of the rivalry."[11]

Campbell refused to establish a base near the Norwegians, so the ship continued west, first to McMurdo Sound to deliver the news and the two unneeded ponies, then to the Victoria Land coast. Sailing north, the party was caught on 12 February in a freshening gale, and, light of ballast, the ship plunged rapidly through the rough seas northward. The *Terra Nova* was soon ninety-six miles north of Cape Adare. Pennell and Campbell had to make a choice: either land at Cape Adare, regrettable since Borchgrevink had already shown that useful journeys from that locale were impossible, or chance landing farther south at Wood Bay or near Coulman Island, failure in which would force a return of the entire party to New Zealand due to the shortage of coal. The company opted for Cape Adare; Campbell's party, now renamed the Northern Party, was left, and Pennell hurried north with the ship.[12]

Scott was now back at Hut Point after the discouraging Depot journey, and the mail was waiting. "Every incident of the day pales before the startling contents of the mail bag which Atkinson gave me—a letter from Campbell setting out his doings and the finding of *Amundsen* established in the Bay of Whales. One thing only fixes itself definitely in my mind. The proper, as well as the wiser, course for us is to proceed exactly as though this had not happened. To go forward and do our best for the honour of the country without fear or panic. There is no doubt that Amundsen's plan is a very serious menace to ours. He has a shorter distance to the Pole by 60 miles—I never thought he could have got so many dogs safely to the ice. His plan for running them seems excellent. But above and beyond all he can start his journey early in the season—an impossible condition with ponies. . . . Well, we have done our best and bought our experience at a heavy cost."[13]

Scott went out again with a party of men, dogs, and ponies to add to the stores at Safety Camp and Corner Camp. The job done, Bowers, Crean, and Cherry-Garrard were sent back from Safety Camp with ponies and sledges. The group, under Bowers's charge, camped on what they thought was safe sea ice. Bowers was awakened by a noise at half past four in the morning, went out of the tent to investigate, and found to his horror that the party was on a floe only thirty yards across. One of the four ponies was gone, and orcas were in the lanes.

"I cannot describe either the scene or my feelings. I must leave those to your imagination. We were in the middle of a floating pack of broken-up ice. ... Long black tongues of water were everywhere."[14] Bowers never considered anything but salvaging all, knowing that losing the remaining ponies could mean the end of Scott's chances for the pole. The men worked their way to the twenty-foot barrier edge, jumping floes with the sledges and trusting animals, but there was more water than ice. While they were debating what to do next, their floe split in half. Crean was able to get across to get help from Scott's party, which would be returning from Corner Camp. Meanwhile, Bowers and Cherry spent an anxious day on the floe, wondering whether a southerly breeze might come and send them irretrievably out to sea.

Crean returned with Scott and Oates. "Scott, instead of blowing me up, was too relieved at our safety."[15] Slowly the sledges and horses were worked closer and closer to the barrier edge; one by one, every article was brought up until at last only the ponies remained while Oates was digging a ramp in the barrier face for bringing them up. Then their floe began to move in a southeasterly air. Scott ordered the men up, and soon the three horses were alone on the floe, increasingly separated from the barrier by a widening water lane. Scott watched his chances for the pole disappear. After making camp and turning in, Bowers went out for a walk and espied the ponies about a mile away. "They saw me, and remained huddled together not the least disturbed, or doubting that we would bring them their breakfast nosebags as usual in the morning. Poor trustful creatures! If I could have done it then, I would gladly have killed them rather than picture them starving on that floe out on the Ross Sea, or eaten by the exultant Killers [orcas] that cruised around."[16]

The following morning was calm. The horses were still visible, and rescue seemed possible; but only one pony could be saved. Of eight ponies taken out on the Depot journey, only two had survived. Six more had remained at Cape Evans, and Campbell had delivered his two. Scott's hopes depended on these ten.

The stay at Hut Point through the middle of April was pleasant while the men waited for the sea ice to freeze so they could cross to Cape Evans. They hunted seals, looked after the dogs and ponies, collected geological specimens, and rested. With improved heating, ventilation, insulation, and good food and clothing, they were relatively comfortable. The Western Party arrived on 15 March, increasing their number to sixteen; the late arrivals provided new intellectual stimulation and stories of their doings. Cherry-Garrard reminisced: "Those Hut Point days would prove some of the happiest in my life. Just enough to eat and keep us warm, no more—no frills nor trimmings: there is many a worse and more elaborate life. . . . The luxuries of civilization satisfy only those wants which they themselves create."[17]

However, Scott, deeply distressed over the ponies and Amundsen, was hardly in the same mood. "In spite of all little activities I am impatient of our wait here. But I shall be impatient also in the main hut. It is ill to sit still and contemplate the ruin which has assailed our transport. . . . The Pole is a very long way off, alas!"[18] Teddy Evans led an eight-day sledge journey in extreme cold, wind, and gloom to increase the stores at Corner Camp. On 7 April, with food variety running short, Scott's impatience increased, and he decided to risk traveling over the new ice to Cape Evans. Within two miles Taylor was in the water, and all backtracked to Hut Point. The next day, all the ice was blown out. Six days later, Scott decided on a hazardous overland trip, one group under his charge and another under Teddy Evans. Both traveled over a precarious land and sea-ice route. The seven men who remained behind to care for dogs and ponies were instructed not to cross until the sea ice had withstood a blizzard. They made the trip on 13 May.

During the winter, Scott worked out the measures for the polar journey and modified his transport. Oates nurtured the remaining ponies, and Meares tended the dogs. The scientists continued their investigations, and lectures were given three times weekly. Ponting's slide lectures of his travels were most popular; Oates spoke on horses to everyone's delight; but of greatest interest was an open discussion Scott led to review plans for the polar journey.

For pleasure, the men enjoyed football, chess, moonlight walks on the sea ice beneath the aurora, and their lively discussions and arguments at mealtime. They found reasons to bet cigarettes, dinners in London, and socks. Their library contained polar books, poetry, modern fiction, and an encyclopedia. Three issues of *The South Polar Times* were produced, in the tradition of the *Discovery* expedition; each issue consisted of poetry and prose, edited by Cherry-Garrard, with illustrations chiefly by Wilson. Scott's birthday (6 June) and Midwinter Day (22 June) were celebrated in conviviality. After a day's bustle, the scene at night was subdued. The acetylene lamp was put out

Captain Scott in his den
Herbert Ponting, from *Scott's Last Expedition*, 1913

at half past ten, and scant light from the stove illuminated the night watchman. The silence was broken by Bowers's snoring, mechanical sounds of the scientific instruments, and occasional noises from the animals.

By wintertime, the men knew each other well. Scott was the energy source of the expedition. He could accomplish an amazing amount of work and organization and was the hardest in harness. "Men never realized Scott until they went sledging with him." Charismatic and sensitive, with strong likes and dislikes, he was fond of his pipe and a good book (usually one on polar exploration). His chief concerns were scientific inquiry, the call to service, and the glory of his country. However, he was dominating and not often open to suggestion; he had little sense of humor, and was prone to profound mood swings. Cherry-Garrard thought he laid himself open to misunderstanding.[19]

Of Wilson, Scott said, "Words must always fail me when I talk of Bill Wilson. I believe he really is the finest character I ever met. . . . There is no member of our party so universally esteemed. . . . [He] has been consulted in almost every effort which has been made towards the solution of the practical or theoretical problems of our polar world. . . . [He] sets an example which is more potent than any other factor in maintaining that bond of good fellowship which is the marked and beneficent characteristic of our community." Cherry-Garrard said about Wilson, "If you knew him you could not like him: you simply had to love him. Bill was of the salt of the earth. . . . He never for one moment thought of himself. [He put the] expedition first and the rest nowhere which others followed ungrudgingly: it pulled us through more than one difficulty. . . . No published reports will give an adequate idea of . . . the tact he displayed in dealing with the difficulties which arose. . . . Those who knew him best will probably remember Wilson by his water-colour paintings rather than by any other form of his many-sided work. . . . If you want accuracy of drawing, truth of colour, and a reproduction of the soft and delicate atmospheric effects which obtain in this part of the world, then you have them."[20]

Bowers was a lieutenant and member of the ship's company aboard the *Terra Nova*, but his adeptness with the stores and his imperturbable nature caused Scott to take him ashore and ultimately to the pole. Bowers refused to admit difficulties or even perceive them as such. At five feet, four inches, he was the shortest man in the main party, but "little Birdie" weighed 168 pounds, had a forty-inch chest, and was seemingly impervious to the cold. Bowers's capacity for work was prodigious, and Scott could not praise him enough: "Bowers is all and more than I ever expected of him. He is a positive treasure, absolutely trustworthy and prodigiously energetic. He is about the hardest man amongst us, and that is saying a good deal . . . and a delightful companion on the march." Cherry-Garrard, who considered Bowers one of the dearest friends of his life, at times "almost hated him for his infernal cheerfulness."[21]

Oates was the most popular officer among the seamen; he understood them and could get work from them. The "cheerful and lovable old pessimist" never believed he would ever be chosen to be a member of the polar party, "never for a moment appreciating his own sterling qualities." Ponting recalled: "He was a man of few words; he spoke with deliberation and never loosely, and he had a fund of dry humour. . . . He always delivered his considered judgment . . . calmly, decisively and positively. . . . His devotion to the indispensable animals in his charge was . . . most inspiring."[22]

Taff Evans was Scott's man of "Herculean strength."[23] Scott was impressed with his petty officer's superior size and power, and had shared with him and

Lashly the arduous journey through the Western mountains onto the high, ice-capped inner plateau of Victoria Land during the *Discovery* expedition. Scott must have had a soft spot for his petty officer: when Evans got drunk and fell overboard when the *Terra Nova* was docked in New Zealand, Scott dismissed him from the expedition but ultimately relented when Evans earnestly pleaded for forgiveness.[24] Scott included Evans in his final polar party.

No winter activity was as dramatic, and no prior sledging experience as harrowing, as the winter journey to Cape Crozier. Ever since the days of the *Discovery* expedition, Wilson had imagined returning there to study the embryology of the emperor penguin, believing he might gain new insights into the relationship between reptiles and birds. To obtain eggs, a midwinter journey was required. Wilson asked Cherry-Garrard, his assistant zoologist, to accompany him, and the two selected Bowers to be the third. Scott considered the choices excellent, although Cherry-Garrard had some reasonable doubts about himself. As part of the program, the three decided to experiment with different balances of dietary fat, protein, and carbohydrate; the information would be used for the upcoming polar journey. To minimize finger exposure in the handling of food bags, only pemmican, biscuit, butter, tea, and salt were taken. With two sledges toggled together, 757 pounds of equipment and provisions including ropes, axes, canvas and board, six weeks of food, and no skis, the men departed on 27 June 1911. Cherry-Garrard commented, "And so we started just after midwinter on the weirdest bird's-nesting expedition that has ever been or ever will be."[25]

The conditions exceeded by far the most rigorous ever experienced by men in the Antarctic. The temperature was regularly below minus 40 degrees Fahrenheit, often much lower, and reached minus 77.5 on 6 July. On the coldest days, butter splintered and kerosene was milky. To touch anything metallic meant instant frostbite. Garments moist from perspiration froze solid within seconds. Because of the men's sweat, balaclavas were soldered to their heads; they had to wait until the stove warmed the tent before they could remove them. Two men were required to dress the third. Routine daily camp work that would have taken only an hour or so in more temperate climes took up to nine hours. Wilson insisted that they spend seven hours in their bags every day "sleeping," which Wilson and Cherry-Garrard often could not do. The air was too cold to keep an opening to breathe through, so exhaled moisture accumulated as ice. All together, the bags weighed 47 pounds at the start and 118 pounds at the finish. The men needed up to forty-five minutes just to thaw their way into the bags, if they could even get in all the way; and if for any reason one had to get out, the bag froze all over again. Once inside, the bag was never warm (Cherry-Garrard shivered the nights through, but Bowers, oblivious to the cold, slept well and never had frostbite).

Leaving in late June and traveling the south side of Ross Island, the men were in virtually complete darkness at the beginning of the trip until midday twilight and moonrise later illuminated their path. The darkness was intolerable. They could not see where they were stepping and could not read a compass. Pulling the sledges on the barrier surface was like pulling through sand; on the outbound trip the men had to uncouple the sledges and relay, tripling the distances. Net progress was as little as one-fifth mile per hour. The men had only candlelight or midday twilight to see their footprints back to the second sledge. Appreciating the difficulty of the conditions, Wilson gave Cherry-Garrard and Bowers on the evening of 6 July the choice of returning to Cape Evans, but they determined to carry on.

As the three approached Terror Point, near their objective at the east end of Ross Island, surfaces and distances improved and temperatures were up to minus 20 degrees, but crevasses and ice jumbled under pressure lay in the way. The last camp, reached on 15 July after a journey of seventy miles, was eight hundred feet up the slope of Mount Terror overlooking Cape Crozier, about four miles from the Ross Sea edge, where the penguins would be. Cherry-Garrard built an igloo of rock and snow with a sledge as a ridge beam and canvas as a roof. The men headed toward the rookery on 19 July, Cherry-Garrard falling repeatedly into crevasses because he could not see, even with his glasses. The ice terrain was exceedingly rugged on account of pressure and precipices. The men confirmed the presence of the emperor colony, but they had no time to approach it that day.

The next day, the trio set out again with high hopes amid a confusion of ice. They arrived safely, and to Wilson's surprise they observed only about a hundred birds, compared with two thousand, nine years earlier. With the light dissipating and a south wind increasing, the men hurried to procure five eggs, to be put in alcohol back at camp; they also took three penguin skins for oil, since they already had consumed more than four of their six kerosene tins. Cherry-Garrard lost his two eggs in falls as they hurried over the horrid surfaces in appalling conditions: "Such extremity of suffering cannot be measured. . . . We groped our way back that night, sleepless, icy, and dog-tired in the dark and the wind and the drift."[26]

Worse was to come. As the blizzard and drift increased, the men moved into the igloo. The blubber stove spurted a blob of hot oil into Wilson's eye, and all night he writhed in pain. The next day the men packed soft snow into gaps in their igloo and revised the roof. The tent was set up in the igloo's lee to store equipment, the stove, and personal gear. The men turned in to their bags. About three in the morning on 22 July, everything changed.

Cherry-Garrard wrote: "It was calm, with that absolute silence which can be so soothing. . . . Then there came a sob of wind, and all was still again. Ten minutes and it was blowing as though the world was having a fit of hysterics. The earth was torn in pieces: the indescribable fury and roar of it all cannot be imagined. 'Bill, Bill, the tent has gone,' was the next I remember—from Bowers shouting at us again and again."[27] At Cape Evans, Scott recorded: "To-day we have another raging blizzard—the wind running up to 72 m.p.h. in gusts—one way and another the Crozier Party must have had a pretty poor time."[28] In the storm, the roof of the igloo rose, fell, and stretched. Bowers was in and out of his bag trying to secure the canvas, but it got loose and shredded in the shrieking wind as the igloo filled with drift and bits of rock. The only solace was that the blizzard was a "warm" one, with above-zero temperatures. The men dove into their bags, turning them so the openings were beneath their bodies. They could not communicate over the noise of the storm; each was privately wondering how to survive a return trip without the tent and gear. Wilson later wrote about the second day: "It happened that this was my birthday—and we spent it lying in our bags without a roof or a meal."[29] On the third day, the storm abated. The men made their first meal in two days—pemmican and tea with incidentals such as reindeer hair, penguin feathers, and dirt, but the repast was memorable.

Expecting never to see the tent again, the men looked for it with little hope. "I followed Bill down the slope. . . . As we searched, we heard a shout . . . and came upon Birdie with the tent, the outer lining still on the bamboos. Our lives had been taken away and given back to us. We were so thankful we said nothing. . . . We made our way back up the slope with it, carrying it solemnly and reverently, precious as though it were something not quite of the earth."[30]

The men headed home; Bowers would have gone back to the rookery, but Wilson said no. Cherry-Garrard had repeated nightmares of being smothered by drift. As the party passed over a pressured surface, Bowers was suddenly down a narrow crevasse. Wedged in, he directed Cherry-Garrard to throw him a rope with a bowline. Bowers got the line under his leg and was gradually hauled out, a tough job at minus 46 degrees Fahrenheit. (The technique repeatedly proved useful later, on the polar journey.) With better surfaces, lightening loads, increasing temperatures, and brightening skies, the men found their situation improved. But it was still winter. Bowers and Cherry-Garrard were so exhausted that they fell asleep on the marches. Cherry-Garrard noted: "I for one had come to that point of suffering at which I did not really care if only I could die without much pain. They talk of the hero-ism of the dying—they little know—it would be so easy to die, a dose of mor-phia, a friendly crevasse, and blissful sleep. The trouble is to go on."[31]

The party arrived at Cape Evans on 1 August 1911. Their food had been ample—the high-fat diets were more robust and the combined weight loss of the three men was only seven pounds—but they were bedraggled. Cherry-Garrard recounted: "I'll swear there was still a grace about us when we staggered in. And we kept out tempers—even with God. . . . The door opened—'Good God! here is the Crozier Party,' said a voice. . . . Thus ended the worst journey in the world."[32]

Teddy Evans remarked, "What forlorn objects they did look: it was pathetic to see them as they staggered into the hut. . . . Wilson . . . was loud in his praise of Birdie and Cherry." Ponting recalled that their look of severe deprivation haunted him for days. When he heard the "quiet and modest way they told of their adventures and achievements, I feel it has been a great privilege to have known these men as comrades." Scott wrote upon their return: "That men should wander forth in the depth of a Polar night to face the most dismal cold and the fiercest gales in darkness is something new; that they should have persisted in this effort in spite of every adversity for five full weeks is heroic. It makes a tale for our generation which I hope may not be lost." Cherry-Garrard wrote praises of his friends: "Always patient, self-possessed, unruffled, he [Wilson] was the only man on earth, as I believe, who could have led this journey. . . . In civilization men are taken at their own valuation because there are so many ways of concealment. . . . Not so down South. They [Wilson and Bowers] were gold, pure, shining, unal-loyed. Words cannot express how good their companionship was. . . . No sin-gle hasty or angry word passed their lips. When, later, we were sure, so far as we can be sure of anything, that we must die, they were cheerful. . . . I am not going to pretend that this was anything but a ghastly journey. . . . I have no wish to make it appear more horrible than it actually was." (Cherry-Garrard, the "Custodian of the Sacred Eggs," delivered them home for scientific scrutiny, but they added nothing to existing knowledge.[33])

[211]

Wilson, Bowers, and Cherry-Garrard on their return from Cape Crozier
Herbert Ponting, from *Scott's Last Expedition*, 1913

The sun returned in late August. Scott wrote, "It was glorious to stand bathed in brilliant sunshine once more. We felt very young, sang and cheered. ... There is little new to be said of the return of the sun in polar regions, yet it is such a very real and important event that one cannot pass it in silence. It changes the outlook on life of every individual."[34] Scott then set to work on details of the southern journey in an optimistic mood. Teddy Evans, Gran, and Forde dug out and supplied the Safety and Corner Camp depots in the bitter cold of mid-September. At about the same time, Scott, Bowers, Taff Evans, and Simpson made a thirteen-day, 175-mile trip to stock the Butter Point depot for Taylor, prepare coastal surveys, and measure glacial ice movement. Teddy Evans, Gran, and Debenham carried out more coastal surveys in late September. Scott returned to Cape Evans to put the final touches on all preparations.

As the date of departure arrived, however, Scott's mood turned anxious. Two horses were in poor condition, another dog died mysteriously, a motor required major repairs, and the cook, Thomas Clissold, fell off a berg while posing for Ponting and sustained a concussion, eliminating him from the southern advance. Scott fretted that he would be leaving late and arriving back late, and dreaded more than ever that Amundsen would get to the pole first.

The motor sledge party (Day, Lashly, Hooper, and Teddy Evans) left for the south on 24 October. The motors had been a dubious prospect all along, and the four men had to weather their mates' taunting gibes. Icy surfaces indeed proved too much for the machines. Engine overheating and mechanical problems soon finished both cars, one after only six days, just short of Corner Camp, and the other two days later, just beyond. Actually happy to be done with the motorcars, Evans remarked, "It seems very cruel to say this, but there's no good in shutting one's eyes to Truth, however unpleasantly clad she may be."[35] In the end, however, the motors did accomplish most of their main objective—namely, to permit the ponies to go light until Corner Camp. The four men, now without transport, man-hauled over two hundred pounds apiece to the planned rendezvous point at 80°32' (Mount Hooper Depot). There they built a large cairn and waited.

The pony and dog parties departed under Scott from Cape Evans on 1 November 1911. Scott had set his heart on the success of the motors, and he experienced quite a blow when he came upon them, ruined and abandoned. To stay within their food allowances, the men would need to average thirteen miles daily from One Ton to The Gateway at the bottom of the Beardmore Glacier. Again, Scott resorted to staggered starts, night marching, and the effort of building ice walls in camp for the ponies. "We men are snug and comfortable enough, but it is very evil to lie here and know that the weather is steadily sapping the strength of the beasts on which so much depends. It requires much philosophy to be cheerful on such occasions."[36] Summer sledging on the barrier was easy and comfortable for the most part, but appalling surfaces tested Scott's patience. In a fit of temper, he accused his dependable Bowers of deliberately giving him an excess load.[37] The horses already showed signs of wear when One Ton was reached on 15 November. So the party rested one day and decided to take just enough food to get some of them to the base of Beardmore Glacier; animals sacrificed along the way would feed both dogs and men. On 21 November, Scott's entourage caught up to the "motor party," which had been expecting them for six days. According to Teddy Evans, "Day facetiously remarked, 'We haven't seen anything of Amundsen'—seeing that the valiant Norseman was in Latitude 85°30'S nearly eleven thousand feet up . . . one is not surprised. For all our peace of mind it was well we did not know it."[38]

In all, the party was now sixteen men with five tents and thirteen sledges, ten ponies, and twenty-three dogs. Teddy Evans's manhauling party started first each day to do fifteen miles, followed by the pony parties, and last by

Meares and the Russian dog handler Demetri Gerof with the dogs, who were fastest. Barrier depots were to be laid about sixty-five miles apart, each holding a week's rations per man for the return. As food and fodder were consumed, a pony was killed when calculations showed that redistribution of weights would permit returning the remaining animals to full loads. The Middle Barrier Depot was laid down at 81°35' on 26 November; Day and Hooper turned home northward, and Atkinson joined Evans and Lashly manhauling. Three days later Scott passed his own previous farthest south. The Southern Barrier Depot was laid down at 82°47' on 1 December. Now the men approached land over great undulations in the barrier surface, and the parties camped thirteen miles from The Gateway on 4 December.

Then for four days, a warm and devastating blizzard blew fine powdery snow; sleet and rain obliterated all visibility and kept the group confined. The men's own words describe their misery. Bowers wrote: "When I swung the thermometer this morning I looked and looked again, but unmistakably the temperature was +33°F. [the temperature ultimately reached 35.5 degrees Fahrenheit], above freezing point (out of the sun's direct rays) for the first time since we came down here. What this means to us nobody can conceive. We try to treat it as a huge joke, but our wretched condition might be amusing to read of it later. We are wet through, our tents are wet, our bags which are our life to us and the objects of our greatest care, are wet; the poor ponies are soaked and shivering far more than they would be ordinarily in a temperature fifty degrees lower. . . . Water trickles down the tent poles. . . . The warmth of our bodies has formed a snow bath in the floor for each of us to lie in. . . . The drifts are tremendous, the rest of the show is indescribable."[39] Scott wrote on successive days from 5 to 8 December: "No foresight—no procedure—could have prepared us for this state of affairs." "Miserable, utterly miserable. We have camped in the 'Slough of Despond.' . . . Oh! but this is too crushing. . . . A hopeless feeling descends. . . . What immense patience is needed for such occasions!" "The storm continues. . . . We have this morning started our summit rations." "Hoped against hope for better conditions. The snow all about us is terribly deep. We tried Nobby and he plunged to his belly in it."[40]

Teddy Evans later wrote that the blizzard "tore our chances of any great success to ribbons—it was the biggest knock-down blow to Scott sustained in the whole history of his expedition to date." Evans described the ponies "standing head down, feet together, knees bent, the picture of despair. . . . Whenever one peeped out of the tent door, there was Oates, wet to the skin, trying to keep life in his charges. I think the poor soldier suffered as much as the ponies."[41] The ponies were to be kept alive only for a final twelve miles of dragging; Cherry-Garrard wrote about them: "All the food is finished. . . . It is a terrible end—driven to death on no more food, to be then cut up, poor devils."[42] Meanwhile, the dogs were quite content during the blizzard and simply curled up in the snow.

The entourage was on the trail again on 9 December, but the blizzard left the worst traveling surfaces the men faced at any time on the expedition. They struggled fifteen hours to camp, where all five remaining ponies were shot. "Poor beasts!" "It was a horrid business, and the place was known as Shambles Camp."[43] This camp marked the end of the barrier stage of the journey. Here the Lower Glacier Depot was laid. The dogs were still doing well, Cherry-Garrard commenting, "It began to look as if Amundsen had chosen the right form of transport."[44] Even so, the dogs were not part of the plan for the Beardmore Glacier and polar plateau. Scott wished to preserve the dogs for sledging work in the upcoming season, but he went on with them to 83°35' instead of 81°15' as originally intended. Meares and Demetri now returned with the two dog teams, arriving at Hut Point four weeks later.

Three teams of four now proceeded by manhauling alone: Scott, Wilson, Oates, Taff Evans; Teddy Evans, Atkinson, Wright, and Lashly; and Bowers, Cherry-Garrard, Crean, and Keohane. The men sank to their knees, at times netting only a tenth of a mile an hour by relaying. Half the men became snow-blind. Bowers wrote: "I am afraid I am going to pay dearly for not wearing goggles. . . . It is painful to look at this paper, and my eyes are fairly burning as if some one had thrown sand into them. . . . I have missed my journal for four days, having been enduring the pains of hell . . . as well as doing the most back-breaking work I have ever come up against."[45] Teddy Evans and Lashly had been manhauling since the breakdown of the second motor at Corner Camp and were slowing down. Scott was bitter as well as worried. He diverted his frustration toward his old nemesis: "Hereabouts Shackleton found hard blue ice. It seems an extraordinary difference in fortune, and at every step S.'s luck becomes more evident."[46]

Gradually the parties ascended, and at two thousand feet they felt blue ice under foot. Now, according to Teddy Evans, began the most enjoyable stage of the journey. The scenery was grand, the science was good, the men were fit, and Scott was filled with the spirit of manhauling without the concern of animals. Scott spurred competition between the teams to catch up to Shackleton's dates. Scott was good at picking a route and avoided all but a few crevasses and culs-de-sac. The Middle Barrier Depot was left at about 3,600 feet, near The Cloudmaker. At 5,800 feet, the men could feel the cold, southerly breezes off the plateau.

On 20 December, the First Supporting (Returning) Party was designated, at 7,000 feet, 85°10', and here the Upper Glacier (Mount Darwin) Depot was fixed. Scott wrote: "I have just told off the people to return to-morrow night: Atkinson, Wright, Cherry-Garrard, and Keohane. All are disappointed— poor Wright rather bitterly, I fear. I dread this necessity of choosing—nothing could be more heartrending.[47] Cherry-Garrard wrote: "It was a sad job saying good-bye . . . and the last we saw of them . . . was a black dot just disappearing over the next ridge and a big white pressure wave ahead of them. . . . Scott said some nice things when we said good-bye."[48] Atkinson's party had a relatively uneventful return, save for crevasses on the glacier. Near The Cloudmaker, Keohane went in the full length of his harness eight times in twenty-five minutes. "Little wonder he looked a bit dazed."[49] Atkinson went into one crevasse head first. Meares had rebuilt all the cairns destroyed by the blizzard, and the dog tracks helped the men. Atkinson's party arrived at Hut Point, completing a journey of 1,164 miles.

Scott retained his team; the other now consisted of Teddy Evans, Bowers, Lashly, and Crean. They left all nonessential supplies to reduce the load to 190 pounds per man. Crevasses were still a problem, Bowers remarking, "It is a bit of a jar when it gives way under you, but the friendly harness is made to trust one's life to. The Lord only knows how deep these vast chasms go down, they seem to extend into blue black nothingness."[50] On Christmas Day, Lashly's forty-fourth birthday, he went down a crevasse, the sledge only just spanning the eight-foot-wide gulf. Lashly was suspended, spinning, with an eighty-foot drop below him. His mates had a tough job hauling him out. Teddy Evans commented, "One of my party wished him a 'Merry Christmas,' and another, 'Many Happy Returns of the Day,' when he had regained safety. Lashly's reply was unprintable." By this time, Evans was aware that everyone was slowing down. "Yes, the strain was beginning to tell, though none of us would have confessed it."[51]

At Christmas dinner, all were in excellent spirits as they shared thoughts of next Christmas at home. Temperatures were now consistently below 0 degrees, and the wind was in their faces. Evans's party slowed even further, and Scott was anxious and unsympathetic. "The structure [of the sledge] has been distorted by bad strapping, bad loading, &c. The party are not done, and I have told them plainly that they must wrestle with the trouble and get it right for themselves."[52] By the next day, the problem was corrected. On 30 December, the members of Evans's team cached their skis and rope to increase speed. The eight men caught up to Shackleton's dates. Now on the polar plateau, Scott got every bit from the men, trying to make up for the blizzard and the surfaces on the lower reaches of the glacier.[53] But leaving the skis was a mistake: "It's been a plod for the foot people and pretty easy going for us."[54] Three Degree Depot was fixed on 31 December. On the same day, Taff Evans injured his hand while stripping a scratched sledge runner; there is no evidence Scott was informed. Remarkably, the men were visited by a skua, hungry but otherwise well, in 87°20' at ten thousand feet.

Scott informed Teddy Evans on 3 January 1912 of his decision to take his team plus Bowers onward. Bowers wrote in his diary: "Teddy was frightfully cut up at not going to the Pole, he had set his heart on it so. I am afraid it was a very great disappointment to him, and I felt very sorry about it. Poor Teddy, I am sure it was for his wife's sake he wanted to go. He gave me a little silk flag she had given him to fly on the Pole."[55] The rearrangement to five-man and three-man parties meant revising the stores and allocations at the depots. In addition, Bowers would have to proceed on foot, while the others were on ski. Teddy Evans, Lashly, and Crean, composing the Last Supporting (Returning) Party, accompanied the Polar Party for a while the following day, then turned home from 87°32' S. Scott commented: "As soon as I was certain we could get along we stopped and said farewell. Teddy Evans is terribly disappointed but has taken it very well and behaved like a man. Poor old Crean wept and even Lashly was affected. I was glad to find their sledge is a mere nothing to them, and thus, no doubt, they will make a quick journey back."[56] Scott would never know that Evans almost lost his life.

Evans, Lashly, and Crean headed north without a sledge meter; they had only cairns to guide them on the featureless plain. They would have to average seventeen miles per day the entire way back to remain on full rations. Evans later wrote: "Throughout our homeward march the three of us literally stole minutes and seconds from each day in order to add to our marches, but it was a fight for life."[57] The men lost three days in a blizzard, and in order to make up the time they went straight down the Shackleton Ice Falls. That they had to make 120 miles in seven days to reach the Upper Glacier (Mount Darwin) Depot justified this enormous risk. They picked up their skis. Crean was snow-blind and lost a ski stick. They got into crevasses with no crampons, having left them at their upcoming depot. They made Mount Darwin with one meal left. Then followed a maze of crevasses with narrow escapes.

Lashly was no longer his stoical self and wrote: "We have to-day experienced what we none of us ever wants to be our lot again. I cannot describe the maze we got into and the hairbreadth escapes we have had to pass through to-day. This day we shall remember all our lives. . . . Often we saw openings where it was possible to drop the biggest ship afloat in."[58] They arrived overdue at their depot. Evans was snow-blind and had to be told directions by his men.

The three were on the barrier on 22 January with 360 miles left to Hut Point. Eight days later, Evans had pain behind the knees and knew it was scurvy. Over the next two weeks, he weakened; eventually he could not pull, began stumbling, and then one day fainted. "Crean thought I was dead. His hot tears fell on my face, and as I came to I gave a weak kind of laugh. . . . Those two gallant fellows held a short council of war. I endeavoured to get them to leave me . . . but it was useless to argue with them."[59] The surface was so bad that the sledge could not be budged with the sick man upon it, so Crean went for help while Lashly stayed to tend Evans. "Crean came in to say good-bye to me. I thanked him for what he was doing in a weak, broken sort of way, and Lashly held open the little round tent door to let me see the last of him."[60]

With two sticks of chocolate and three biscuits in his pockets, Crean made the solo thirty-five-mile walk to Hut Point in eighteen hours; if he dropped into a crevasse or were hit by a blizzard, both he and Evans likely would not survive. A blizzard sprang up half an hour after his arrival at Hut Point. Atkinson and Demetri started out in thick weather with two dog teams, carrying fresh food. A day later they reached the tent; Evans, who was still alive, was fed and carried in his bag on a sledge. They were all back at Hut Point on 22 February. (Lashly and Crean were later awarded the Albert Medal by the king for their heroic effort.)

The Polar Party, consisting of Scott, forty-three; Wilson, thirty-nine; Bowers, twenty-eight; Oates, thirty-two; and Taff Evans, thirty-seven, had left the Last Supporting Party behind. These five were the culmination of years of experience and preparation. They had enough food for full rations on the plateau back to the Beardmore. The worries of motors, animals, and crevasses were behind them. Spirits were high, and Scott was confident. His team had been the strongest, but they did not yet realize the toll taken on them to make up lost time after the blizzard. Little or nothing was to be gained with five instead of four men, so Scott's choice was a sign of his self-assurance and desire to take as many men as possible. Scott was delighted with his choices. He had his dear friend Wilson at his side; the indispensable and indefatigable Bowers; his old, strong, *Discovery* companion Taff Evans; and the dependable Oates, who would represent the Army. Scott was willing to overlook certain difficulties: the tent was cramped, and the bags on the edges were partly off the floor cloth, collecting rime from the tent lining; the extra time to cook meals would have to be taken away from sleeping or marching; the sledge was top-heavy and less safe on crevasse lids; and they had only four sets of skis.

On 9 January, Scott wrote: "Lat. 88°25', beyond the record of Shackleton's walk. All is new ahead."[61] They fixed One and a Half Degree Depot the next day, departing with eighteen days' food. Ice crystals and sastrugi made the pulling exhausting. Evans was weakening in the cold and his cut hand was not healing. Soon all were feeling the cold, although temperatures had not dropped. On 15 January, they left their Last Depot thirty miles from the pole and took with them nine days' provisions. Scott wrote, "It ought to be a certain thing now, and the only appalling possibility the sight of the Norwegian flag forestalling ours."[62]

At the South Pole: Oates, Scott, and Evans standing,
Bowers and Wilson seated (left to right)
Scott, *Scott's Last Expedition*, 1913

On 16 January, Scott recorded: "The worst has happened. . . . Bowers' sharp eyes detected what he thought was a cairn. . . . It was a black flag tied to a sledge bearer; near by the remains of a camp; sledge tracks and ski tracks going and coming and other clear trace of dogs' paws—many dogs. This told us the whole story. The Norwegians have forestalled us and are first at the Pole. It is a terrible disappointment, and I am very sorry for my loyal companions. Many thoughts come and much discussion have we had. To-morrow we must march on to the Pole and then hasten home with all the speed we can compass." On 17 January, Scott wrote: "The Pole. Yes, but under very different circumstances from those expected. We have had a horrible day. . . . Great God! this is an awful place and terrible enough for us to have laboured to it without the reward of priority. . . . Now for the run home and a desperate struggle. I wonder if we can do it." On the following day, 18 January, Scott recorded: "We have just arrived at this tent. . . . We find a record of five Norwegians having been here. . . . Left a note to say I had visited the tent with companions. . . . We built a cairn, put up our poor slighted Union Jack, and photographed ourselves—mighty cold work all of it. . . . Well, we have turned our back now on the goal of our ambition and must face our 800 miles of solid dragging—and good-bye to most of the daydreams!"[63]

Astoundingly, Scott and Amundsen had fixed the South Pole only one-half mile apart, equal to a single theodolite gradation representing a half-minute of arc. Scott picked up Amundsen's letter to King Haakon VII. Forlorn and cold, the men hurried home with the aid of a sail, and followed their cairns. Exhaustion, hunger, and snow blindness plagued them. Bowers remarked, "I sometimes spend much thought on the march with plans for making a pig of myself on the first opportunity. As that will be after a further march of 700 miles they are a bit premature."[64] At One and a Half Degree Depot, the general tone of Scott's writing was gloomy and anxious, and he began to mention many little hardships. All the joy of sledging was gone, despite some superb marches of almost twenty miles.

Evans, Scott's "giant worker with a remarkable headpiece,"[65] began to show signs of trouble with his injured hand, now frostbitten and infected. (Gran later believed Evans was demoralized because he had hoped that being first at the pole would guarantee him future financial independence, but now that security was uncertain.[66]) Then Evans fell into a crevasse with Scott, sustained a concussion, and became "dull and incapable."[67] Oates had severe frostbites and a gangrenous toe. Wilson, too, was cold. Scott and Bowers were relatively fit, although Bowers ceased keeping his diary on 4 February.

They reached the Upper Glacier (Mount Darwin) Depot on 7 February.

On 8 and 9 February, the weather was fine. Wilson could not resist the temptation to sketch and geologize under the Mount Buckley cliffs. Gloom gave way to enthusiasm as Wilson procured thirty-five pounds of outstanding geologic and fossil specimens, and the men dried their garments in the sun. But only two days later, the men lost their way in thick weather and cold, got into terribly pressured ice and crevasses, fell repeatedly, and had to cut rations because of uncertainty when they might arrive at the next depot. The following day brought unrelentingly poor conditions. "In a very critical situation. . . . one meal only remaining in the food bag; the depot doubtful in locality. We *must* get there to-morrow. Meanwhile we are cheerful with an effort." Getting away the next morning after only a biscuit apiece, Wilson spotted the depot flag. "The relief to all is inexpressible."[68]

Scott wrote, "There is no getting away from the fact that we are not going strong. . . . We are pulling for food. . . . Evans has nearly broken down."[69] The party was taking as long to descend the Beardmore with light sledges as they had taken to go up with full sledges. On 17 February, Evans was delirious, unable to ski, and could not keep up. He was brought unconscious into camp on the sledge and died quietly. At one time Scott had considered him the strongest of the five. "It is a terrible thing to lose a companion in this way, but calm reflection shows that there could not have been a better ending to the terrible anxieties of the past week."[70] Clearly Scott knew that Evans's breakdown had jeopardized the survival chances of the entire party. Evans, for his part, had suffered without complaint. Cherry-Garrard later speculated that because Evans was such a large man, his equal but proportionately smaller ration left him underfed.

The remaining four men were now on the barrier and able to maintain full rations. The line of cairns was lost, and opinions were divided as to whether they were too far west or east; anxiety was increasing when Bowers spotted a cairn. Temperatures dropped steadily in late February to below minus 30 degrees Fahrenheit, with no tail wind to assist the sledge. Wilson stopped writing in his diary on 27 February, leaving Scott the sole chronicler. No one had ever been very far south on the barrier in March, but from all previous records near Hut Point, the weather could have been anticipated. On 1 March, they reached the Middle Barrier Depot; oil was short owing to evaporation from containers with poorly fitting seals.[71] Oates's frostbitten feet were very bad, and the temperature was below minus forty. With a strong wind and full sail, they made only five and a half miles. "God help us, we can't keep up this pulling, that is certain. Amongst ourselves we are unendingly cheerful, but what each man feels in his heart I can only guess." The surfaces worsened, and again they lost the line of cairns. "I don't know what I should do if Wilson and Bowers weren't so determinedly cheerful over things."[72]

On 6 March, Oates could no longer pull. "The poor Soldier has become a terrible hindrance, though he does his utmost and suffers much I fear. . . . He is wonderfully brave." Three days later, they arrived at the Mount Hooper Depot, again with shortages. Scott felt sure Oates had no chance of survival, and he doubted their own. "Titus Oates is very near the end, one feels. What we or he will do, God only knows. We discussed the matter after breakfast; he is a brave fine fellow and understands the situation, but he practically asked for advice. Nothing could be said but to urge him to march as long as he could."[73] Scott ordered, over Wilson's resistance, that opiates be distributed so that each man could end his own life if he chose to. The men had only seven days' food for the fifty-five miles to One Ton Depot, but their endurance seemed to be only six miles per day. Until 12 March, Scott repeatedly implored: "Pray God," "Providence to our aid!" and "God help us."[74] Then there were no more supplications—Scott evidently understood and had accepted his fate.

The seventeenth of March was Oates's birthday. The soldier had hoped he would not wake in the morning, but he did, to whirling drift outside the tent. Scott recorded the remarkable sacrifice that followed. "He said, 'I am just going outside and may be some time.' He went out into the blizzard and we have not seen him since. . . . We knew that poor Oates was walking to his death, but though we tried to dissuade him, we knew it was the act of a brave man and an English gentleman. We all hope to meet the end with a similar spirit, and assuredly the end is not far. . . . The cold is intense, -40° at midday . . . and though we constantly talk of fetching through I don't think anyone of us believes it in his heart."[75]

On 19 March, they made the camp they would never leave, eleven miles from One Ton. Scott's right foot was severely frostbitten, and he knew that amputation is needed in such cases. The men had only enough fuel to cook or make water for one day, and only two days' food. A long gale and blizzard began, and for the three men it would never let up. On 21 March: "To-day forlorn hope, Wilson and Bowers going to depot for fuel."[76] But in fact they were never able to go. Scott, knowing all was lost, wrote his final, emotionally stirring letters, his "Message to the Public," and diary entries until 29 March.

Of Wilson, Scott wrote to his companion's wife, Oriana: "His eyes have a comfortable blue look of hope and his mind is peaceful with the satisfaction of his faith in regarding himself as part of the great scheme of the Almighty." Of Bowers, Scott wrote: "As the troubles have thickened his dauntless spirit ever shone brighter and he has remained cheerful, hopeful, and indomitable to the end. The ways of Providence are inscrutable, but there must be some reason why such a young, vigorous and promising life is taken." In his climactic and immortal "Message to the Public," he wrote: "We have been unable to leave the tent—the gale howling about us. We are weak, writing is difficult, but for my own sake I do not regret this journey, which has shown that Englishmen can endure hardships, help one another, and meet death with as great a fortitude as ever in the past. We took risks, we knew we took them; things have come out against us, and therefore we have no cause for complaint, but bow to the will of Providence, determined still to do our best to the last. . . . Had we lived, I should have had a tale to tell of the hardihood, endurance, and courage of my companions which would have stirred the heart of every Englishman. These rough notes and our dead bodies must tell the tale." His last written words—"For God's sake look after our people."[77]

Back at base in late February, Atkinson had sent Cherry-Garrard and Demetri to resupply One Ton. If Scott had not arrived, Cherry-Garrard was to decide whether to proceed farther south. Scott had stated that he was not dependent on the dogs for his return and that the animals were not to be risked in view of sledging plans for the next season. With good runs and extra food for the dogs at Corner Camp, Cherry-Garrard and Demetri reached One Ton in seven days. They remained for six. On four days the men could not go south for fear of missing Scott in thick weather. With no dog food at One Ton, Cherry-Garrard and Demetri would have to kill some dogs to feed the others if they were to travel more than a single day south. Demetri was feeling the cold, which was below minus 30 degrees Fahrenheit, so they headed northward on 10 March. The dogs charged home in wild career for a six-day return. Demetri was in a state of near collapse, and the dogs were done for the season. Cherry-Garrard later second-guessed his decision not to go south from One Ton to leave food and fuel on a cairn, even though Teddy Evans fully supported his judgment to return as he had done.

The *Terra Nova* returned. Pennell had picked up the second Western Party (Taylor, Debenham, Gran, and Forde) in the middle of February. The Western Party had succeeded in arduous explorations despite stern hardships. But Pennell was unable to pick up the Northern Party, thus Campbell's group was stranded. The ship delivered two new men, fresh dogs, and mules, and took Teddy Evans, Simpson, Taylor, Ponting, Meares, Forde, Day, Clissold, and Anton Omelchencko, the Russian pony boy, home.

At Cape Evans anxiety for Scott increased. On 27 March, Atkinson and Keohane man-hauled south. Three days later, eight miles beyond Corner Camp in autumn conditions, their route was obscured and the men were used up. They left a week's provisions and turned north. All hope for the Polar Party ran out. Atkinson led a party on 17 April to Butter Point to attempt a rescue of the Northern Party. Ice was tenuous, and temperatures were minus forty with no sun to dry garments and bags. At Butter Point, the ice was going out north, so Atkinson's party was forced to return to Cape Evans after their courageous effort. Back at the hut, Cherry-Garrard described how they were plagued by mirages of the missing parties' arrivals.

Thirteen worn-out men, with Atkinson in charge, made up the party at Cape Evans. Those who went home had no hint of the tragedy; the men of the Cape Evans party had to bear it alone. On a bright scientific note, Debenham discovered fossils of plants and marine animals in rocks brought back by Atkinson from the Beardmore Glacier, but, as Cherry-Garrard put it, "A second winter, with some of your best friends dead, and others in great difficulties, perhaps dying, when all is unknown and every one is sledged to a standstill, and blizzards blow all day and all night, is a ghastly experience."[78] The strongest prevailing opinion was that the Polar Party had perished in a crevasse on the Beardmore. Less likely was scurvy. The chance the Cape Evans party could ever find them seemed slim, but the missing men's families, the British nation, and the world would want to know what had happened. A search party would have to get as far as the Upper Glacier (Mount Darwin) Depot, which meant investing all their resources in the endeavor. Considering that this left no assistance for Campbell, whose party might be alive and in need of help, the unanimity of opinion to go south was remarkable.

With the passing of winter, "God sent His daylight to scatter the nightmares of the darkness."[79] Two runs were made to stock Corner Camp in October. "Those of us who had borne the brunt of the travelling of the two previous sledge seasons were sick of sledging . . . but the job had to be done."[80] When wildlife returned to McMurdo Sound, the summer season was officially under way.

The search party set out from Hut Point on 29 October 1912 with eleven men plus mules and dogs; Debenham and W. W. Archer stayed behind at Cape Evans. The party reached One Ton on 11 November. The next day, eleven miles farther south, Wright spotted something suspicious and decided to investigate. Only through this good fortune did he discover the tent, for it could easily have been overlooked. "I saw a small object projecting above the surface on the starboard bow but carried on the chosen course until we were nearly abreast of this object. . . . I decided [it] had better be investigated more closely, but did not expect it was of great interest so told the mule train to continue south while I went over the 1/2 mile or so to examine what it was. It was the 6 inches or so tip of a tent and was a great shock."[81] When the snow was removed and they entered the tent, the drama and tragedy of the Polar Party was finally known to the men, and would be known to the world and posterity.

Cherry-Garrard described the scene: "Bowers and Wilson were sleeping in their bags. Scott had thrown back the flaps of his bag at the end. His left hand was stretched over Wilson. . . . Beneath the head of his bag, between the bag and the floor-cloth, was the green wallet in which he carried his diary. . . . Everything was tidy. The tent had been pitched as well as ever. . . . Near Scott was a lamp. . . . I think that Scott had used it to help him to write up to the end. I feel sure that he had died last. . . . [Atkinson] read the diary. . . . We never moved them. We took the bamboos of the tent away, and the tent itself covered them. . . . The sun was dipping low above the Pole. . . . The Lord gave and the Lord taketh away. Blessed be the name of the Lord. . . . A great cairn has been built over them. . . . A cross has been fixed, made out of ski."[82]

Cherry-Garrard was deeply stirred by Scott's diary. "You have only to read one page of what he wrote towards the end to see something of his sense of justice. . . . Indeed I think you must read all those pages; and if you have read them once, you will probably read them again. You will not need much imagination to see what manner of man he was."[83] Teddy Evans related what Gran later told him: "When I saw those three poor souls the other day, I just felt that I envied them. They died having done something great. How hard death must be for those who meet it having done nothing."[84] About eighteen miles further south, Oates's body was sought but not found. A cairn was erected for him with another note, signed by Atkinson and Cherry-Garrard: "Hereabouts died a very gallant gentleman."[85]

Through the years since the expedition, historians have vigorously debated why the Polar Party failed. Many factors contributed: faulty transport; failure to place One Ton Depot farther south; the exhausting efforts of the winter and spring journeys that depleted the men's strength; their late start on the polar trail; the warm, early December blizzard; the fatiguing competition between the manhauling parties on the Beardmore Glacier; the composition of the Polar Party; the demoralizing effect of arriving second at the South Pole; the time lost collecting specimens at Mount Buckley and carrying the extra weight; the oil evaporation from the depots; the proportionately smaller ration for Taff Evans; travel on the barrier in March; and Cherry-Garrard's decision not to go south from One Ton Depot. The margin of failure was small enough that reversal of any one of these alone might have made the difference. Arguably, faulty transport was Scott's greatest undoing, for excellent transport would have amply compensated for all the other problems; what Amundsen did with dogs alone Scott could not do with a combination of dogs, ponies, motors, and manhauling. But perhaps above all, the root of the downfall was Scott's tragically flawed leadership.

The search party arrived back at Hut Point and learned that the Northern Party was safe. For the main party, this was the happiest news they had gotten in a long time. They were to learn how the story of Campbell's party had dramatically unfolded.

The Northern Party landed at Cape Adare on 17 February 1911; they unloaded in two days and dug out Borchgrevink's snowed-up hut, using it as temporary quarters during the two weeks that their own hut was under construction. The new hut was twenty feet square and was secured with three wire hawsers. Stores were piled to windward as a weather guard. Each man had a six-foot-square cubicle delineated by pencil marks on the wall and was free to decorate it as he chose. There were two windows, a large communal table, a stove, and acetylene plant. The hut was spacious and cozy.

Priestley was the only scientist, but all the men were trained to make the needed observations. Campbell improvised two kayaks out of sledges fitted with blubber-sealed canvases in which they were able to carry out short journeys in the vicinity. Browning cleaned and leveled Hanson's grave, and inscribed Hanson's name in block letters out of quartz. The winter proceeded uneventfully. To ensure that the weather observation was taken at two every morning, Browning invented an ingenious alarm clock that was accurate to a few minutes: a candle burned down, releasing a string attached to a taut bamboo stick, which in turn activated the arm on their gramophone.

The ship picked up Campbell's party on 4 January 1912 and left them four days later at a point farther south, Evans Cove in Terra Nova Bay. They were to be picked up on 18 February. During the interval, they sledged around Mount Melbourne making collections, observations, and surveys, and discovered previously unknown glaciers. The ship returned for them, but ice kept the vessel thirty miles out. The men came to realize they were stranded.

Thus began one of the most remarkable tales of Antarctic survival on record. The men had been landed with only six weeks' provisions, two sledges, a small supply of oil, a spare tent and sleeping bag, and some spare summer clothing. Now the tents were split, threadbare, and nearly useless. The men cut their rations drastically, set up camp on what they named Inexpressible Island in Terra Nova Bay, and took the few seals and penguins they could find. Biscuits, sugar, chocolate, and cocoa were diligently set aside as half-rations for an eventual trip next spring down the Victoria Land coast and across the frozen sound to Hut Point. They also set aside finnesko (padded boots of reindeer hide and fur), windproofs, and woolen underwear. Hope for relief ran out in the middle of March.

The men dug out a nine-by-thirteen-foot cave for shelter, covered the entrance with sealskin, employed snow blocks for insulation, and laid down pebbles, seaweed, and tent cloths for flooring in the sleeping chamber. About three feet of snow accumulated overhead, which kept the interior warmer. They could not stand upright inside, and developed "igloo back" from crouching. The stove was fashioned from a tin can; oil from heated blubber was dripped onto seal bones and burned. Black, oily smoke filled their quarters, covering them with soot and irritating their lungs and eyes. As the men's hair and beards grew long and their clothing deteriorated, they took on a ghastly appearance. Snowdrifts above ground occasionally choked off the ventilation, and the men were warned just in time of impending asphyxiation when the blubber light or stove went out. For lack of warm clothing, they were largely confined to the cave, except when on mandatory seal patrols. For entertainment they had virtually nothing—three books and a bible, and Priestley's journal to read from. The men pieced together their recollections of various songs and hymns to while away time when conversations became worn.

Food reserves were woefully meager, and the infrequency of seals and penguins was a matter of constant anxiety through the winter. Nothing from an animal was wasted; all the organs were eaten, blood frozen in the snow was recovered for the hoosh, and even the bones were set aside in the event of dire need. Their usual diet was two meals per day consisting of some seal or penguin, pemmican, a single biscuit, some very thin cocoa amounting to an average of two and a half teaspoons weekly per man, one and a half ounces of chocolate three times in two weeks, and twelve lumps of sugar weekly. Seaweed was the only vegetable. Sea water was used to salt the hoosh, and ginger and citron tablets from the medicine chest provided occasional flavor variety. Tea leaves were brewed on Sundays, reboiled on Mondays, and smoked on Tuesdays. Biscuit rations were halved in June, then for over a month eliminated altogether. Their Midwinter Day celebration was merely full rations and some saved tobacco. Food fantasies became unrelenting.

Priestley recalled the preciousness of the extra morsel allowed at special times: "As I had taken the precaution to allow for six birthdays and as many other festive occasions, I was always able to advance some little trifle, a biscuit apiece, a stick of chocolate, or half a dozen raisins, to mark the occasion. It was little enough, but . . . such gala days were looked forward to for a week or more and remembered for as long. . . . One of our biscuits . . . would give more pleasure than a City dinner." The finding of thirty-six fresh fish in a seal's stomach made "a dish fit for a king."[86]

The men maintained discipline and amiable spirits, made no complaints, and were loyal to Campbell's command. Abbott had an accident with a slippery knife while slaying a seal and severed three tendons in a hand. Toward the end of winter, diarrhea affected most of them, especially Browning and Dickason. The resulting scene in the cave was indescribable.

The party left the cave for Cape Evans on 30 September. Browning had to be carried on the sledge part of the way, and the others feared for his life. About 110 miles south, in the vicinity of Tripp Island, they sought for and found Professor David's depot of letters and specimens from Shackleton's expedition, and these they took with them. After another twenty-five miles, at Cape Roberts, four weeks after setting out, they found a food cache with biscuit, raisins, tea, cocoa, butter, and lard left by the Western Party the previous year, and they gleefully enjoyed a large feed and took a day off from travel, which helped Browning considerably. They also received news from the main party: it was last year's news, but it was sheer joy to have this contact with their comrades. Three days later they had made another forty miles and were at the Butter Point depot; they found Atkinson's note from April concerning the failed attempt to relieve them. The six men crossed the sea ice, arriving at Hut Point on 6 November.

The hut was empty, but they found a note from Atkinson to the ship's commanding officer informing him of the loss of the Polar Party and the search journey then under way. They proceeded to Cape Evans, where Debenham and Archer welcomed them with a feast, bath, and change of clothes, which brought about a major transformation in their appearance. Later, Priestley recalled: "The winter of 1912 has undoubtedly left its mark on all of us, and none of us would care to repeat the experience; but in my own case, the "Call of the South" remains a force . . . which is probably rather increased than decreased by the hardships."[87] Remarkably, Priestley led a group of six men to the summit of Mount Erebus in December. (Priestley returned to the Antarctic with Prince Philip on *R.Y. Britannia* in 1957, and he served as United Kingdom advisor to the American Deep Freeze IV project in Antarctica in 1958–59).

Teddy Evans had recovered from his illness in England and now returned with the *Terra Nova* for the final relief. The wardroom was decorated with flags, ribbons, letters, champagne, chocolates, cigars, and cigarettes, and the ship was scrubbed. Evans met Campbell with a sense of relief, but also learned of Scott's tragedy. Flags on the masthead were lowered in honor of the lost men, all the festive decorations were taken down, and the undeliverable letters were set aside. A year's stores for twelve men were deposited at Cape Evans for use by any future expedition, and on 19 January 1913, all were aboard after twenty-eight hours of loading. Cherry-Garrard wrote: "I leave Cape Evans with no regret: I never want to see the place again. The pleasant memories are all swallowed up in the bad ones."[88]

The party first went to Hut Point. The carpenter made a great memorial cross of Australian jarrah wood, inscribed with the names of the Polar Party. At Cherry-Garrard's suggestion, he added the concluding line of Alfred Lord Tennyson's *Ulysses*: "To strive, to seek, to find, and not to yield"—words that could not better have suited such men as Scott, Wilson, Bowers, Oates, and Taff Evans. On 22 January, the cross was erected atop the 750-foot Observation Hill, standing nine feet out of the rocks, well secured to endure, overlooking the barrier and the resting place of the dead men.

The ship sailed to Evans Cove to pick up the geological treasures gathered by the Northern Party. Upon seeing the cave, Evans commented, "No cell prisoners ever had such discomforts. . . . Campbell's simple narrative I read aloud. . . . It was a tale of altruism and grit, so simply told, full of disappointments and privations, all of which they accepted with fortitude and never a complaint. I had to stop reading it as it brought tears to my eyes and made my voice thick."[89]

The ship endured a rough passage northward amid gales and icebergs, arrived in New Zealand on 10 February, and eventually in England. "We landed to find the Empire—almost the civilized world—in mourning. It was as though they had lost great friends."[90]

21

WILHELM FILCHNER AND THE
SECOND GERMAN ANTARCTIC EXPEDITION
(1911–1912)

Obwohl wir nunmehr durch unsere Entdeckungen auch für das Weddell-
Meer die Ausgangsbasis für die Landerkundungen geschaffen haben . . .
[werden die] schwierigen [Eisverhältnisse] . . . schon ein Herankommen
an die Basis nur wenigen Sterblichen gestatten.

[Although through our discoveries we have now provided a point of
departure for overland exploration from the Weddell Sea . . . the difficult
ice conditions . . . will permit few mortals to reach the starting point.]

Wilhelm Filchner, *Zum Sechsten Erdteil*

BEFORE LAUNCHING HIS ANTARCTIC ADVENTURE, Wilhelm Filchner
(1877–1957) had the experience of leading a hazardous expedition to Tibet in
1903–4 for geographical and scientific discovery. He envisioned an Antarctic
expedition to unravel the mystery of whether land or frozen sea ran between
the Weddell Sea and the Ross Sea, an undertaking that would require two
ships and separate parties to examine the respective regions. The land parties would keep in contact by wireless communication and would cross the
continent by way of the South Pole. Financial circumstances, however,
forced Filchner to abbreviate his plan to a single ship that would explore the
deepest recess of the Weddell Sea; then he would proceed by sledge toward
the Ross Sea.

By the expedition's end, Filchner could claim only to have discovered the
southernmost point of the Weddell Sea, certainly no small accomplishment
given the hazardous ice conditions. The rest of the voyage was a disastrous
failure, owing largely to the ship's captain, Richard Vahsel, who divided the
staff and crew and went so far as to sabotage the expedition's principal aims.
Filchner, in his official expedition account and even in his late-in-life auto-

biography, scarcely addressed the enmity of the relationships, although the acrimony had been well appreciated in Germany for years. His reserve and patience were finally broken by the publication of an untruthful article against him. He took direct aim at his rivals in a dramatic manifesto that he requested not be published until after his death.[1]

As a child Filchner was unruly, and he was sent to a boarding school at age ten. He was later enrolled in the Munich Cadet Corps; the discipline agreed with him, and by age fifteen he had settled on a military career and proceeded to earn his promotions. On a visit to Russia in 1900 he developed an insatiable wanderlust, became interested in science, and met some of Germany's finest scientists. His first major expedition was a scientific journey to northeast Tibet in 1903–4. Expedition members faced four and a half months of enormous hardships of terrain, weather, and hostile native peoples. To Filchner's credit, the party succeeded in its scientific objectives. The physician on that expedition, Albert Tafel, was, however, to become Filchner's nemesis—Tafel assaulted and slyly maligned Filchner's character whenever the opportunity arose. Filchner's life was further complicated by a bad marriage: soon after his wife had a child she left him, and the marriage dissolved. Filchner kept himself busy with work.

Filchner developed his idea for an Antarctic expedition in 1909 and received firm support in scientific and military circles. He consulted with Bruce, Scott, and Shackleton, and obtained valuable endorsements from Nordenskjöld and from the Gesellschaft für Erdkunde in Berlin. Prinzregent Luitpold of Bavaria became the expedition's patron. To obtain polar experience, Filchner went to Spitzbergen with a small party of men that included Erich Przybyllok, Heinrich Seelheim, and Erich Barkow, who figured later in the Antarctic expedition. Filchner's Antarctic mission was essentially geographical, with some efforts in other branches of science.

The assemblage of thirty-five men included five scientists: Filchner, Przybyllok (astronomy, magnetism), Barkow (meteorology), Wilhelm Brennecke (oceanography), and Fritz Heim (geology, glaciology). Vahsel, the captain, had been one of the second officers of the *Gauss* under Drygalski. Aboard ship were a hundred tons of provisions, explosives, and hut-building materials. Filchner adopted the transport philosophy of the British: ponies and dogs (motor sledges were abandoned in Buenos Aires for lack of necessary modifications). A generous sledging ration was planned (5,238 kcal. per day, almost a third more than other polar explorers considered feasible to carry).

The expedition ship was the Norwegian barque *Bjørn,* built in 1905, and renamed *Deutschland.* The vessel had actually been Shackleton's choice, but it was too expensive for his budget. The ship was modified for the ice by strengthening the hull and making the screw retractable. The auxiliary engine could run on coal or blubber (seal blubber was cut in strips, and, in rather barbaric fashion, penguins were fed in whole). Each scientist had a private room to work in, and laboratories were heated.

The expedition departed Germany on 3 May 1911, with Seelheim in charge; Filchner remained behind to complete arrangements for the scientific program. In Buenos Aires, the Argentineans lent assistance, and the men of the *Deutschland* met Capt. Thorvald Nilsen of the *Fram* and others of Amundsen's party. The German party, now under Filchner and Vahsel, departed Buenos Aires on 4 October for South Georgia. En route, an emergency appendectomy was performed on Dr. Ludwig Kohl, who remained at South Georgia to recover. Carl A. Larsen, who had explored the region of the Antarctic Peninsula in the *Jason* in 1892–94, was now head of the whaling station at Grytviken, and he welcomed the party.

Filchner's group prepared charts, made scientific observations, and ran a brief voyage to the South Sandwich Islands to determine the islands' geological relationship to the Antarctic Peninsula and South America. Severe weather, motion sickness, ice, and poor visibility frustrated the men as they explored the northerly Traversey island group. They returned to South Georgia, where Walter Slossarczyk, the third officer, took his own life during the evening of 26 November.[2] Filchner had a cross erected in Slossarczyk's memory near the waterfall at the Grytviken whaling station and named a bay at South Georgia after his lost comrade. The watch-keeping officer Alfred Kling arrived from Buenos Aires with the party's Manchurian ponies, and the group departed on 11 December.

Filchner was aware how treacherous the Weddell Sea ice conditions could be, now having experienced his own difficulties at the South Sandwich Islands. And he was, by now, increasingly at odds with Vahsel. Not surprisingly, Filchner was hardly sanguine about his future prospects. "It is therefore expedient to lay out the schedule only in its broad outlines. If one later succeeds in achieving these broad goals even approximately one can with a clear conscience consider the polar enterprise in question as successful."[3] The first ice was encountered at 57°30' S, 33°4' W; Filchner was pleased with the ship. An ice anchor was lost, however, and interior lighting was cut to save coal. A 30 December "census" gave thirty-three men, seventy-five dogs (including thirty-seven pups), eight ponies (four having been left behind), and a cat. "Total 117 living creatures."[4] On New Year's Eve, Filchner gave a heartfelt toast to his patron Luitpold.

The ice of the Weddell Sea proved difficult, as expected, and by 62° S the ship was periodically beset. On 18 January, at 72°20' S, the ice opened, and the men made a quick fifty-one-mile run to the south, only to be virtually imprisoned again. After several days hoping for current and wind to jostle and dislodge the floes, Filchner formulated a contingency plan that ultimately he did not have to execute—he would settle on determining the southern extension of Coats Land if they could get no farther. Based on the number of bergs, Filchner speculated correctly that there must still be a vast stretch of open water to the south: the Weddell Sea must extend farther than previously known. At six in the morning on 29 January, the party passed Weddell's record of 74°15' S in open sea. Depth soundings revealed a rising ocean floor as the men headed south-southwest.

On 30 January, at 76°40' S, 31°32' W, a sounding showed only 1,800 feet. In poor visibility the ship steamed slowly northwest. Then, "when the fog lifted at 3.00 p.m. a shout of 'Land to the southeast!' rang out."[5] Drifting amid a magnificent gallery of bergs, the men saw an ice-covered slope rising over 2,600 feet that they assumed (correctly) to be the extension of Coats Land. They immediately drafted plans to survey the coast, which was fittingly named after Luitpold, and to land and set up winter quarters. The land was seen swinging off to the west, and in bright sunshine the men proceeded south-southwest along an ice front. At 77°41' S, the front swung south-south-east, and they saw an open bay measuring three by four miles, bounded by a high cliff on the east and the ice barrier twenty-five to sixty-five feet high on the south and west. This broad inlet, the most southerly point navigable by ship in the Weddell Sea, was named Vahsel Bay. The party attained a farthest south of 77°44' S, at 34°38' W.

When Vahsel declared the bay suitable for mooring, two parties of three men set out to search for a wintering site. The surface of the ice barrier was found to be too rough for transporting provisions and animals to the ice cap covering Luitpold Land, so the men proceeded west by ship along the ice front a distance of 179 miles. No better wintering site was found, however, and pack ice threatened to entrap them. Filchner accurately concluded that currents along the eastern coast of the Weddell Sea swung southwest then north toward Graham Land, creating a vortex of current and ice movement. The men reversed course for Vahsel Bay; a southerly wind blew ice into their previously open track, and only after much anxiety and battle did they succeed in their return. Filchner aimed to erect a winter station and find another route to the interior, but reconnaissance parties had discouraging news: the barrier was "a severely shattered chaos of ice rubble and crevasses."[6]

The Austrian mountaineer Felix König and seaman Paul Wolff climbed to an altitude of a thousand feet on the ice cap and, based on their views, advised Filchner on a wintering site, a spot two miles across the sea ice about sixty feet up. Ninety tons of provisions were to be moved there. Vahsel, however, refused to release his men to do the work because he declared the plan unfeasible. Filchner was forced instead to choose the ice shelf forming the south and western boundary of Vahsel Bay, which appeared solidly attached to the inland ice. Vahsel agreed to remain the winter with the ship as a security measure. Just as unloading was to begin, a northeast wind came up and broke up a quarter-mile of sea ice into a jostling sheet, raising doubts about whether wintering on the ice shelf would be possible after all. So, once more, the party explored west to search for a better site.

The men succeeded in getting farther, to 76°56' S, 40°54' W; but the ice pileup was worse than before. They returned to Vahsel Bay after a futile two-day excursion and moored the ship to the barrier. Soundings showed that the ice barrier, and an attached iceberg measuring four-tenths of a square mile, were afloat. Even so, Vahsel proclaimed the berg stable; it was chosen as the hut site and named "Station Iceberg." Animals and hut-building materials were landed.

Two days later, a gale broke up the sea ice fronting Station Iceberg. "Then a grandiose spectacle occurred: the entire surviving section of the sea ice cover, about 10 km² [about 4 square miles] in area and 2 m [6.5 feet] thick, was converted by the swell into a field of debris within a few moments, as if at the utterance of a magic word."[7] Equipment had been left on the sea ice near Station Iceberg, and bergs were sweeping into the bay. Four men salvaged the equipment from the heaving floes just before the wind swung south and the sea ice sped north. Soon all was open water, and Filchner thought they were once again safe.

On 9 February, the men proceeded to unload the ship in earnest. An uncrevassed site was chosen on which to erect the hut, and most of the construction was completed within a week. Filchner optimistically developed plans for three spring sledging trips the following season; the most important one would determine whether their present locale was connected to the Ross Ice Shelf. Filchner later recalled: "Late on the evening of 17 February,

The partially completed building on Station Iceberg
Filchner, *Zum Sechsten Erdteil*, 1922

full of encouragement and in an elated mood, I contemplated what we had achieved. . . . Admittedly all my fine hopes and all the carefully developed plans were to be in vain."[8]

At four in the morning on 18 February, the weather and sea were comfortably calm, but this was the time of an especially high spring tide, and the rising sea quickly destabilized all the shelf ice in the vicinity. A series of cannon-like sounds, a "hellish cacophony,"[9] announced the abrupt deterioration of Station Iceberg and its separation from the fixed ice mass. The berg slowly rotated clockwise as it began to drift. The seven men asleep on the berg were awakened by the sounds but were so exhausted from their work that they declined to take account of it and went back to sleep. Meanwhile, the ship's company launched an aggressive rescue operation. By eight in the evening, shuttling two boats back and forth from ship to berg, the men had removed all materials except a small amount of coal and lumber. The seven ponies were taken off; one dog among the seventy-five refused to come and was left to his fate with a case of biscuits. The effects of the tide on the regional ice topography were far greater than the men imagined possible, and the scientists charted the breakup. An ice sheet measuring more than 250 square miles was set loose: Vahsel Bay now became part of a much vaster Herzog Ernst Bay (although referred to now as Vahsel Bay). The men contemplated their next actions as they stood off, waiting for southerly winds to blow the ice out.

The bay offered no shelter, so no further operations would be possible until the sea froze over. When the freeze came, the men would land at what was previously Vahsel Bay and spend the autumn, as Filchner had originally intended, hauling provisions and equipment to the ice cap in preparation for the next season's sledging. On 25 February, they laid a depot at the foot of the ice cap about one and a half miles from ship. Filchner commented: "I was really glad to have finally set foot on Prinzregent Luitpold Land and to know that I had *terra firma* beneath my feet."[10] The men redoubled their efforts as the ice conditions improved, transporting over a metric ton of provisions and materials to the depot. A thin layer of ice appeared on the ocean surface, and Filchner excitedly awaited the final solidification of the sea.

Then a northerly wind swept old ice into the bay and forced a halt to operations. Scientists Brennecke and Heim were stranded ashore. Vahsel, fearing the ship would be carried west and splintered by the pressure, reversed his earlier decision to remain in the vicinity and told Filchner that they had to leave for South Georgia as soon as the stranded men were picked up. Filchner was devastated. "For me as leader this announcement means nothing less than abandoning my landing on the ice cap!"[11]

In a favorable moment on 4 March, the two men ashore were rescued, and the ship set a course for Grytviken. "So near to our goal and to have to retreat! We had not deserved such a fate."[12] Aided by southerly winds amid only loose ice, Filchner hoped to follow the Luitpold Coast north to extend his observations, but ice the following day forced the ship west. Filchner now realized that getting out of the Weddell Sea was a race against time. Progress north diminished, and on 7 March, at 73°19' S, 30°16' W, no advance could be made. A week later the party was beset, and the fire in the ship's main boiler was let out.

As the *Deutschland* slowly drifted north-northwest, the men settled into a schedule of science and day-to-day living. The crew was accountable to Vahsel, and the scientists to Filchner. Small observation huts were set up within two hundred feet of ship. The ship carried an extensive library— "Only somebody who knows from his own experience what it means to spend hundreds of days through a polar winter in a little cabin aboard an icebound ship, can sympathise with how precious it is to have a varied mental diet."[13] The dogs, kenneled off ship, were sometimes wild and cannibalistic; they attacked the horses, ate their dung, and hunted seals without mercy. Some of the ponies did not survive the winter.

Filchner organized a midwinter sledge journey of Kling, König, and himself to corroborate the existence of land seen about forty miles west of the ship's position by Benjamin Morrell in 1823.[14] Kling remarked, "Admittedly the idea of making a sledge trip from a drifting ship across the sea ice in the middle of the polar night and with an average temperature of -35°C [minus 31 degrees Fahrenheit] was not exactly alluring; but we had come on the expedition to achieve and experience something."[15]

Their departure date was 23 June. The hardships of their journey are reminiscent of the midwinter journey to Cape Crozier by Wilson, Bowers, and Cherry-Garrard on Scott's expedition. Ice surfaces were extremely difficult because of the pressure, and leads were covered only in thin ice. Often the dogs got tangled in their traces. Once out of sight of the ship, the men could only guess its position, since the ship's drift was not necessarily the same as their own. The men depended on the theodolite to determine where they were, but it was difficult to use. Kling had to bare his fingers to manipulate it, and frostbite was the result. His freezing breath iced up the lenses. In the dark, which comprised all but a few hours of twilight each day, he needed the flashlight to read the figures, but often the battery was too cold to function. Kling wrote: "In the tent, by the meagre glow of the candle, I refused to let myself be dispirited by the uncertainty of our position, but cheered up my companions and gave them the assurance that I could find the ship again."[16]

Temperatures were so cold that sausage and meat had to be chiseled, then warmed in the mouth before chewing. The unlucky man who touched bare metal with his fingers found the two soldered together. Sometimes the men shivered uncontrollably; their faces were covered with rime in the mornings. Once the dogs sprinted off with the sledge, cooker, and theodolite; Kling caught up with them after falling on his face several times, and he "cursed the dogs eloquently."[17] Kling turned thirty years old and celebrated with two cigars.

The men's position on 27 June was 70°33' S, 44°48' W, where they should have seen Morrell's land. Morrell's positions had previously been held in some doubt; Filchner, Kling, and König now disproved the existence of land at the position Morrell had claimed. The men began their return journey. A spring tide, which threatened to open cracks and leads, was due in two days. By skill and some luck, the men found their old tracks and rejoiced; they were back at the ship on 30 June, having covered a total of ninety-eight miles (including drift), with a lowest temperature of minus 39 degrees Fahrenheit. Theirs was one of the most creditable achievements of the expedition. The sun returned on 18 July.

In his official narrative, Filchner began mentioning Vahsel's ill health on 5 June, noting the captain's cough, breathing difficulties, and suffusion of the head. Vahsel, who was attended by the ship's physician for his serious heart condition, steadily worsened, and he died on 8 August. The funeral and burial were presided over by the first officer, Wilhelm Lorenzen, who, according to maritime law, became captain.

By early September, cracks in the ice were appearing around the ship, and plans were made to bring the dogs and equipment aboard at a moment's notice. The ship's drift swung eastward; the vessel occasionally groaned in the pressure but escaped harm. Not until the middle of November did release finally seem possible. The huts and kennels were dismantled, and the men blasted themselves clear of the ice, gaining their freedom on 26 November at 63°37' S, 36°34' W. They arrived at last in Grytviken on 19 December.

Filchner placed the *Deutschland* under the command of Kling while he returned to Berlin on an Italian ship to raise funds for a second season. Filchner's attempts were unsuccessful, however, and he had to be satisfied with what he had already achieved. "Although through our discoveries we have now provided a point of departure for overland exploration from the Weddell Sea too, the Ross Sea will still form the more convenient port of entry for exploration in Antarctica in the future. The reason for this is the difficult ice conditions of the Weddell Sea, which will permit few mortals to reach the starting point."[18] (At the time of his writing, Filchner was aware of the fate of Shackleton's expedition in the *Endurance* [see chapter 24].)

These principal events, described by Filchner in his official account, *Zum Sechsten Erdteil*, were only part of the expedition's story. Intense interpersonal dramas told heavily on the outcome, as Filchner later revealed in "Teststellungen." Tafel, Filchner's slandering enemy from his earlier Tibetan excursion,[19] wanted so desperately to join the Antarctic voyage that he blackmailed the leader by threatening to destroy the expedition from its inception. Filchner refused to have anything to do with him, and Tafel got even by spreading evil rumors about Filchner's character both before the expedition's departure and upon its return.

A far more consequential conflict unfolded between Filchner and Vahsel. Filchner had wanted the Norwegian Jørgensen as captain, but German naval officials, on whose goodwill Filchner depended, exerted a large influence on the choice of personnel and demanded a German captain, even if less qualified. Vahsel was chosen by the Committee of the German Antarctic Expedition in spite of Filchner's distrust, and Filchner found him arrogant and obstreperous. Hans Ruser, who had captained the *Gauss* on Drygalski's expedition, warned Filchner that Vahsel was "greedy for power and an out-

and-out schemer."[20] Ruser was right—Filchner lost control and was forced to look on as Vahsel secured the right to choose the ship's officers, thus turning the expedition into a naval enterprise. On the voyage to Buenos Aires, Vahsel made Seelheim, a Filchner loyalist, so miserable that Seelheim left the expedition.

Kling was captain of the *Cap Ortega,* on which Filchner voyaged to Buenos Aires to join the *Deutschland* party; these two men cooperated well. Upon arrival of the *Cap Ortega* in Argentina, conflict between Filchner and Vahsel escalated so rapidly that Filchner considered abandoning the project. Only his ideals and the support he received from several key expedition members, including Kling, kept the party from disintegrating. Filchner persuaded Kling to remain with him as a buffer against Vahsel. "I was neither an independent expedition leader nor a shipowner, nor could I control anything aboard the polar vessel according to maritime law. . . . Undoubtedly the most rational thing would have been to resign. But I was an explorer, and an explorer operates not simply on the basis of reason. I had had a dream and had pushed it through and worked at it by means of months of exhausting activity. Who abandons a 'child,' as it were, without first having tried and risked everything to save it?"[21]

After embarking for the south, Vahsel lived up to his reputation as a schemer. He insidiously manipulated the ship's officers and crew against Filchner, who eventually found support only in a meager minority. He fell victim to one injustice after another. One night he found feces in his cabin. Later, Vahsel signed the official expedition record formally admitting that Filchner was the one who had encouraged a landing on the ice cap, but he later took credit and accused Filchner of rejecting the proposal, as if it had been his own.

In determining whether Station Iceberg would be safe as the wintering site, Filchner considered the opinion of his fine Norwegian ice pilot Paul Bjørvik paramount and asked Vahsel to obtain it. (Vahsel understood Norwegian, whereas Filchner did not.) Vahsel lied to Filchner, saying Bjørvik believed Station Iceberg to be satisfactory, when in fact Bjørvik had warned Vahsel against building the hut there. Filchner learned the truth only several days into the landing and building operations. Kling, Przybyllok, and König all rallied around Filchner once they learned of Vahsel's duplicity. Until the Bjørvik affair, Filchner did not imagine that Vahsel would deliberately jeopardize the men and the expedition's objectives by such debased conduct. Filchner and Kling believed that there was enough time left in the season to establish a base on the ice cap as Filchner had originally intended, but Vahsel found reasons for objecting. Kling was of the opinion that Vahsel wasted twelve days at anchor.

The official expedition record documents that Vahsel insisted that the two stranded scientists, Brennecke and Heim, be picked up and Vahsel Bay be quit for the year. But once the scientists were back on board and the ship was heading north, Lorenzen and Brennecke at a "Great Ship's Council" accused Filchner of prematurely evacuating the scientists and the ship's position in Vahsel Bay. Apparently, Vahsel had put Lorenzen and Brennecke up to this accusation.[22] So effective was he that even König, who was loyal to Filchner, was led to doubt his leader until trust was re-established during the winter sledging journey.

In a harmless but unfortunate winter incident, Filchner was shooting at seals from the ship, and a bullet struck near König, who, unbeknownst to Filchner, was at work in an igloo off ship. König recognized Filchner as the marksman, approached him, and the two men privately cleared the matter up quickly and resolved to keep it secret to protect Filchner. Filchner reassured König: "I am really not in the habit of shooting at expedition members, least of all at those whom I count among my few friends on board."[23] But word leaked that a bullet had been fired near König, and König was brought before another Great Ship's Council, whose members tried to catch him in contradictions as he successfully concealed Filchner's involvement. Filchner lamented, "In order to maintain one's nerves in this incredible wasteland of lies and hostilities, to advance one's work according to plan during the long polar night while the ship lay beset in the pack and to control oneself and maintain essential working contacts with an opposition which abused my trust in a shameful fashion, all this consumed my will power almost to the point of exhaustion and I would have collapsed under this mental strain had I not had friends at my side and had I not known that I was entirely right in what I was doing."[24] The turmoil undoubtedly explained why the social functions and bonhomie that helped other expeditions pass the difficult autumn and winter seasons were scarcely in evidence on this expedition.

Vahsel was thought to have syphilitic heart disease; his symptoms and signs were compatible with that diagnosis. Przybyllok observed that Vahsel was already sick en route to Buenos Aires.[25] Vahsel's condition deteriorated rapidly during the Antarctic winter of 1912. Gottlob Kirschmer, archivist at the Deutsche Geodätische Kommission in Munich, who arranged for the publication of "Feststellungen," believed Vahsel may have attempted to sabotage the expedition in part to hasten his return to civilization, where he could obtain treatment.[26]

Vahsel's death did little to ease the conflict aboard ship, because by then, the two opposing camps were firmly entrenched. Lorenzen, who had been loyal to Vahsel, was in charge. Upon the ship's arrival in Grytviken, Filchner's opposition virtually ran riot against him: Filchner, with Larsen's assistance, isolated the parties. (Filchner later dedicated *Zum Sechsten Erdteil* to Larsen "in sincere gratitude.") Filchner had his enemies housed on shore until they could be transported to Buenos Aires. Soon the press learned of the party's deplorable infighting and became more interested in the invectives than the science. The Court of Honor in Germany investigated the incidents and issued a final report that Filchner considered inconclusive because König and Kling had not been interviewed. In spite of the flawed report, Filchner obtained the moral support of Kaiser Wilhelm, Amundsen, and others, but accusations continued to fly for many years. Kling wrote: "We all greatly regretted that such a national enterprise, which the entire world was watching, had to be abandoned in such a miserable fiasco, one which was caused solely by the sloppiness of a single person [Vahsel]."[27]

After the expedition, Filchner served Germany in World War I. He was transferred to Norway, where he became close with Amundsen and Nansen. Amundsen asked Filchner to join what became the *Maud* expedition to the Arctic, and Filchner accepted. However, wartime suspicions against Germany led to Filchner's deportation from Norway as relations between the two countries deteriorated. Filchner conducted another arduous expedition to Tibet in 1926–28 and wrote a number of books, but he spent most of his life in near poverty. Late in his life, reflecting on his experiences, he wrote: "Today, as I look retrospectively over my work I may say with pleasure and pride that I have been awarded honours and recognition in rich measure. But I admit in the same breath that I have been dealt no small measure of hostility, hostility in every conceivable variation from open dealings to malicious intrigue, malice dictated by envy and jealousy and vicious lies."[28]

22

DOUGLAS A. MAWSON AND THE AUSTRALASIAN ANTARCTIC EXPEDITION (1911–1914)

> Science and exploration have never been at variance; rather, the desire for the pure elements of natural revelation lay at the source of that unquenchable power—the "love of adventure."
>
> Douglas A. Mawson, *The Home of the Blizzard*

THIS COMPLEX ANTARCTIC VENTURE was led by Douglas A. Mawson (1882–1958), a twenty-nine-year-old Australian geologist who had been a member of Shackleton's 1907–9 expedition. In brief, the ship *Aurora*, under the command of John King Davis (1884–1967), departed for the south from Australia on 2 December 1911. A scientific base with wireless radio transmission was established on Macquarie Island. Two of three planned bases were then established in the Antarctic, the main one at Commonwealth Bay, a site previously unknown, and another fifteen hundred miles to the west at the Shackleton Ice Shelf. The ship returned to Hobart to refit, and oceanographic investigations were carried out south of Australia and New Zealand. In December 1912 the ship returned to pick up the two Antarctic parties. Mawson's party afield had met with disaster: his two companions had died. Mawson returned to base too late to be picked up that season, thus he and six others remained at Commonwealth Bay for the winter of 1913. Meanwhile, Davis went to London to secure additional support for a relief voyage. The following season, both the Commonwealth Bay and Macquarie Island parties were relieved, and the expedition ended when the ship returned to Adelaide on 26 February 1914.

Mawson received his education at the University of Sydney and became a geologist under the tutelage of T. W. Edgeworth David. Mawson did fieldwork in the New Hebrides and Australia, and became curator of minerals at the South Australian Museum. He joined Shackleton's *Nimrod* expedition and proved himself highly capable on the three-man trek to the south magnetic pole during which David, who led, assigned him numerous responsibilities. Mawson became known as one who would not ask of another something he would not do himself.

After the Shackleton expedition, Mawson harbored the idea of returning to the Antarctic, and the notion of a purely Australian endeavor to explore the region south of Australia between Cape Adare and Gaussberg became firmly set in his mind early in 1910. Scott, impressed with Mawson's abilities, asked him to join his own expedition and offered him a position in the polar party. But Mawson declined, in part because he was more interested in pure science than in such a grandiose plan as pole-seeking. But out of deference to Scott, Mawson declined to raise funds for an expedition of his own until Scott's needs had been fully satisfied.[1] Mawson was both a serious scientist and a determined explorer: "The polar regions . . . may be said to be paved with facts." "Science and exploration have never been at variance; rather, the desire for the pure elements of natural revelation lay at the source of that unquenchable power—the 'love of adventure.'"[2]

For his own expedition, Mawson obtained the approval of the Australian Association for the Advancement of Science in January 1911. David was president-elect, but even with his influence, the society granted Mawson only £1,000. Within a year, however, Mawson had gathered institutional and private donations, including £18,500 from the governments of Sydney, Melbourne, Adelaide, and Hobart, and a commonwealth grant of £5,000. He went to London for several months, collecting donations through Shackleton's support, advertisements in the London *Daily Mail,* and the Royal Geographical Society. With funds now totaling almost £38,000, the expedition had a solid financial basis, but fund-raising continued after the expedition's departure; another £8,000 came in, including a second commonwealth grant of £5,000.[3]

Davis, who was twenty-eight, had been aboard the *Nimrod* a few years earlier; Mawson selected him as ship's master and second in command. Davis arranged the purchase and refitting of the *Aurora,* a three-masted Dundee sealer built in 1876. Large for a polar vessel of the day (165 feet long, 30 feet abeam, 386 tons), and equipped with only a modest ninety-six-horsepower steam engine, the vessel still managed a speed of six to ten knots. The reinforced hull was oak, sheathed in greenheart and steel. Davis brought the ship to Hobart, and 150 tons of supplies were loaded. Mawson procured an airplane, a thirty-four-foot Vickers I that could remain airborne for five hours and travel three hundred miles, but an accident during a test flight in Australia ruined plans for the first flight on the last continent. The party had no way of knowing that the craft could not have flown under the windy conditions at Commonwealth Bay, but they did try to use it as an air-tractor.

A full gale and enormous seas quickly besieged the southbound party, contaminating their fresh water and flooding the galley. In nine days the men arrived at Macquarie Island, a long, narrow isle abounding with seals, penguins, and pelagic birds. A boatload of men investigated Caroline Cove at the southern end, after which Davis found a good anchorage at the northern end in what he named Hasselborough Bay after the island's discoverer. The men erected a hut for a party of five in the lee of a rocky mass at the north end of the spit amidst the wildlife. Meanwhile, Frank Hurley (1885–1962), the Mawson expedition photographer, discovered that he had left a choice lens behind at Caroline Cove and, after being scolded by Mawson, was assigned to fetch it; that involved an overland trip of some twenty miles each way over difficult terrain. The *Aurora* then departed on 23 December. The ship party's last effort at Macquarie Island was to secure a supply of fresh water at Caroline Cove; as the ship held a tenuous anchorage on the weather side of the island, the men ashore made an unpleasant search for clean runoff amid penguin guano and the mire of elephant seals.

Three Antarctic bases were initially planned, but the season's advance and difficult ice conditions caused Mawson to give up the idea of an Adélie Land base. (Adélie Land is now known as the Adélie Coast.) He reorganized into two parties, a Main Base and a Western Base. The Main Base had to be as close to the south magnetic pole as possible for the magnetic work, and close enough to Macquarie Island for wireless communication. Sailing west along a coast never before seen, they entered a bay on 8 January 1912, at 67° S, 142° E. Numerous islets there were covered with Adélie penguins and Weddell seals. Mawson's men were the first humans to step ashore on the eighteen-hundred-mile coast between Cape Adare and Gaussberg. Commonwealth Bay, Cape Denison, and the Mackellar Islets were all given their names. "The land was so overwhelmed with ice that, even at sea-level, the rock was all but entirely hidden. We were led to surmise that the snowfall must be excessive. The full truth was to be ascertained by bitter experience."[4]

Indeed, their first encounter with Commonwealth Bay was wholly unusual: the weather was magnificent. But even that night, as the men were attempting to secure the ship's anchorage and get supplies ashore, cold winds and showers of fine, driving snow caused frostbite and severed the motorboat from its mooring as seawater shorted the motor. Gales prevented further movements for two days; deliveries ashore could be made only when the winds moderated. Eventually, materials for two huts, a magnetic observatory, a wireless, the sledges, the air-tractor, twenty-three tons of coal, and over two thousand packages were landed, along with the eighteen men who composed the Main Base party.

Davis then departed with the ship on 19 January to take Frank Wild and seven companions westward to another site. Sailing south of land positions recorded by Wilkes, Dumont d'Urville, and Balleny, Davis and his company described Queen Mary Land (now Coast) at 94°25' E, just east of Drygalski's Wilhelm II Coast. Running short on coal, Davis and Wild agreed to establish the Western Base on the large ice shelf at hand, first seen by Wilkes and now named after Shackleton. Thirty-six tons of materials, equipment, and stores were landed in four days. The hut site was ten miles north of the Antarctic Circle at 95° E, and 175 miles east of Gaussberg. The ship left the Western Base on 21 February and arrived safely in Hobart on 12 March 1912, where the *Fram* was in the Derwent with news of Amundsen's South Pole conquest. In Sydney the ship was refitted while the scientists took on equipment and performed oceanographic studies south of Australia. The Macquarie Base was resupplied during a two-week stay from 7 to 22 June; the ship's party examined the Auckland Island group and arrived in Lyttleton on 11 July.

Back at the Main Base, the immediate range of sledging operations would be limited until the following spring. Cape Denison was only a mile wide, projecting seaward to the north half a mile from the ice cliffs to the east and west. To the south was the upsloping inland ice sheet. A boat harbor one-quarter mile deep penetrated the cape in roughly a north-to-south direction. The men set up four temporary tents; building two huts for permanent residence was the next priority. Stout blocks of wood were embedded into the gneiss as a foundation. The larger hut was twenty-four feet square, with bunks, dining table, acetylene gas plant, and scientific instruments. The smaller hut, adjoined downwind, was twenty-one and a half by eighteen feet and had a workroom, veranda, outer living area for the nineteen dogs, engine, wireless operating area, sewing machine, and areas for scientific work. With sloping roofs and an arrangement of storage boxes to windward, the structures were well prepared to withstand high winds. The men also erected instrument sheds nearby. These were pleasant days for the men; Weddell and crabeater seals, penguins, and skuas were in bustling abundance. Mawson recalled: "We worked hard, ate heartily, and enjoyed life."[5]

As the summer progressed, Cape Denison laid bare the truth of its winds. Mawson had noted that even in early February, "after having experienced nothing but a succession of gales for nearly a month, I was driven to conclude that the average local weather must be much more windy than in any other part of Antarctica."[6] By early March, winds laden with snow blew up to eighty miles per hour. Drift got in through every crack but insulated the hut against drafts. Snow had to be shoveled off the veranda every morning. A fish trap and whaleboat were carried away by the wind. "The equinox arrived, and the only indication of settled weather was a more marked regularity in the winds. Nothing like it had been reported from any part of the world. Any trace of elation we may have felt at this meteorological discovery could not compensate for the ever-present discomforts of life. Day after day the wind fluctuated between a gale and a hurricane."[7] The winds severely limited the scientific work and autumn sledging. Whirlwinds were regular phenomena; one lifted and destroyed the three-hundred-pound lid to the air-tractor case. Anything left loose outside was blown away. Men generally went out only on scientific business, and walking, which was impossible without crampons or boots modified with one-and-a-half-inch spikes, was achieved by leaning steeply into the wind.

Lulls were uncommon, and "an abating wind suddenly gave way to intense, eerie silence."[8] Mawson recorded on 24 March that the men's spirits were lifted because of lighter winds, yet the mean wind velocity that day was forty-five miles per hour. Storage tunnels were excavated to avoid having to go out of doors: "Outside, the crude and naked elements of a primitive and desolate world flowed in writhing torrents."[9] One night the watchman, leaving the hut to get coal, was blown down in a gust, and lost his bearings. In hurricane-force winds at minus 7 degrees Fahrenheit, he sheltered as best he could and waited for daylight. He was found alive a mere sixty feet from the hut. Mean wind velocities for March, April, and May ranged from forty-nine to sixty-one miles per hour. On the evening of 24 May, a two-hundred-mile-per-hour gust raced through as the hut creaked. Bizarre electrical effects were produced by the extraordinary dryness of the wind. The edges of the screens outside the hut and the wire stays gave off electrical displays, and rocky points emitted a pale blue glow at night. Sparks jumped a half to a full inch, to the acute displeasure of those not wearing gloves. The locale had very active auroral displays. With the penguins and seabirds long since gone and seals making only occasional appearances, the scene had become starkly desolate.

In the blizzard
Frank Hurley, from Mawson, *The Home of the Blizzard,* 1915

The hut was an unpretentious scene of bunks and worktables; clothing and garments were hung all about, books were disorganized, and dishes were piled high in the galley. Life was punctuated by amusing mishaps and the evolution of a delicious local humor. For entertainment, the men had a library, games, a gramophone, and celebrations. The midwinter feast included such delicacies as "Noisettes de Phoque," "Champignons en Sauce Antarctique," and "Pingouin à la Terre Adélie," with a fourteen-year-old burgundy. Meanwhile the winds roared at ninety-five miles per hour outside.

At the Western Base the wind was not as extreme, but autumn and winter conditions were still severe. The party consisted of Frank Wild, who was in charge; G. Dovers (cartography); C. T. Harrisson (biology); C. A. Hoadley (geology); S. E. Jones (medical officer); A. L. Kennedy (magnetics); M. H. Moyes (meteorology); A. D. Watson (geology); and nine dogs. Temporary quarters were set up in tents while a hut was built in a week about a third of a mile from the landing site. The men labored twelve hours a day constructing it, while a blizzard left six feet of drift around their stores and coal at the landing site, greatly compounding the work. The dwelling was twenty feet square with a veranda on three sides for stores and insulation. A wireless mast was erected nearby. A case of nuts and bolts was missing, but snowdrifts reinforced the building against the wind.

Wild and five men relayed 1,233 pounds of supplies under severe autumn weather and surface conditions to lay a depot for the next season. Half the days the men were confined by ferocious blizzards that collapsed the tents and filled the interiors with drift; the stove was too dangerous to use under the circumstances, and the men either fasted or ate their food frozen. Hoadley was knocked over in a gust only six feet from his tent and could not find his way until he heard Dovers and Wild respond to his yells. Still, the men achieved an altitude of twenty-six hundred feet. They returned to the hut on 6 April, having been away for twenty-five days.

Heavy drifts had virtually buried the hut by April. During the winter Wild assigned specific chores, and the night watch was shared. Bridge was their favorite game, and each Saturday night the men toasted "sweethearts and wives." The auroral displays were impressive, and the taking of an infrequent Weddell seal in early June brought a welcome change in their diet. Mid-winter Day was proclaimed a holiday throughout the land. The hut was decorated with flags, and the men had a special dinner feast with wine, cigars, speeches, and toasts, while the gramophone played. Just north of the Antarctic Circle, they had about six hours of usable daylight and twilight, even in the middle of June. That month they recorded their lowest mean monthly temperature, minus 14.5 degrees Fahrenheit. In July, each member was encouraged to write an article or poem; these were read aloud one evening to great amusement and published in camp as *The Glacier Tongue*. In the middle of August, four men went off to examine a thirty-mile-long capsized berg fifteen miles away. Embedded stones denoted what had once been the berg's bottom; these rocks were the first evidence of terra firma in the otherwise ice-covered land of their vicinity.

Plans for two depot journeys were drawn up in earnest. The first was carried out to the east, commencing 20 August 1912. This journey proved to be one of the most difficult spring ventures ever undertaken in the Antarctic. Six men departed with the three remaining dogs and 1,440 pounds on three sledges. After two days, the Gillies Nunataks (now Islands) were sighted, the first actual land seen since arrival. Other new points of interest were Henderson Island, the Bay of Winds, Alligator and Hippo Nunatak (now Island), Delay Point, and Avalanche Rocks (a bold vertical face four hundred feet high over which two hundred feet of glacial ice flowed). At a point eighty-four miles from the hut, in bitter cold of minus 47 degrees, the men turned homeward on 4 September after erecting a depot marked with bamboo and a flag; at the depot they left a sledge and six weeks' food and other provisions for three men. High winds forced the party to bivouac a quarter-mile from Avalanche Rocks. The men dug a snow cave, using sledges and tents as a roof. Winds gusted over one hundred miles per hour, and Harrisson was lifted and thrown twenty feet. The site lived up to its name. Avalanches were a "fearful crash resounding above the roar of the wind."[10] After being holed up for five days, the men made good distances and were back at the hut on 15 September.

Another spring depot journey was run to the west, this one consisting of five men, Jones leading. When, after four weeks, the party had not returned, a search party set out on 26 October. Jones's party was found nine miles out. Frustrated by a blizzard, they had been confined for seventeen days.

The main expeditions were finalized in a hurry. Wild, Kennedy, and Watson composed the Eastern party; Jones, Dover, and Hoadley were the Western party. Harrisson was to help the Eastern party during a portion of its outward trek, then return to join Moyes; the two were to tend the hut and scientific instruments. The Eastern party with the dogs followed its former path over the shelf ice to Hippo Island and arrived at their depot, where the men were shocked to find that it had been destroyed in storms: the sledge blown away, food bag stays broken, and bags scattered. The loss of the sledge was a serious matter, since 1,180 pounds could not be hauled on one sledge. The only option was to include Harrisson in the party for his sledge, although that left Moyes alone, back at the hut, believing that Harrisson had died on his return. Wild recalled: "I was extremely sorry for Moyes, but it could not be helped."[11]

Ahead was a new land projection, named David Island, about one thousand feet high, its steep sides covered with mosses and lichens; snow petrels were abundant. The men's object now was to go as far east as possible, and possibly south. As the men approached the previously unknown Denman Glacier, pressure turned the ice into a chaotic jumble, and the men camped among crevasses and "hell-holes"; "during the night . . . sounds of movement were distinctly heard; cracks like rifle shots and others similar to distant heavy guns, accompanied by a weird moaning."[12] The Denman Glacier, twelve miles wide, poured down three thousand feet from the interior, tearing into the Shackleton Ice Shelf. On approaching an infinitely crevassed ravine, three to four hundred feet deep and one thousand feet wide, Wild remarked with amazement, "The sides were splintered and crumpled, glittering in the sunlight with a million sparklets of light. Towering above were titanic blocks of carven ice. The whole was the wildest, maddest and yet the grandest thing imaginable."[13]

They tried to pass over this pressure, but for four days the men were thwarted by crevasses; on one day the total distance achieved was only two-thirds of a mile. Disappointed, they turned around on 27 November. The return over the glacier ice was "a series of Z's, S's, and hairpin turns."[14] Wild's party headed south from Cape Gerlache (at the western edge of the Denman Glacier outflow), crossed the outflow of the Northcliffe Glacier (a tributary from the southwest), and ascended Mount Barr Smith, about forty miles south, on 19 December. They discovered Mounts Barr Smith, Sandow, Amundsen, and Strathcona, and the Possession Nunataks (now Rocks). On the return, one of the three dogs was killed for want of enough food to feed them all; under the bluff of David Island, the men camped and took snow petrels and their eggs for food. "It seemed a fearful crime to kill these beautiful, pure white creatures, but it meant fourteen days' life for the dogs and longer marches for us."[15] Skuas were lured with dog flesh and made an excellent stew, the centerpiece of the men's Christmas dinner. The party arrived back at the hut on 6 January. Moyes was found to be well, but the nine weeks he had spent alone were the worst of his life. He had made a six-day solo trip searching vainly for Harrisson, whom he indeed had presumed to be dead.

Jones's Western party had no dogs, so they manhauled nine weeks' provisions by sledge. Crossing a narrow crevasse, Hoadley and Jones just missed a terrible fate. "About forty feet of the bridge collapsed lengthwise under the leading man, letting him fall to the full extent of his harness rope. Hoadley and myself had passed over the same spot, unsuspecting and unroped, a few minutes previously."[16] The men rediscovered ice-covered Drygalski Island about fifty miles to the northwest (first sighted by Drygalski from balloon). They also discovered a cluster of twelve islets that were a biological paradise. The men camped on Haswell Island, the largest outcrop of these Haswell Islands, which abounded in nesting penguins and seabirds, Weddell seals, and marine life. Nearby was an enormous emperor penguin colony of seventy-five hundred birds, one of the few known colonies at the time. The men arrived at Gaussberg, the westernmost limit of their travel, 215 miles from the hut, on 22 December. They found the two summit cairns and the bamboo poles left by members of Drygalski's expedition; they were unable to find the German expedition's bottle-sealed narrative. The party was back at the hut on 20 January 1913, in plenty of time for the expected arrival of the ship some ten days later.

At the Main Base, early spring sledging campaigns had been organized. The daily food ration was thirty-four ounces, which included biscuit, pemmican, butter, chocolate, dried milk, sugar, cocoa, and a quarter ounce of tea. The biscuits were made very hard to avoid splintering during rough sledging, but the men "should have preferred something less like a geological specimen."[17] (Wild's party created a biscuit incorporating dried milk that was so good as to be an inducement to sledging.)

On 9 August 1912, Mawson, Belgrave E. S. Ninnis (dog handler), and C. T. Madigan (meteorology) headed south into a forty-mile-per-hour wind for a distance of five and a half miles; the ice was so hard that the dogs' feet were cut. To avoid the wind a shelter was excavated beneath the ice surface. All of the sledging parties would be able to use the cave, as their paths radiated outward from this point. "Inside the silence was profound; the blizzard was banished. Aladdin's Cave it was dubbed—a truly magical world of glassy facets and scintillating crystals."[18] The cave had its amenities: ice shelves were chipped out of the walls, daylight filtered through from above, a small crevasse within was a natural waste disposal site, ventilation came through a small fissure, and the ice within was pure enough for consumption. Unsettling, however, were the occasional sharp crackling sounds of ice movement, and the ventilation was not very good—later, asphyxiation nearly finished two parties. Mawson, Ninnis, and Madigan went only two and a half miles further, to an elevation of two thousand feet, before realizing that the season had not progressed far enough for any further travel. On 15 August, a blizzard raging, they dashed back to the hut. The dogs suffered terribly. At the hut, a five-day spell of perfect weather in September cheered the men and led to a burst of outdoor productivity. The men gathered scientific data, repaired the wireless masts, amplified their stores of seal meat, and hauled supplies to Aladdin's Cave.

A southern reconnoitering party of Eric N. Webb (chief of magnetics), A. L. McLean (bacteriology, chief medical officer), and F. L. Stillwell (geology) departed on 7 September 1912, but cold and high winds stalled them three miles beyond Aladdin's Cave. They made a forced return with dangerous tail winds of seventy-five miles per hour. Another party, consisting of Ninnis, Xavier Mertz (dog handler), and H. D. Murphy (in charge of stores), headed out to the southeast on 11 September. They, too, encountered severe head winds on the way to Aladdin's Cave. They covered almost thirteen miles in three days before they were halted with a badly damaged tent in raging hurricane-force winds. They had no choice but to make a dash home in a forced march.

Madigan, J. H. Close (assistant collector), and L. A. Whetter (surgeon) set out for the west on 12 September. Anxiety at the hut arose for the three when, despite relatively fine weather, they had not returned in fourteen days. Ninnis and Mertz went out to search and found the weather-worn men who had made an arduous journey of one hundred miles. They achieved an altitude of forty-five hundred feet, out of sight of the sea. The trip had been made difficult by smooth ice, high winds that blew down their tent as they slept, and severe cold, to 35 degrees below zero Fahrenheit. The men repaired their wind-torn tent with bare hands and at times ate their food frozen. A bottle of port wine to celebrate Close's birthday had frozen solid. "After being shaken and held over the primus for a good half-hour it began to issue in lumps . . . in what we voted to be the finest draught it had ever been our good fortune to drink."[19] Aladdin's Cave was a haven on their return: "Never was the Cave a more luxurious place. The cooker was kept busy far into the night, while we drank and smoked and felt happy."[20]

With the arrival of spring and lengthening days, Mawson recounted: "It was a splendid sight to watch the birds sailing in the high winds of Adélie Land. In winds of fifty to seventy miles per hour, when with good crampons one had to stagger warily along the ice-foot, the snow petrels and Antarctic petrels were in their element. Wheeling, swinging, sinking, planing and soaring, they were radiant with life—the wild spirits of the tempest."[21] The first Adélie penguin arrived on 12 October against a seventy-five-mile-per-hour wind; the bird was brought into the hut and hailed as the harbinger of spring.

The men did not forsake the hut humor of winter, even though they were now busier. A farce was staged to great applause, and an extemporaneous opera in five acts was staged by eight men (and one dog) to an audience of the other men, who made their own extemporaneous remarks. Admission was free, with children at half price. As the days became less windy and the temperatures warmer, Mawson designated several sledging parties for the November campaigns. C. F. Laseron, the expedition's taxidermist and biologist, observed: "It was obvious from the very beginning that Adelie Land was not going to yield its geographical secrets without a bitter struggle."[22]

Several parties made substantial accomplishments in the field. The Southern party of R. Bage (astronomy, tides, assistant in magnetics), Webb, and Hurley was to make magnetic observations as near as possible to the south magnetic pole; a support party of Murphy, J. G. Hunter (biology), and Laseron would go with them as far as possible. Bage, Webb, and Hurley said good-bye to Mawson, Ninnis, and Mertz at Aladdin's Cave on 10 November and met up with their support team at an eleven-and-three-quarter-mile cave. The support team accompanied the main party for about sixty miles. They struggled uphill into frigid head winds of sixty miles per hour or more. Even in a tiny tent so small that there was barely enough room to move, the men had to shout to be heard over the wind. Hurley wrote: "Drifting snow! How soft it sounds. But 'drifting' is a misnomer, for when snow 'drifts' before a blizzard it resembles a sand-blast. Its flying particles will polish a metal surface till it shines, will cut into a board like coarse sandpaper, and will wear ice projections to smooth and shining knife-edges. These tiny particles, bombarding the eyeballs if goggles are left off, burn like sparks of white-hot metal, and cause an agony worse than snow blindness."[23] Two snow petrels and a skua, in seeming defiance of the severe conditions, had flown fifty miles inland—they just avoided being taken for the hoosh pot.

On 12 December, the men reached their two-hundred-mile camp at an altitude of forty-eight hundred feet. They left a depot and set out with seventeen days' provisions, three more than they thought they needed. In the vicinity of an 89-degree dip in the needle, wide swings in the east-west determinations made the men speculate there might be a subsidiary pole in the region. The party's line of travel passed over concealed crevasses. Hurley went through one with a sickening feeling; he emerged convinced that a calm crevasse was even worse than a windy surface. But this man who captured splendor on film also caught the splendor of the crevasse interior in words: "I could not help noticing the unearthly beauty of the abyss. . . . Its walls, about thirty feet apart, were the colour of jade at the top, gradually shading down through sapphire to pure cobalt and then, below, to blackness. The sheer faces were covered with exquisite crystals that scintillated as I moved.[24]

On 21 December, by taking careful magnetic and sun altitude readings, the party determined a magnetic dip of 89°43.5', at 70°36.5' S, 148°10' E, altitude fifty-nine hundred feet. The men had not reached the vertical dip, but they could not trust that their remaining rations would sustain them for the additional week they reckoned might be needed to establish the spot. So the Union Jack and Commonwealth Ensign were raised, and with nothing in sight but sastrugi and yet another ridge, the men gave three cheers for the king. David, Mawson, and Mackay had stood at a spot 175 miles away to the southeast in 1909. Bage, Webb, and Hurley now hurried downslope with wind in a sail; large daily distances were the rule as the men picked up their tracks and ice mounds. The three arrived back at the hut in good condition on 11 January after a creditable journey of more than six hundred miles.

The Western Sledging party consisted of F. H. Bickerton (in charge of the air-tractor), A. J. Hodgeman, and Whetter. They were assigned the duty of testing the air-tractor, which failed on its first day. The men succeeded in a 158-mile trek to the west along the coast and by 25 December got as far as Cape Robert, sighted first and named by Dumont d'Urville. A meteorite was found—a particularly remarkable discovery. The men endured days of blinding drift and travel delays and were back at Aladdin's Cave on 17 January.

The Eastern Coastal party, consisting of Madigan, McLean, and P. E. Correll (mechanic, assistant physicist), departed on 8 November. After lending support to Mawson's party, their charge was to examine as much of the coast east of the Mertz Glacier as possible. They made their farthest east camp on 18 December, at 68°18' S, 150°12' E, having traversed the Mertz and Ninnis Glacier Tongues and the intervening solid floe ice along the way. From their farthest east, the party headed southwest to Horn Bluff, where they encountered a magnificent basaltic coastal headland rising to a thousand feet. Madigan wrote: "Awed and amazed, we beheld the lone vastness of it all and were mute. . . . a mammoth vertical barrier of rock rearing its head to the skies above. The whole face for five miles was one magnificent series of organ-pipes. . . . Here was indeed a Cathedral of Nature, where the 'still, small voice' spoke amid an ineffable calm. Far up the face of the cliff snow petrels fluttered like white butterflies. . . . These majestic heights had gazed out across the wastes of snow and ice for countless ages, and never before had the voices of human beings echoed in the great stillness nor human eyes surveyed the wondrous scene."[25]

Fossilized plants were collected at Organ Pipe Cliffs. In the middle of the Ninnis Glacier Tongue, the party celebrated Christmas elegantly: McLean, the cook, presented his two companions with a formal menu written in French. At a granite buttress called Penguin Point, in Murphy Bay, the men found tiny live insects. A nerve-racking crossing of the Mertz Glacier Tongue followed; the men were exhausted and virtually without food by the time they retrieved their depot, fifty-three miles from the hut. At Aladdin's Cave they found fresh oranges and pineapple, a sure sign of the ship.

The first Near Eastern party consisting of Close and Hodgeman (cartography, artist) left Madigan's party and spent a week surveying Mount Hunt and Madigan Nunatak before returning to Cape Denison. In the second phase, Close and Laseron made detailed surveys of the vicinity near Commonwealth Bay, returning to base on 5 January. W. H. Hannam (mechanic, wireless operator) spent most of the time at the hut.

The Far Eastern party, consisting of Mawson, Ninnis, Mertz, and dogs, became by far the most interesting of the campaigns because it produced an exceptional struggle for survival. The plan was to proceed "overland" to the east as far as possible. The group set off with sixteen dogs and three sledges weighing over seventeen hundred pounds in all. Mawson had two fine companions whom Laseron described thus: "Ninnis . . . we at once christened 'Cherub,' partly on account of his complexion, which was as pink and white as that of any girl. He was tall and rather ungainly in build, and had more boxes of beautiful clothes than seemed possible for one mere man. He took our chaff good-naturedly enough, and afterwards we learnt to love him for the thoroughbred he was." "Xavier Mertz . . . was a Swiss, A Doctor of Law and a magnificent athlete, having won the world's championship in ski-running in Switzerland just prior to leaving. We took Mertz to our hearts at once. His Christian name did not sound well to Australian ears, and was soon abbreviated to 'X,' by which he was known to the end."[26] Mawson was thirty, Ninnis was twenty-three, and Mertz was twenty-eight.

The initial phase of their journey was straightforward. The dogs were eager, and the weather and surfaces were good. Sometimes two men could ride the sledges while the other broke trail for the dogs in front. Mawson believed that dogs were the superior form of transport in the polar regions and that manhauling was preferable only over very rugged or crevassed areas or during extremely bad weather. Soon the party saw the Mertz Glacier Tongue off to the east and the valley of its glacier they would have to cross. Rare patches of rock poked out of the ice (the Madigan and Correll Nunataks); Aurora Peak stood prominently.

The Mertz Glacier presented difficult and foreboding moments. "Studded about on the icy plain were immense cauldrons. . . . Crevasses became correspondingly more numerous. The dogs frequently broke through them but were easily extricated. . . . Mertz prepared the lunch and Ninnis and I went to photograph an open crevasse near by. Returning . . . I heard a bang on the ice, and swinging round, could see nothing of my companion but his head and arms. . . . How narrowly he had escaped."[27] Ice was pressured into chaotic folds two hundred feet high and a little over a quarter-mile from crest to crest. The worst twenty miles was traversed in just two days, the men usually managing to keep the dogs from entangling or dragging the sledges sideways over crevasses. But once Ninnis's especially heavy sledge broke through a crevasse lid and jammed; one wrong move would have sent it to the bottom.

Now the party traversed a relatively level plain, the ice field between the Mertz Glacier they had just crossed and the Ninnis Glacier, which lay some fifty miles ahead. On 26 November, the men commenced a four-day crossing of the crevassed Ninnis Glacier. Three dogs no longer pulling well were killed, and one disappeared, leaving twelve. Soon the party was traveling easily, parallel to the coast, about fifteen miles inland. On 10 December, the men discerned Cape Freshfield to the east-northeast from an altitude of two thousand feet. All was well except that Ninnis was troubled by an inflamed finger; Mawson lanced it. On 13 December, the men cached one sledge and rearranged the other two. They assumed that if crevasses became troubling and a sledge were lost, it would more likely be the lead one. Thus, in a fateful decision, the rear sledge was loaded with most of the food, hauled by the six best dogs.

The next day, 14 December 1912, the party was on smooth ice far from the coastal cliffs, and the men expected no crevasses. However, the surface became suspicious to Mertz, who was in the lead, and he signaled back to Mawson to be alert. Mawson got on his sledge, noted "the faint indication of a crevasse,"[28] and called out to Ninnis a warning. Mawson recorded: "I then went on with my work. There was no sound from behind except a faint, plaintive whine from one of the dogs which I imagined was in reply to a touch from Ninnis's whip. . . . When I next looked back, it was in response to the anxious gaze of Mertz who had turned round and halted in his tracks. Behind me, nothing met the eye but my own sledge tracks. . . . I hastened back. . . . I came to a gaping hole in the surface about eleven feet wide. . . . Two sledge tracks led up to it on the far side but only one continued on the other side. . . . I leaned over and shouted into the dark depths below. No sound came back but the moaning of a dog, caught on a shelf just visible 150 feet below. The poor creature appeared to have broken its back, for it was attempting to sit up with the front part of its body while the hinder portion lay limp. Another dog lay motionless by its side. Close by was what appeared in the gloom to be the remains of the tent and canvas tank containing food for three men for a fortnight. We . . . took turns leaning over secured by a rope, calling into the darkness in the hope that our companion might be still alive. For three hours we called unceasingly but no answering sound came back. The dog had ceased to moan and lay without a movement. A chill draught was blowing out of the abyss. . . . Why had the first sledge escaped the crevasse? . . . Ninnis had walked by the side of his sledge, whereas I had crossed it sitting on the sledge. The whole weight of a man's body bearing on his foot is a formidable load."[29]

Stunned, helpless, and heavy-hearted, Mawson and Mertz now realized their own desperate situation. "We considered it a possibility to get through . . . but terribly handicapped. . . . May God Help us."[30] Food that would have served them for three weeks and all of the dog food was lost in the crevasse, along with their only tent. They were three hundred miles from Cape Denison. All that was left on the remaining sledge was one and a half weeks' food. No depots had been laid on the way out. A descent to the sea was out of the question.

They discarded everything unnecessary to lighten the load. Not a single edible morsel could be wasted; Mawson and Mertz made a thin soup of the contents of all the used food bags. Occasionally the men called down into the crevasse in case Ninnis might have regained consciousness, but there was no response. "When comrades tramp the road to anywhere through a lonely blizzard-ridden land in hunger, want and weariness the interests, ties and fates of each are interwoven in a wondrous fabric of friendship and affection. The shock of Ninnis's death struck home."[31] Mawson read the burial service beside the crevasse, and Mertz thanked him. Now they harnessed the six remaining dogs, the poorest of the lot, for a forlorn return.

The next day, the discarded sledge came into view, and Mertz fashioned a tent out of a cut sledge runner, a spare tent cover, and his skis. Floor space was just adequate to accommodate two sleeping bags; the tent's height permitted nothing more than sitting. Mertz carved spoons out of the sledge wood as well, and spare metal containers served as pannikins. Mawson and Mertz opted for a high inland route home to avoid the crevassed surfaces of the two glaciers. They sacrificed the weakest dog, George, deciding how much to feed the other dogs to keep them strong for transport and future food, and how much to have for themselves. The next day, another dog, Johnson, became so weak that he was hauled on the sledge until he, too, was sacrificed. Mawson wrote: "Their meat was tough, stringy and without a vestige of fat. For a change we sometimes chopped it up finely, mixed it with a little pemmican, and brought all to the boil in a large pot of water. We were exceedingly hungry, but there was nothing to satisfy our appetites. . . . Each animal yielded so very little, and the major part was fed to the surviving dogs. They crunched the bones and ate the skin, until nothing remained."[32]

Within several days, Mary, who had performed splendidly, had to be killed. Another dog, Haldane, fell into a crevasse; he was so thin that he slipped out of his harness and was barely rescued. Haldane "took to the harness once more but soon became uncertain in his footsteps, staggered along and then tottered and fell. Poor brutes! that was the way they all gave in—pulling till they dropped."³³ Two days later, Pavlova was sacrificed. The hungry men dreamt of fantastic food orgies while the reality was a soup from Pavlova's bones. None of the fuel had been lost, so there was enough kerosene to render every serviceable part, down to the gristle and bones. "The paws took longest of all to cook, but, treated to lengthy stewing, they became quite digestible."³⁴

The men's compass was useless so close to the magnetic pole, so course was set by dead reckoning. On Christmas Day, the men were half way through the upper reaches of the Ninnis Glacier, having covered less than half the distance home. The men had dog stew, wished each other better Christmases in the future, divided two scraps of biscuit, and had an extra ounce of butter each in celebration. Their usual daily ration was about fourteen ounces. (By comparison, Shackleton's party had about twenty ounces per day when experiencing starvation on the return from their farthest south.) The men sacrificed their last dog, dispensed with all but the barest necessities, lightened the tent frame, discarded the camera and films, weather instruments, rifle and ammunition, and retained only the theodolite so they could determine their position. On 28 December, "we had breakfast off Ginger's skull and brain. I can never forget the occasion. As there was nothing available to divide it, the skull was boiled whole. Then the right and left halves were drawn for by the old and well-established sledging practice of 'shut-eye,' after which we took it in turns eating to the middle line, passing the skull from one to the other. The brain was afterwards scooped out with a wooden spoon."³⁵

By 30 December, Mertz's personality was changed: he had lost his cheer. The next day, he said that he suspected that the diet of dog was making him ill and suggested a return to usual sledging rations. He continued to weaken, and on 6 January, Mawson persuaded him to ride on the sledge. Mawson knew that his own chances of survival were slipping away with Mertz's incapacity. For four days they could not move, still one hundred miles from the hut. Both men were now losing skin, exposing raw surfaces beneath. They were unaware that their affliction was hypervitaminosis A, a toxic excess of vitamin A from eating dog liver.³⁶ Mertz, in the end delirious and insensible, died on 8 January. Mawson, some of his toes gangrenous and festering, lay alone in the tent next to Mertz's still body. He considered giving in but defied inaction. He modified the sledge, sawing it in half with a pocket tool, and fashioned a sail out of Mertz's burberry jacket. He buried

Dr. Xavier Mertz (left) and Lt. B. E. S. Ninnis (right)
Mawson, *The Home of the Blizzard,* 1915

his friend under snow blocks and erected a rough cross out of the remaining sledge runners.

High wind and thick drift prevented Mawson from getting on his way for three days. To his diary, he confided: "My whole body is apparently rotting . . . frost-bitten fingertips festering, mucous membrane of nose gone, saliva glands of mouth refusing duty, skin coming off whole body." Later, in his official expedition account, *The Home of the Blizzard,* Mawson wrote: "My feet . . . had become so painful after a mile of walking that I decided to make an examination of them. . . . The sight of my feet gave me quite a shock, for the thickened skin of the soles had separated in each case as a complete layer, and abundant watery fluid had escaped into the socks. The new skin underneath was very much abraded and raw."[37] He wrapped his feet in lanolin and bandages and struggled on, revived by a spell of absolutely glorious weather. But bad weather soon stopped him again. The next day he spotted Aurora Peak across the Mertz Glacier, a welcome landmark. That night he camped on the glacier and listened to the cannonlike sounds of slowly grinding ice. On 15 January, he was officially overdue back at the hut, but he was just starting to cross the trying, broken surface of the upper reaches of the Mertz Glacier. A jelly soup of dog sinews was an "acute enjoyment."[38]

The seventeenth of January brought an episode that should have ended Mawson's life. "Going up a long, fairly steep slope, deeply covered with soft snow, broke through lid of crevasse but caught myself at thighs, got out . . . a few moments later found myself dangling fourteen feet below on end of rope in crevasse—sledge creeping to mouth—had time to say to myself, 'so this is the end,' . . . but as the sledge pulled up without letting me down, thought of Providence giving me another chance. . . . I hung freely in space, turning slowly round. A great effort brought a knot in the rope within my grasp, and, after a moment's rest, I was able to draw myself up and reach another, and, at length, hauled myself on to the overhanging snow-lid into which the rope had cut. Then, when I was carefully climbing out on to the surface, a further section of the lid gave way, precipitating me once more to the full length of the rope. Exhausted, weak and chilled (for my hands were bare and pounds of snow had got inside my clothing) I hung with the firm conviction that all was over except the passing. Below was a black chasm; it would be but the work of a moment to slip from the harness . . . a rare temptation . . . to pass from the petty exploration of a planet to the contemplation of vaster worlds beyond. . . . My strength was fast ebbing; in a few minutes it would be too late. It was the occasion for a supreme attempt. New power seemed to come as I addressed myself to one last tremendous effort. The struggle occupied some time, but by a miracle I rose slowly to the surface. This time I emerged feet first, still holding on to the rope, and pushed myself out, extended at full length, on the snow—on solid ground."[39]

Now he constructed a rope ladder that ran from the bow of the sledge to his harness. If he fell into a crevasse again, the exit would be easier, assuming the sledge stayed on top. Two days later, he broke through crevasse lids twice in quick succession. The sledge held, and the ladder proved a great success. Now finished with the glacier but weakening, Mawson discarded his spare alpine rope, crampons, and worn socks to lighten the load even further. He could only cover a few miles a day. Twice he had to lay over a day for bad weather while he attended to his raw skin. Every camp's tent floor was covered with fallen hair.

On 29 January, with only about thirty-two ounces of food left, and still twenty-three miles from Aladdin's Cave, Mawson spotted a dark object ahead. It was a cairn erected by McLean, Hodgeman, and Hurley, who had come that far searching for his party. Of all ironies, the three men had departed from that spot a scant five hours earlier. Food in the cairn was plentiful, and McLean's party left news that the ship had arrived and was waiting.

Hurley later recorded: "Well did I remember piling up that cairn. Had only the weather been clear when I swept the horizon with the glasses I would have seen the tent in which he was resting!"[40]

Mawson quickly felt revived by the extra food and proceeded on. But soon he found himself on hard ice with no crampons, and the wind was too strong for the sledge sail. Thus he cut up the box that housed the theodolite for its tacks and raided the sledge meter for its screws in order to create crampons of a sort. His new footgear lasted only six miles; Mawson took three days more to arrive at Aladdin's Cave. There, a mere five and a half miles from the hut, Mawson was confined for a week by a drawn-out hurricane and blinding drift; he spent the time eating, sleeping, and making new crampons for the final descent. He made that final leg on 8 February 1913, though the wind had not slackened.

The *Aurora*, meanwhile, had left Hobart on 12 November 1912, landed stores and mail at the Macquarie Base, discovered the submarine Mill Rise two hundred miles south of Tasmania, and was back in Hobart on 14 December. Two days later, the ship departed again to relieve the two Antarctic parties. The ship's party carried a large supply of coal, the mail, twenty-one dogs presented by Amundsen, and thirty-five sheep. Sydney N. Jeffryes was to relieve Hannam as wireless operator at the Main Base. On 11 January the ship entered the pack ice, and two days later the vessel was anchored in Commonwealth Bay. Davis wrote: "At 2.30 P.M. the launch was hoisted over and the mail was taken ashore. . . . We were greeted most warmly by nine wild-looking men. . . . They danced about in joyous excitement."[41]

With Mawson's party overdue, Davis ordered a search party. Based on the prior year's experience of increasingly persistent high winds in March, Davis knew that he would not be able to return to Commonwealth Bay after relieving the Western Base. Thus he resolved to remain at Commonwealth Bay as long as possible. He assigned a party to stay another year under the command of the dependable and respected twenty-three-year-old Madigan, along with Bage, Bickerton, Hodgeman, McLean, and Jeffryes. Coal, food, and equipment were landed. Toward the end of January, occasional high winds and increasing darkness at midnight made for anxious times on ship. By the first week in February, continuous winds blew up to eighty miles per hour. Davis tried to shelter under cliffs where the sea was not so heavy, but waves broke overboard with freezing spray. On 6 February, "the wind became very violent with the most terrific squalls I have ever experienced. Vessel absolutely unmanageable, driving out to sea. I was expecting the masts to go overboard every minute."[42] Two days later, the wind slackened, and the launch went ashore to take off ten members of the Main party. Good-byes were necessarily brief.

The ship departed. Mawson arrived at the hut a few hours later. Davis received a wireless message from the Main Base informing him that Mawson had arrived and that Ninnis and Mertz were dead. Davis returned to Commonwealth Bay on the morning of 9 February and tried for his anchorage; but a gale kept the ship out, and the party roamed back and forth waiting for a letup. Davis lamented: "So near, and yet so far!"[43] Now the captain had to make a decision. He knew the shore party was safe and that gales often lasted for days at a time. He also knew that further delay would jeopardize Wild's relief, since they had fifteen hundred miles to the Shackleton Ice Shelf in the closing season of increasingly dark nights and autumn weather. Additionally, he was afraid that the ship could be frozen in for the winter, for which it was not provisioned.

Laseron recalled Davis's consternation: "Captain Davis came to the wardroom. . . . He laboured under repressed emotion, the only time we had seen him so affected. He spoke curtly in low tones. He said that a grave responsibility rested upon him, and before deciding, he wished to take us into his confidence, and would welcome any suggestions or criticism of his action."[44] Davis simply recorded: "There was no time to lose, in hastening to the relief of Wild's party. . . . I went down to the ward room and announced my decision to the officers. I invited them to suggest any alternative measures, but none were forthcoming. . . . Sincere regret for the detention of our Leader and his six comrades was combined with grave anxiety as to being able to reach the Western Base in time. . . . I was convinced . . . I was acting as Dr. Mawson would have wished."[45] Davis had never received Mawson's wireless permitting him to depart.

Mawson was ecstatic to have arrived back at the hut. He hoped Davis might still have enough coal and time to relieve him after picking up the Western Base party, but the ship never materialized. The six men who had stayed to search for Mawson's missing party now heard their leader's extraordinary tale. Davis eloquently wrote many years later: "I can never read the chapters of Mawson's book describing that journey without being profoundly moved. And the chapter 'Alone' with its carefully restrained words and phrases,[46] describing without any dramatics the remainder of that ghastly journey, is to me the most moving of all. Survival! Nature, for its own inscrutable purpose, has implanted most deeply in every living organism the instinct to survive. . . . And yet there may come a time . . . when . . . the tides of life run out to their uttermost ebb and a conscious man may choose between life or death. . . . There are circumstances and moments when it is easier to die than to live and it is then, when instinct itself is dead, that the willpower and the spirit of man is glorious indeed and the exercise of it one of man's greatest virtues."[47]

At the Western Base, the expected date of the ship's arrival had passed. The men harvested seals, anticipating a second winter. The twenty-second of February was the anniversary of their arrival; it passed without sign of the ship, and their concern grew. The next day, the ship arrived and anchored to the floe ice, which extended a mile further north than the previous year. The ship was loaded and watered, and the entire party, healthy and well, hurriedly departed the same day. Davis recalled: "It was with a feeling of profound relief that I shook hands with Wild, and realized that, although we had left them in a perilous position, we had, in spite of all difficulties, been able to welcome them heartily on board the 'Aurora' to-day."[48] Any lingering thought of returning to Commonwealth Bay was dissolved by the reality of a dwindling coal supply. The ship arrived in Australia on 14 March.

The company of seven men settled in at Commonwealth Bay. Mawson wrote: "It was a dreary and difficult time for the five [sic] men who had volunteered to remain behind in order to make a thorough search for myself and comrades. They were men whom I had learned to appreciate during the first year, and I now saw their sterling characters in a new light. To Jeffreys [sic] all was fresh, and we envied him the novelties of a new world, rough and inhospitable though it was."[49] The men had contact with Macquarie Island by wireless, and even occasionally with points in Australia and New Zealand when transmission and reception were not obscured by auroral activity, static, and wind. By wireless they learned of the Scott tragedy. Food assumed an important part of their winter existence, and each man became known for some bit of special cuisine. The men spent the winter at odd jobs, science, and preparing scientific reports. A monthly publication, *The Adelie Blizzard*, was initiated in April and ran for seven months through October. McLean was editor. Mawson stated: "Light doggerel to heavy blank verse was welcomed, and original articles, letters to the Editor, plays, reviews on books and serial stories were accepted within the limits of our supply of foolscap paper and type-writer ribbons."[50] (Mawson was impressed with McLean's editorship and later obtained considerable assistance from him in writing *The Home of the Blizzard*.)

The winds were at their worst throughout July, the mean velocity for the month an astounding 63.6 miles per hour. Over an eight-hour period on 5 July the wind averaged 107 miles per hour, the highest recorded throughout their entire stay. On 22 July the barometer fell to 28.4 inches, and "the wind ran riot." However, Mawson described how "it was a grand sight to witness the sea in a hurricane on a driftless, clear day. . . . One could watch the water close inshore blacken under the lash of the wind, whiten into foam farther off, and then disappear into the hurrying clouds of spray and sea-smoke."[51]

The men were cheered by the arrival of penguins in the middle of October. A memorial to Ninnis and Mertz was erected on a nearby hill, and a brief sledging trip was run in late November to try, unsuccessfully, to recover instruments cached during the Southern and Eastern coastal parties. The *Aurora* arrived and relieved the party on 12 December 1913 in an "indescribable moment. . . . The two long years were over—for the moment they were to be effaced in the glorious present. We were to live in a land where drift and wind were unknown, where rain fell in mild, refreshing showers, where the sky was blue for long weeks, and where the memories of the past were to fade into a dream—a nightmare?"[52] As tempting as it might have been to head north directly, Mawson and Davis used the peak season to perform detailed coastal surveys from the Mertz Glacier Tongue westward to Gaussberg, which they approached within twenty-five miles. Backtracking eastward, the men examined the Shackleton Ice Shelf, Drygalski Island, and the Queen Mary Coast. Finally, on 6 February, the ship turned north, and the men were home on 26 February 1914.

Upon the return of the expedition, Mawson married his fiancée, Francesca Adriana "Paquita" Delprat (1891–1974), and soon was knighted. He served in the Ministry of Munitions in London and as an advisor to the Russian government during the war. He became professor of geology at the University of Adelaide in 1921 and went on to assume the chair. Following the Imperial Conference of 1926 in London concerning whaling in the Antarctic, the Australian Antarctic Committee selected Mawson to lead what became the British Australian New Zealand Antarctic Research Expedition (BANZARE) of 1929–31, which accumulated a wealth of new scientific data. He became president of the Australian Association for the Advancement of Science in 1935. He promoted the preservation of Macquarie Island wildlife but paradoxically encouraged Australia to partake in the profitable Antarctic whaling industry. He was involved with the Australian National Antarctic Research Expedition (ANARE) from its inception in 1946 and followed with great interest Australia's participation in the International Geophysical Year of 1957–58. With so many professional activities, Mawson still found time to retreat into the Australian outback north of Adelaide, where he and his wife found refuge and spent much of their leisure time. He died of a stroke in 1958 and was honored with a state funeral. The church bell tolled seventy-six times, once for each year of the life of this distinguished scientist, explorer, and humanitarian.

23

ERNEST H. SHACKLETON AND THE IMPERIAL TRANSANTARCTIC EXPEDITION (1914–1917)

"She's gone, boys."
Ernest H. Shackleton, *South*

THE SOUTH POLE having been attained by Amundsen and Scott, Shackleton envisioned one remaining grand Antarctic conquest—crossing the continent via the pole. Thus was conceived the last great expedition of the heroic era. And a great expedition it was, not for its success—because it failed—but rather for Shackleton's indomitable leadership and for his men's courage and perseverance. The story has been told and retold, the thrilling and timeless tale of hope and survival ever fresh and dramatic.

According to Shackleton's original plan, his party was to head into the Weddell Sea. Upon landing in the deep south at Vahsel Bay, six men were to cross the continent, three more were to head west toward Graham Land, another three were to strike east toward Enderby Land, and two were to remain at base in a hut. They were to explore broad territories and make scientific observations in several fields. On the other side of the continent, a support party was to use previously established huts on Ross Island and lay depots for the crossing party.

Funding for the expedition came from private sources, principally from Sir James Caird (who contributed £24,000), Dudley Docker, and Dame Janet Stancomb Wills, Shackleton's friend and confidante. Shackleton's three lifeboats were named after these benefactors and were immortalized in Antarctic lore. Limited funding was also received from the British government and the Royal Geographical Society. When word of a new Shackleton expedition was announced, five thousand applicants stepped forward, from among whom a total of fifty-six men were chosen to constitute the two parties. The *Endurance* was newly constructed in Norway at a cost of £14,000; it weighed 350 tons and could be powered by sail, coal, or oil. The second ship, the *Aurora*, was the same one that Mawson had used; Shackleton purchased it from him. As the expedition was about to depart, the threat of World War I loomed. At the last minute, Shackleton placed the expedition's resources at the service of England in war, but he was instructed by the Admiralty, Winston Churchill, and the king to proceed with his plans. The expedition, the only one to the Antarctic to take place during the war, departed on 5 August 1914.

THE WEDDELL SEA PARTY

The twenty-eight men who composed the party aboard the *Endurance* departed South Georgia on 5 December 1914. They could not have realized that their ship would become ensnared in the ice, foiling their plans, and that an epic tale of perseverance and survival would follow. Shackleton wrote in his classic narrative, *South*: "Though failure in the actual accomplishment must be recorded, there are chapters in this book of high adventure, strenuous days, lonely nights, unique experiences, and, above all, records of unflinching determination, supreme loyalty, and generous self-sacrifice on the part of my men."[1] The events following the entrapment of the ship were, of course, unplanned, but in retrospect they somehow seem preordained, pursuing an inscrutable, unmistakable logic.

The whaling captains at South Georgia advised Shackleton to take on extra coal on account of difficult ice conditions in the Weddell Sea, and to sail east before heading south to avoid some of the heavy pack. This advice he heeded. Two days later the party sighted the South Sandwich Islands and quickly ran into pack at the northerly 59° latitude of Saunders Island. Belts of pack gave way to open water, but ice and bergs became the rule as the ship proceeded south. Christmas Day was celebrated with a decorated wardroom, grog and a special meal, and a sing song with the witty Leonard Hussey (1894–1965) playing an improvised one-string violin or banjo. The ship crossed the Antarctic Circle on 30 December.

The party received a forewarning of pressure the following day, when the ship was briefly squeezed and heeled 6 degrees. Progress was periodically stalled, and the crew banked the engine fires to conserve coal. From 3 to 8 January 1915, the party made no progress and remained at latitude 70°. Then the men struck open water and in two days reached 72°2' S and sighted Coats

Land. The scientists made soundings, dredged the ocean floor for specimens, and noted birds, seals, and whales. On 12 January, the *Endurance* was at 74°4' S, 22°48' W, approaching an ice barrier, and the following day the men could have landed without trouble where the barrier swept low to the sea. But Shackleton spurned this opportunity for a better site farther south, in order to cut the land distance across the continent. The crew described glacier fronts up to five hundred feet high and seventeen to forty miles wide spilling out from the inland ice. The party also discovered an ice-covered coast connecting Coats Land and the Luitpold Coast; Shackleton named it the Caird Coast after his supporter.

The men were held up by pack ice and had to wait for opportunities to zigzag farther south. At 76°34' S, 31°30' W, on 19 January in the height of summer, a northeast gale drove ice around the ship. The *Endurance* would never be free again. The men could see land sixteen miles away to the southeast. Wind changes and swells shifted the ice teasingly, and mirages sometimes deceived the men into thinking that they were near open water; but the pack remained closed as the ship drifted. On 24 January, and again on 8, 11, and 14 February, the crew stoked the engine and raised steam, hoping to enter leads. On 14 February, all men were on the floe working with chisels, saws, and picks to get into a lead six hundred yards away. They cut the distance by two hundred yards in one day, but low temperatures froze the sea in the openings, and the disappointed party abandoned its work. The first sunset came on 17 February, and five days later the ship reached the most southerly point of its drift, 77°0' S, at 35° W. With land still in sight but beyond reach, Shackleton acknowledged that he and his men were confined for the winter; but with his typical unrestrained optimism, he hoped for an early spring release and arrival at Vahsel Bay.

On 24 February the ship was officially declared a winter station, and new daily routines were adopted. The men laid in stores of seal meat to feed themselves and the dogs; seal blubber was used for fuel. Kennels were placed on the floes, and the dogs were put into training. New pups were born. To occupy themselves the men played hockey and football, and they carried out scientific studies in meteorology and marine biology. They set up quarters between decks; cubicles were given such names as "The Ritz," "Billabong," "Auld Reekie," and "The Fumarole." The men tried unsuccessfully to receive radio Morse-code signals from Port Stanley. They had no transmitter.

By the middle of March, they were drifting northwest. They heard ice grinding in the distance, and occasionally the ship creaked and vibrated. The

The *Endurance* frozen in
Frank Hurley, from Shackleton, *South*, 1919

sun departed in early May. Shackleton now realized that the extent of the drift would prevent him from ever reaching Vahsel Bay. Alone, he lamented: "We seem to be drifting helplessly in a strange world of unreality."[2]

The deepest part of winter approached and passed uneventfully. When weather was clear, the men enjoyed the moonlight and the colorful glow of twilight at noon. "Perhaps never did the ship look quite so beautiful as when the bright moonlight etched her in inky silhouette, or transformed her into a vessel from fairy-land."[3] The ship's drift was out of their control, but the floes were frozen solid; the party was at peace and the ship safe, despite their helplessness. The men tried to imagine how the war was faring and fought mock campaigns on a map. They raced their dog teams in an "Antarctic Derby" and bet chocolate and cigarettes on their favorites. They festively celebrated Midwinter Day.

Their relative bliss soon was interrupted. In the middle of July, a storm-force blizzard left five feet of drift and snow piled against the bow and port side of the ship. The floe was forced down under the snow's weight. Later in the month the floes began to move, and the crew set up watches in case the dogs had to be evacuated from the ice. The men were cheered by the return of the sun on 26 July, but on 1 August their floe broke up, the ship listed 10 degrees in the pressure, and the dogs were brought on board. The men watched the mighty forces of pressure lift huge ice blocks, and they somberly realized that the ship could be crushed in an instant. They heard the roar of the pressure in the distance; several times the noise approached, the ship straining as the timbers creaked.

In the vortex of the Weddell Sea, the ice delivered a dramatic shock on 30 September. Shackleton noted: "It was the worst squeeze we had experienced. The decks shuddered and jumped, beams arched, and stanchions buckled and shook. I ordered all hands to stand by in readiness. . . . But the ship resisted valiantly, and . . . the huge floe that was pressing down upon us cracked across and so gave relief."[4] Frank Worsley (1872–1943), commander of the ship, wrote, "She has been strained, her beams arched upwards, by the fearful pressure; her very sides opened and closed again as she was actually bent and curved along her length, groaning like a living thing."[5] The ship was subjected to repeated attacks of pressure throughout October and once abruptly listed to 30 degrees, to the chaotic shifting of stores and pandemonium of dogs.

"Then on Sunday, October 24," wrote Shackleton, "there came what for the *Endurance* was the beginning of the end. The position was lat. 69°11' S., long. 51°5' W. . . . The onslaught was all but irresistible. The *Endurance* groaned and quivered as her starboard quarter was forced against the floe. . . . The ship was twisted and actually bent by the stresses. She began to leak dangerously at once."[6] The pressure relaxed, but the men held out little hope for the ship. They worked the pumps; stores and dogs were made ready for evacuation. The men witnessed the enormous forces of the ice all around them. Shackleton recalled: "Listening below, I could hear . . . the faint, indefinable whispers of our ship's distress."[7]

The vessel was evacuated on the evening of 26 October. Shackleton wrote the following day: "After long months of ceaseless anxiety and strain, after times when hope beat high and times when the outlook was black indeed, the end of the *Endurance* has come. But though we have been compelled to abandon the ship, which is crushed beyond all hope of ever being righted, we are alive and well, and we have stores and equipment for the task that lies before us. The task is to reach land with all the members of the Expedition. It is hard to write what I feel. To a sailor his ship is more than a floating home, and in the *Endurance* I had centred ambitions, hopes, and desires. Now, straining and groaning, her timbers cracking and her wounds gaping, she is slowly giving up her sentient life at the very outset of her career."[8]

Camp was set up on the floes nearby, but no sooner had this been done than at midnight a crack ran right through the camp, forcing a frenzied move to the larger portion of the floe. The men selected a larger, stronger floe about two hundred yards away, which they called Dump Camp, for there they discarded many nonessential items. All the while they witnessed the progressive annihilation of the ship in the pressure. The men established routines for daily living, worked the dog teams, and prepared the boats. They decided to march across the sea ice, hoping to make five to seven miles daily toward land to increase their chances of safe arrival once they took to the boats. Perhaps it was unrealistic to plan such travel, but for the psychological well-being of the party, Shackleton thought it the right thing to do. Each man was permitted to carry only two pounds of personal articles, so only the most precious items were chosen. Worsley described how Shackleton "himself set the example, throwing away, with a spectacular gesture, a gold watch, a gold cigarette case, and several golden sovereigns."[9] But Shackleton preserved a book of Browning's poetry. Photographer Frank Hurley selected 120 photographic plates to preserve, along with his kinematographic films; he smashed several hundred plates more, to make his decisions absolutely final.

The first day's going was difficult. The party cut through pressure ridges twice a man's height. They covered only one mile the first day, so the group abandoned any further attempt at travel. They selected a large, solid floe about a mile and a half from the ship, established Ocean Camp on 1 November, then returned to Dump Camp and the ship to recover equipment, supplies, and food cases. The men particularly enjoyed farinaceous foods, which broke the monotony of seal and penguin. Hunting, cooking, reading, conversation, and observations of weather and their drift occupied the men's time. The weather was sometimes too warm for life on a floe; the surface became a honeycomb from irregular melting, and expletives flew as the men unpredictably stepped through melting ice up to their knees.

For a time the ship remained visible, though only the stern and a tangle of wood splinters, ropes, and rigging. On 21 November, the remains of the *Endurance* finally sank and disappeared forever. A wave of gloom hit the camp as Shackleton, atop a lookout, sadly announced, "She's gone, boys."[10] The men's spirits rose soon enough, however, encouraged, no doubt, by a modest increase in rations. On 20 December, Shackleton, after reconnoitering to the west and consulting with his second in command, Frank Wild, decided to make for Paulet Island, where he knew not only that Nordenskjöld's party had left supplies but also precisely what those provisions were.

Wild taking a last look at the wreckage of the *Endurance*
Frank Hurley, from Shackleton, *South,* 1919

Shackleton himself had ordered and dispatched them. On 22 December the men prepared an early Christmas feast of all the luxuries they could not transport. As they set out the following morning, they ardently hoped for better traveling than two months earlier.

They were stopped after seven days. The hummocked and honeycombed surfaces, the increasingly brittle state of the floes, and the difficulty in negotiating cracks and water lanes defeated them as they hauled their supplies and two boats, the *James Caird* and the *Dudley Docker.* They had made no great distance when they were forced again to abandon travel and set up a new home, Patience Camp. Remaining supplies and the *Stancomb Wills,* left behind at Ocean Camp, were now retrieved. Summer weather was generally fair, but the wind and currents were the all-important determinants of their fate. During this long period of waiting, Shackleton never betrayed his own wavering confidence in overcoming their setbacks, but attended to each man's needs, giving hope and cheer to all. Because the men needed the dog pemmican for food and would eventually be unable to carry the dogs in the boats, most of the dogs were shot. "It was the worst job," commented Shackleton, "that we had had throughout the Expedition."[11]

In late February 1916, the party was only eighty miles from Paulet Island. By the middle of March, however, the ship had drifted past it to the east, and the floes were too broken for the men to sledge to the island. Shackleton turned his attention to Elephant Island or Clarence Island, both of which lay about one hundred miles to the north. The men reserved their sledging rations for an eventual boat journey and ate a monotonous and unsatisfying diet of seal and penguin meat, as they carefully rationed out the remaining provisions. All the remaining dogs were killed.

The eighth of April was a fateful day. Late in the afternoon, the floe that the party called home received a heavy shock, causing a crack that ran through the camp. Shackleton watched as the rent cut through the depression his body had made in the ice during many nights of sleep at Patience Camp. The men launched themselves into the sea the following day as the floe split under the boats. Hurley exclaimed, "At last we were Free! Free!! No more idle captives."[12] Two lifeboats, the *James Caird* and the *Dudley Docker,* were under the respective commands of Shackleton and Worsley, carrying thirteen and ten men. The third lifeboat, the *Stancomb Wills,* carried five men; command was shared by two of the *Endurance*'s second officers, Hubert Hudson and Tom Crean. (Crean, along with William Lashly, had saved the life of Lt. Edward Evans on Scott's 1910–13 expedition.)

During their ensuing five-day journey, there were few good daylight hours. All the boats were heavily laden. Cold wind, freezing spray, riptides, and sea ice made navigation difficult, especially for the *Stancomb Wills,* which was slower than the others. Orcas were a constant danger. Camps at night, when possible, were on precarious, unstable floes. One night, a floe split under the camp, and fireman Ernest Holness dropped into the water in his sleeping bag. He was hauled out just before the ice edges crashed back together. Sometimes the men had only a makeshift "kitchen" in which to prepare a hot meal or milk as the boats were constantly attended in the water aside the floes. When the weather was windy and bad, the men shouted to be heard. Some nights members of the party had little or no sleep, and when the temperatures dropped below zero, the men clung to each other in their icy clothing for extra warmth. Hurley recounted an episode he considered typical of Shackleton: "The leader noticing my endeavours to restore circulation took off his warm gloves and handed them to me. 'Take these until your hands are right,' he said. As he was suffering himself I refused. But he was determined that I should have them. 'All right,' he replied, 'if you don't take them I'll throw them into the sea.'"[13]

On 13 April, Shackleton decided on a run to Elephant Island. Sensing the men's exhaustion, and realizing that stores would have to be jettisoned anyway once they entered open sea, he permitted a meal of unlimited rations of which all but the seasick took advantage. They reached open water at noon, set sail, and were soon shipping seas and burning with a thirst relieved only by occasional pieces of ice. Percy Blackborrow and first officer Lionel Greenstreet had frostbitten feet. The night of 14 April was particularly miserable—in a snow squall the boats were separated; temperatures were low, the winds high, and the seas fierce. The men crouched low and huddled. The following morning, 15 April, the boats were reunited as the three separate parties cruised along the coast of Elephant Island in uncertain seas.

The men arrived at Cape Valentine, where Shackleton bestowed on Blackborrow, the youngest member of the expedition—and a stowaway at that—the honor of being the first documented human being to set foot on Elephant Island. He collapsed in the surf on frostbitten feet. Shortly all the men were on shore, their first experience of solid land in sixteen months. Shackleton described some of the men "laughing uproariously, picking up stones and letting handfuls of pebbles trickle between their fingers like misers gloating over hoarded gold."[14] The men ate seal meat and drank water luxuriously until each had had his fill; then came a "safe and glorious sleep."[15] As most of the men slumbered, Shackleton, Wild, Worsley, and Hurley surveyed the beach and realized to their dismay that a gale would bring the seas right up to the cliffs and swamp their camp. They knew they must leave Cape Valentine.

The following morning, Wild and four others set out in the *Stancomb Wills* to seek another site. They returned that night announcing the discovery of a suitable sandy spit seven miles to the west. The next morning, the entire party once again entered the sea and promptly had a gale on their bows. Struggling at oars in the raging ocean, wet to the skin and blistered from chafing, the men made their landing at what they named Cape Wild (now Wild Point), an inhospitable patch of rock and shingle. Reasoning that penguins would establish a rookery only above the highest water mark, they accordingly set up their camp of five tents. They harvested for food the few penguins and seals that still remained at season's end. The scene was desolate: winter was approaching, food was monotonous and uncertain, fuel was limited, and their rescue seemed at best remote. The heat of their bodies as they slept on the ground melted the ice and guano into a foul-smelling yellow mud. No wonder some of the men were apathetic and listless.

On these grounds Shackleton justified the enormous risk of a boat journey to South Georgia. Many volunteered. Shackleton selected himself, Worsley as navigator, Crean, the carpenter Harry McNeish, and seamen Tim McCarthy and J. Vincent. The keel of the *James Caird,* a boat twenty-three feet, six inches long[16] was strengthened for the journey with the mast of the *Stancomb Wills.* A covering to keep out the seas was fashioned of case lids and canvas. The boat was readied with one month's food for the six men, water casks, ice for additional fresh water, equipment, sleeping bags, and stones as ballast. Shackleton had his last words with Wild, whom he left behind in charge of the Elephant Island party. Shackleton gave him instructions, including a course of action should no rescue party appear by spring. The party of six launched into choppy waters on 24 April and sailed away to the northeast. On shore, Hurley recounted: "We stood on the beach watching the tiny sail grow smaller and smaller until it diminished to a minute speck. How lonely it looked. Then it disappeared from sight."[17] In Shackleton's words, "The men who were staying behind made a pathetic little group on the beach, with the grim heights of the island behind them and the sea seething at their feet, but they waved to us and gave three hearty cheers. There was hope in their hearts and they trusted us to bring the help that they needed."[18]

Launching the *James Caird*
Frank Hurley, from Shackleton, *South,* 1919

What happened during the sixteen days of that small, open boat's journey to South Georgia in tempestuous autumn seas is an enduring tale of supreme hardship, courage, and improbable survival. Seldom was the weather good. Each day was ruled by about thirteen hours of complete darkness. Overcast skies, gale- to hurricane-force winds, enormous waves, and freezing spray were with them nearly constantly. The sail of the tiny boat flapped idly in the calm of the troughs between waves, suddenly to catch the onslaught of the wind as the boat rose to the crests. The men were constantly apprehensive, and moment-to-moment life in the boat was comfortless. Three men at a time were on four-hour watch, one at the tiller, one managing the sails, and one pumping or bailing water. Below the decking, space was cramped, requiring that any movements be carefully coordinated. When not on watch, sleep was no true reward, because the sleeping bags were soaked, the men were bumped by shifting stores and rock ballast, and their bodies were chafed and lips cracked. Their only compensations were the hot meals and hot milk they managed to prepare on a stove that was always at risk of being overturned in the heavy motion.

By the sixth day, so much ice had accumulated from frozen spray that the boat was dangerously losing its buoyancy. The men chipped ice away everywhere. Spare oars and two sleeping bags encased in ice were jettisoned. The painter and sea anchor were lost, and handling became very difficult. A spell of good weather on the seventh day was the men's only respite, and that was soon interrupted.

On the eleventh day, the party came within a breath of perishing. Shackleton tells us: "At midnight I was at the tiller and suddenly noticed a line of clear sky between the south and south-west. I called to the other men that the sky was clearing, and then a moment later I realized that what I had seen was not a rift in the clouds but the white crest of an enormous wave. During twenty-six years' experience of the ocean in all its moods I had not encountered a wave so gigantic. It was a mighty upheaval of the ocean, a thing quite apart from the big white-capped seas that had been our tireless enemies for many days. I shouted, 'For God's sake, hold on! It's got us!' Then came a moment of suspense that seemed drawn out into hours. White surged the foam of the breaking sea around us. We felt our boat lifted and flung forward like a cork in breaking surf. We were in a seething chaos of tortured water; but somehow the boat lived through it, half-full of water, sagging to the dead weight and shuddering under the blow. We bailed with the energy of men fighting for life, flinging the water over the sides with every receptacle that came to our hands, and after ten minutes of uncertainty we felt the boat renew her life beneath us. She floated again and ceased to lurch drunkenly as though dazed by the attack of the sea. Earnestly we hoped that never again would we encounter such a wave."[19]

The following day, a new hardship confronted them: the drinking water was brackish from seawater contamination. The men were preoccupied by thirst, water was rationed, and Vincent became useless. In the final approach to South Georgia, the men were attacked by hurricane-force winds driving them toward a lee coast, and they battled with a double-reefed mainsail to remain offshore. As the boat strained, the men bailed without ceasing and were racked with thirst—all of their drinking water was now gone. Darkness came, and their chances of surviving the night seemed slim. A shift in the wind was their salvation. Because the boat had weakened under the stress of the ocean crossing, and because McNeish and Vincent were in poor condition, they could not make it to Stromness Bay, 150 miles around the island by sea. Shackleton, very concerned about his men's health, decided that they had to land immediately, anywhere possible.

The next day saw more difficulties delaying a landing. Finally, at dusk, the party tacked in an easterly direction into King Haakon Bay. Just beyond the southern headland, they found a small cove with a beach. Here, on 10 May, the six men set foot ashore for the first time since leaving Elephant Island. Shackleton recounted: "We heard a gurgling sound that was sweet music in our ears, and, peering around, found a stream of fresh water almost at our feet. A moment later we were down on our knees drinking the pure, ice-cold water in long draughts that put new life into us. It was a splendid moment."[20] A small concavity in the rock wall at the left (eastern) end of the beach was sufficient shelter. Stores were landed and the boat's ballast was discarded, but the men were too weak to haul the boat out of the water; they took watches that night guarding it. The *James Caird* was eventually brought up to safety, but its rudder was lost, only to be washed into the cove, as if by a miracle, and retrieved three days later. Meanwhile, the men rested, dried their clothes, and ate well, though they regretted destroying the albatross chicks they found in nests on the tussock slopes above.

Refreshed, the men left their cove in the *James Caird* and cruised eastward in high spirits to the head of the bay. On the north side, they beached the boat, inverted it for shelter, secured it with tussocks, and named their site Peggotty Camp. Abundant elephant seals were a promise of unlimited food and fuel. Shackleton and Worsley scouted a crossing and estimated a seventeen-mile trip for help. No one had ever crossed the uncharted interior of South Georgia. Shackleton, Worsley, and Crean would go, leaving McCarthy in charge of McNeish and Vincent. Shackleton, Worsley, and Crean planned to make the trip nonstop, taking three days' rations, a Primus stove with enough oil to cook six meals, forty-eight matches, some tobacco, a pair of binoculars, a chronometer, an adze, and rope. They took screws from the *James Caird* and converted their boots into crampons.

At two in the morning on 19 May, after a quick meal and good-byes, they left Peggotty Camp. Peaks and glaciers were set in crisp relief against a cloudless, moonlit sky. The men ascended the east side of the glacier above the camp and gained what seemed to Shackleton to be an altitude of twenty-five hundred feet in just two hours. The first glimpse of the interior revealed a formidable terrain broken with peaks, steep slopes, glaciers, and snow plains. In increasingly misty weather, on treacherous surfaces in knee-deep snow, they roped up and navigated by compass, Worsley at the rear shouting out directions. Deceived in the poor early-morning light, they began a descent from atop a saddle to a huge frozen lake, only to discover that it was distant ocean, an error that cost a precious hour. After sunrise, the weather clearing, the men found themselves climbing upward through soft snow in the direction of a transverse mountain range with five peaks. They chose the lowest, most rightward gap, cutting steps with the adze to make the final ascent. They were crestfallen to find their way blocked by a sheer fifteen-hundred-foot precipice on the other side of the ridge, but at least they could now see that their correct path lay between the glaciers that flowed northward and the outfalls of the inland ice that dropped southward.

They had to retrace steps, canceling out three precious hours of work; they ascended the next crest to the left, and then left again, only to find similar precipices blocking their way. Their fourth attempt, at the most leftward gap, came as a fog was rising from behind, effectively preventing another retrograde descent. Worsley recounted: "Down below us was an almost precipitous slope, the nature of which we could not gauge in the darkness and the lower part of which was shrouded in impenetrable gloom." Dangerous rocks or a precipice could have been in their way. The men had cut only a few steps down when Shackleton said, as recounted by Worsley, "We must go on no matter what is below. To try to do it in this way is hopeless. We can't cut steps down thousands of feet. It's a devil of a risk, but we've got to take it. We'll slide." Worsley and Crean agreed. They each coiled a portion of the single rope as a pad to sit on, Shackleton in front, Worsley behind with his arms around Shackleton, and Crean behind Worsley.

"Then Shackleton kicked off. We seemed to shoot into space. For a moment my hair fairly stood on end. Then quite suddenly I felt a glow, and knew that I was grinning! I was actually enjoying it. It was most exhilarating. We were shooting down the side of an almost precipitous mountain at nearly a mile a minute. I yelled with excitement, and found that Shackleton and Crean were yelling too. It seemed ridiculously safe. To hell with the rocks! The sharp slope eased out slightly toward the level below, and then we knew for certain that we were safe. Little by little our speed slackened, and we finished up at the bottom in a bank of snow. We picked ourselves up and solemnly shook hands all round."[21] Their descent had taken only two or three minutes. Now, at six in the evening, they had finally arrived at their long and gentle ascent between the glaciers and outfalls.

Darkness came, but at eight the moon rose directly in front of them like a benevolent beacon, illuminating a "silver pathway,"[22] throwing crevasse edges in shadow to help guide them safely along. By midnight, at four thousand feet, their path swung to the northeast, and the moon in its course swung around, too, continuing as their guide. The men fancied that Stromness Bay was close at hand as they wistfully identified certain landmarks, but as they descended, they realized that they were on a crevassed glacier northwest of their destination. They backtracked. A southward-running jagged line of peaks lay in their eastbound path. At five in the morning, exhausted, they briefly lay in the lee of a rock. Worsley and Crean fell asleep, but Shackleton, recognizing the danger of sleep and hypothermia, wakened them after five minutes, convincing them that they had dozed half an hour. At the ridge an hour later, the three men prepared their last hot meal and abandoned the Primus.

At seven they could hear the distant whaling station whistle blow. Shackleton remarked, "It was the first sound created by outside human agency that had come to our ears since we left Stromness Bay in December 1914. . . . It was a moment hard to describe."[23] Their hardships were not over. They set out with one remaining ration and biscuit apiece, descended two thousand feet easily in soft snow, but then encountered very steep, blue ice. They cut steps, roped up, and in two hours descended the treacherous five-hundred-foot slope. At the bottom, they found themselves on the beach and tussocks of Fortuna Bay. They climbed the slope on the other side, crossed a lake frozen only at the surface, went into water above their knees, and by half past one in the afternoon were twenty-five hundred feet up on the last ridge overlooking Husvik Harbor, their destination.

They began their last downward trek but were forced to descend a waterfall some twenty-five to thirty feet high by rope, through the icy water. When the rope stuck, they abandoned it. The brass screws they had placed in their boots were by now worn level with their soles, and they had some slips on the ice as they ended their journey. Scruffy, heavily bearded, and generally uncivilized in appearance, they reentered the outside world. The Norwegian whaling station personnel were cautious of them at first, but once they realized who the three were and had heard their incredible story, their doubt turned to stupefaction, then to effusive generosity. The three bathed and shaved and were fed and dressed.

Shackleton's final thought about the journey was that Providence had guided them. "I know that during that long and racking march of thirty-six hours over the unnamed mountains and glaciers of South Georgia it seemed to me often that we were four, not three."[24] Writer Harold Begbie, an acquaintance of Shackleton's who wrote a sensitive memorial tribute about the great leader, had queried Shackleton about the "fourth presence." Shackleton is said to have replied, "There are some things which never can be spoken of. Almost to hint about them comes perilously near to sacrilege. This experience was eminently one of those things."[25]

By ten that night, Worsley was accompanying the whalers west around the island to pick up McCarthy, McNeish, and Vincent at Peggotty Camp, while Shackleton immediately set about a plan to rescue the Elephant Island party. The relieved men at Peggotty Camp were exalted that their companions had succeeded in their crossing but were disappointed that no member of the crossing party had returned with the whalers. They simply did not recognize the new Worsley. Camp was dismantled, and the James Caird was taken on board the whaler. (The James Caird is now preserved at Dulwich College in London.)

Shackleton now began what would become a series of four rescue attempts on the Elephant Island party. The men departed South Georgia under Captain Thom in the English whaler Southern Sky on 23 May. On the third night out, their speed was slowed by sea ice of increasing thickness. The steel-built steamer could not take the shocks of the ice, so it was diverted north. Two more attempts on separate days fell short of Elephant Island by about seventy miles. Shackleton proceeded to the Falklands in search of a better vessel, arriving in Port Stanley on 31 May. The governor offered assistance, but no suitable ship was available. The British minister in Montevideo telegraphed Shackleton that the Uruguayan government would provision the trawler *Instituto de Pesca No. 1*. The ship arrived in Port Stanley on 10 June, and the party immediately went south. Elephant Island was sighted on 12 June, but, again, they were stopped twenty miles short by impenetrable ice, out of sight of the stranded party.

Shackleton, Worsley, and Crean then traveled by British mail boat to Punta Arenas. The British Association of Magellanes had raised money to charter and equip the schooner *Emma*. The Chilean government lent the steel-hulled *Yelcho* to tow the *Emma* partway, but the *Yelcho* was designed for the ice, and the tow rope snapped in the strain of a gale. The *Yelcho* returned on 14 July, laboring in rough weather. The *Emma* encountered the ice on 21 July and handled it poorly—the ship was too buoyant and bounced dangerously. An engine malfunctioned, and, in miserable winter weather, the crew were dependent on the sails, which, along with the rigging, became encased in freezing spray. The crippled ship could not penetrate the pack; only a little over a hundred miles from Elephant Island, they turned north to Port Stanley, arriving 8 August.

Shackleton, increasingly anxious for the safety of his stranded men, asked the Chileans to send the *Yelcho* to pick them up in Port Stanley, and they obliged. Shackleton started south on 25 August, hoping the ice had opened up. Weather was, for once, fine; the ice was open, and the men spotted the camp at twenty minutes before noon on 30 August. Shackleton saw the castaways scrambling out to the beach, waving, and recounted: "I saw a little figure on a surf-beaten rock and recognized Wild. As I came nearer I called out, 'Are you all well?' and Wild answered, 'We are all well, boss,' and then I heard three cheers."[26] With no guarantee that ice might not drift in and bar the ship's exit, all hurried aboard within an hour. Exhilarated, the entire party steamed north.

Shackleton learned how the Elephant Island party had clung to life and hope. Hurley described the scene: "Here we were, a party of twenty-two, maintaining a precarious foothold on an exposed ledge of barren rock, in the world's wildest ocean. Our leader had departed, taking with him the pick of the seamen. Of our party, one was a helpless cripple, a dozen were more or less disabled with frostbite, and some were, for the moment, crazed by their privations. Our refuge was like the scrimped courtyard of a prison—a narrow strip of beach 200 paces long by 30 yards wide. Before us, the sea which pounded our shores in angry tumult. . . . Behind us, peaks rose 3000 feet into the air, and down their riven valleys . . . the wind devils raced and shrieked, lashed us with hail, and smothered us with snowdrift. . . . Inhospitable, desolate and hemmed in."[27] Even when weather was good, the high cliffs blocked most of the direct sunlight.

The party erected a hut called "The Snuggery" by building two stone walls four feet high and nineteen feet apart, over which the men placed the *Stancomb Wills* and the *Dudley Docker* upside down. They caulked the walls and lashed down the boats to resist the gales, and they were quite satisfied with the design as a shelter. But the floor area was only eighteen by twelve feet; fine snow got in through crevices; and the hut was perpetually dark, except for feeble outside light or a flame from burning oil. Nine or ten men slept up in the thwarts, and the rest slept on the ground. For entertainment, they had only conversation and a few books, including the account of Nordenskjöld's expedition, which must have been dear to them given the similarities of the Paulet Island castaways' circumstances to their own predicament. When the weather warmed above freezing, water from the surrounding hills drained into the hut, which was "bailed" of over a hundred gallons of water on some days. A calving glacier across the bay regularly sent huge waves up to thirty feet ashore, on one occasion flooding the hut. The interior and all contents became increasingly grimy from the soot given off by the blubber stove. One of the men recounted, "Our shingle floor will scarcely bear examination by strong light without causing even us to shudder and express our disapprobation at its state. Oil mixed with reindeer hair, bits of meat, sennegrass, and penguin feathers form a conglomeration which cements the stones together. . . . Our ceiling, which is but four feet six inches high at its highest part, compels us to walk bent double or on all fours."[28] Surgeons Alexander Macklin and James McIlroy amputated Blackborrow's five frostbitten toes in the filthy conditions.

Each man took turns as cook for the week. Seal and penguin was their diet, with little else. "Enough barley and peas for one meal all round of each had been saved, and when this was issued it was a day of great celebration."[29] To celebrate Midwinter Day with a feast, the men brought out their hidden reserves. But they craved variety and fantasized their favorite dishes. When finally rescued, they were spinning out a dwindling supply of penguin, seal, limpets, and seaweed, and had only four days of rations left. They had worn the same clothing for six months.

Every man spoke admiringly of Wild's leadership. With rescue uncertain and conditions deplorable, Wild kept the "demons of depression" away.

When the ice was open, Wild would announce, "Lash up and stow, boys, the boss is coming today!"[30] Hussey entertained on his violin. Nearly every week a concert was held, and one would sing a song about some other member of the party. If the recipient objected to the lyrics, even worse lyrics were contrived for the following week.

George Marston first spotted the ship on 30 August. "Wild, there's a ship!"[31] The men rushed the door of the hut, tearing down the canvas walls and knocking over the lunch hoosh pot in their excitement. One recounted, "Again and again we cheered, though our feeble cries could certainly not have carried so far. Suddenly . . . a boat was lowered, and we could recognize Sir Ernest's figure as he climbed down the ladder. Simultaneously we burst into a cheer. . . . Blackborrow, who could not walk, had been carried to a high rock and propped up in his sleeping-bag so that he could view the wonderful scene. . . . We were like men awakened from a long sleep. . . . We intend to keep August 30 as a festival for the rest of our lives."[32] Shackleton remarked: "You readers can imagine my feelings as I stood in the little cabin watching my rescued comrades feeding."[33] Many years later, Hussey was still inspired to remark, "August 30th, 1916, will always stand out in my memory as the most wonderful day in my life."[34]

The men were met in Punta Arenas on 3 September by enormous throngs and given a hearty reception. Shackleton, on learning that the government of New Zealand was arranging relief of the Ross Sea Party, went directly there with Worsley, while the rest of the men returned to England.

THE ROSS SEA PARTY

Among the heroes of the Antarctic, the members of Shackleton's Ross Sea Party have yet to receive their honored place in history. Their story has been overshadowed both by the remarkable events that occurred simultaneously on the other side of the continent and by the extraordinary accomplishments of earlier expeditions in the Ross Sea area. The fact that they were a support party stripped them of the glamour and romance of previous expeditions based at Ross Island. The company also lacked a highly visible and charismatic leader, although the group was certainly not wanting in capable men.

These men, in fact, constituted the only Ross Island–based party of the heroic era that actually accomplished its southward objective. When their ship *Aurora* went adrift during the first autumn, leaving them extremely short of supplies, they demonstrated remarkable will and ingenuity to persevere with the little they had under extremely harsh circumstances. They never lost sight of the fact that the lives of Shackleton's party crossing the continent depended on them for survival. Their morale was continually assaulted by adverse conditions, lack of consistent leadership, loss of contact with the ship, scurvy, the deaths of three men, the absence of Shackleton's party, and uncertainty about their own rescue. Meanwhile, the men adrift on the *Aurora* almost shared the same fate experienced by the men of the *Endurance*. The final irony of all this effort and suffering is that their labor was for naught.

The group in the *Aurora* was under the command of Capt. Aeneas Mackintosh. Mackintosh was enthusiastic and loyal to Shackleton, having served under him on the 1907–9 expedition, but he was, at times, impetuous. Shackleton had instructed that a base be set up in the McMurdo area. Transport was to be accomplished by manhauling, dogs, and a motor-tractor. Scientific studies were planned. Mackintosh had been instructed to use the remainder of the first season to cache stores south to latitude 80°.

The *Aurora* sailed uneventfully from Hobart on 24 December 1914, with two years' provisions. The men visited Macquarie Island and passed safely through the Ross Sea pack ice. They intended to erect a hut and leave provisions at Cape Crozier for a party that would winter there to study emperor penguins. But when Ernest Joyce and Lt. J. R. Stenhouse (1887–1941) went ashore on the ice cliff to scout for a site, no suitable place was found. Joyce nevertheless observed, "Stenhouse was delighted with his first landing on 'Antarctica.' It is truly fascinating to the uninitiated, and gratifying to an old penguin like myself to share in his enthusiasm."[35]

Mackintosh headed the party into McMurdo Sound for Hut Point, but sea ice kept them seven miles out. On 17 January 1915, the discharge of men, dogs, supplies, and the motor-tractor began in earnest. The men left Hut Point for the south eleven days later. Blizzards, soft snow, an exhausting job of relaying, and trouble with the dogs, including the loss of one, made progress difficult. On 11 February, Mackintosh, Joyce, and Ernest Wild went on with the strongest remaining dogs, while the Reverend Arnold Patrick Spencer-Smith and the Australians A. Keith Jack and Irvine O. Gaze returned.

Mackintosh's party reached its goal of 80° S on 20 February, left a depot of supplies in a large cairn, and laid out smaller marker cairns to the east and west. They were held up by inclement weather at 80° S for three extra days and lost two dogs. After only four and a half miles' progress northward, fog and blizzards halted them again for three days. Food became short and was rationed; ironically, Mackintosh and Joyce had to return to the 80° depot to take one-third of the food for their own return trip.

On their trek north, surfaces improved and the weather was occasionally fine, but the closing season brought cold and blizzards. The remaining dogs either died or became so feeble that they had to be abandoned. Richard W. Richards, the third Australian member of the shore party, was later critical of Mackintosh for subjecting the unacclimatized dogs to the rigors of sledging so soon into the first season. Despite the hardships, the men found the resolve to relocate the Bluff Depot, which on the outbound journey in thick weather had been misplaced by four miles.

The remainder of the return trip to Hut Point was marked by weather delays, increasing cold, agonizingly painful frostbites, and food shortages. On 24 March, Mackintosh wrote in his diary: "We have some biscuit-crumbs in the bag and that is all."[36] At last they made it to Safety Camp, feasted, and reached Hut Point the following day; the other party had arrived there on 10 February.

Meanwhile, the *Aurora*, wintering at Cape Evans, was secured forty yards offshore by six hawsers, a cable, and two anchors. Mackintosh believed that the ship would hold fast and so did not hurry the delivery of supplies ashore. On 6 May 1915, a gale stripped the ship from its moorings and swept it out of sight. Richards recounted: "It was moonlight when I left the hut at 4 am and a moderate blizzard was blowing. . . . Automatically I looked seaward and was startled at not being able to see the top-masts of the ship. . . . I walked down to the shore line and found all hawsers loose and the cable bent back twice sharply. . . . Whatever hopes we entertained . . . for the return of the ship were shattered when the worst blizzard we had experienced so far raged violently on 10, 11, and 12 May."[37] The ship's safety and whereabouts were unknown to the men ashore until their ultimate rescue over one and a half years later.

The four men on shore, John L. Cope, Alexander O. Stevens, V. G. Hayward, and Richards, were short of coal and meat. Provisions and clothing for the upcoming sledging season had not been landed. So the men took as many seals as possible—meat for food, and blubber for fuel. The six men isolated at Hut Point by open water now made a risky return to Cape Evans over uncertain sea ice on 2 June, increasing the party to ten. They economized on clothing and footgear, made shoes out of canvas and leather found in the hut, and resolved to complete the next season's work. A small fire in the hut on 12 August was fortunately extinguished quickly. Life in the hut was unpleasant: oily smoke from the burning of blubber permeated everything, even the leaves of books. Without soap the men became black with grease. Mackintosh and Stevens crossed the Barne Glacier to visit the Cape Royds hut on 13 August, secured a small stash of tobacco, and found a year's supply of various foods for six men and used garments.

For the southward spring sledging of the 1915–16 season, Mackintosh divided nine men into three parties of three; one man remained behind at Cape Evans. Four thousand pounds of provisions were to be carried south. As had happened on previous expeditions in the same vicinity, the motor-sledge failed immediately and was abandoned. By 1 October, all provisions had been moved to Hut Point and Safety Camp. On 9 October, the men began moving supplies seventy miles south to the Minna Bluff depot. Joyce and Mackintosh argued over how to accomplish this task. Mackintosh prevailed; the job was to be completed in four runs lasting to early January. Soft surfaces, crevasses, and blizzards were sporadic but formidable. One of the Primus stoves became defective south of the Bluff depot, and three men had to be sent back permanently to Cape Evans with the faulty device.

By 8 January the final phase began, with a party of six setting out from a point south of Minna Bluff. This group was made up of Mackintosh, Joyce, Spencer-Smith, Richards, Hayward, and Wild. The party had to move supplies to Mount Hope at the foot of the Beardmore Glacier, at about 83°30' S. Richards described the sledging: "There was no conversation. . . . All our energies were needed for the job in hand. The silence was profound, the soft crunch of feet in the snow and the faint swish of the sledge-runners merely serving to emphasize it. Profound silence, that is unless a blizzard was raging, and then the tiny party was lost in a howling shrieking wilderness of whirling snow. The hours of a day's march seemed endless. I do not know what went on in my companions' minds over these months while on the march. . . . In my case I used to perform long useless computations of one sort and another in my head . . . an automatic reaction to the monotony."[38]

Trouble soon surfaced: Mackintosh and Spencer-Smith were fatiguing too easily. Mackintosh turned the leadership over to Joyce. Spencer-Smith showed signs of scurvy by the third week of January. He asked to be left behind with a tent and provisions and encouraged the others to go on; he insisted that the rest would make him fit for the return journey. The other five went ahead. As they approached the Beardmore Glacier, Joyce wrote: "We came across very wide crevasses . . . had several drops, and many shudders in consequence, Skipper and Richy hauling me out. All around us was such a scene . . . beyond realization in life. . . . We seemed to be in the centre of a vortex of ice . . . the pressure 3 to 400 feet."[39]

They established the final depot, then turned north on 27 January. They reached Spencer-Smith two days later and found him unable to walk, "limbs black, extending from ankle to hip."[40] They carried him in his sleeping bag on a sledge. Mackintosh weakened but could still march. Hayward was the next victim, showing blackened gums and swollen knees. The men made good progress under favorable conditions through 13 February with great help from the dogs: Con, Oscar, Gunner, and Towser. North of the 80° depot, surfaces turned bad, and a blizzard halted the party for six days. "We are frozen by night and starved by day," wrote Joyce.[41] Men and dogs were virtually without food on 23 February. Spencer-Smith was hallucinating. Joyce wrote: "We often talk about poor Captain Scott and the blizzard that finished him."[42] The next depot was eleven miles away, the same distance that Scott's party fell short of One Ton Depot.

The blizzard let up, and the men prepared to move on only to find that Mackintosh could not proceed on his feet. They pitched a tent, and Wild stayed to look after Mackintosh and Spencer-Smith while Joyce, Richards, and Hayward headed north. In storm-force winds and snow, the dogs without food and the men with only scant tea and biscuits, they reached the depot on 26 February. Joyce wrote: "I do not think there has ever been a weaker party arrive at a depot. . . . If ever a person owed their life to anyone, we owe ours to the dogs."[43] After the men and dogs were fully fed, they backtracked south with a sledge loaded with provisions for Wild and the two sick men. Stalled by weather and bad surfaces, they did not reach their companions until 29 February. They found the three out of food, Spencer-Smith doing very badly, and Mackintosh barely able to walk. Mackintosh said to them, "I want to thank you for saving our lives."[44] They headed north with two men on the sledges and Hayward now scarcely capable of proceeding on his feet. "No mistake it is scurvy," wrote Joyce, on 4 March.[45] By this time Joyce, Richards, and Wild were all affected.

On 7 March, Mackintosh volunteered to stay behind with a tent and three weeks' provisions even though they were only forty miles out. Mackintosh's aim was to hurry Spencer-Smith back to fresh food as quickly as possible, but Spencer-Smith, who had never complained, died on the morning of 9 March. He was buried in his sleeping bag under a snow cairn topped with a cross. The remaining men arrived at Hut Point two days later. They gorged themselves and secured ample seal meat and blubber before the sea ice would blow out and the seals with it. On 14 March the men set out with fresh food for Mackintosh. They found him disoriented; he had been talking to imaginary men in the tent. The party arrived back at Hut Point four days later. (Richards, Wild, and Joyce were later awarded the Albert Medal for their journey.) By now they were expecting Shackleton's arrival from the south, but there was no sign of him.

The men were eager to cross to Cape Evans as soon as possible—the Cape Evans hut provided more comfort, an improved diet (they had nothing but seal meat at Hut Point), reunion with their companions, and news of the *Aurora*. But new sea ice bridging the two points was repeatedly blown out during April. On 8 May, Mackintosh and Hayward set out across the frozen sea close to shore; uncertain weather caused strong misgivings among their companions who stayed behind. Conditions worsened. Not until 12 May could Joyce, Richards, and Wild check on Mackintosh's and Hayward's path. They found footsteps ending abruptly at open water, proof that the ice they had tread upon had been blown out. The three men retreated to Hut Point and could not cross to Cape Evans until the full moon of 15 July, in eclipse for part of the journey.

They joined Stevens, Cope, Gaze, and Jack and found that Mackintosh and Hayward had never arrived. That they had perished was terribly obvious. The efforts of Joyce, Richards, and Wild to save the two men had ultimately been futile. In addition, it had long since become clear that Shackleton had not completed his transantarctic crossing, so all their depot efforts had been in vain as well. The depressed men got along well together and waited out the remainder of winter and spring until their rescue, six months later.

The story of the *Aurora* was unfolding simultaneously. After the ship's moorings parted on 6 May 1915, the eighteen men aboard were adrift and helpless in the shifting sea ice. They never achieved their hope of returning to Cape Evans to land more supplies. Indeed, they were uncertain of their own survival. As the ship drifted northwest, the men struggled to maintain supplies of fresh water and attempted but failed to radio Macquarie Island or Cape Evans. The ship was strained and jammed by the ice, groaning and listing severely. Stenhouse, in command, described "the beauty and loneliness of our surroundings, and uselessness of ourselves, while in this prison."[46] On Midwinter Day, he wrote: "Wind howling and whistling through rigging. Outside, in glare of moon, flying drift and expanse of icefield. Desolation!"[47] On 21 July, south of Coulman Island, heavy pressure smashed the rudder, and the men, fearing for the ship's integrity, made ready to abandon ship with four sledges loaded with a month's rations so they could try for the nearest land. The pressure eased, however, and the ship was spared. Off Cape Adare on 6 August, the men celebrated the sun's return.

Still trapped, the ship continued its northward drift and passed the Balleny Islands. As spring advanced, the crew saw seals and penguins frequently and took them for food. Although the ice began breaking up on 12 February 1916, it remained closely packed, and the ship was not clear until 14 March, at 62°27′ S, 157°32′ E. The *Aurora*, without a rudder and short on coal in the region's rough seas, struggled northward and arrived in Port Chalmers, New Zealand, on 3 April, after eleven months adrift.

The vessel was repaired, and the government placed it under the command of Capt. John K. Davis, who appointed the officers, staff, and crew. The Australian government was indignant over Shackleton's handling of the finances of the Ross Sea expedition, so when he arrived in December 1916, he had to sign on. But by force of personality he secured a loyal following in New Zealand, cleared his debts, and resumed psychological leadership of the ship's party.

The seven men at Cape Evans were relieved on 10 January. A sheet of ice kept the ship almost eight miles off the cape, but three men left the ship and approached the shore. "Joycey, old man, more than pleased to see you," was Shackleton's greeting.[48] Richards reminisced: "We must have appeared a most disreputable and piratical crew. We were greasy and black from the prolonged contact with blubber, we were unwashed and unshorn, and our clothes were in the last stages of disrepair."[49] The men learned for the first time the fate of the *Endurance* and the drift of the *Aurora*. A final vain search was made for the bodies of Mackintosh and Hayward, and a cross was erected near the Cape Evans hut in memory of the two, as well as Spencer-Smith. The ship headed north again on 17 January and arrived in Wellington. Their journey, and one of Antarctica's greatest tales, came to an end on 9 February 1917.

24

JOHN L. COPE AND THE
BRITISH IMPERIAL EXPEDITION
(1920–1922)

> We had realized for some time that, as far as the Expedition was con-
> cerned, we had come to a dead end.
>
> Thomas W. Bagshawe, *Two Men in the Antarctic*

IN AN ERA OF HEROIC EXPEDITIONS carried out by large numbers of individuals with multilayered organizations and towering budgets, the venture
of four men under the grandiose title of the British Imperial Expedition of
1920 was an anomaly. The enterprise had almost no funds; its leader was
incapable, and its second in command bailed out as soon as the opportunity
presented itself.[1] But two inexperienced, young, and naive men remained in
the Antarctic—foolishly perhaps—to winter alone in the name of duty and
science on a lonely, remote islet on the Danco Coast of Graham Land. They
bewildered their contemporaries by proving highly ingenious at surviving in
the shelter of an abandoned boat with almost no resources, and by gathering
useful scientific data on weather, tides, and penguins at considerable personal inconvenience, discomfort, and risk.

The expedition's original party consisted of John Lachlan Cope, the nomi-
nal leader who had been a member of Shackleton's Ross Sea shore party; G.
Hubert Wilkins (1888–1958), who later served on Shackleton's *Quest* expedition and then distinguished himself as an Antarctic aviator; Maxime Charles
Lester, a navigator in his early twenties; and Thomas Wyatt Bagshawe, a nine-
teen-year-old geologist. Cope put forth ambitious ideas in his prospectus for
the expedition, which included a first flight over the South Pole. But funds
were insufficient to consider such an undertaking, or even to purchase a single
airplane. So he whittled down his objectives to mapping the west coast of the
Weddell Sea between the area examined by Nordenskjöld south to Shackleton's Caird Coast. On a shoestring budget, Cope had no expedition ship; each

man obtained individual passage to the South Shetlands. They made their rendezvous at Deception Island on 24 December 1920.

Cope arranged passage aboard the *Svend Foyn I*, a Norwegian whaler, under the charge of Capt. O. Andersen. The plan called for the four-man party to be dropped at Hope Bay. From there the group would proceed to Snow Hill Island and use Nordenskjöld's hut as a base, but ice blocked Antarctic Sound. So instead Andersen dropped them off with their equipment and stores on a tiny islet just south of the entrance to Andvord Bay in the Gerlache Strait, at 64°48' S, 62°43' W. Their little island measured only about 700 by 350 feet, with a maximum height of 18.5 feet; it was connected to two more islets that were home to breeding gentoo and chinstrap penguins. Where the men were dropped off, a water-boat had been left eight years earlier by whalers; they accordingly named the spot Waterboat Point. The abandoned vessel, 27.5 feet long, 10.5 feet in greatest breadth, and only 3.75 feet high, but covered by a deck, served as part of their shelter. Its unsatisfactory dimensions prompted the men to build an adjacent hut alongside, fashioned of packing cases and sacks of coal and sennegrass.

Summer weather was fairly good, and the temperature once reached 49.8 degrees Fahrenheit. The men managed only a few sledge journeys from their camp, however, and the party was never able to reach the east side of the Antarctic Peninsula to carry out its original goals. With the season advancing and their plans unraveling, Bagshawe wrote: "We had realized for some time that, as far as the Expedition was concerned, we had come to a dead end. Our prospects of getting across Danco Land were small, and of carrying out the intended work of exploring the west coast of the Weddell Sea practically hopeless."[2] Thus Cope would return to Montevideo to secure a vessel so the party could reach Snow Hill the following year. Wilkins, who had become entirely disenchanted with Cope's leadership and the enterprise in general, promptly joined Cope as a way out. Lester and Bagshawe opted to remain behind in the Antarctic for the winter to carry out scientific studies.

Bagshawe was temporarily left at Waterboat Point as the others went off to notify the Norwegians of their new plans. They returned and exchanged final farewells. Lester and Bagshawe declined to leave when a last-chance visit from Andersen materialized on 4 March 1921. As Andersen departed, he vowed to send a boat for them early the following year. To the two men, food seemed ample and varied, with pemmican, jam, marmalade, biscuits, a sack of flour, tea, onions, sardines, baked beans, various condiments, and two hundred penguins plus some cormorants, skuas, and seals in reserve. They had a few books to help pass the time.

Autumn and winter were to bring all their ferocity and hardships, however. When the boat leaked rain, the two men sealed a canvas with blubber to keep the water out. In a heavy gale and rain on 18 April, Bagshawe celebrated his twentieth birthday with an English pudding and cigar. The two men had no forks—they had forgotten them! By late April, dampness had spoiled a third of their biscuit supply, so what remained of this satisfying food had to be rationed. Temperatures were sometimes high enough to spoil their meat and produce thaws that yielded a conglomerate of mud and guano underfoot. And they had dogs to care for, even though the animals were of no use sledging. In spite of all this, the men faithfully carried out various scientific observations whatever the conditions, and sometimes at highly inconvenient hours.

As the cold of winter set in, Bagshawe recorded: "Everything freezes. Tonight my ink-pot has frozen up and the mince froze as we were eating it. We sit and shiver and try to laugh at our discomforts; it's not much use to moan and groan."[3] Everything gradually became impregnated by seal oil, smoke, guano, flour, and reindeer hair. Having heat was always attended by the anxiety their shelter could catch fire, but the promise of warmth, even for a brief period, was too tempting. By great effort, the men managed a bath apiece in July.

The men were aware of how much they depended on each other for sanity and survival. Bagshawe ruminated: "It would have been terrible for the other if one of us had died. The thought of being left in the Antarctic alone, wondering whether rescuers would ever come was a nightmare on which we dared not dwell. If the choice had come, I would unhesitatingly have chosen the lot of the one doomed to die; I could not have faced the ghastly loneliness of being left behind."[4] Relief came on 18 December—not from Cope, who was never able to obtain a ship, but from the Norwegians. "Such handshakes, they almost conveyed our joyous feelings."[5] The dogs were taken off, and the men made final preparations for their departure on 13 January 1922. Bagshawe and Lester remained at Nansen Island (in the Biscoe Islands group lying to the southwest) with the Norwegians until 29 March. They departed the Antarctic for good the following day.

Bagshawe later stated of Lester: "My happiest memory will always be of his cheery good-humour. On those dismal days when things had gone all wrong and we stared at each other in rueful dismay, a quizzical smile would creep over his face and expand into a broad grin so infectious that we would both burst into hearty laughter."[6]

25

Shackleton's Last Voyage— The Shackleton–Rowett Expedition (1921–1922)

"We want to wake you up thoroughly, for we have some bad news to give you—the worst possible." I sat up, saying: "Go on with it, let me have it straight out!" He replied: "The Boss is dead!"

Frank Wild, *Shackleton's Last Voyage*

SHACKLETON, EVER RESTLESS IN HUMDRUM SOCIETY and eager to set out again on another polar expedition, planned a voyage to the Arctic with funding from the Canadian government. But after he had lined up private contributors, obtained the commitment of his personnel, and arranged for equipment and supplies, the Canadian government backed out. Other supporters followed suit. The project was on the verge of collapse when it was salvaged single-handedly by John Q. Rowett, who supported an expedition purely for scientific research with no expectation—or even the possibility— of financial reward.

By the time Rowett stepped in, however, time had run out for the Arctic season; so Shackleton turned his attention once again to the Antarctic, proposing a broad program—too much to be accomplished in the two years planned—including the study of subantarctic islands, a search for islets and reefs of questioned existence, and examination of the Enderby coast. Preparations were hurried and completed in just three months so as to get an early start on the Antarctic season, but Shackleton was frustrated by a shipyard workers' strike that postponed departure for four weeks. The party left St. Katherine's Dock to supportive crowds on 17 September 1921.

Eight undaunted survivors of the *Endurance* expedition signed on, including Frank Wild (second in command), Frank Worsley (hydrography, sailing master), Alexander H. Macklin (surgeon, stores and equipment), James A. McIlroy (surgeon, meteorology), Leonard D. A. Hussey (assistant surgeon, meteorology), A. J. Kerr (chief engineer), C. J. Green (cook), and T. F. McLeod (seaman). Shackleton also selected the experienced seaman James Dell (electrician, boatswain), his close acquaintance on the *Discovery*. These constituted the nucleus of the party.

Applicants for the remaining positions numbered in the thousands and included women. The final party that departed from Rio de Janeiro included D. G. Jeffrey (navigator), G. V. Douglas (geology), G. Hubert Wilkins (natural history), C. R. Carr (aviator), James W. S. Marr (one of two boy scouts selected from among a flood of applicants), and six crewmen. Shackleton chose no women. The work was to include observations of weather and sea temperatures, balloon and kite ascents, magnetism studies, hydrography and surveys, and biological collections. The party also planned to have a small seaplane. Shackleton brought along a beautiful and friendly Alsatian wolfhound puppy named Query as a mascot; the animal had been presented to him by a friend.

The ship was a small 111-foot, 125-ton wooden Norwegian ketch with a steel-sheathed, reinforced bow, a 125-horsepower steam engine that promised seven knots, and a coal capacity of 120 tons permitting four to five thousand miles of travel. The ship was refitted, and Lady Emily Shackleton suggested the name *Quest*.

The *Quest* was undoubtedly one of the most uncomfortable vessels ever taken to the southern oceans. Although Shackleton made it clear that no work was too lowly for anyone, it appears that Marr, the scout, was given a disproportionate number of menial chores, which he carried out cheerfully, efficiently, and with great pluck. When the ship leaked, he was often at the hand pumps. He commented, "The bilges [are] extraordinarily unpleasant, for the stench of putrefying sea water is about the most stomach-turning odour I know."[1] In the coal bunker, dust was part of the air to be breathed. Space was severely restricted because of room set aside for the laboratories. Marr was allotted a seven-by-two-foot sleeping shelf, "at least as roomy as a coffin."[2] Even Shackleton's space was only seven by six feet. Heat was poorly distributed—the bridge was drafty and cold, and the men's feet suffered especially.

Worst of all, the ship was highly animated and rolled severely. During a roll, water would come over the decks, filling the boots of anyone above. The cook served scrambled eggs, for, as Green put it, "If I did not scramble them, they would have scrambled themselves."[3] Macklin wrote: "It has been impossible to stand without holding firmly to some support. . . . Meals are a screaming comedy . . . endeavouring to guide some food into our mouths. Suddenly, during a particularly violent roll, the bench was torn from its fastenings, and we were thrown backwards into the lee of the wardroom, intimately mixed with knives, forks, plates and treacle dough. . . . Wild was talking . . . when suddenly he shot away into the darkness, and a few moments later sounds the reverse of complimentary were heard issuing from the end of the bridge-house. . . . The *Quest* is a little 'she-devil,' lively as they are made. She has many uncomplimentary things said of her, and deserves all of them."[4] Bee Mason, the photographer, and Norman E. Mooney, one of the two boy scouts, were sent home from Madeira because they were unable to withstand the rigors, although both wanted to carry on. Marr wrote, "Even the hardiest veterans . . . succumbed to *mal-de-mer;* or, as this particular brand was even more atrocious than seasickness, let's call it *mal-de-Quest.*"[5]

The engine had the triple fault of weak thrust, coal inefficiency, and mechanical malfunction. Maximum steaming speed was not the seven knots expected but usually five and a half knots, forcing Shackleton to omit island stops on the way south to save time. Stocking enough coal became a preoccupation. The engine required repairs in Lisbon for a misaligned crankshaft, resulting in a week's delay. More engine repairs were needed in St. Vincent, still failing to remedy the trouble. Thus Shackleton decided on a major overhaul in Rio de Janeiro. The party arrived on 22 November, and Shackleton immediately went about his plans, including a major redesign of the living quarters. Four weeks would be needed, so he canceled plans that year for the Antarctic via the Cape of Good Hope and instead would confine his work to the South Georgia environs. The airplane and many other articles sent ahead to Cape Town were now unavailable.

When they left Rio, the engine seemed to be working better. Wild wrote: "If the reader will but . . . think of how, since the inception of the expedition, one difficulty after another had risen to baulk the enterprise, and how on board the ship one thing after another had gone wrong and required repair, he will agree that the Boss might well have thrown in his hand and retired from the unequal struggle. But nothing could have been more foreign to his mind."[6] Nevertheless, Wild recognized that the toll on Shackleton had been substantial. On 17 December at Rio, Shackleton had briefly "felt a slight faintness,"[7] for which Macklin was summoned. Worsley was also concerned about Shackleton's condition. "It struck me that he was thinking a good deal about the past, which was unusual for him, since he was a man who liked to leap forward mentally and who would generally dismiss memories in favour of speculations as to the future. I was vaguely worried by this strange and new attitude, which seemed to me to have a significance that I could not define."[8]

Despite all the difficulties, the men experienced a happy camaraderie. Wild noted: "Sir Ernest seemed to be enjoying the quiet, the freedom and the mental peace of our small self-contained little world. I think he liked to find himself surrounded by his own men, and he was always at his best when he had a definite objective to go for."[9] Lively ship motion forced the men to postpone their Christmas celebration, and in a gale and heavy sea, the ship made nine knots before the men were forced to heave to. "During the bad weather he [Shackleton] was almost constantly on the bridge, though his officers, sensing that all was not well with him, repeatedly urged him to go below and rest. But instead of resting he actually stood another officer's watch in addition to his own in order that his subordinate might secure what he considered to be much-needed rest. That, of course, was Shackleton all over, one of the qualities that made him a leader."[10]

Now the boiler was malfunctioning, but the problem could not be investigated until they arrived in South Georgia where Kerr, the chief engineer, could enter the boiler and determine if the problem was minor and reparable or meant the end of the expedition. Shackleton took the news quietly and calmly, but Wild was sure it worried him.

Setting aside all concerns, Shackleton became increasingly excited and optimistic as they approached South Georgia. Marr noted: "The old-timers amongst the crew were in their element now; you'd have thought they had suddenly come in sight of home. Particularly was the Boss exultant; he kept on pointing out familiar sights, and the weight of depression that had recently troubled him was quite shaken off. He was brimming over with vigour and energy, as happy as a sand-boy, and sniffed the air like a war-horse scenting a far-off battle. . . . He could hardly restrain himself from rushing ashore at once."[11] They arrived at Grytviken on 4 January 1922 and were met by the whaling station manager. Little could anyone have imagined the sadness the following day would hold.

Wild related the events: "On Thursday, January 5th, I was awakened about 3.0 A.M. to find both of the doctors in my cabin—Macklin was lighting my oil lamp. McIlroy said: 'We want you to wake up thoroughly, for we have some bad news to give you—the worst possible.' I sat up, saying: 'Go on with it, let me have it straight out!' He replied: 'The Boss is dead!' It was a staggering blow. . . . At 8.0 A.M. I mustered all hands on the poop, and told them the bad news. Naturally it was a great shock to them all, especially to those who had served with him before."[12] Marr recalled that "it was a dismal morning; the South Georgia sky was weeping copiously. . . . Whole volumes of dramatic rhetoric could not have conveyed the sad, sad truth to our hearts. . . . His name will live when many others are forgotten; for the men he led, who were his friends, must necessarily pass down to the generations the truth of his greatness."[13]

Wild informed the rest of the party that he was now their leader. News was sent to Lady Shackleton and Rowett. Macklin performed an autopsy on his friend; the cause of death was arteriosclerotic coronary artery disease, hardening of the arteries to the heart. Shackleton's body was carried ashore and taken to the little church. Wild recalled, "Here I said good-bye to the Boss, a great explorer, a great leader and a good comrade. . . . I had served with him in all his expeditions. . . . No one knew the explorer side of his nature better than I, and many are the tales I could tell of his thoughtfulness and his sacrifices on behalf of others, of which he himself never spoke."[14] Wild planned to send the body home to England, assuming that would be the wish of Shackleton's wife. Hussey was entrusted to accompany the remains and see this responsibility through.

Hussey's first stop was Montevideo, where a memorial service was held. The attendees, who included officials and well-wishers, represented many of the world's nations. There Hussey received a message from Lady Shackleton that she thought it most fitting her husband be buried in South Georgia, a place dear to his heart, the land he last trod, and the scene of his greatest exploit. By the time the coffin was returned, the *Quest* had already departed for the Weddell Sea. On 5 March, all five whaling station managers and a hundred whalers and seamen paid their last respects at Grytviken. The coffin was taken to the tiny cemetery and lowered into the ground. Hussey was the Boss's only former companion at the burial. The wife of the Norwegian doctor on South Georgia, the only woman on the island, made a wreath from flowers she had cultivated and placed it upon the grave.

Meanwhile, Wild and his men were distressingly limited by the fact that much of their equipment and stores remained in a Cape Town warehouse; but Wild was determined to carry on. To give up would have been intolerable. Wild, with the party in agreement, decided on exploration of the Weddell Sea. He obtained all needed food and clothing from the Leith Harbor whaling station manager. The manager at Husvik Harbor gave Wild 105 tons of coal, all he needed. In Larsen Harbor, fresh meat was taken on.

The ship and its company of twenty men departed from South Georgia at dawn, 18 January.

The heavily laden ship dipped its gunwales with each roll, seas ran over the decks, and the pumps were manned. The floes and bergs brought smiles to some of the old hands for whom the ice was not a danger but a homecoming. In a freak accident during a huge roll, one of the boats suspended over the deck drove Worsley into a wall of the bridge house. Only because the wall gave way and splintered with the force of the crash did Worsley avoid being crushed to death, but he was covered with bruises and abrasions and suffered fractured ribs. This tough old man of the sea could not be kept down, however; he made a rapid recovery. The party surveyed and sounded in the vicinity of Zavadovski Island, and the men disproved the existence of Pagoda Rock, reported by T. E. L. Moore in 1845. A typewritten shipboard magazine, *Expedition Topics,* was put out on 1 February 1922 for the amusement of all on board.

As the men proceeded southward the air became colder, and the sea threatened to freeze. The *Quest* could not survive being frozen in, being unable to withstand lateral pressure. Wild would soon have to retreat. The men reached 69°17' S, 17°9' E, where shallow soundings indicated that they were approaching the continent. But like Dumont d'Urville and Ross, who were stalled at relatively northerly latitudes in the Weddell Sea, Wild had to turn north on 12 February. Wild, who had more experience in the Antarctic than anyone else on board, revealed his philosophy amid the endless ice expanse before him: "Much of our finest art is surpassed by Nature. . . . Once wedded to Nature there is no divorce—separate from her you may and hide yourself amongst the flesh-pots of London, but the wild will keep calling and calling for ever in your ears. You cannot escape the 'little voices.'"[15]

In the advancing season, fog, mist, and high winds made progress difficult, and darkness filled the middle of the night. In open pack, the danger of being beset was past. On 22 February, Worsley celebrated his fiftieth birthday. Green pulled a gag on him by presenting a beautifully iced "cake" and an ax to cut it with; a fifty-four-pound metal sinker was concealed beneath the frosting. After the ensuing unrestrained words had settled down, "Wuzzles" was presented with his real birthday cake, a masterpiece.

By late February, the men were running short on coal. So Wild decided only to check on Ross's very tentative land sightings in the western Weddell Sea,[16] visit Elephant Island for seals and blubber and Deception Island to coal the ship, then return to South Georgia. Wild was aware of a "discordant element" among the men that he needed to purge, especially if they were to winter over or a catastrophe were to occur. He attributed the discontent to discomfort, a difficult time in the Weddell Sea, the monotony of the activities, and the fact that some of the ship's officers and crew did not feel especially loyal to him. But Wild was no stranger to leadership; he had been in charge of the twenty-two-man party cast away on Elephant Island during the *Endurance* expedition. The "old, tried men" who had been with him there helped preserve harmony. Wild met individually with each person and threatened harsh treatment if there were any further dissension. "I pointed out that although I would at all times welcome suggestions from the officers and scientific staff, and would consider any reasonable complaints, I could consider no selfish or individual interests, and my own decision must be final and end discussion of the matter. I was glad to notice an immediate improvement."[17]

At 64°11' S, 46°4' W, a search in clear weather for Ross's possible land was fruitless. Then from 15 to 21 March, the ship was frozen in the ice. Wild thought they might have to winter where they were. He confided only in Macklin for fear of upsetting the fragile harmony aboard. But the ship was freed, and discomfort again took hold as the *Quest* rolled in the swells, ice decorating the rigging. Macklin quoted Wild: "'The man who comes down here for the sake of experience is mad; the man who comes twice is beyond all hope; while as for the man who comes five times (himself)—' Words failed him."[18]

The men approached Elephant Island, the sea dotted with bergs and ice, the sky fiery gold and crimson. Sight of the island touched the hearts of the *Endurance* men, who animatedly picked out landmarks and reminisced. The ship was put in tenuous anchorage on the southwest side at Cape Lookout, and a landing was made on 26 March. The scene was lonely and forlorn. A few seals were taken, Wild commenting, "I loathed having to slaughter all these creatures, but the matter was one of the direst necessity, and I had to put aside any feelings of sentiment."[19]

For emotional reasons, Wild was eager to visit Wild Point, the tiny spit where his party had been stranded; McIlroy wanted to retrieve his diary. But inclement conditions prohibited a landing. Winds now picked up, perfect for a run to South Georgia; the men would not have to beat to Deception Island, and course was set. The *Quest* was ever lively and footing was treacherous. The ship was swept repeatedly by heavy seas from astern, one wave carrying away the after-scuttle, breaking the skylights, and filling the after-cabin with several feet of water. Marr was assigned the job of making the damaged sites watertight; the seas soaked him through, and his garments froze into a suit

The Shackleton memorial cairn at Grytviken
Taken by the author, 19 November 1996

of ice. One day's run was a phenomenal 197 miles on sail alone. The ship put in to Leith Harbor on 6 April, where the party was greeted by Hussey and the station manager.

The men's most important gesture yet to be undertaken was the building of a memorial cairn for Shackleton. They selected a prominent site on the headland projecting out on the lower slopes of Mount Duse at the entrance to Grytviken Harbor. Stones were quarried with picks and shovels from a hill a quarter-mile away. The cairn was surmounted with a cross, and a memorial brass plate was affixed. The work was done out of love and respect, Wild commenting, "It was the last job we should do for the Boss."[20] Wild directed that only those who served on the *Endurance* would make the last visit to the grave. He did not consider his decision a slight to the others; rather, he felt that the very last respects should be paid by those who were welded by their commonality and special intimacy with the Boss.

The ship departed from South Georgia on 8 May. They stopped at Tristan da Cunha and Gough Island. Theirs was only the second scientific visit to Gough Island; the first had been Bruce's. Course was then set for Cape Town. Query, the dog, who had tolerated alongside the men all the rigors of the ship, was washed overboard in a heavy roll. His death was a sadness to all. The men arrived in Cape Town on 18 June, where the party was welcomed by officials and prominent citizens. Here the men collected their mail from family and friends at home. They departed on 14 July, made stops at St. Helena, Ascension Island, St. Vincent, and the Azores, and arrived quietly in Plymouth Sound on 16 September 1922. Rowett was the first person to meet them.

In fulfillment of the scientific objectives of the voyage, the expedition brought back a body of scientific data. The expedition also was notable for its great hardships on account of the poor vessel. But in the men's hearts and the public's perception, Shackleton's death outweighed any other significance the voyage might have had. Mankind had lost one of its greatest and best loved explorers. Many tributes have been heaped on Shackleton during and after his lifetime, but Roald Amundsen's surpasses them all. "Sir Ernest Shackleton's name will always be written in the annals of Antarctic exploration in letters of fire."[21]

MAPS

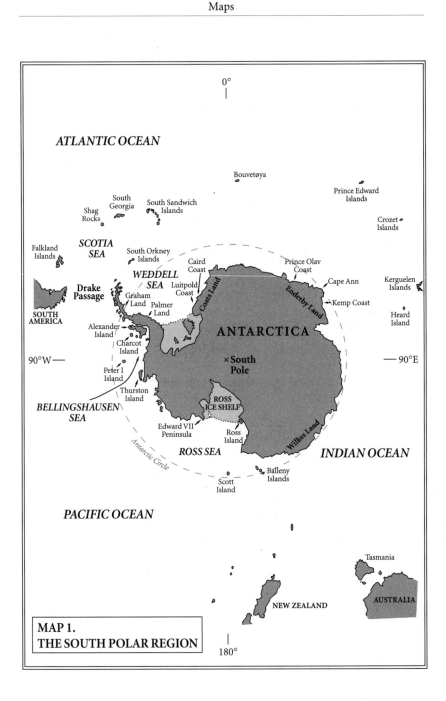

ATLANTIC OCEAN

Bouvetøya

Prince Edward
Islands

South
Georgia

Shag
Rocks

South Sandwich
Islands

Crozet
Islands

SCOTIA
SEA

Falkland
Islands

South Orkney
Islands

Caird
Coast

Prince Olav
Coast

Cape Ann

Kerguelen
Islands

WEDDELL
SEA

Luitpold
Coast

Coats Land

Enderby Land

Drake
Passage

Graham
Land

Palmer
Land

Kemp Coast

Heard
Island

SOUTH
AMERICA

Alexander
Island

Charcot
Island

ANTARCTICA

90°W

× South
Pole

90°E

Peter I
Island

Thurston
Island

ROSS
ICE SHELF

BELLINGSHAUSEN
SEA

Edward VII
Peninsula

Ross
Island

Wilkes Land

ROSS SEA

INDIAN OCEAN

Antarctic Circle

Balleny
Islands

Scott
Island

PACIFIC OCEAN

Tasmania

NEW ZEALAND

AUSTRALIA

MAP 1.
THE SOUTH POLAR REGION

180°

55°W

Clarence
Island

Elephant
Island

Cape Valentine

Cape Lookout

Joinville
Island

D'Urville
Island

Danger
Islands

Dundee Island   Paulet Island

King George
Island

SOUTH SHELTLAND ISLANDS

Bransfield Strait

Antarctic Sound

Erebus and Terror Gulf

Vega Island   Hope Bay

Cockburn Island

Nelson
Island

Tower
Island

Seymour Island

Snow Hill Island

Livingston
Island

Deception
Island

Trinity Peninsula

Prince Gustav Channel

Admiralty Sound

Lockyer Island

Orleans Strait

James Ross Island

Hoseason
Island

Trinity
Island

Christensen Nunatak

Smith
Island

Liège
Island

Robertson Island

Low
Island

Brabant
Island

GRAHAM

Nordenskjöld Coast

Cape Disappointment

Cape Framnes

65°W

Andvord
Bay

Gerlache Strait

LARSEN

Jason Peninsula

limit of ice shelf

55°W

Anvers
Island

LAND

Danco Coast

Graham Coast

ICE
SHELF

Cape
Tuxen

Wiencke
Island

Booth
Island

Wilhelm
Archipelago

Loubet Coast

Biscoe Islands

Matha Strait

Fallières Coast

PALMER LAND

Adelaide
Island

65°S

Marguerite
Bay

65°W

75°W

Alexander
Island

Charcot
Island

MAP 2. REGION OF THE
ANTARCTIC PENINSULA

70°S

75°W

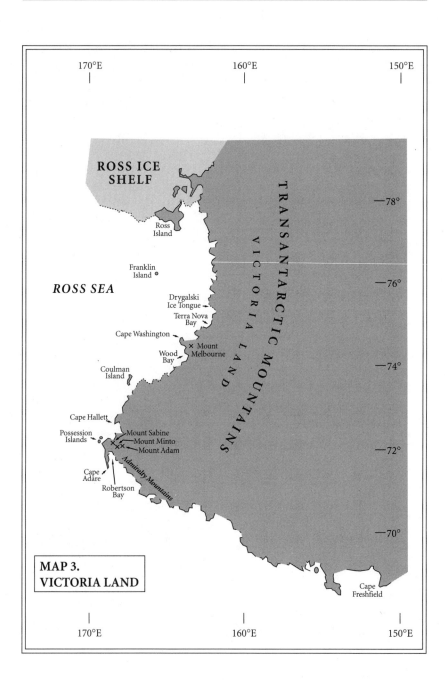

170°E   160°E   150°E

ROSS ICE SHELF

—78°

Ross Island

Franklin Island

—76°

ROSS SEA

Drygalski Ice Tongue

Terra Nova Bay

Cape Washington

× Mount Melbourne

Wood Bay

Coulman Island

—74°

Cape Hallett

Possession Islands

Mount Sabine
Mount Minto
Mount Adam

Cape Adare

—72°

Admiralty Mountains

Robertson Bay

TRANSANTARCTIC MOUNTAINS

VICTORIA LAND

—70°

MAP 3. VICTORIA LAND

Cape Freshfield

170°E   160°E   150°E

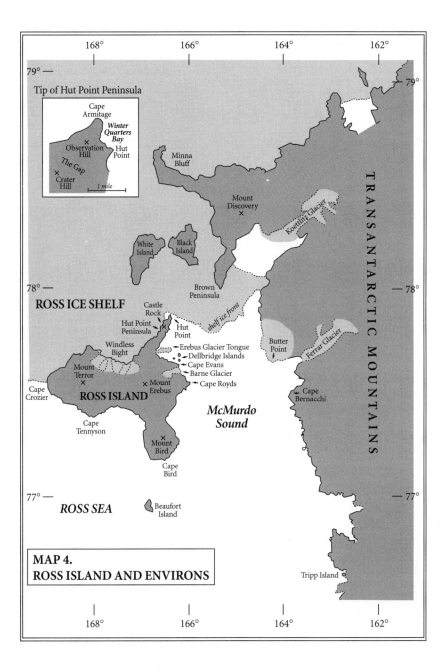

168°   166°   164°   162°

79°

Tip of Hut Point Peninsula

Cape
Armitage

*Winter
Quarters
Bay*

Observation
Hill

Hut
Point

The Gap

Crater
Hill

1 mile

79°

Minna
Bluff

Mount
Discovery

Koettlitz Glacier

T R A N S A N T A R C T I C

78°

White
Island

Black
Island

Brown
Peninsula

78°

ROSS ICE SHELF

Castle
Rock

shelf ice front

Hut Point
Peninsula

Hut
Point

Butter
Point

Ferrar Glacier

Windless
Bight

Erebus Glacier Tongue

Dellbridge Islands

Cape Evans

Barne Glacier

Mount
Terror

Mount
Erebus

Cape Royds

Cape
Bernacchi

M O U N T A I N S

Cape
Crozier

ROSS ISLAND

*McMurdo
Sound*

Cape
Tennyson

Mount
Bird

Cape
Bird

77°

ROSS SEA

Beaufort
Island

77°

**MAP 4.
ROSS ISLAND AND ENVIRONS**

Tripp Island

168°   166°   164°   162°

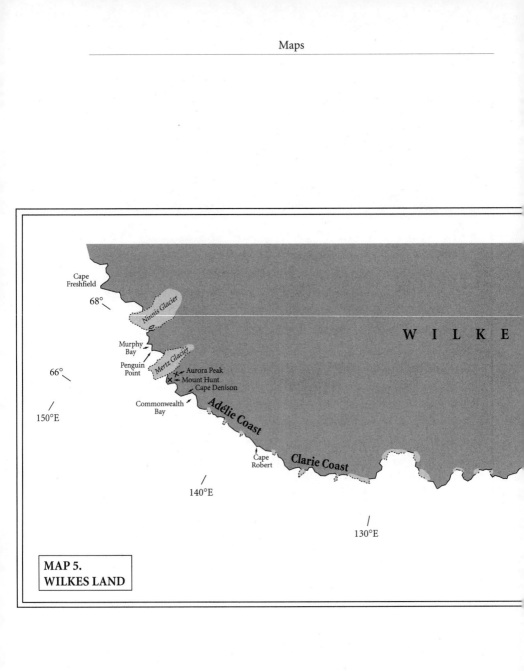

Cape
Freshfield

68°

Ninnis Glacier

Murphy
Bay

Penguin
Point

Mertz Glacier

66°

Aurora Peak
Mount Hunt
Cape Denison

150°E

Commonwealth
Bay

Adélie Coast

W I L K E

Cape
Robert

Clarie Coast

140°E

130°E

**MAP 5.
WILKES LAND**

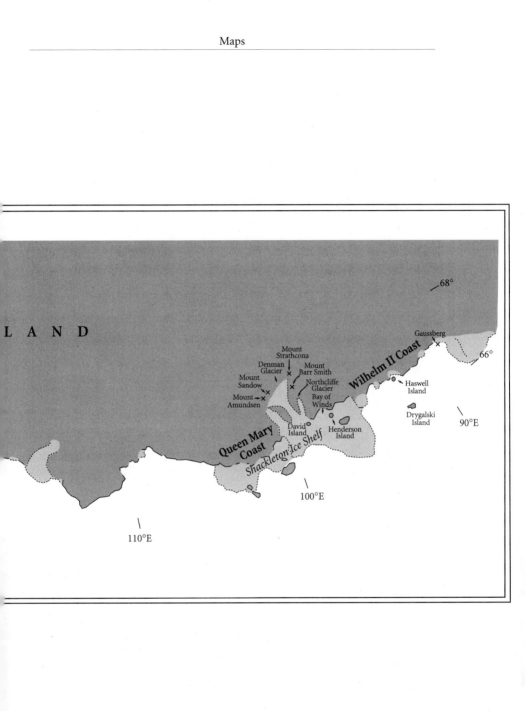

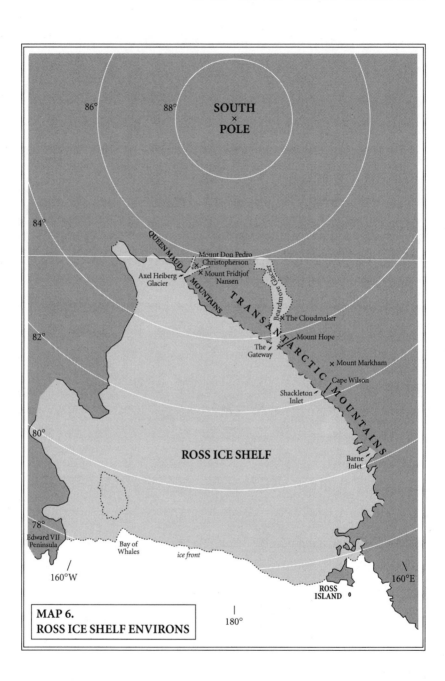

86°   88°   **SOUTH**
              ×
              POLE

84°

QUEEN MAUD

Mount Don Pedro
Christopherson
× Mount Fridtjof
Nansen
Axel Heiberg
Glacier

MOUNTAINS

Beardmore Glacier

T R A N S A N T A R C T I C   M O U N T A I N S

× The Cloudmaker

82°

Mount Hope

The
Gateway

× Mount Markham

Cape Wilson

Shackleton
Inlet

80°

ROSS ICE SHELF

Barne
Inlet

78°

Edward VII
Peninsula

Bay of
Whales

ice front

160°W

ROSS
ISLAND

160°E

MAP 6.
ROSS ICE SHELF ENVIRONS

180°

NOTES

CHAPTER 1. JAMES COOK, 1772–1775

1. [J. Cook], *Voyage of the* Resolution *and* Adventure, 2:clxviii.
2. [J. Marra], *Journal of the Resolution's Voyage,* 8.
3. [J. Cook], *Voyage of the* Resolution *and* Adventure, 2:80.
4. G. Forster, *Voyage round the World,* 1:109.
5. J. Cook, *Voyage towards the South Pole,* 1:56.
6. [Elliott and Pickersgill], *Journals of Lieutenants Elliott and Pickersgill,* 65.
7. J. Cook, *Voyage towards the South Pole,* 2:254–60.
8. [Burney], *With Captain James Cook in the Antarctic and Pacific,* 92.
9. Jones, *Antarctica Observed,* 21–27.
10. G. Forster, *Voyage round the World,* 1:535.
11. J. Cook, *Voyage towards the South Pole,* 1:264.
12. Ibid., 1:268.
13. Ibid.
14. [J. R. Forster], *Resolution Journal,* 3:451.
15. G. Forster, *Voyage round the World,* 1:544.
16. [Sparrman], *Voyage round the World,* 121.
17. Jones, *Antarctica Observed,* 49–55.
18. J. Cook, *Voyage towards the South Pole,* 2:213–14.
19. Ibid., 2:231.

CHAPTER 2. FABIAN GOTTLIEB VON BELLINGSHAUSEN, 1819–1821

1. Mill, *Siege of the South Pole,* 114.
2. Bellingshausen, *Voyage of Captain Bellingshausen,* 1:117.
3. Fricker, *Antarctic Regions,* 50; Mill, *Siege of the South Pole,* 121.
4. Bellingshausen, *Voyage of Captain Bellingshausen,* 1:xvi; Jones, *Antarctica Observed,* 101–2.
5. [Reader's Digest], *Antarctica,* 83.
6. Bellingshausen, *Voyage of Captain Bellingshausen,* 1:117.
7. Jones, *Antarctica Observed,* 101.
8. Ibid., 92.
9. Ibid., 92.

10. Ibid., 99.
11. Bellingshausen, *Voyage of Captain Bellingshausen,* 2:410.
12. Ibid., 2:410.
13. Ibid., 2:420.
14. Fanning, *Voyages round the World,* 437.
15. Bellingshausen, *Voyage of Captain Bellingshausen,* 2:425–26.
16. Mill, *Siege of the South Pole,* 130.
17. Bellingshausen, *Dvukratnyya Izyskaniya v Yuzhnom Ledovitom Okeane.*
18. Bellingshausen, *Forschungsfahrten im Südlichen Eismeer 1819–1821;* Fricker, *Antarctic Regions,* 49–53.
19. Bellingshausen, *Voyage of Captain Bellingshausen.*

CHAPTER 3. SEALING AND EARLY SCIENTIFIC VOYAGES, 1819–1830
1. Matthews, *Penguin,* 94–95.
2. Smith, *Narrative of the Life,* 161.
3. Webster, *Voyage to the Southern Atlantic Ocean,* 1:157.
4. Mill, *Siege of the South Pole,* 98–99.
5. Miers, "Discovery of New South Shetland," 369.
6. Jones, *Antarctica Observed,* 64.
7. Mill, *Siege of the South Pole,* 94.
8. Jones, *Antarctica Observed,* 63–64; Miers, "Discovery of New South Shetland," 370.
9. Jones, *Antarctica Observed,* 59–83.
10. Miers, "Discovery of New South Shetland," 369–70.
11. Mill, *Siege of the South Pole,* 94–95.
12. Balch, *Antarctica,* 96–97.
13. Jones, *Polar Portraits: Collected Papers,* 213.
14. Powell, *Notes on South Shetland,* 7.
15. Matthews, *Penguin,* 88.
16. Ibid., 92.
17. Weddell, *Voyage towards the South Pole* (1825), 30.
18. Ibid., 36.
19. Ibid., 37.
20. Ibid., 120.
21. Ibid., 48; ibid., (1827), 314.
22. J. C. Ross, *Voyage of Discovery and Research,* 2:357.
23. Stackpole, *Voyage of the Huron and the Huntress,* 51.
24. Mill, *Siege of the South Pole,* 111.
25. Morrell, *Narrative of Four Voyages,* 67.
26. Eights, "New Crustaceous Animal Found," 53–69.

CHAPTER 4. JOHN BISCOE, JOHN BALLENY, AND THE ENDERBY VOYAGES, 1830–1850

1. [Messrs. Enderby], "Recent Discoveries in the Antarctic Ocean," 105–12; Murray, *Antarctic Manual,* 305–35.
2. Murray, *Antarctic Manual,* 315–16. [Biscoe referred to these two species as brown eaglets and snow-birds, respectively.]
3. Ibid., 320.
4. Ibid., 322.
5. Ibid., 323.
6. Ibid., 330.
7. Ibid., 331.
8. Ibid., 332; and Sheet No. 2 [map] in rear pocket.
9. Balch, *Antarctica,* 123.
10. Murray, *Antarctic Manual,* 336–45, 348–59.
11. Ibid., 340.
12. Ibid., 343.
13. Ibid., 355.
14. Ibid.

CHAPTER 5. JULES S.-C. DUMONT D'URVILLE, 1837–1840

1. Dumont d'Urville, *Two Voyages to the South Seas,* 2:339.
2. Quoted by Dumont d'Urville, in Murray, *Antarctic Manual,* 437.
3. Ibid., 445.
4. Dumont d'Urville, *Two Voyages to the South Seas,* 2:478.
5. Quoted by Dumont d'Urville, in Murray, *Antarctic Manual,* 448.
6. Dumont d'Urville, in ibid., 454.

CHAPTER 6. CHARLES WILKES, 1838–1842

1. Wilkes, *Narrative of the United States Exploring Expedition,* 1:3.
2. Poesch, *Titian Ramsay Peale,* 75.
3. Palmer, *Thulia: Tale of the Antarctic,* 71.
4. Ibid., 65.
5. Colvocoresses, *Four Years in a Government Exploring Expedition,* 112–13.
6. Wilkes, *Narrative of the United States Exploring Expedition,* 2:292.
7. Clark, *Lights and Shadows of Sailor Life,* 103.
8. Wilkes, *Narrative of the United States Exploring Expedition,* 2:295–96.
9. [Reynolds], *Voyage to the Southern Ocean,* 131.
10. Colvocoresses, *Four Years in a Government Exploring Expedition,* 114.
11. Clark, *Lights and Shadows of Sailor Life,* 104.
12. Erskine, *Twenty Years before the Mast,* 109–10.

13. Clark, *Lights and Shadows of Sailor Life,* 107.
14. Wilkes, *Narrative of the United States Exploring Expedition,* 2:320.
15. Ibid., 2:325–26.

Chapter 7. James Clark Ross, 1839–1843

1. M. J. Ross, *Ross in the Antarctic,* 11.
2. L. Huxley, *Sir Joseph Dalton Hooker,* 1:79.
3. J. C. Ross, *Voyage of Discovery and Research,* 1:346–52.
4. Ibid., 165.
5. McCormick, *Voyages of Discovery in the Arctic and Antarctic Seas,* 1:145.
6. J. C. Ross, *Voyage of Discovery and Research,* 1:176.
7. M. J. Ross, *Ross in the Antarctic,* 82.
8. Mill, *Siege of the South Pole,* 273.
9. Amundsen, *South Pole,* 1:12.
10. McCormick, *Voyages of Discovery in the Arctic and Antarctic Seas,* 1:156.
11. M. J. Ross, *Polar Pioneers,* 211.
12. J. C. Ross, *Voyage of Discovery and Research,* 1:209.
13. Ibid., 1:216.
14. Ibid., 1:217–19.
15. L. Huxley, *Sir Joseph Dalton Hooker,* 1:117–18.
16. McCormick, *Voyages of Discovery in the Arctic and Antarctic Seas,* 1:168–69.
17. J. C. Ross, *Voyage of Discovery and Research,* 1:247.
18. L. Huxley, *Life and Letters of Sir Joseph Dalton Hooker,* 1:109–13.
19. J. C. Ross, *Voyage of Discovery and Research,* 2:138.
20. Ibid., 2:169–70.
21. J. E. Davis, *Letter from the Antarctic,* 19.
22. Ibid., 27–28.
23. J. C. Ross, *Voyage of Discovery and Research,* 2:217–18.
24. Ibid., 2:218–19.
25. McCormick, *Voyages of Discovery in the Arctic and Antarctic Seas,* 1:276.
26. J. C. Ross, *Voyage of Discovery and Research,* 2:219–20.
27. J. E. Davis, *Letter from the Antarctic,* 28.
28. Ibid., 30.
29. J. C. Ross, *Voyage of Discovery and Research,* 2:303.
30. Fricker, *Antarctic Regions,* 114–15.
31. Hayes, *Antarctica,* 125.
32. Drygalski, *Southern Ice Continent,* 223.
33. M. J. Ross, *Polar Pioneers,* 211–14; *Ross in the Antarctic,* 212.
34. M. J. Ross, *Polar Pioneers,* 385–86.

Chapter 8. Whaling, Sealing, and Scientific Voyages, 1841–1899

1. Balch, *Antarctica,* 186–87.
2. Murdoch, *From Edinburgh to the Antarctic,* 68.

3. Ibid., 212.
4. Ibid., 230.
5. Ibid., 233.
6. Ibid., 278.
7. Mill, *Siege of the South Pole*, 376.
8. Ibid., 377.

CHAPTER 9. HENRYK JOHAN BULL, 1893–1895

1. Bull, *Cruise of the 'Antarctic,'* 30.
2. Ibid., 52.
3. Baughman, *Before the Heroes Came*, 36, 38.
4. Bull, *Cruise of the 'Antarctic,'* 126.
5. Ibid., 175–76.
6. Borchgrevink, "First Landing on the Antarctic Continent," 432–48.
7. Translated from Kristensen, *Antarctic's Reise til Sydishavet*, 222.
8. Quartermain, *New Zealand and the Antarctic*, 9.
9. Bull, *Cruise of the 'Antarctic,'* 181.
10. Ibid., 181–83.
11. Ibid., 234.

CHAPTER 10. ADRIEN V. J. DE GERLACHE, 1897–1899

1. [Keltie and Mill], *Report of the Sixth International Geographical Congress*, 176.
2. Amundsen, *My Life as an Explorer*, 19–20.
3. F. A. Cook, *Through the First Antarctic Night*, 127.
4. Ibid., 127.
5. Ibid., 151–52.
6. Ibid., 177, 178.
7. Ibid., 191.
8. Gerlache de Gomery, *Quinze mois dans l'Antarctique*, 164–65; Lecointe, *Au pays des manchots*, 191.
9. Amundsen, *My Life as an Explorer*, 26.
10. F. A. Cook, *Through the First Antarctic Night*, 207.
11. Amundsen, *My Life as an Explorer*, 27.
12. F. A. Cook, *Through the First Antarctic Night*, 231.
13. Translated from Gerlache, *Quinze mois dans l'Antarctique*, 200.
14. F. A. Cook, *Through the First Antarctic Night*, 284, 288.
15. Ibid., 339–41.
16. Arctowski, *Programme scientifique de la seconde expédition Antarctique Belge.*

CHAPTER 11. CARSTEN E. BORCHGREVINK, 1898–1900

1. [Keltie and Mill], *Report of the Sixth International Geographical Congress*, 169–76.
2. Baughman, *Before the Heroes Came*, 77–113.
3. Borchgrevink, *First on the Antarctic Continent*, 1.

4. Bernacchi, *To the South Polar Regions*, 50–51.

5. Borchgrevink, *First on the Antarctic Continent*, 84.

6. Ibid., 102.

7. Bernacchi, *To the South Polar Regions*, 117–18.

8. Borchgrevink, *First on the Antarctic Continent*, 128–29.

9. Ibid., 190.

10. Ibid., 139, 184, 189.

11. Bernacchi, *To the South Polar Regions*, 190.

12. [Borchgrevink], *Report on the Collections of Natural History*, 221–23.

13. Ibid., 174–89.

14. Bernacchi, in Borchgrevink, *First on the Antarctic Continent*, 310–12.

15. Ibid., 250.

16. Ibid., 279.

17. Ibid., 294.

CHAPTER 12. ROBERT F. SCOTT, 1901–1904

1. Huntford, *Scott and Amundsen*, 129.

2. Bernacchi, *Saga of the "Discovery,"* 22.

3. Scott, *Voyage of the Discovery*, 1:95.

4. [Wilson], *Diary of the Discovery Expedition*, 93.

5. Scott, *Voyage of the Discovery*, 1:139.

6. [Wilson], *Diary of the Discovery Expedition*, 99.

7. Reginald Pound, *Scott of the Antarctic*, 55.

8. [Wilson], *Diary of the Discovery Expedition*, 111.

9. Hydrogen [Skelton], "Ballooning in the Antarctic," in [Scott], *South Polar Times* (1907), 1:2–8.

10. Allan, *Hookers of Kew*, 247.

11. [Wilson], *Diary of the Discovery Expedition*, 130.

12. Armitage, *Two Years in the Antarctic*, 84.

13. Scott, *Voyage of the Discovery*, 1:268.

14. Ibid., 1:290.

15. Ibid., 1:149.

16. [Wilson], *Diary of the Discovery Expedition*, 150–51.

17. Scott, *Voyage of the Discovery*, 1:298; and [Wilson], *Diary of the Discovery Expedition*, 135.

18. Armitage, *Two Years in the Antarctic*, 99–100.

19. Scott, *Voyage of the Discovery*, 1:299.

20. Ibid., 1:392.

21. Ibid., 1:467–68.

22. Ibid., 1:507.

23. Ibid., 2:8.

24. Ibid., 2:20.

25. Ibid., 2:23.
26. Ibid., 2:60.
27. Ibid., 2:32.
28. Ibid., 2:104.
29. Seaver, *Scott of the Antarctic*, 53.
30. Scott, *Voyage of the Discovery*, 2:79.
31. Doorly, *Voyages of the 'Morning,'* 59.
32. Doorly, *In the Wake*, 95; Scott, *Voyage of the Discovery*, 2:158.
33. Scott, *Voyage of the Discovery*, 2:92.
34. Ibid., 2:99.
35. Ibid., 2:118.
36. Ibid., 2:121.
37. Armitage, *Two Years in the Antarctic*, 191.
38. Bernacchi, *Saga of the "Discovery,"* 57.
39. [Markham], *Antarctic Obsession*, 13
40. Doorly, *Voyages of the 'Morning,'* 27.
41. Ibid., 58.
42. Armitage, *Two Years in the Antarctic*, 195.
43. Scott, *Voyage of the Discovery*, 2:171.
44. Ibid., 2:172.
45. [Wilson], *Diary of the Discovery Expedition*, 245.
46. Armitage, *Cadet to Commodore*, 132.
47. E. Huxley, *Scott of the Antarctic*, 104–5.
48. Armitage, *Cadet to Commodore*, 132.
49. [Evans] Mountevans, *Adventurous Life*, 67.
50. Scott, *Voyage of the Discovery*, 2:192.
51. Armitage, *Cadet to Commodore*, 131–33.
52. Ibid., 130–31.
53. Huntford, *Scott and Amundsen*, 180–81.
54. Scott, *Voyage of the Discovery*, 2:258–59.
55. Ibid., 2:269.
56. Ibid., 2:264–5.
57. Ibid., 2:278.
58. Ibid., 2:282–85.
59. [Lashly], *Under Scott's Command: Lashly's Antarctic Diaries*, 81.
60. Scott, *Voyage of the Discovery*, 2:296.
61. [Wilson], *Diary of the Discovery Expedition*, 330–31.
62. Armitage, *Two Years in the Antarctic*, 283.
63. Doorly, *Voyages of the 'Morning,'* 173–74.
64. Scott, *Voyage of the Discovery*, 2:356; Armitage, *Two Years in the Antarctic*, 289.
65. Scott, *Voyage of the Discovery*, 2:361–62.

Chapter 13. Erich D. von Drygalski, 1901–1903

1. Drygalski, *Southern Ice Continent*, 17.
2. Ibid., 18.
3. Ibid., 20.
4. Ibid., 21.
5. Ibid., 324.
6. Ibid., 178.
7. Ibid., 283.
8. Ibid., x (modern historical introduction).
9. Ibid., 370, 372–73.

Chapter 14. Otto Nordenskjöld, 1901–1904

1. Sobral, *Dos Años entre los Hielos 1901–1903*.
2. Nordenskjöld, *Antarctica*, 24–25.
3. Ibid., 34.
4. Ibid., 112.
5. Ibid., 158.
6. Ibid., 230, 232.
7. Ibid., 264.
8. Ibid., 289–90.
9. Andersson, in ibid., 464, 466, 469.
10. Ibid., 310.
11. Ibid., 510, 512.
12. Skottsberg, in ibid., 532–33.
13. Skottsberg, in ibid., 543.
14. Skottsberg, in ibid., 546.
15. Skottsberg, in ibid., 554.
16. Larsen, in ibid., 576–77.
17. Skottsberg, in ibid., 582.
18. Skottsberg, in ibid., 583.
19. Charcot, *Voyage of the "Why Not,"* 272.
20. Nordenskjöld, *Antarctica*, 584.

Chapter 15. William S. Bruce, 1902–1904

1. Bull, *Cruise of the 'Antarctic,'* 106.
2. Brown, *Naturalist at the Poles*, 97.
3. Ibid., 103.
4. Ibid., 115.
5. Bruce, in [Brown et al.], *Voyage of the "Scotia,"* viii.
6. Ibid., 59.
7. Ibid., 71.
8. Ibid., 80.

9. Ibid., 78.

10. Ibid., 106.

11. [Bruce], *Log of the Scotia Expedition,* 133–34.

12. [Brown et al.], *Voyage of the "Scotia,"* 153.

13. Ibid., 128.

14. Ibid., 154.

15. Ibid., 160.

16. Ibid., 161.

17. Brown, *Naturalist at the Poles,* 148.

18. Ibid., 158.

19. [Brown et al.], *Voyage of the "Scotia,"* 236–37.

20. Brown, *Naturalist at the Poles,* 178.

21. [Bruce], *Log of the Scotia Expedition,* 220.

22. [Brown et al.], *Voyage of the "Scotia,"* 253.

CHAPTER 16. JEAN-BAPTISTE CHARCOT, 1903–1905

1. Oulié, *Charcot of the Antarctic,* 52.

2. Ibid., 57.

3. Ibid., 60.

4. Ibid., 63–64.

5. Ibid., 67–68.

6. Translated from Charcot, *Le "Français" au Pole Sud,* 297–98.

7. Translated from ibid., 303.

8. Translated from ibid., 317–18.

CHAPTER 17. ERNEST H. SHACKLETON, 1907–1909

1. Shackleton, *Heart of the Antarctic,* 1:1.

2. Huntford, *Shackleton,* 202, 203, 206, 212, 216, 219–20.

3. Mill, *Life of Sir Ernest Shackleton,* 128.

4. Murray and Marston, *Antarctic Days,* 105–7.

5. John Millard, in the introduction to [Shackleton], *Aurora Australis,* vii–xx.

6. Shackleton, *Heart of the Antarctic,* 1:230.

7. Ibid., 1:297.

8. Ibid., 1:308.

9. Ibid., 1:342. [Tibetan plateau is actually higher.]

10. Ibid., 1:346.

11. Ibid., 1:347.

12. Ibid., 1:348.

13. Ibid., 1:354.

14. Huntford, *Shackleton,* 280.

15. Ibid., 285.

16. Shackleton, *Heart of the Antarctic,* 1:359.

17. Ibid., 1:360.
18. Ibid., 1:363.
19. Ibid., 1:366.
20. Mill, *Life of Sir Ernest Shackleton*, 150.
21. [Mackintosh], *Shackleton's Lieutenant*, 100.
22. David, in Shackleton, *Heart of the Antarctic*, 2:181–82.
23. David, in ibid., 2:186.

CHAPTER 18. JEAN-BAPTISTE CHARCOT, 1908–1910

1. Charcot, *Voyage of the "Why Not,"* 27.
2. Ibid., 266.
3. Ibid., 65.
4. Ibid., 79.
5. Ibid., 89–90.
6. Ibid., 99.
7. Ibid., 171.
8. Ibid., 189.
9. Ibid., 198.
10. Ibid., 214.
11. Ibid., 217–18.
12. Ibid., 270.
13. Ibid., 284–85.
14. Ibid., 286.
15. Ibid., 289.
16. Ibid., 296.
17. Ibid., 302.

CHAPTER 19. ROALD AMUNDSEN, 1910–1912

1. Cherry-Garrard, *Worst Journey in the World*, 2:544–55.
2. Nansen, in Amundsen, *South Pole*, 1:xxviii–xxix.
3. Ibid., 1:52.
4. Nilsen, in ibid., 2:310.
5. Ibid., 1:57.
6. Ibid., 1:92–93.
7. Ibid., 1:102–3.
8. Huntford, *Scott and Amundsen*, 261–63.
9. Hanssen, *Voyages of a Modern Viking*, 87–88.
10. Amundsen, *South Pole*, 1:129–30.
11. Ibid., 1:110.
12. Ibid., 1:120.
13. Ibid., 1:186.
14. Priestley, *Antarctic Adventure*, 40.
15. Amundsen, *South Pole*, 1:238.

16. Ibid., 1:370.
17. Ibid., 1:378.
18. Ibid., 1:384.
19. Ibid., 1:389.
20. Hanssen, *Voyages of a Modern Viking,* 101–2.
21. Huntford, *Scott and Amundsen,* 261–63, 410–15.
22. Amundsen, *South Pole,* 2:1.
23. Prestrud, in ibid., 2:204.
24. Ibid., 2:22.
25. Ibid., 2:28.
26. Ibid., 2:43.
27. Ibid., 2:53–54.
28. Huntford, *Scott and Amundsen,* 448.
29. Amundsen, *South Pole,* 2:57.
30. Ibid., 2:57–58.
31. Ibid., 2:60.
32. Ibid., 2:62–63.
33. Ibid., 2:69–71.
34. Ibid., 2:81.
35. Ibid., 2:97.
36. Ibid., 2:100.
37. Ibid., 2:113.
38. Ibid., 2:114.
39. Hanssen, *Voyages of a Modern Viking,* 106–7.
40. Amundsen, *South Pole,* 2:121–22.
41. Alexander, in ibid., 2:400–403.
42. Ibid., 2:132.
43. Ibid., 2:134.
44. Ibid., 2:164.
45. Ibid., 2:172.
46. Ibid., 2:174.
47. Hanssen, *Voyages of a Modern Viking,* 112–13.
48. Amundsen, *South Pole,* 1:vii–xix.
49. Nansen, in ibid., 1:xxxi.
50. Shirase, *Nankyoku-ki.*
51. Hayes, *The Conquest of the South Pole,* 307–8; [Reader's Digest], *Antarctica,* 206–7.

CHAPTER 20. ROBERT F. SCOTT, 1910–1913

1. Cherry-Garrard, *Worst Journey in the World,* 2:543.
2. Ibid., 1:50, 2:548.
3. Ibid., 1:2.
4. [Scott], *Scott's Last Expedition,* 1:7.
5. Evans, *South with Scott,* 34 36.

6. [Scott], *Scott's Last Expedition*, 1:25; Ponting, *Great White South*, 29; Cherry-Garrard, *Worst Journey in the World*, 1:63, 83–84.
7. Evans, *South with Scott*, 95.
8. Ibid., 55–56.
9. [Scott], *Scott's Last Expedition*, 1:92–93.
10. Ibid., 1:99–100.
11. Priestley, *Antarctic Adventure*, 40; Priestley, in Cherry-Garrard, *Worst Journey in the World*, 1:132–33.
12. [Campbell], *Wicked Mate*, 47–48; and Priestley, *Antarctic Adventure*, 43–44.
13. [Scott], *Scott's Last Expedition*, 1:187–88, 192.
14. Bowers, in Cherry-Garrard, *Worst Journey in the World*, 1:140.
15. Bowers, in ibid., 1:144.
16. Bowers, in ibid., 1:146.
17. Ibid., 1:177.
18. [Scott], *Scott's Last Expedition*, 1:205.
19. Cherry-Garrard, *Worst Journey in the World*, 1:200, 202.
20. [Scott], *Scott's Last Expedition*, 1:295, 432–33; Cherry-Garrard, *Worst Journey in the World*, 1:204, 206, 207.
21. [Scott], *Scott's Last Expedition*, 1:433; Cherry-Garrard, *Worst Journey in the World*, 1:210.
22. Ibid., 1:218; Evans, *South with Scott*, 125; Ponting, *Great White South*, 161–62.
23. Scott, *Voyage of the Discovery*, 2:258.
24. Huntford, *Scott and Amundsen*, 328–29.
25. Cherry-Garrard, *Worst Journey in the World*, 1:234.
26. Ibid., 1:272.
27. Ibid., 1:275–76.
28. [Scott], *Scott's Last Expedition*, 1:357
29. Wilson, in ibid., 2:49.
30. Cherry-Garrard, *Worst Journey in the World*, 1:284–85.
31. Ibid., 1:237.
32. Ibid., 1:297, 299.
33. Evans, *South with Scott*, 120; Ponting, *Great White South*, 156; [Scott], *Scott's Last Expedition*, 1:366–67; Cherry-Garrard, *Worst Journey in the World*, 1:240, 246, 247, 299.
34. [Scott], *Scott's Last Expedition*, 1:393.
35. Evans, *South with Scott*, 171.
36. [Scott], *Scott's Last Expedition*, 1:456.
37. Bowers, in Cherry-Garrard, *Worst Journey in the World*, 2:325.
38. Evans, *South with Scott*, 178.
39. Bowers, in Cherry-Garrard, *Worst Journey in the World*, 2:345–46.
40. [Scott], *Scott's Last Expedition*, 1:487, 488, 489, 490–91.
41. Evans, *South with Scott*, 184, 186, 187.

42. Cherry-Garrard, *Worst Journey in the World,* 2:348.
43. [Scott], *Scott's Last Expedition,* 1:493; Cherry-Garrard, *Worst Journey in the World,* 2:349.
44. Ibid., 2:351.
45. Ibid., 2:353.
46. [Scott], *Scott's Last Expedition,* 1:496.
47. Ibid., 1:511.
48. Cherry-Garrard, *Worst Journey in the World,* 2:381.
49. Ibid., 2:382.
50. Bowers, in ibid., 2:366.
51. Evans, *South with Scott,* 201–2.
52. [Scott], *Scott's Last Expedition,* 1:523.
53. Cherry-Garrard, *Worst Journey in the World,* 2:376–77.
54. [Scott], *Scott's Last Expedition,* 1:528.
55. Bowers, in Evans, *South with Scott,* 228.
56. [Scott], *Scott's Last Expedition,* 1:529.
57. Evans, *South with Scott,* 208–9.
58. Lashly, in Cherry-Garrard, *Worst Journey in the World,* 2:390.
59. Evans, *South with Scott,* 223–24.
60. Ibid., 224.
61. [Scott], *Scott's Last Expedition,* 1:536.
62. Ibid., 1:543.
63. Ibid., 1:543–46.
64. Bowers, in Cherry-Garrard, *Worst Journey in the World,* 2:512–13.
65. [Scott], *Scott's Last Expedition,* 1:534–35.
66. [Gran], *Norwegian with Scott,* 216–17.
67. [Scott], *Scott's Last Expedition,* 1:560.
68. Ibid., 1:568, 569.
69. Ibid., 1:570, 571.
70. Ibid., 1:573.
71. Cherry-Garrard, *Worst Journey in the World,* 2:550.
72. [Scott], *Scott's Last Expedition,* 1:584, 585.
73. Ibid., 1:587, 589.
74. Ibid., 1:551, 552, 576, 581, 584, 585, 586, 588, 590.
75. Ibid., 1:592–93.
76. Ibid., 1:594.
77. Ibid., 1:595, 597, 598, 606–7.
78. Cherry-Garrard, *Worst Journey in the World,* 2:454.
79. Ibid., 2:459.
80. Ibid., 2:465.
81. [Wright], *Silas: Antarctic Diaries,* 345–46.
82. Cherry-Garrard, *Worst Journey in the World,* 2:480–84.

83. Ibid., 2:202.
84. Evans, *South with Scott,* 252.
85. Cherry-Garrard, *Worst Journey in the World,* 2:487.
86. Priestley, *Antarctic Adventure,* 229, 243.
87. Ibid., 375–76.
88. Cherry-Garrard, *Worst Journey in the World,* 2:565.
89. Evans, *South with Scott,* 282–83.
90. Cherry-Garrard, *Worst Journey in the World,* 2:573.

CHAPTER 21. WILHELM FILCHNER, 1911–1912

1. Filchner, *Zum Sechsten Erdteil;* Filchner, *Ein Forscherleben;* Filchner, "Feststellungen," in [Filchner] *Dokumentation über die Antarktisexpedition 1911/12.*
2. "Feststellungen" [translation], in Filchner, *To the Sixth Continent,* 210.
3. Filchner, *To the Sixth Continent,* 69.
4. Ibid., 75.
5. Ibid., 84.
6. Ibid., 97.
7. Ibid., 104.
8. Ibid., 114.
9. Ibid., 115.
10. Ibid., 126.
11. Ibid., 134.
12. Ibid., 136.
13. Ibid., 142.
14. Morrell, *Narrative of Four Voyages,* 69.
15. Kling, in Filchner, *To the Sixth Continent,* 159.
16. Kling, in ibid., 164.
17. Ibid., 162.
18. Ibid., 195.
19. "Feststellungen," in Filchner, *To the Sixth Continent,* 196–98.
20. Ibid., 202.
21. Ibid., 204.
22. Ibid., 208.
23. Ibid., 209.
24. Ibid., 205.
25. Barr, in ibid., 214; Pyrzybyllok, "Handwritten notes . . ." [translation], in ibid., 231.
26. Barr, in ibid., 9, 214.
27. Kling [translation], in ibid., 234.
28. "Feststellungen," in ibid., 196.

Chapter 22. Douglas A. Mawson, 1911–1914

1. P. Mawson, *Mawson of the Antarctic*, 43.
2. D. Mawson, *Home of the Blizzard* (1915), 1:6, 1:ix.
3. Ibid., 1:xvi–xvii, 2:311–12.
4. Ibid., 1:61.
5. Ibid., 1:88.
6. Ibid., 1:95.
7. Ibid., 1:111.
8. Ibid., 1:113.
9. Ibid., 1:130.
10. Wild, in ibid., 2:82.
11. Wild, in ibid., 2:92.
12. Wild, in ibid., 2:95.
13. Wild, in ibid., 2:96.
14. Wild, in ibid., 2:100.
15. Wild, in ibid., 2:101.
16. Jones, in ibid., 2:111.
17. Ibid., 1:188.
18. Ibid., 1:195.
19. Madigan, in ibid., 1:205.
20. Madigan, in ibid., 1:207.
21. Ibid., 1:161.
22. Laseron, *South with Mawson*, 115.
23. Hurley, *Argonauts of the South*, 68.
24. Ibid., 78–79.
25. Madigan, in D. Mawson, *Home of the Blizzard*, 1:334–35.
26. Laseron, *South with Mawson*, 21, 22.
27. D. Mawson, *Home of the Blizzard*, 1:227–28.
28. Ibid., 1:239.
29. Ibid., 1:239–40.
30. [D. Mawson], *Mawson's Antarctic Diaries*, 148.
31. D. Mawson, *Home of the Blizzard*, 1:242.
32. Ibid., 1:247.
33. Ibid., 1:249.
34. Ibid., 1:251.
35. Ibid., 1:254.
36. Bickel, *This Accursed Land*, 109–11, 207.
37. [D. Mawson], *Mawson's Antarctic Diaries*, 159; D. Mawson, *Home of the Blizzard*, 1:261.
38. Ibid., 1:264.
39. Ibid., 1:264–65.

40. Hurley, *Argonauts of the South*, 119.

41. Davis, in D. Mawson, *Home of the Blizzard*, 2:35.

42. Ibid., 2:43.

43. J. K. Davis, *High Latitude*, 216.

44. Laseron, *South with Mawson*, 201.

45. J. K. Davis, *With the "Aurora" in the Antarctic*, 95, 98–99.

46. D. Mawson, *Home of the Blizzard* (1930), 186–203.

47. J. K. Davis, *High Latitude*, 208–9.

48. Ibid., 103.

49. D. Mawson, *Home of the Blizzard* (1915), 2:134.

50. Ibid., 2:140.

51. Ibid., 2:149, 150.

52. Ibid., 2:165–66.

Chapter 23. Ernest H. Shackleton, 1914–1917

1. Shackleton, *South*, vii.

2. Ibid., 43.

3. Hurley, *Argonauts of the South*, 158–59.

4. Shackleton, *South*, 65.

5. Worsley, in ibid., 66.

6. Ibid., 71–72.

7. Ibid., 73–74.

8. Ibid., 74–75.

9. Worsley, *Endurance*, 23.

10. Shackleton, *South*, 99.

11. Ibid., 108.

12. Hurley, *Argonauts of the South*, 223.

13. Ibid., 237.

14. Shackleton, *South*, 143.

15. Ibid., 144.

16. Dunnett, *Shackleton's Boat: The James Caird*, 25.

17. Hurley, *Argonauts of the South*, 251.

18. Shackleton, *South*, 164.

19. Ibid., 174–75.

20. Ibid., 179–80.

21. Worsley, *Endurance*, 155–56.

22. Shackleton, *South*, 200.

23. Ibid., 202.

24. Ibid., 209.

25. Begbie, *Shackleton: A Memory*, 61.

26. Shackleton, *South*, 219.

27. Hurley, *Argonauts of the South*, 252.

28. Shackleton, *South,* 229–30.
29. Ibid., 234.
30. Hurley, *Argonauts of the South,* 274.
31. Shackleton, *South,* 239.
32. Ibid., 240.
33. Ibid., 240.
34. Hussey, *South with Shackleton,* 151.
35. Joyce, *South Polar Trail,* 47–48.
36. Shackleton, *South,* 259.
37. Richards, *Ross Sea Shore Party,* 15.
38. Ibid., 24–25.
39. Joyce, *South Polar Trail,* 136–37.
40. Ibid., 140.
41. Ibid., 149.
42. Shackleton, *South,* 287.
43. Joyce, *South Polar Trail,* 156–57.
44. Shackleton, *South,* 290.
45. Joyce, *South Polar Trail,* 164
46. Stenhouse, in Shackleton, *South,* 312.
47. Stenhouse, in ibid., 315.
48. Joyce, *South Polar Trail,* 203.
49. Richards, *Ross Sea Shore Party,* 41.

CHAPTER 24. JOHN L. COPE, 1920–1922

1. Thomas, *Sir Hubert Wilkins,* 127–39.
2. Bagshawe, *Two Men in the Antarctic,* 57.
3. Ibid., 89.
4. Ibid., 114.
5. Ibid., 160–61.
6. Ibid., xx–xxi.

CHAPTER 25. ERNEST H. SHACKLETON, 1921–1922

1. Marr, *Into the Frozen South,* 72.
2. Ibid., 4.
3. Green, in Wild, *Shackleton's Last Voyage,* 20.
4. Macklin, in ibid., 141–42.
5. Marr, *Into the Frozen South,* 173.
6. Wild, *Shackleton's Last Voyage,* 47–48.
7. Ibid., 48.
8. Worsley, *Endurance,* 276.
9. Wild, *Shackleton's Last Voyage,* 26–27.
10. Marr, *Into the Frozen South,* 93–94.

11. Ibid., 98.
12. Wild, *Shackleton's Last Voyage*, 64, 66.
13. Marr, *Into the Frozen South*, 102, 103.
14. Wild, *Shackleton's Last Voyage*, 68.
15. Ibid., 136, 165.
16. M. J. Ross, *Ross in the Antarctic*, 201.
17. Wild, *Shackleton's Last Voyage*, 117, 138, 139.
18. Macklin, in ibid., 153.
19. Ibid., 160.
20. Ibid., 193.
21. Amundsen, *South Pole*, 2:114.

BIBLIOGRAPHY

Alberts, Fred B. *Geographic Names of the Antarctic.* 2d ed. Reston, Va.: United States Board on Geographic Names, 1995.

Allan, Mea. *The Hookers of Kew, 1785–1911.* London: Michael-Joseph, 1967.

Amundsen, Roald. *My Life as an Explorer.* Garden City, N.Y.: Doubleday, Page, 1927.

———. *The South Pole: An Account of the Norwegian Antarctic Expedition in the "Fram," 1910–1912.* Translated by A. G. Chater. 2 vols. London: John Murray, 1912.

———. *Sydpolen: Den Norske Sydpolsfærd med Fram, 1910–1912.* 2 vols. Kristiania [Oslo]: Jacob Dybwads, 1912.

Arctowski, Henryk. *Programme scientifique de la seconde expédition Antarctique Belge.* Bruxelles: Veuve Ferdinand Larcier, 1907.

Armitage, Albert B. *Cadet to Commodore.* London: Cassell, 1925.

———. *Two Years in the Antarctic: Being a Narrative of the British National Antarctic Expedition.* London: Edward Arnold, 1905.

Bagshawe, Thomas Wyatt. *Two Men in the Antarctic: An Expedition to Graham Land, 1920–1922.* Cambridge: Cambridge University Press, 1939.

Balch, Edwin Swift. *Antarctica.* Philadelphia: Allen, Lane and Scott, 1902.

Baughman, T. H. *Before the Heroes Came: Antarctica in the 1890s.* Lincoln: University of Nebraska Press, 1994.

Beaglehole, J. C. *The Life of Captain James Cook.* London: Adam and Charles Black, 1974.

Begbie, Harold. *Shackleton: A Memory.* London: Mills and Boon, 1922.

Bellingshausen, Fabian G. von. *Dvukratnyya Izyskaniya v Yuzhnom Ledovitom Okeane i Plavanie Vokaug Sveta, v Prodolzhenii 1819, 20 i 21 Godov.* St. Petersburg: 1831.

———. *Forschungsfahrten im Südlichen Eismeer 1819–1821.* Leipzig: Verlag von S. Hirzel/Max Weg, 1902.

———. *The Voyage of Captain Bellingshausen to the Antarctic Seas 1819–1821.* Edited by Frank Debenham. 2 vols. London: Hakluyt Society, 1945.

Bernacchi, Louis C. *Saga of the "Discovery."* London: Blackie and Son, 1938.

———. *To the South Polar Regions: Expedition of 1898–1900.* London: Hurst and Blackett, 1901.

Bertrand, Kenneth J. *Americans in Antarctica, 1775–1948.* New York: American Geographical Society, 1971.

Bickel, Lennard. *This Accursed Land.* Melbourne: Macmillan, 1977.

Borchgrevink, C. E. "The First Landing on the Antarctic Continent: Being an Account of the Recent Voyage of the Whaler 'Antarctic.'" *Century Illustrated Monthly Magazine* 51 (November 1895–April 1896): 432–48.

———. *First on the Antarctic Continent: Being an Account of the British Antarctic Expedition, 1898–1900.* London: George Newnes, 1901.

[———.] *Report on the Collections of Natural History Made in the Antarctic Regions during the Voyage of the "Southern Cross."* Edited by E. Ray Lankester and Jeffrey Bell. London: Printed by Order of the Trustees [of the British Museum], 1902.

Brown, Robert N. Rudmose. *A Naturalist at the Poles: The Life, Work, and Voyages of Dr. W. S. Bruce the Polar Explorer.* London: Seely, Service, 1923.

[Brown, Robert N. Rudmose, R. C. Mossman, and J. H. Harvey Pirie.] *The Voyage of the "Scotia": Being the Record of a Voyage of Exploration in Antarctic Seas by Three of the Staff.* Edinburgh: William Blackwood and Sons, 1906.

[Bruce William Speirs.] *The Log of the Scotia Expedition, 1902–4.* Edited by Peter Speak. Edinburgh: Edinburgh University Press, 1992.

———. "The Proposed Scottish National Antarctic Expedition." *Scottish Geographical Magazine* 16 (1900): 352–57.

Bull, H. J. *The Cruise of the 'Antarctic' to the South Polar Regions.* London: Edward Arnold, 1896.

[Burney, James.] *With Captain James Cook in the Antarctic and Pacific: The Private Journal of James Burney, Second Lieutenant of the Adventure on Cook's Second Voyage 1772–1773.* Edited by Beverley Hooper. Canberra: National Library of Australia, 1975.

[Campbell, Victor.] *The Wicked Mate: The Antarctic Diary of Victor Campbell.* Edited by H. G. R. King. London: Bluntisham Books, Erskine Press, 1988.

Charcot, Jean-B. E. A. *Journal de l'expédition Antarctique française, 1903–1905: Le "Français" au Pole Sud.* Paris: E. Flammarion, 1906.

———. *Le "Pourquoi-Pas?" dans l'Antarctique: Journal de la deuxième expédition au Pole Sud 1908–10.* Paris: E. Flammarion, 1910.

———. *The Voyage of the "Why Not" in the Antarctic: The Journal of the Second French South Polar Expedition, 1908–1910.* Translated by Philip Walsh. London: Hodder and Stoughton, 1911.

Cherry-Garrard, Apsley. *The Worst Journey in the World: Antarctic, 1910–1913.* 2 vols. London: Constable, 1922.

[Chun, Carl.] "The German Deep-Sea Expedition in Antarctic Waters." *Geographical Journal* 13 (1899): 640–50.

Clark, Joseph G. *Lights and Shadows of Sailor Life.* Boston: John Putnam, 1847.

Colvocoresses, George M. *Four Years in a Government Exploring Expedition.* New York: Cornish, Lamport, 1852.

Cook, Frederick A. *Through the First Antarctic Night, 1898–1899: A Narrative of the Voyage of the "Belgica" among Newly Discovered Lands and over an Unknown Sea about the South Pole.* New York: Doubleday and McClure, 1900.

[Cook, James.] *The Journals of Captain James Cook on His Voyages of Discovery: The Voyage of the* Resolution *and* Adventure *1772–1775.* Vol. II. Edited by J. C. Beaglehole. Cambridge, U.K.: Published for the Hakluyt Society at the University Press, 1961.

———. *A Voyage towards the South Pole and round the World: Performed in His Majesty's Ships the Resolution and Adventure, in the Years 1772, 1773, 1774, and 1775.* 2 vols. London: W. Strahan and T. Cadell, 1777.

Crawford, Janet. *That First Antarctic Winter: The Story of the Southern Cross Expedition of 1898–1900, As Told in the Diaries of Louis Charles Bernacchi.* Christchurch, New Zealand: South Latitude Research Limited, in association with Peter J. Skellerup, 1998.

Dallmann, Eduard. "Explorations in South Polar Regions." *Nature* 7 (1872): 21–23, 62–66, 138–40.

Davis, J. E. *A Letter from the Antarctic.* London: William Clowes and Son, 1901.

Davis, John King. *High Latitude.* Parkville: Melbourne University Press, 1962.

———. *With the "Aurora" in the Antarctic.* London: A. Melrose, n.d. [ca. 1919].

Debenham, Frank. *In the Antarctic: Stories of Scott's Last Expedition.* London: John Murray, 1952.

[———.] *The Quiet Land: The Antarctic Diaries of Frank Debenham.* Edited by June Debenham Back. Harleston, Norfolk: Bluntisham Books, Erskine Press, 1992.

Doorly, Gerald S. *In the Wake.* London: Sampson Low, Marston, n.d. [ca. 1936].

———. *The Voyages of the 'Morning.'* London: Smith, Elder, 1916.

Drygalski, Erich von. *The Southern Ice Continent: The German South Polar Expedition aboard the Gauss 1901–1903.* Translated by M. M. Raraty. Alburgh, Harleston, Norfolk: Bluntisham Books and Erskine Press, 1989.

———. *Zum Kontinent des Eisigen Südens: Deutsche Südpolarexpedition, Fahrten und Forschungen des "Gauss" 1901–1903.* Berlin: Georg Reimer, 1904.

Dumont d'Urville, Jules S. C. *An Account in Two Volumes of Two Voyages to the South Seas by Captain (later Rear-Admiral) Jules S-C Dumont d'Urville.* Edited by Helen Rosenman. 2 vols. Melbourne: Melbourne University Press, 1987.

———. *Voyage au Pole Sud et dans l'Océanie sur les corvettes l'Astrolabe et la Zélée, exécuté par ordre du roi pendant les années 1837–1838–1839–1840.* 10 vols. Paris: Gide, 1841–46.

Dunnett, Harding McGregor. *Shackleton's Boat: The Story of the James Caird.* School Farm, Benenden, Cranbrook, Kent: Neville and Harding, 1996.

Eights, James. "Description of a New Crustaceous Animal Found on the Shore of the South Shetland Islands." *Transactions of the Albany Institute* 2 (1833): 53–69.

[Elliott, John, and Richard Pickersgill.] *Captain Cook's Second Voyage: The Journals of Lieutenants Elliott and Pickersgill.* Edited by Christine Holmes. London: Caliban Books, 1984.

Enderby, Charles. "Note on Sabrina Land." *Proceedings of the Royal Geographical Society of London* 2 (1858): 171–73.

[Enderby, Messrs.] "Recent Discoveries in the Antarctic Ocean. From the Log-Book of the Brig Tula, Commanded by Mr. John Biscoe, R. N." *Journal of the Royal Geographical Society of London* 3 (1833): 105–12.

Erskine, Charles. *Twenty Years before the Mast: With the More Thrilling Scenes and Incidents While Circumnavigating the Globe under the Command of the Late Admiral Charles Wilkes 1838–1842*. Boston: published by the author, 1890.

[Evans, Edward R. G. R.] Mountevans, Admiral Lord. *Adventurous Life*. London: Hutchinson, n.d.[ca. 1946].

———. *South with Scott*. London: W. Collins Sons, 1921.

Fanning, Edmund. *Voyages round the World: With Selected Sketches of Voyages to the South Seas, North and South Pacific Oceans, China, etc.*. New York: Collins and Hannay, 1833.

———. *Voyages to the South Seas, Indian and Pacific Oceans, China Sea, North-west Coast, Feejee Islands, South Shetlands, &c &c. with an Account of the New Discoveries Made in the Southern Hemisphere, between the Years 1830–1837*. New York: William H. Vermilye, 1838.

[Filchner, Wilhelm.] *Dokumentation über die Antarktisexpedition 1911/12 von Wilhelm Filchner*. Zusammengestellt und Kommentiert von Gottlob Kirschmer. Munich: Bayerischen Akademie der Wissenschaften, 1985.

———. *Ein Forscherleben*. Munich: Eberhard Brokhaus, 1950.

———. *To the Sixth Continent: The Second German South Polar Expedition 1911–1912*. Edited and translated by William Barr. Bluntisham, Huntingdon: Bluntisham Books; Banham, Norfolk: Erskine, 1994.

———. *Zum Sechsten Erdteil: Die Zweite Deutsche Südpolar-Expedition*. Berlin: Ullstein, 1922.

Fisher, Margery, and James Fisher. *Shackleton*. London: James Barrie Books, 1957.

Forster, George. *A Voyage round the World in His Britannic Majesty's Sloop, Resolution, Commanded by Capt. James Cook, during the Years 1772, 3, 4, and 5*. 2 vols. London: B. White, J. Robson, P. Elmsley, and G. Robinson, 1777.

[Forster, Johann Reinhold.] *The Resolution Journal of Johann Reinhold Forster 1772–1775*. Edited by Michael E. Hoare. 4 vols. London: Hakluyt Society, 1982.

Fricker, Karl. *The Antarctic Regions*. Translated by A. Sonnenschein. London: Swan Sonnenschein, and New York: Macmillan, 1900.

Gerlache de Gomery, Adrien V. J. de. *Voyage de la "Belgica": Quinze mois dans l'Antarctique*. Bruxelles: Ch. Bulens, 1902.

[Gran, Tryggve.] *The Norwegian with Scott: Tryggve Gran's Antarctic Diary, 1910–1913*. Edited by Geoffrey Hattersley-Smith. London: National Maritime Museum, 1984.

Gwynn, Stephen. *Captain Scott*. London: John Lane, 1929.

Hanssen, Helmer. *Voyages of a Modern Viking*. London: George Routledge and Sons, 1936.

Hayes, J. Gordon. *Antarctica: A Treatise on the Southern Continent*. London: Richards Press, 1928.

Huntford, Roland. *Scott and Amundsen*. London: Hodder and Stoughton, 1979.

———. *Shackleton*. London: Hodder and Stoughton, 1985.

Hurley, Frank. *Argonauts of the South: Being a Narrative of Voyagings and Adventures in the Antarctic with Sir Douglas Mawson and Sir Ernest Shackleton*. New York: G. P. Putnam's Sons, 1925.

Hussey, L. D. A. *South with Shackleton.* London: Sampson Low, 1949.

Huxley, Elspeth. *Scott of the Antarctic.* London: Weidenfeld and Nicolson, 1977.

Huxley, Leonard. *Life and Letters of Sir Joseph Dalton Hooker.* 2 vols. London: John Murray, 1918.

Jones, A. G. E. *Antarctica Observed: Who Discovered the Antarctic Continent?* Whitby, U.K.: Caedmon of Whitby, 1982.

————. *Polar Portraits: Collected Papers.* Whitby, U.K.: Caedmon of Whitby, 1992.

Joyce, Ernest E. M. *The South Polar Trail: The Log of the Imperial Trans-Antarctic Expedition.* London: G. Duckworth, 1929.

[Keltie, J. Scott, and Hugh Robert Mill, eds.] *Report of the Sixth International Geographical Congress, Held in London, 1895.* London: John Murray, 1896.

Kristensen, L. *Antarctic's Reise til Sydishavet: Eller Nordmœndenes Landing paa Syd Victoria Land.* Tønsberg [Norway]: Forfatterens Forlag, 1895.

Lansing, Alfred. *Endurance: Shackleton's Incredible Voyage.* New York: McGraw-Hill, 1959.

Larsen, C. A. "The Voyage of the 'Jason' to the Antarctic Regions." *Geographical Journal* 4 (1894): 333–44, 466–67.

Laseron, Charles F. *South with Mawson: Reminiscences of the Australasian Antarctic Expedition 1911–1914.* Sydney: Australasian Publishing, 1947.

[Lashly, William.] *Under Scott's Command: Lashly's Antarctic Diaries.* Edited by A. R. Ellis. London: Victor Gollancz, 1969.

Lecointe, Georges. *Expédition Antarctique Belge: Au Pays des Manchots; Récit du voyage de la "Belgica."* Bruxelles: Oscar Schepens, 1904.

[Mackintosh, A. L. A.] *Shackleton's Lieutenant: The Nimrod Diary of A. L. A. Mackintosh, British Antarctic Expedition, 1907–9.* Edited by Stanley Newman. Auckland, New Zealand: Polar Publications, 1990.

[Markham, Clements.] *Antarctic Obsession: A Personal Narrative of the Origins of the British National Antarctic Expedition 1901–1904.* Edited by Clive Holland. Alburgh, Harleston, Norfolk: Bluntisham Books, Erskine Press, 1986.

Marr, James W. S. *Into the Frozen South.* London: Cassell, 1923.

[Marra, John.] *Journal of the Resolution's Voyage, in 1772, 1773, 1774, and 1775.* London: F. Newbery, 1775.

Matthews, L. Harrison. *Penguin: Adventures among the Birds, Beasts and Whalers of the Far South.* London: Peter Owen, 1977.

[Mawson, Douglas.] *The Home of the Blizzard: Being the Story of the Australasian Antarctic Expedition, 1911–1914.* 2 vols. London: William Heinemann, 1915, Philadelphia: J. B. Lippincott, 1915.; 1 vol. rev. ed. London: Hodder and Stoughton, 1930.

————. *Mawson's Antarctic Diaries.* Edited by Fred Jacka and Eleanor Jacka. Sydney: Allen and Unwin, 1988.

Mawson, Paquita. *Mawson of the Antarctic: The Life of Sir Douglas Mawson.* London: Longmans, Green, 1964.

McCormick, Robert. *Voyages of Discovery in the Arctic and Antarctic Seas, and round the World.* 2 vols. London: Sampson Low, Marston, Searle, and Rivington, 1884.

Miers, J. "Account of the Discovery of New South Shetland, with Observations of Its Importance in a Geographical, Commercial and Political Point of View." *Edinburgh Philosophical Journal* 3 (1820): 367–80.

Mill, Hugh Robert. *The Life of Sir Ernest Shackleton.* London: William Heinemann, 1923.

———. *The Siege of the South Pole: The Story of Antarctic Exploration.* London: Alston Rivers, 1905.

Mitterling, Philip I. *America in the Antarctic to 1840.* Urbana: University of Illinois Press, 1959.

Moore, T. E. L. "Magnetic Voyage of the Pagoda." *Nautical Magazine, London* (1846): 21–22.

Morrell, Benjamin. *A Narrative of Four Voyages, to the South Sea, North and South Pacific Ocean, Chinese Sea, Ethiopic and Southern Atlantic Ocean, Indian and Antarctic Ocean. From the Year 1822 to 1831.* New York: J. and J. Harper, 1832.

Murdoch, W. G. Burn. *From Edinburgh to the Antarctic: An Artist's Notes and Sketches during the Dundee Antarctic Expedition of 1892–93.* London: Longmans, Green, 1894.

Murray, George, ed. *The Antarctic Manual for the Use of the Expedition of 1901.* London: Royal Geographical Society, 1901.

Murray, James and George Marston. *Antarctic Days: Sketches of the Homely Side of Polar Life, by Two of Shackleton's Men.* London: Andrew Melrose, 1913.

Nordenskjöld, Otto. *Antarctic: Två År bland Sydpolens Isar.* 2 vols. Stockholm: Albert Bonniers Forlag, 1904.

Nordenskjöld, N. Otto G., and Joh. Gunnar Andersson. *Antarctica, or Two Years amongst the Ice of the South Pole.* London: Hurst and Blackett, 1905.

Oulié, Marthe. *Charcot of the Antarctic.* London: John Murray, 1938.

Palmer, J. C. *Thulia: A Tale of the Antarctic.* New York: Samuel Colman, 1843.

Poesch, Jessie. *Titian Ramsay Peale, 1799–1885, and His Journals of the Wilkes Expedition.* Philadelphia: American Philosophical Society, 1961.

Ponting, Herbert G. *The Great White South: Being an Account of Experiences with Captain Scott's South Pole Expedition and of the Nature Life of the Antarctic.* London: Duckworth, 1921.

Pound, Reginald. *Scott of the Antarctic.* London: Cassell, 1966.

Powell, George. *Notes on South Shetland, Printed to Accompany the Chart of the Newly Discovered Lands.* London: R. H. Laurie, 1822.

Priestley, Raymond E. *Antarctic Adventure: Scott's Northern Party.* London: T. Fisher Unwin, 1914.

Quartermain, L. B. *New Zealand and the Antarctic.* Wellington, New Zealand: A. R. Shearer, Government Printer, 1971.

[Reader's Digest.] *Antarctica: Great Stories from the Frozen Continent.* Sydney: Reader's Digest, 1985.

[Reynolds, William.] *Voyage to the Southern Ocean: The Letters of Lieutenant William Reynolds from the U.S. Exploring Expedition, 1838–1842.* Edited by Anne Hoffman Cleaver and E. Jeffrey Stann. Annapolis, Md.: Naval Institute Press, 1988.

Richards, R. W. *The Ross Sea Shore Party 1914–17*. Cambridge, U.K.: Scott Polar Research Institute, 1962.

Ross, James C. *A Voyage of Discovery and Research in the Southern and Antarctic Regions, during the Years 1839–43*. 2 vols. London: John Murray, 1847.

Ross, M. J. *Polar Pioneers: John Ross and James Clark Ross*. Montreal: McGill-Queen's University Press, 1994.

———. *Ross in the Antarctic*. Whitby, U.K.: Caedmon of Whitby, 1982.

[Scott, Robert F.] *Scott's Last Expedition: In Two Volumes*. Arranged by Leonard Huxley. 2 vols. London: Smith, Elder, 1913.

———. *The South Polar Times*. 3 vols. London: Smith, Elder, 1907, 1914.

———. *The Voyage of the 'Discovery.'* 2 vols. London: Smith, Elder, 1905.

Seaver, George F. *'Birdie' Bowers of the Antarctic*. London: John Murray, 1938.

———. *Edward Wilson of the Antarctic: Naturalist and Friend*. London: John Murray, 1933.

———. *Scott of the Antarctic: A Study in Character*. London: John Murray, 1940.

Shackleton, Ernest H. *The Heart of the Antarctic: Being the Story of the British Antarctic Expedition, 1907–1909*. 2 vols. London: William Heinemann, 1909.

———. *South: The Story of Shackleton's Last Expedition, 1914–1917*. London: William Heinemann, 1919.

[———, ed.] *Aurora Australis*. Alburgh, Harleston, Norfolk: Bluntisham Books, Paradigm Press, 1986.

Shirase, Nobu. *Nankyoku-ki*. Tokyo: Hakubunkan, 1913.

Smith, Thomas W. *A Narrative of the Life, Travels and Sufferings of Thomas W. Smith*. New Bedford: Wm. C. Hill, Portsmouth: Thomas W. Smith, Exeter: B. B. and T. Q. Lowd, and Boston: A. R. Brown, 1844.

Sobral, José M. *Dos Años entre los Hielos 1901–1903*. Buenos Aires: J. Tragant, 1904.

Sparrman, Anders. *A Voyage round the World with Captain James Cook in H.M.S. Resolution*. Edited by Owen Rutter. Translated by Averil Mackenzie-Grieve. London: Golden Cockerel Press, 1944.

Stackpole, Edouard A. *The Voyage of the Huron and the Huntress: The American Sealers and the Discovery of the Continent of Antarctica*. Mystic, Conn.: Marine Historical Association, 1955.

Stanton, William. *The Great United States Exploring Expedition of 1838–1842*. Berkeley: University of California Press, 1975.

Taylor, Thomas Griffith. *With Scott: The Silver Lining*. London: Smith, Elder, 1916.

Thomas, Lowell. *Sir Hubert Wilkins: His World of Adventure; A Biography*. New York: McGraw-Hill, 1961.

Webster, W. H. B. *Narrative of a Voyage to the Southern Atlantic Ocean, in the Years 1828, 29, 30, Performed in His Majesty's Sloop Chanticleer under the Command of the Late Captain H. Foster*. 2 vols. London: Richard Bentley, 1834.

Weddell, James. *A Voyage towards the South Pole, Performed in the Years 1822–24*. London: Longman, Rees, Orme, Brown, and Green, 1825. 2d ed., 1827.

Wild, Frank. *Shackleton's Last Voyage. The Story of the "Quest": From the Official Journal and Private Diary Kept by Dr. A. H. Macklin*. London: Cassell, 1923.

Wilkes, Charles. *Narrative of the United States Exploring Expedition, during the Years 1838, 1839, 1840, 1841, 1842.* 2d ed. 5 vols. Philadelphia: Lea and Blanchard, 1845.

[Wilson, Edward.] *Edward Wilson: Diary of the Discovery Expedition to the Antarctic Regions 1901–1904.* Edited by Ann Savours. London: Blandford Press, 1966.

[————.] *Edward Wilson: Diary of the 'Terra Nova' Expedition to the Antarctic 1910–1912.* Edited by H. G. R. King. London: Blandford Press, 1972.

Worsley, Frank Arthur. *Endurance: An Epic of Polar Adventure.* London: P. Allan, 1931.

[Wright, Charles S.] *Silas: The Antarctic Diaries and Memoir of Charles S. Wright.* Edited by Colin Bull and Pat F. Wright. Columbus: Ohio State University Press, 1993.

INDEX

Abbott, George, 200, 202–3
Académie des Sciences, Charcot expeditions and, 140, 164
Acuña, H., 135, 136
Adams, Jameson: first ascent of Mount Erebus, 149; "No. 1 Park Lane," 150; southern journey, 152–56; spring (1908) depot journey, 151
Adare, Cape: first sighted, 44; landing by Bull, 64–65; summit climbed, 77; landing by Scott, 85; Scott's Northern Party at, 226
Adelaide Island, discovery of, 25
Adelie Blizzard, The (expedition magazine), 263. *See also* publications, shipboard and expedition
Adventure (ship), 1–2
airplanes, 87, 243–44, 294
Åkerlund, Gustav, 118, 120, 125
Aladdin's Cave, 251
albatrosses, 6, 57; as food, 277
Alexander, Anton, 192
Alexander Island: discovery by Bellingshausen, 11 sighting by Evensen, 58; sighting by Gerlache, 70; sighting by Charcot, 169
Amundsen, Leon, 177
Amundsen, Roald: comment on Ross's entering pack ice, 44; first mate on Gerlache's voyage, 68; participates in first Antarctic sledge journey, 69; on Gerlache's wintering over, 70, 71; on

Gerlache's aversion to fresh meat, 72; moral command on Gerlache's voyage, 73; early achievements, 74; expedition, 176–95; reputation, 177; objectives of expedition, 178; dogs as transport, 179, 180, 183; reveals South Pole plans, 180–81; conflict with Johansen, 180, 185–86; sentiments over dogs, 181–82, 183, 188–89; encounters Scott, 181; establishment of Framheim, 182; depot journeys, 182–84; trail and depot markers, 182, 183, 186, 193, 194; encounter with Scott's Eastern Party, 182, 202, 203; anxiety over Scott, 184, 191; belief in preparation, 184, 186; southern journey false start, 184–85; southern journey, 186–94; "The Butcher's Shop," 188–89; regard for polar party comrades, 189, 192; passes Shackleton's farthest south, 191; at the South Pole, 191–93; life after expedition, 195; Amundsen's cairn at Mount Betty, 194, death, 195; letter for Scott at the South Pole, 220; meets with Filchner's party, 232; gives dogs to Mawson, 261; tribute to Shackleton, 301; quotations from writings, 44, 70–71, 72, 178, 179, 181–82, 183, 184–85, 186, 187, 188–89, 190, 191, 192, 193, 194, 301
Andersen, O., 291
Anderson, Betty, 187
Andersson, Johann Gunnar: responsibilities in Nordenskjöld's expedition, 115;

ABOUT THE AUTHOR

Dr. Rosove was born in Los Angeles in 1948 and is Clinical Professor of Medicine at the University of California, Los Angeles. He is author of numerous research papers in peer-reviewed medical journals and books, and recipient of distinguished teaching awards. His interest in the history and wildlife of the Antarctic dates back twenty years; he has visited the Antarctic on several occasions, acquiring firsthand knowledge of the regions referred to in his book. Dr. Rosove lives in Santa Monica, California.